NATIONALISMS IN
INTERNATIONAL POLITICS

Princeton Studies in Political Behavior
Tali Mendelberg, Series Editor

Nationalisms in International Politics

Kathleen E. Powers

PRINCETON UNIVERSITY PRESS

PRINCETON AND OXFORD

Published by Princeton University Press
41 William Street, Princeton, New Jersey 08540
99 Banbury Road, Oxford OX2 6JX

press.princeton.edu

All Rights Reserved

ISBN (cloth) 978-0-691-224572
ISBN (pbk) 978-0-691-224565
ISBN (e-book) 978-0-691-224589

British Library Cataloging-in-Publication Data is available

Editorial: Bridget Flannery-McCoy and Alena Chekanov
Jacket/Cover Design: Lauren Smith
Production: Danielle Amatucci
Publicity: Kate Hensley (US) and Kathryn Stevens (UK)

Jacket/Cover Credit: Shutterstock

This book has been composed in Adobe Text and Gotham

10 9 8 7 6 5 4 3 2 1

CONTENTS

ACKNOWLEDGMENTS

Nationalisms are fundamentally social phenomena—they exist because people connect to groups. Although writing a book involves a lot of solo time at a computer, other people and groups play essential roles in the process.

Like many first books, this project began as a dissertation. Rick Herrmann, Kathleen McGraw, Chris Gelpi, and William Minozzi provided generous feedback, encouragement, and advice throughout my time at the Ohio State University. I was lucky that my dissertation committee challenged me to transform my jumble of ideas about nationalism into a meaningful contribution, and fostered an open intellectual environment that allowed me to pursue a project outside traditional disciplinary niches.

My broader Ohio State community also shaped this project. Many faculty members shared insights, read early drafts, and asked questions that made me stop, think, and refine my work—particularly Larry Baum, Bear Braumoeller, Jennifer Mitzen, Tom Nelson, Mike Neblo, Alex Thompson, Randy Schweller, and Alex Wendt. My graduate student colleagues provided perfect outlets for testing my ideas. Nyron Crawford, Jessy Defenderfer, Paul DeBell, Marina Duque, Erin Graham, Matt Hitt, Josh Kertzer, Emily Lynch, Sebastien Mainville, Eleonora Mattiacci, Vittorio Merola, and Carolyn Morgan merit special thanks for both friendship and feedback.

This book project took shape at Dartmouth's Dickey Center for International Understanding and the University of Georgia. I'm indebted to Steve Brooks, Ben Valentino, and Bill Wohlforth for providing transformative feedback throughout multiple revisions—starting as mentors at the Dickey Center and now as departmental colleagues at Dartmouth. Steve and Bill also provided invaluable guidance on the practical side of publishing. A cohort of brilliant post-doctoral fellows at the Dickey Center provided feedback that enriched this project, including Dan Altman, Kate Geoghegan, Mauro Gilli, Alexander Lanoszka, and Josh Shifrinson. At UGA, I am especially grateful to Chad Clay, Maryann Gallagher, and Cas Mudde for camaraderie and many illuminating conversations that improved my work. Thanks also to Alexa Bankert, Jeff Berejikian, Leah Carmichael, Danny Hill, Loch Johnson, Hannah Kleider, and Andy Owsiak for helpful discussions.

I completed the book back at Dartmouth College, where I am lucky to be surrounded by outstanding scholars who have influenced this book with formal feedback and casual conversation—including Deb Brooks, John Carey, Jeremy Ferwerda, Jeremy Horowitz, Jenny Lind, Jay Lyall, Nick Miller, Herschel Nachlis, Brendan Nyhan, Daryl Press, Julie Rose, Luke Swaine, and Sean Westwood. Jeff Friedman served as a particularly cheerful and consistent sounding board—his critical and actionable feedback profoundly improved this work. A virtual writing group with Lisa Baldez, Mia Costa, and Michelle Clarke pushed this book through the final stages during the pandemic, and their dogs offered additional incentives for daily writing.

Throughout the research and writing process, I received formative feedback from audiences at Christopher Newport University, Dartmouth, Harvard, Ohio State, SUNY Albany, UCLA, University of Georgia, University of Illinois, Utah State, University of Virginia, Yale, and various conferences. I'm grateful to more people than I can list, including Scott Althaus, Andrew Bertoli, Suparna Chaudhry, Stephen Chaudoin, Amber Curtis, Alex Debs, Stacie Goddard, Hein Goemans, Brian Greenhill, Pete Gries, Josh Gubler, Maria Jose Hierro, Rob Johns, Sabrina Karim, Jiyoung Ko, Debbie Larson, Dalton Lin, Dani Lupton, Aila Matanock, Nuno Monteiro, Mark Peffley, Ryan Powers, Didac Queralt, Aaron Rapport, Jason Reifler, David Rousseau, Thania Sanchez, Tom Scotto, Meghan Stewart, Rob Trager, Jessica Weeks, and George Yin. Ciara Comerford, Taylor Holley, Steven Li, and Ryan Waaland provided intrepid research assistance.

Several institutions and individuals made the empirical portions of this book possible. Support from Ohio State's Mershon Center for International Security Studies and Decision Science Collaborative and Dartmouth's Dickey Center for International Understanding allowed me to fund the experiments in chapters 3 and 4. I am also grateful to Pierangelo Isernia for graciously sharing comprehensive data and codebooks for the IntUne surveys analyzed in chapter 5.

The Dickey Center also hosted a manuscript workshop. I offer my profound gratitude to Rose McDermott and Jack Snyder for traveling to rural New Hampshire in the middle of winter and attending the workshop. Rose and Jack provided encouraging, critical, and constructive advice throughout their visit. I returned to their feedback often, each time awed by how deeply they engaged with my work, identifying potential problems alongside ways to develop solutions. I am eternally grateful for this time and generosity from two top scholars who know quite a bit about nationalisms; their input left imprints throughout the book. Thanks also to Melody Burkins for organizing the workshop and for constant encouragement, and to Dan Benjamin, Tom Candon, and Sharon Tribou-St. Martin, whose unfailingly generous administrative and other support made this book possible.

At Princeton University Press, Bridget Flannery-McCoy shepherded me through the submission and publication process, patiently answering my many questions and offering valuable guidance. I am thankful that she and Tali Mendelberg saw promise in my manuscript amid the rising sea of nationalism research. Tali also provided tremendous feedback that improved chapter 1, and it is a sincere privilege to publish this work in the Political Behavior series. Alena Chekanov, Brigitte Pelner, and the rest of the PUP team provided fantastic support. I am also thankful to three anonymous reviewers who provided concrete, constructive, and encouraging feedback. A paragon of peer review, their comments are responsible for many of this book's redeeming qualities.

Thank you to my parents, Judi and Bernie, for fostering my endless academic pursuits and to Kelley, Kerry, and Courtney for enduring years of conversations and complaints about this project. Thanks also for knowing when to change the topic, and to all of my nieces and nephews just for being you.

My deepest appreciation to Dani Lupton, Brian Rathbun, Jason Reifler, Jonathan Renshon, Elizabeth Saunders, and Keren Yarhi-Milo, who provided comments, guidance, and encouragement at critical junctures. Committed to reciprocity, I owe them. Josh Kertzer and Eleonora Mattiacci have provided a decade of friendship, feedback, and professional advice. They helped bring this book to fruition, and their contributions could alone fill many pages. I am profoundly grateful.

Finally, Dave Lieberman offered more help than I had any right to expect, serving variously as a note-taker, copyeditor, intellectual sounding board, and barista. We weathered the pandemic and final stretch of book-writing together from our home in the woods, and Dave was an outstanding partner and home office-mate throughout. For responding every time I asked for a word, and for an endless reservoir of encouragement: Thank you.

NATIONALISMS IN
INTERNATIONAL POLITICS

1

Nationalisms in International Politics

Just because the circumstances of the war have brought the idea of the nation and the national to the foreground of every one's thoughts, the most important thing is to bear in mind that there are nations and nations, this kind of nationalism and that.
—JOHN DEWEY, 1916

On November 11, 2018, world leaders gathered in Paris to mark the 100th Armistice Day observation. Standing under the Arc de Triomphe, French President Emmanuel Macron exhorted his audience to stem the rising tide of nationalism flooding the globe. Nationalism helped to incite World War I, and he warned that the "old demons are coming back . . . to wreak chaos and death." It would be a "grave error" to succumb to nationalism with "isolationism, violence, and domination."[1] Instead, Macron implored people to embrace supranational bodies, like the United Nations and European Union, as bastions of enduring cooperation. Bitter enemies can become close friends through supranational unity—a point he underscored when he tweeted "*Unis*" alongside a photo of himself holding hands

---

1. Full English language transcript available from C-SPAN. "World War I Armistice Centennial Commemoration," 11 November 2018. See also Nakamura, Kim, and McAuley, 2018. "Macron denounces nationalism as a 'betrayal of patriotism' in rebuke to Trump at WWI remembrance," *Washington Post*, 11 November.

with German Chancellor Angela Merkel.[2] French and German citizens could bind together as Europeans to face threats from terrorism, climate change, and economic strife.

Macron stood in good company when he drew a connection between nationalism and militarism, and between *supra*nationalism—nationalist attachment to an entity that reaches across country borders[3]—and co-operation. When scholars warn that modern-day Chinese "hypernationalism" could spark a great power war (Mearsheimer, 2014), praise shared democratic identification for its pacifying effect (Kahl, 1998), or connect growing European identification to regional security cooperation (Koenig-Archibugi, 2004), they recite two stories that constitute the accepted wisdom in international politics. The first ties nationalism to increased international competition and conflict: Nationalists demonize outsiders, inflate threats, and escalate disputes. These tendencies create a deadly combination, leading to nationalism's notorious reputation as "inherently prone toward war" (Mylonas and Kuo, 2017, 10) and "one of the most dependable culprits for conflict between nations" (Gruffydd-Jones, 2017, 700). And in line with Macron's prescription for peace, the second story contends that supranational attachments subdue nationalism's destructive capacity. French and German nationalism fueled the two world wars, for instance, but a European identity helped citizens in both countries overcome their historic animosity. Supranationalism allows people to think of themselves as part of an overarching group that stretches across borders, such that they stop dividing "us" from "them" along national lines (Cronin, 1999; Acharya, 2001). Citizens across the continent can say that as co-Europeans, "we" trust one another to resolve disputes without force.

These accepted views rest on a misunderstanding: They treat nationalism as one-dimensional, yet nationalisms vary. When people embrace national or supranational identities, they commit to an idea about how people who share that identity think and behave. Those norms carry distinct implications for foreign policy attitudes. Some nationalist norms prescribe foreign policy aggression just as some supranationalist norms prescribe cooperation within the transnational group. Others stipulate measured, reciprocal conflict or undermine support for regional security cooperation.

---

2. Macron, Emmanuel (@EmmanuelMacron). "Unis." 10 November, 2018, 11:24am. Tweet. See also Baker, Peter and Rubin, Alissa J. 2018 "Trump's Nationalism, Rebuked at World War I Ceremony, Is Reshaping Much of Europe," *New York Times*, 11 November, URL: www.nytimes.com/2018/11/11/US/politics/macron-trump-paris.wwi.html.

3. I use supranational, transnational, and regional interchangeably to refer to identities or areas that encompass two or more countries.

For instance, U.S. President Barack Obama invoked nationalism when he claimed that the United States was "the greatest country on earth,"[4] but he largely "eschew[ed] a muscle-bound foreign policy"[5] vision and avoided describing U.S. adversaries with punitive rhetoric (Macdonald and Schneider, 2017). And while 86% of Norwegians were "quite proud" or "very proud" of their nationality in 2018[6]—and more than 70% agreed that Norway is a better country than others in 2013[7]—they seem to assert their superiority through foreign aid, not war (Prather, 2014; Wohlforth et al., 2018). Some scholarship, too, shows that nationalism occasionally corresponds to weaker threat perceptions and less hawkishness (Jones, 2014; Ko, 2019). Meanwhile, support for deeper security cooperation in the EU remains strong amid doubts that many residents identify as European at all (Schilde, Anderson and Garner, 2019; Schoen, 2008; Risse, 2004; McNamara and Musgrave, 2020), and despite evidence that European identification sometimes heightens negative biases against continental neighbors (Mummendey and Waldzus, 2004). Treating all nationalisms as equal fails to account for these complexities.

Faced with inconsistent answers about *whether* nationalism amplifies individual appetites for external belligerence—and whether supranationalism prompts support for cooperation—this book develops an overarching theory to explain *which* nationalisms shape support for conflict and which supranationalisms encourage cooperation. It also confronts three problems that limit most previous work on nationalisms in international politics:

4. Barack Obama, 2013. "Remarks by the President at a DNC Event—New York, NY," 13 May. Obama White House Archives. Available at: www.obamawhitehouse.archives.gov /the-press-office/2013/05/13/remarks-president-dnc-event-new-york-ny-0. He decreased ambiguity about whether he meant to invoke American superiority later in the speech, asserting that "objectively, . . . we are poised for a 21st century that is as much the American century as the 20th century." Related, Gilmore, Sheets and Rowling (2016, 515) find that President Obama invoked American exceptionalism in public speeches more than any of his predecessors since 1945.

5. Landler, Mark and Mark Mazzetti, 2013. "For Obama's Global Vision, Daunting Problems," *New York Times*, 24 March. URL: www.nytimes.com/2013/05/25/us/politics/for-obamas -global-vision-daunting-problems.html.

6. Data from the World Values Survey, Wave 7, available at worldvaluessurvey.org. The question (Q254) asks participants, "How proud are you to be Norwegian?" A majority (61.3%) of respondents selected "very proud," 24.9% chose "quite proud," and 3.6% and 0.3% chose "not very proud" and "not at all proud," respectively.

7. Data from the 2013 ISSP National Identity Survey. The question (V20) asks participants whether they agree or disagree that "Norway is a better country than most other countries," a standard indicator for nationalist attitudes in existing research. Among respondents, 20.5% agreed strongly, and 49.8% agreed. For comparison, 69.9% of U.S. respondents agreed or strongly agreed that the U.S. is a better country than others.

Research often reduces nationalism to a single dimension, lacks generalizable foundations that apply across problems and levels, or explains either the conventional wisdom *or* aberrations—but not both. This book offers conceptual, theoretical, and empirical contributions to overcome these challenges.

First, my conceptualization incorporates two dimensions of nationalism: The strength of someone's nationalist identity (*commitment*) and the norms that define what it means to be a nationalist (*content*). Scholars often conceptualize nationalism as synonymous with external hostility and supranationalism as synonymous with transnational cooperation (Kosterman and Feshbach, 1989; Koenig-Archibugi, 2004).[8] But when people commit to national and supranational identities, they embrace an idea about what it means to be American, French, or European. For example, nationalism sometimes entails committing to nonviolence—a view that the Indian National Congress expressed in the early twentieth century (Tudor and Slater, 2020, 6)—whereas other equally fervent nationalists demand violence against outsiders to protect their country. Such content shapes how people interact with others inside and outside their group's boundaries, and how they respond to challenges and opportunities in the foreign policy realm. Content differentiates nationalists who prefer to use all available military force from those who would engage in more limited exchanges with adversaries, and likewise differentiates supranationalists who crave deeper security integration from those wary about ceding national foreign policy autonomy to potentially untrustworthy partners. Elevating content can explain variation in nationalist foreign policy attitudes that we otherwise miss when we treat nationalisms as a monolith.

Second, I combine IR (International Relations) scholarship with interdisciplinary insights to explain how *unity* and *equality* provide distinct bases for nationalisms and supranationalisms in international politics. My framework builds from psychology's relational models theory (Fiske, 1991). Unity and equality represent two distinct relational models. Relational models are "relational" in the sense that they apply to *social* interactions—relationships with other people, including fellow national or supranational group members. They are "models" because they provide implicit rules of thumb for how we think about and behave toward other people and groups.

8. For notable exceptions that I discuss in more detail later on, see, e.g., Snyder (2000); Schrock-Jacobson (2012); Schoen (2008); Katzenstein and Checkel (2009); Risse (2010); Saideman (2013).

For example, a group of people tasked with making a joint decision needs to set guidelines. Will the decision rest on majority voting (equality), a consensus position (unity), or another rule? The models facilitate social life by providing a baseline for what to expect. They play a similar role in structuring nationalisms.

Unity norms prioritize in-group homogeneity—a shared culture, history, or other material that binds people as one. Unity requires a binary separation between "us" and "them," where a "feeling of kinship" allows people to embrace national or supranational insiders as family and guard against outsiders. Those who describe their nation as a "collective individual" embrace unity. For example, nineteenth century Russian elites demanded conformity to the "fatherland" (Greenfeld, 1992, 261), and Jean Monnet asserted that Europe would be strongest when Europeans stand together to enact the "common will" (qtd. in Fursdon, 1980, 118). When we use kinship myths, religion, ethnicity, or other cultural bonds to demarcate national or regional boundaries, we depend on unity.

By contrast, equality requires reciprocity and fairness, and manifests in peer-like interactions. Equality accommodates heterogeneity—creating more flexible group boundaries that avoid the binary separation that corresponds to unity. This variety of nationalism flows from notions of equality rather than kinship; from friendship rather than family. The Federalist papers, for example, reveal efforts to define American nationalism using respect and individual freedom (Sinopoli, 1996, 6), and many modern Americans claim the liberal "American Creed" as the foundation for their nationalism (Smith, 1997; Theiss-Morse, 2009, 18). European citizens whose political identity depends on democratic participation and valuing diversity express equality-oriented supranationalisms—like when Jean-Claude Juncker described the EU as a "cord of many strands," rather than a unified family.[9] Juncker's words illustrate the idea of equality nationalism by connecting corresponding descriptive norms to the European group.[10]

To my knowledge, this is the first study to adapt insights from relational models theory for research on nationalisms. And this framework brings several advantages. Unity and equality provide generalizable foundations that apply across issues and across two levels of categorization

9. Jean-Claude Juncker, 2016. "Jean-Claude Juncker European Parliament speech in full," *Independent*, 14 September. URL: www.independent.co.uk/news/world/europe/jean-claude-juncker-european-parliament-speech-full-a7298016.html.

10. Of course, understanding Juncker's supranationalism would require systematic research beyond a single public speech.

that matter in international politics. These *fundamental* models structure interactions across a variety of social settings, setting different expectations within friendships (often predicated on equality) than families (unity), for example. In turn, they apply to both nationalisms and supranationalisms, bridging the artificial divide between research that connects identification to conflict or cooperation. Indeed, synthesizing theories about nationalisms and supranationalisms—which I refer to collectively as nationalisms—constitutes one of this book's contributions.

Building from relational models theory also avoids the trap of defining bespoke nationalisms for each new puzzle;[11] rather, unity and equality have implications for a range of foreign policy problems. Related, these pre-political norms guard against the inclination to infer nationalisms from outcomes, like separating "good" from "bad" nationalisms based on whether they increase the chance of war. Finally, some scholars ascribe different nationalisms to whole countries or regions—comparing French "civic" nationalism to Japanese "ethnic" nationalism. But my theory accounts for the substantial disagreements about content that occur among *individuals* within the same national and transnational groups—that is, among fellow Americans or fellow Europeans.

Third, *unity* and *equality* together account for nationalism's inconsistent relationship to foreign policy attitudes. Nationalisms centered on unity and equality—my primary independent variables—carry distinct implications for attitudes about militarism in international conflict and security cooperation in transnational groups. In a nutshell, I argue that equality-oriented nationalism mitigates aggressive foreign policy attitudes because group members commit to reciprocity and extend this norm to outsiders. Their unity-oriented counterparts instead inflate external threats and demand disproportionate force to defeat adversaries. As to international cooperation, a supranational identity built on unity undermines trust and support for security integration. Pressures for unity lead supranationalists to reject deepening ties to "deviants" inside the group's boundaries. Equality, by contrast, accommodates intragroup heterogeneity and encourages cooperation with any co-regionals who reciprocally commit to those same principles. In this respect, my theory both explains the conventional wisdom and challenges it.

And indeed, this book provides empirical evidence to show that the character of nationalisms matters as much as commitment—unity and

11. See Mylonas and Kuo (2017) for a review of different varieties of nationalism.

equality have distinct effects on foreign policy attitudes. Two original experiments manipulate nationalist identity content with treatments that describe how unity or equality comprises the definition of one's membership in a national group. I then evaluate how beliefs about national superiority correspond to foreign policy attitudes, and the degree to which nationalism manifests in different outcomes when it centers on unity versus equality. I find that unity nationalism corresponds to militarism and escalatory aggression in a foreign policy crisis, per the standard story. But equality alters these relationships. Nationalists express less hawkish foreign policy attitudes and more measured escalation when their national group commits to equality, compared to unity.

Recognizing that experiments comprise one part of the inquiry, this book adopts a multi-method approach and tests my hypotheses about supranational cooperation using observational survey data from Europe. I take advantage of the gains in scale from cross-national surveys to test the theory's implications for supranational cooperation in a sample of elites alongside members of the public. Europeans who envision the region as a set of equals or peers trust fellow Europeans, support a common foreign policy, and endorse a European army to a greater degree than their counterparts for whom Europe constitutes a united family. Together, my results underscore the central role played by content; to understand how nationalisms affect foreign policy, we must first know what being a nationalist means to individuals.

Before I present and test my theory in detail, I make the case that we need one. In the remainder of this chapter, I dive into the conventional wisdom on nationalism and foreign policy attitudes and then highlight puzzling contradictions in the scholarship. Next, I preview my conceptual framework by defining nationalism and disaggregating the concept into its unity- and equality-oriented variants. I then summarize my primary argument and this book's contributions. I conclude with an outline of the proceeding chapters.

Two Stories about Nationalisms in International Politics

International relations scholars tell two stories about nationalisms in international politics, both of which Macron highlighted when he decried the perils of nationalism and touted the promise of European unity. The logic that connects nationalism to war is the same logic that ties supranational identification to cooperation, despite the paradigmatic gulf that typically separates the two research programs. Nationalism scholarship explains how group members react to outsiders; theories about supranational identities address how group members relate to insiders. The two stories share the same mechanisms and assumptions: Lines that separate "us" from "them" cause nationalist hawkishness and war, but when they break down—when French and German citizens no longer see themselves as egoistic adversaries but as fellow Europeans—the trust once reserved for co-nationals expands to people in other countries who share the umbrella identity. To understand how nationalisms shape conflict and cooperation in international politics, we must synthesize these two stories.

In the following section, I first introduce the conventional wisdom that connects nationalism to militarism and supranationalism to cooperation. Ample scholarship supports Macron's pessimism about nationalism and his correspondingly optimistic take on supranationalism. But these standard stories—while convincing in some respects—neglect crucial information. Individual studies provide empirical evidence that strong or salient nationalism sometimes corresponds to *less* hawkish attitudes, compared to weaker nationalism, and that certain types of nationalism inspire peace rather than war. And in the case of supranationalism, some researchers conclude that European citizens with the strongest commitments to the continent express as much hostility toward fellow Europeans in other countries as those who reject supranationalism. If we take a closer look at both the empirical evidence and theoretical assumptions beneath the standard stories, the foundations start to crack.

THE STANDARD STORY ABOUT NATIONALISM AND MILITARISM

Nationalist conflicts litter our history books and prediction lists—from Bismarck advancing German unification via war against France (Sambanis, Skaperdas and Wohlforth, 2015) to both World Wars, the 1969 Football War (Bertoli, 2017), and ominous warnings that nationalism drives China's extraverted foreign policy (Schweller, 2018).[12] IR scholars accordingly treat nationalism as a pernicious force in world politics (Van Evera,

---

12. Yet Schweller (2018) argues that the U.S. can manage China's assertive foreign policy posture if they adopt the more restrained and isolationist grand strategy implicated by nationalism in a declining power. See Johnston (2017) for an argument that Chinese nationalism is not rising and Mearsheimer (2014) for an argument connecting Chinese "hypernationalism" to predictions about the next great power war.

1994), in part because it animates militaristic attitudes (Mylonas and Kuo, 2017, 10).

The standard story: National identities bring people together within countries (Sambanis and Shayo, 2013; Robinson, 2016),[13] but tear them apart in the international arena (Mercer, 1995).[14] Nationalism creates a bond among citizens who see their own group as superior. This process situates those who reside outside the nation as threatening "others" (Schrock-Jacobson, 2012). Driven by our human tendency toward groupism—which has both neurological and evolutionary roots (Sapolsky, 2019; Brewer and Caporael, 2006)[15]—we view outsiders with suspicion. "They" are more threatening when they differ from "us." Nationalist pride can blind people to their country's strategic or material shortcomings, leading to overconfidence and myths about incompetent rivals (Snyder, 1991; Druckman, 2001; Walt, 1996).[16] "We" are powerful and righteous, whereas "they" are weak. Scholars presume that nationalists display their superiority with aggression.

Research designed to test these propositions often finds that nationalist individuals support foreign policy aggression more than those who reject sentiments about national greatness (Druckman, 1994; De Figueiredo and Elkins, 2003; Kemmelmeier and Winter, 2008; Federico, Golec and Dial, 2005). Indeed, proponents of the conventional wisdom point out that stronger nationalism correlates with support for nuclear armament (Feshbach, 1987), "hard-line" policies toward the Soviet Union (Hurwitz and Peffley, 1990), and both dispositional militarism and foreign policy aggression (Herrmann, Isernia and Segatti, 2009). Experiments reveal similar patterns. For example, when Chinese participants watch a nationalistic video depicting a struggle between China and outside enemies, they support hawkish responses to China's territorial disputes (Ko, 2019). Leaders

---

13. Normative theorists and comparative politics scholars often prescribe nation-building and nationalism to resolve civil strife, emphasizing nationalism's "light side." See, for example, Emerson (1960); Horowitz (1985); Kymlicka (1998); Osaghae (1999); Goodson (2006); Diamond (2006); Johnston et al. (2010); Sambanis and Shayo (2013); Robinson (2014, 2016); Tamir (2019). See Mylonas (2012) on the politics of nation-building and variation in state nation-building strategies.

14. For more macro-level research on nationalism and international conflict, see Mansfield and Snyder (2002)—and the exchange between Narang and Nelson (2009) and Mansfield and Snyder (2009)—Schrock-Jacobson (2012); Wimmer (2013); Bertoli (2017); Gruffydd-Jones (2017).

15. See, e.g., Lopez, McDermott and Petersen (2011) on how coalitions and community groups conferred important advantages for our ancestors' survival.

16. For more on the relationship between optimism and war, see, e.g., Blainey (1988); Altman (2015).

can be nationalists too, and research from the Leadership Trait Analysis tradition suggests that leaders who favor their national in-groups incline toward using force (Hermann, 1980). In short, nationalism corresponds to "authoritarianism, intolerance, and warmongering" (Li and Brewer, 2004, 728), consistent with its status as a *casus belli*.

These patterns create a dynamic relationship, whereby scholars assume that nationalism both causes and incentivizes foreign aggression (Sambanis, Skaperdas and Wohlforth, 2015; Hixson, 2008). Misplaced confidence and threat inflation might lead nationalist leaders to start a war, and nationalist masses might demand confrontational displays that provoke conflict (Gruffydd-Jones, 2017, 705). Nationalist hawkishness theoretically enables leaders to mobilize support for their foreign policy adventures, overcome collective action problems, prepare citizens to sacrifice, or signal resolve to their adversaries (Posen, 1993; Weiss, 2013, 2014). According to the conventional wisdom, nationalism provides both the tinder and the spark for war.

THE STANDARD STORY ABOUT SUPRANATIONALISM AND COOPERATION

Supranationalism offers a ray of hope for those concerned that nationalism makes "war, conflict, and misery natural and inevitable products of international politics" (Mercer, 1995, 252). And the standard story about supranationalism seems shrewdly simple: Building bigger groups combats nationalist competition by turning outsiders into insiders. Arguments about nationalist conflict and transnational cooperation go hand in hand.

Supranationalism facilitates cooperation by redefining self-interest, assuaging animosity, and strengthening interstate trust. Individuals trust and favor their fellow in-group members. And when people "recategorize" themselves into an overarching group that bridges two or more otherwise competitive subgroups (Gaertner and Dovidio, 2000), their in-group expands. When a group transcends national boundaries—forming a supranational identity (see, e.g., Adler and Barnett, 1998; Cronin, 1999)—members look out for each other. Rather than advance only their national interest, French citizens care about protecting Europe as a whole. Citizens also trust each other to resolve disputes without force and no longer view co-regionals as outsiders even though they fly a different national flag.[17]

17. Within the group, they display what Uslaner (2002) and Rathbun (2009) call "particularized" trust—two or more parties trust each other implicitly.

Turning Americans and Canadians into "North Americans" transfers the trust previously reserved for co-nationals up to a higher level of categorization (Rousseau and Garcia-Retamero, 2007). Group members expect that others will preserve regional peace rather than pursue myopic national gains. These assurances provide a pathway to security cooperation and integration: If we trust one another, we can redirect our energies to protecting the region, rather than protecting our borders from each other.

If supranationalism fosters cooperation, we should see its effects on full display among Europeans (Risse, 2010).[18] Europe provides "an important test for determining whether a supranational identity is possible" (Curtis, 2014, 522), and whether supranationalism promotes trust and support for security cooperation. The EU has expanded beyond a monetary union to shape everything from human rights practices to foreign policy via a joint diplomatic corps. Common symbols and practices permeate citizens' everyday lives, designed to foster shared identification,[19] making it a most-likely case for the accepted wisdom. Indeed, IR scholars overwhelmingly emphasize Europe when they present the argument that regional identities facilitate cooperation.

And again, some evidence from Europe supports the story that supranationalism promotes cooperation.[20] European identification can overcome the nationalist impulse for autonomy in the security realm. People who identify as European view the common defense and foreign policies more favorably (Citrin and Sides, 2004; Schoen, 2008), support deeper integration (Hooghe and Marks, 2005; Risse, 2010), and endorse intra-European immigration at greater rates than those who reject supranationalism

18. IR scholars also use supranationalism to explain why democracies avoid conflict with other democracies (Rousseau, 2006; Risse-Kappen, 1995; Kahl, 1998; Hayes, 2009; Tomz and Weeks, 2013), or how states can create the conditions for peaceful conflict management in security communities (Deutsch, 1957; Adler and Barnett, 1998; Cronin, 1999; Wendt, 1999; Acharya, 2001). These research traditions typically use countries, regions, or the international system as units of analysis, though many rely on psychological insights to explain how these encompassing identities tear down seemingly fortified borders. Scholars disagree about whether identification precedes cooperation (Hemmer and Katzenstein, 2002; Schimmelfennig, 2007) or emerges from it (Haas, 1958; Deutsch, 1961), but they agree that these two phenomena reinforce each other.

19. Though see, e.g., McNamara (2015a) and McNamara and Musgrave (2020) for research on why those symbols have limited efficacy.

20. Although some constitutive arguments rely on social processes that cannot be reduced to micro-foundations (Wendt, 1999; Fearon and Wendt, 2002), much research on supranational cooperation attributes causal mechanisms to the same individual-level theories and dynamics that explain nationalist conflict (Cronin, 1999; Hayes, 2012). See Kertzer (2017) for more on micro-foundations and macro-arguments in IR.

(Curtis, 2014).[21] European identification also seems to infuence policy: When larger proportions of the general public and opinion leaders identified as European, their country was more likely to support treaty reforms that centralized foreign and security policies at the 1996 Intergovernmental Conference (Koenig-Archibugi, 2004). Politicians exhibit the same tendencies. For example, stronger European identification corresponds to a greater willingness to comply with nationally costly EU laws among German parliamentarians (Bayram, 2017).

Scholars expect supranationalism to develop outside Europe, too—whereupon it should lead to increased cooperation within those regions. For example, Asia is known more for its divisions than binding supranational identities. Distance, geography, wartime resentments, and geopolitical fissures foment competition (Hagström and Gustafsson, 2015; Glosserman and Snyder, 2015).[22] At the same time, the region does possess ingredients for supranationalism. For example, scholars argue that identification with the Association of Southeast Asian Nations (ASEAN) could foster peace (Jones, 2004; Kivimäki, 2010), or that their shared Confucian or Buddhist heritage might facilitate trust in Northeast Asia (Clements, 2018, 7). And indeed, public opinion data show signs that citizens in ASEAN countries increasingly identify with the region—though it may take time for ASEAN supranationalism to match its European benchmark (Moorthy and Benny, 2012, 2013; Acharya, 2016a; Lee and Lim, 2020). Arguments about the cooperative effect of supranationalism theoretically apply just as well outside Europe, but the comparatively less-established identities in other regions limit the inferences we can draw about them using contemporary evidence.

In short, the conventional story about supranationalism presents an optimistic foil for research on nationalist conflict. Building international cooperation and stifling conflict requires shifting people's commitments to a different and more inclusive level of categorization.

INTERLOCKING PUZZLES

On first pass, these stories seem to shed light on persistent patterns in foreign policy attitudes and international politics. But on both empirical

21. See Hobolt and De Vries (2016) for a recent review that discusses identification in the context of European integration.

22. Though cf. Katsumata and Iida (2011) on an emerging Asian identity.

and theoretical grounds, the conventional wisdom falls short. The standard stories skip over contradictory evidence that fails to link nationalism to consistent militarism and limits nationalism's explanatory power. Moreover, the notion that supranationalism suppresses conflict ignores the fact that such broadly inclusive identities can paradoxically magnify intragroup animosity toward fellow regional residents who depart from the mold—thereby undermining the trust required for security integration.

What's puzzling about nationalism?

A closer look at the empirical record reveals that nationalism does not always increase support for conflict, threat inflation, and hawkish foreign policy attitudes.

First, inconsistencies in public opinion data contradict notions that nationalism must coincide with militarism. For example, some American study-abroad students return from their experiences *more* nationalistic but *less* threatened by the prospect that their host country might overtake the United States militarily (Jones, 2014).[23] Nationalism and threat perceptions moved in opposite directions. Others find that national affirmation helps build trust—not suspicion—between citizens in rival countries like China and Japan (Chung, 2015). And one experiment showed that although depictions of China's struggle against enemies increased both nationalism and bellicose responses to conflict, watching a video about China's strong economy caused nationalism but not militarism (Ko, 2019).

Some nationalists reject militarism and even promote international cooperation. Many Canadian nationalists embrace their reputation as a " 'kinder and gentler' country" invested in peace-keeping, mediation, and international law: "One is a good Canadian nationalist by being a good internationalist" (Kymlicka, 2003, 364, 361). In one important study, Bonikowski and DiMaggio (2016) analyze data from a representative sample of Americans who completed the 2004 General Social Survey. Using latent class analysis to inductively derive four varieties of nationalism based on how people responded to questions about their national identity, the

---

23. The students in Jones's (2014) sample studied in a variety of host countries. The five most popular host countries included Spain, the UK, France, Italy, and Australia, but the data also included people who studied in countries with more adversarial relationships with the U.S.—including China, Cuba, and Russia. Importantly, the host countries are evenly distributed between the control and treatment groups in the study, and results are based on pooled estimates.

researchers found one group of nationalists who were less militaristic than key others. These "creedal" nationalists expressed unquestionable nationalism—"they strongly endorsed the ideas that America is a better country than most" and "a plurality agreed that the world would be better if others were more like Americans and that one should support one's country even if it is wrong" (Bonikowski and DiMaggio, 2016, 963). They also embraced key elements from the liberal American Creed alongside pride in American institutions, democracy, and commitment to treating groups equally. But compared to at least one other nationalist class, respondents in this "creedal" nationalism class—more than 20% of the sample—expressed more opposition to the idea that the United States should pursue its interests even if it might mean war (Bonikowski and DiMaggio, 2016, 966). If nationalism and militarism go hand in hand, how do we account for these relatively dovish nationalists?

Second, similar empirical inconsistencies characterize research linking nationalism to actual foreign policy outcomes and demand scrutiny. Indeed, many scholars argue that "the relationship between nationalism and warfare is largely contingent" (Hutchinson, 2017, 2), such that "civic" nationalisms are less prone to conflict than their "ethnic" counterparts (Snyder, 2000; Schrock-Jacobson, 2012), for example. France's Vichy regime contained nationalists who aimed to promote French interests and greatness, maintain sovereignty, and protect the country—yet engaged in "paradoxical behavior" (Kocher, Lawrence and Monteiro, 2018, 118), per the standard story, when they chose to collaborate with Nazi Germany to suit their partisan aims (Kocher, Lawrence and Monteiro, 2018, 131–35). Nationalism sometimes even corresponds to efforts to foster peace through international institutions or foreign aid. For a state like Ireland, expressing superiority might mean advancing human rights or strengthening international law rather than pursuing great power status (Hutchinson, 2017, 180)—just as the predominant strain of Norwegian nationalism prescribes foreign aid, not war, as an expression of Norway's superiority (Wohlforth et al., 2018, 532). Although we are not used to thinking about nationalism as something expressed through external collaboration, cooperation, or aid, people can display their national commitment and superiority without domination.

Nationalism does not inexorably drive support for conflict. Resolving the empirical divide between the standard story and puzzling evidence against it requires a comprehensive theory of nationalisms in international politics; ad hoc explanations cannot smooth over these anomalies.

What's puzzling about supranationalism?

The flip side of nationalist belligerence, we tell a straightforward story about how and why supranational identities drive international cooperation. Scholars rely heavily on the European Union to evaluate claims about identification as a basis for cooperation, due to its status as the most well-integrated contemporary international security community. If supranationalism has universally positive implications for cooperation, they should manifest in Europe. But empirically, we know that support for European cooperation persists despite shortcomings in the European identity project. Moreover, supranationalism provides an insufficient foundation for trusting cooperation as it sometimes *enhances* animosity toward subgroups who share the same umbrella identity.

First, European citizens and elites resoundingly endorse security integration *despite* apparent shortcomings in the European identity project. The Maastricht Treaty introduced the Common Foreign and Security Policy as one of the three EU pillars in 1992 (Schoen, 2008), and large majorities of the public support integrating European defense. Indeed, Schilde, Anderson and Garner (2019, 153) contend that "no other policy domain is as popular and robust as the idea of pooling national sovereignty over defence." But this popularity stands against a backdrop of disagreement about whether Europeans hold "fundamentally fragile" commitments to the region or even identify with Europe at all (McNamara and Musgrave, 2020, 175; Risse, 2004; Bruter, 2003; Cram, 2012; McNamara, 2015a). This disconnect could indicate that other factors account for European security cooperation, of course. But given scholars' preoccupation with identity as the foundation for international cooperation, why should we see one without the other?

Second, psychological theories about overarching identities come with important scope conditions. For one, many people find it difficult to sustain identities like "Europe," "the West," or "all of humanity" (Brewer, 1991; though cf. McFarland, Webb and Brown 2012; McFarland et al. 2019)—which might make them dubious candidates for the foundations of a security community designed to outlive its founders.

But most importantly, supranationalism often creates an in-group caste system that exacerbates negative biases rather than mitigating them. Recall that the conventional story assumes that supranational commitments dampen nationalist distrust and animosity. When French and German people belong to the same larger group, they extend the compatriotism they typically reserve for those inside their borders to a broader group of

Europeans. But some supranationalists challenge this claim. Some Germans who identify as both German and European impugn citizens from Poland or Italy precisely *because* the latter are part of their European in-group, for example. When they identify with a group, people form an implicit (or sometimes explicit) idea about what it means to be a "good" member (Turner, 1985). Indeed, social identification requires these group prototypes—people judge their connection to a group based on how closely they align with their image of the standard member. For German citizens who associate Europeanness with their own cultural ideals, Italians and Poles serve as poor exemplars for the group (Mummendey and Waldzus, 2004). Bad in-group members are worse than out-group members.[24] If supranationalism often undermines trust within groups, what explains the relatively consistent relationship between European identification and support for cooperation on the continent?

Again, I take a close look at the empirical and theoretical record to find that supranationalism fails to pave the unobstructed path to in-group trust and support for security cooperation that scholars have come to expect.

Resolving the Puzzles

Against the conventional wisdom's intuitive appeal, questions about *whether* nationalisms inspire cooperative or conflictual foreign policy attitudes produce an unsatisfying answer: "Maybe." A theory about nationalisms in international politics must be able to account for the standard stories alongside the puzzling contradictions. This book resolves these challenges—first by taking seriously the notion that nationalisms are social identities. Doing so offers several advantages, which I outline below. Chief among them, when we recognize that nationalisms "exist in the plural" (Katzenstein and Checkel, 2009, 213), we can identify which nationalisms drive support for intergroup conflict and intragroup cooperation.

CONCEPTUALIZING NATIONALISM IN INTERNATIONAL POLITICS

I treat nationalisms as social identities. Social identities refer to the "part of the individual's self-concept which derives from his knowledge

---

24. To use a more familiar example, "we" may be researchers. But if someone determines that a "good" researcher uses quantitative data, she might direct resources away from or impugn colleagues (in-group members) who do qualitative research—while she nevertheless applauds investigative journalists (out-group members) who rely on qualitative interviews.

of his membership of a social group (or groups)" (Tajfel, 1981, 255).[25] Nationalism denotes a commitment to one's nation and its superiority (De Figueiredo and Elkins, 2003; Herrmann, Isernia and Segatti, 2009), whereas supranationalism translates that commitment to a broader categorization level—with boundaries that cross state borders (Herrmann and Brewer, 2004). In both cases, individuals claim membership in a collective and navigate the world in terms of what "we" as Germans or Europeans think, want, and do. Defining each of these powerful forces as social identities is more than a lexical twist. This approach offers four advantages for understanding nationalisms in international politics.

First, this conceptualization removes the artificial separation between nationalisms and supranationalisms. Scholars tend to engage one level at a time to develop and test theories about nationalist conflict and supranational cooperation, often sorting along paradigmatic lines. Realists agree that "groupism" matters in international politics (Wohlforth, 2008), and cite nationalist status-seeking as a cause of conflict (Mearsheimer, 2014; Wohlforth, 2009). Liberal and constructivist scholars draw different lessons to argue that shared identities facilitate a democratic peace (Hermann and Kegley Jr, 1995; Kahl, 1998; Oneal and Russett, 2001; Hayes, 2009, 2012) or provide the glue that binds security communities (Adler and Barnett, 1998). Yet French and European nationalisms rest on the same psychological micro-foundations: Humans sort the world into groups, and define themselves in part by their membership in these larger social organizations. Group commitments shape attitudes and behavior toward fellow group members and outsiders.

Treating nationalisms as social identities emphasizes the common dynamics that underlie national and supranational commitments. Someone can identify with her family, neighborhood, state, nation, and global region at the same time—"superordinate" groups, like Americans or Westerners, contain small "subgroups," like Californians. The fact that people can identify with groups that span levels of categorization highlights shortcomings in research that treats nations as objects of "terminal loyalty" (Cottam and Cottam, 2001, 93), that "supersedes their loyalty to other groups" (Van Evera, 1994, 6).[26] Such conceptualizations preclude

25. I return to discussing nationalisms as social identities in chapter 2. Although pinning down a definition for these ubiquitous concepts entails "sweeping a conceptual minefield" (Levy, 1994, 279), see Druckman (1994), Theiss-Morse (2009), Huddy and Khatib (2007), Herrmann and Brewer (2004), and Risse (2010) for thorough discussions of national and European identities as social identities.

26. See also, e.g., Emerson (1960); Citrin et al. (1994).

supranationalisms, because they imply that people cannot identify with groups that encompass multiple national communities. That assertion goes against well-accepted evidence to the contrary: "That individuals hold multiple identities is not controversial" (Risse, 2010, 23). My approach treats nationalisms and supranationalisms as separate, sometimes complementary, objects of identification that share psychological foundations (Herrmann and Brewer, 2004; Risse, 2010).

Second, this conceptualization—based on the degree to which an individual embraces national or supranational superiority—reflects colloquial use. When we refer to nationalists waving flags, donning face paint, or saluting their military (Gruffydd-Jones, 2017; Schatz and Lavine, 2007), we describe people who embrace symbols and actions that connect them to their country. The same applies when European citizens and elites display the EU's twelve gold stars, describe themselves as "European," or distinguish European civilization from their North American or Asian counterparts. People place themselves within social categories and declare their allegiance both internally and via outward signals.

This description departs from scholarship that explicitly incorporates nationalisms' political goals into the definition.[27] For instance, some definitions of nationalism emphasize borders and ideology (Gellner, 1983). Such definitions provide important insights—nationalist demands for political, cultural, and territorial congruence help explain Zionists' quests for a Jewish homeland, Quebecois secessionist movements, Russia's twenty-first-century irredentism (Saideman, 2013), and Milosevic's exploitation of institutional weaknesses to advance claims about Serbian persecution in Kosovo (Snyder and Ballentine, 1996). But privileging political ends understates the cognitive and emotional bonds that most people associate with nationalist passions—the force that permeates daily life and explains why UK citizens cheer for British Olympians or why American support for President Roosevelt soared after the attacks on Pearl Harbor (Berinsky et al., 2011).

Third, and related, my conceptualization separates cause from effect. If we want to explain how nationalism influences foreign policy attitudes, we must excise foreign policy attitudes from our definitions. Existing research often conflates the two. Examining nationalism's relationship to Iraq war

---

27. Van Evera (1994, 6) laments that "the academic literature defines nationalism in an annoyingly wide range of ways," a statement that remains true 25 years after it first appeared in print. See also Hechter (2000) and Hutchinson (1994) on some of the challenges to defining nationalism.

attitudes, for example, Federico, Golec and Dial (2005, 623) define nationalism in terms of the "hostile 'conflict schema'" it is meant to predict: "nationalism" is a "form of ethnocentrism" that entails "hostility toward other national groups" and the desire for "dominance over other nations" (see also Kosterman and Feshbach, 1989; Osborne, Milojev and Sibley, 2017). Herrmann, Isernia and Segatti (2009) similarly argue that "national chauvinists" necessarily hold an extreme and intolerant ideology that pits "us" against threatening, inferior enemies.[28] Others argue that nationalism describes a population's desire to restrict foreign influence in internal affairs (Woodwell, 2007, 16). The latter again embeds the dependent variable into the definition—leaving us flummoxed by examples of nationalists who instead embrace foreigners or reject conflict.

Indeed, researchers diminish nationalism's causal role when they suggest that nationalism and militarism represent co-constitutive attitudes. As Weiss (2019, 680) declares in her research on Chinese hawkishness, "feelings of national identification are not the same as foreign policy beliefs and attitudes." Measuring nationalism on its own cannot tell us whether the Chinese public supports an aggressive posture in the East China Sea, because some "nationalists may support liberal international policies out of deference to the government."[29] The same pattern holds for supranationalism, where constructivist scholars make explicitly constitutive claims that transnational identification redefines states' interests to prioritize the whole—though they focus on countries rather than people (Adler and Barnett, 1998; Wendt, 1999). In that respect, "a state's interests merge with the collective interests of the community" (Pouliot, 2007, 608). But some supranationalists do not trust each other enough to cede their foreign policy autonomy (Risse, 2004), just as some nationalists display their superiority vis-á-vis outsiders without force.

Fourth, shifting from the political to the psychological allows me to embrace the fruits of interdisciplinary engagement and construct a theory of nationalist identity content from the ground up. Psychologists have

---

28. See Kinder and Kam (2010) for more on ethnocentrism and political attitudes. Many scholars separate in-group love from out-group hate when they treat national attachment and nationalism as distinct dimensions and claim that only the latter causes conflict (Brewer, 1999; Kosterman and Feshbach, 1989; De Figueiredo and Elkins, 2003; Rathbun, 2015), but even this distinction "is far too simple to capture the many variants of national ideology" (Reicher and Hopkins, 2001).

29. See, e.g., Gries (1999, 2004, 2005); Gries et al. (2011); Gries, Steiger and Wang (2016); Weiss (2014); Johnston (2017) for additional research on Chinese nationalism.

spent decades building on Tajfel and Turner's (1986) social identity theory to explain that people trust, favor, and cooperate with people who share their identity. And people distrust, dismiss, and sometimes degrade outsiders. In short, our conventional stories about supranational cooperation and nationalist competition rely on fundamental insights about how group memberships affect human behavior.

But these theories tell us that identification, on its own, only tells part of the story: Nationalisms and supranationalisms motivate people to conform with their group's norms. To understand when and how group memberships affect in-group trust or out-group aggression, we need to know what it means to be part of a particular group. Who "we" are shapes what "we" do: Some Christian religious groups, for example, prescribe "benevolence toward strangers" (Thomsen, 2010, 5). In that case, a group member might believe that being a good Christian means committing to out-group kindness, not out-group hostility.[30] Importantly, such benevolence stems from the same moral superiority we associate with nationalist calls to dominate via force. "We" Christians are better than "those" secular people precisely *because* "we" are more committed to helping others. Moreover, the same group membership can mean different things to different people—some American nationalists think that Americans must speak English, whereas others do not (Theiss-Morse, 2009).

Conceptualizing nationalisms as social identities allows me to synthesize insights from across disciplinary divides and provides solid psychological micro-foundations for studying nationalism*s* in international politics—and for filling gaps in the conventional stories. Notably, some scholars might disagree with my characterization of nationalisms as social identities. But decisions to separate "identification" from patriotism, attachment, or national chauvinism often smuggle content into the definitions—describing nationalism as uniquely divisive, for example (Huddy and Del Ponte, 2019). My conceptualization engages the cognitive component of social identification—people assess the degree to which they relate to typical group members (Turner, 1985)—alongside the affective component whereby claiming membership in the national group makes nationalists feel good. Moreover, nationalisms entail the sense of moral superiority common when people compare their own group to other groups (Brewer, 1999, 2001*b*). Whether nationalist superiority manifests in conflictual or

---

30. See also, for example, Postmes and Spears (1998); Reicher, Spears and Postmes (1995); Ellemers, Spears and Doosje (2002).

cooperative foreign policy attitudes, however, depends on what it means to be a nationalist.

THE ARGUMENT: UNITY, EQUALITY, AND FOREIGN POLICY ATTITUDES

Nationalisms vary.[31] Factors in the environment—like dueling historical narratives and respected elites—combine with dispositional traits to create disagreement between individuals. Some people perceive their country or region as committed to equality, whereas others think that the same group requires unity. Variation in these norms explains whether nationalism increases militarism and support for escalation in foreign policy, and whether supranationalism increases or undermines transnational trust and support for security cooperation.

Unity drives nationalist militarism and undermines support for international cooperation

Unity, solidarity, and consensus constitute unity-oriented nationalism. Unity implies that group members share important characteristics. These qualities might include familial ties, ethnicity, religion, national myths, or other elements that provide glue to bind the "imagined communities" central to standard definitions of nationhood (Anderson, 1983). Unity norms encourage people to help their compatriots.[32] What's good for the group is good for all of us. And because "we" are all the same—unity assumes homogeneity—an attack on one is an attack on all.

In-group solidarity comes with a cost, though. Unity implies a sharp distinction between "us" and "them." It creates a binary that encourages suspicion against outsiders, and against insiders whose differences introduce problematic heterogeneity (Fiske, 1992; Fiske and Rai, 2015). German scholars once defined German nationalism by the stark contrast between Germans and Frenchmen, for example (Greenfeld, 1992, 373), but also between the "real" Germans and German Jews whose Western values threatened the group's unity (ibid., 379). References to nationalist

---

31. For other frameworks that differentiate nationalisms by content, see, e.g., Barnett (1995); Snyder (2000); Risse (2004); Saideman (2013). See chapter 2 for a discussion about how my theory resolves theoretical and empirical challenges associated with applying the civic/ethnic framework to individual nationalisms and foreign policy attitudes.

32. This observation corresponds to research on national identities and preferential in-group biases. See, e.g., Theiss-Morse (2009); Wong (2010); Mutz and Kim (2017).

unity span time and place—from John Jay's description of America as "one united people ... descended from the same ancestors, speaking the same language, professing the same religion, attached to the same principles of government" (Hamilton, Madison and Jay, 2009, 12) to UKIP's 2015 manifesto demanding that their "amazing" country reject "divisiveness through multiculturalism" and instead integrate to create a more harmonious society (Burst et al., 2020).[33] Others elide explicit references to homogeneity, but nevertheless emphasize that "we" must join together and stifle differences to meet threats—like former Labour Party leader Jeremy Corbyn's insistence that UK citizens "stand united ... united in our determination not to let triumph those who would seek to divide us"[34] and Jean Monnet's declaration that "without unity," nationalist power-seeking doomed Europe. The "architect of European Unity" (Whitman, 1979, 1), Monnet contended that supranational unity would foster continental peace: "What we have to do first of all is make people aware that they're facing the future together" (Jean Monnet qtd. in Fursdon, 1980, 118). Cooperation will follow.

What does this mean for foreign policy? On one hand, unity primes people for militarism. During an external attack or foreign policy crisis, unity norms imply that people should band together and fight, escalating conflicts to eliminate threats: "*we must all join* in the fight to protect *our* nation, indivisible, because it is *our* land" (Fiske and Rai, 2015, 100). When George W. Bush addressed the nation after the September 11 attacks, he crafted a narrative predicated on unity-oriented nationalism. He built a stark contrast between good, "civilized" people and "evildoers" who must be punished (Krebs and Lobasz, 2007; Bostdorff, 2003), and alluded to American exceptionalism as he called for citizens to "remain strong and united" against terrorist threats.[35] Disunity via dissent was un-American (Krebs and Lobasz, 2007), and the public initially rewarded his message with widespread support for the wars in Afghanistan and Iraq (Hutcheson et al., 2004; Foyle, 2004). Unity norms can account for evidence that

33. See UKIP's 2015 platform in the Comparative Manifestos Project database. Party identifier 51951.

34. Jeremy Corbyn, 2017. "Jeremy Corbyn speech on terrorism and foreign policy: Full text," *New Statesman*, 26 May. URL: www.newstatesman.com/politics/staggers/2017/05/jeremy -corbyn-speech-terrorism-and-foreign-policy-full-text.

35. George W. Bush, 11 September 2001, "Statement by the President in His Address to the Nation." Transcript available at georgewbush-whitehouse.archives.gov/news/releases/2001/09 /20010911-16.html.

connects nationalism to support for war (Druckman, 1994; De Figueiredo and Elkins, 2003; Herrmann, Isernia and Segatti, 2009).

On the other hand, unity undermines intragroup trust and threatens interstate cooperation when it underlies supranationalism. Unity implies that group members share an obligation to help each other—to look out for their figurative "brothers and sisters."[36] But in heterogeneous groups, some people inevitably deviate from whichever characteristics purportedly unite people who share that group membership. Just as I might hesitate to trust the family outcast to watch my house,[37] unity leads supranationalists to demur when asked to rely on people with different ideals for their own security. This pattern played out at the European project's inception. Prominent Western European policymakers began promoting European unity by 1949—on the basis of their shared Western philosophy and Christian values (Fursdon, 1980, 49, 52)—but negotiations for the European Defence Community broke down when French leaders ultimately balked during the final stages (Parsons, 2002). Despite enthusiasm for the project, they viewed security guarantees with suspicion and feared that granting parity to the Germans would backfire. The Germans were unreliable Europeans, after all. Moreover, integrating the French army into a united force would mean losing an institution that made them unique,[38] too high a price to pay (Fursdon, 1980, 200).

The same dynamics that shattered the EDC persist in the twenty-first century. European citizens who proclaim that "Europe is for Europeans" clearly embrace their supranational community. But I nevertheless expect them to reject opportunities to deepen continental security cooperation. If "we" must share kinship ties or religious traditions (Checkel and Katzenstein, 2009; Risse, 2004), then "we" will view non-Christians or citizens from newer EU member-states with suspicion (Waldzus, Mummendey and Wenzel, 2005). In this way, unity creates Euroskeptics—and explains the seemingly puzzling levels of intragroup animosity among some European supranationalists (Mummendey and Waldzus, 2004). Figure 1.1

36. See, e.g., Wong (2010) for more on how Americans define their community boundaries and the conditions under which they feel obligated to support fellow American in-group members.

37. See Rai and Fiske (2011) and Fiske and Rai (2015) for a moral psychology perspective on how protecting a group's unity can justify violence against deviants.

38. See Mols and Weber (2013) for a discussion about how distinctiveness threats can undermine European cooperation.

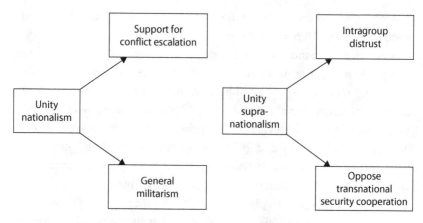

FIGURE 1.1. Unity drives nationalist militarism and undermines support for international cooperation.

summarizes the argument about unity-oriented nationalisms in international politics.

Equality mitigates support for nationalist militarism and promotes support for transnational cooperation

Equality, balance, and reciprocity create distinct nationalist norms. Common among peers or co-workers, these norms accommodate heterogeneity. When our group demands that "all are created equal," we will cooperate so long as members maintain a commitment to fairness. Importantly, people can maintain strong commitments to equality even while viewing their national or supranational group as superior to others—"our" commitment to equality is good and virtuous, whereas "their" commitments are bad. Many Canadian nationalists, for example, view themselves as more tolerant, accepting, and committed to global cooperation than their American neighbors to the south (Kymlicka, 2003).[39] Like unity, political leaders make regular references that connect equality to national identities: For example, the early twentieth century National Congress defined Indian nationalism by its commitment to equality and nonviolence (Tudor and Slater, 2020, 6), Justin Trudeau recently proclaimed that being Canadian demands "openness, respect, compassion, a willingness to work hard,"[40]

39. Of course, not all Canadians share these values, and scholars are quick to point out that the government's formal commitment to diversity sometimes falls short—especially with respect to indigenous communities (Kymlicka, 2004).

40. Justin Trudeau, 2015. "'Differences should be a source of strength': Trudeau at G20," *CBC*, 15 November. Available at www.cbc.ca/player/play/2678854482.

and Jean-Claude Juncker remarked that Europe is a "cord of many strands" that offers a "fair playing field." As these examples suggest, nationalisms vary—Juncker's vision of the EU clashes with Monnet's. The EU may be "United in Diversity," but even contemporaries place different emphases on these two ideals (Risse, 2010).

Equality mitigates the militaristic impulse that we typically associate with nationalism. Equality does not create pacifists—committing to reciprocity means that nationalists will respond to violence targeting people in their national group with equivalent force. But relative to unity, equality mutes reflexive hawkishness and escalatory aggression. Rather than condemn all outsiders as evildoers after 9/11 and support war with Iraq, equality might instead encourage nationalists to advocate limited strikes against al Qaeda targets. Such strikes differentiate between responsible parties and everyone else. Equality discourages people from interpreting an attack against one New York target as an attack on all Americans. They respond as if someone attacked coworkers, not family members. Following the 2015 terrorist attack in San Bernardino, Barack Obama relied on equality-laden rhetoric to call for *inaction* during an Oval Office address—to tamp down public enthusiasm for large-scale retaliation (Yglesias, 2015). His speech reinforced his early claims on the campaign trail that American nationalism centers on justice, equality, and diversity (Augoustinos and De Garis, 2012). Noting that the United States was founded on the idea that "you are equal in the eyes of God and equal in the eyes of the law,"[41] he asked American citizens to extend those values outward. Obama's appeal invited the American public to distinguish perpetrators from ordinary outsiders and to create opportunities for mutual peace (Prokop, 2015). Seen in this light, the relatively dovish "creedal" American nationalists from Bonikowski and DiMaggio's (2016) analysis no longer seem puzzling—committed to internal equality, they seek reciprocity in foreign policy rather than militaristic dominance.

Moreover, equality creates the conditions for supporting supranational cooperation. Because it accommodates heterogeneity—people must share a commitment to fairness but differences do not threaten the group—equality facilitates trust. Reciprocity can turn enemies like France and

41. Obama, Barack. 2015. "President Obama's address to the nation on the San Bernardino terror attack and the war on ISIS," 6 December. Transcript available from at www.cnn.com/2015/12/06/politics/transcript-obama-san-bernardino-isis-address/index.html.

Germany into friends:[42] One state extends a hand, and the two sides build trust over time in tandem with supranationalism. Canada again serves as an instructive analog, insofar as the Canadian state comprises many separate nations—English-speaking Canadians, French-speaking Quebecois, and numerous indigenous communities.[43] Though few Quebecers support political independence—a 2016 poll found that 82% of Quebecers support remaining in Canada[44]—they have long resisted unity within a pan-Canadian identity (Kymlicka, 2003, 373). Many nevertheless retain strong trust in and support for Canadian institutions—in part because they believe that Canadian law treats them fairly (ibid.). And if European supranationalism does not depend on ascriptive characteristics, like adapting to certain religious or cultural standards or giving up a native tongue, concerns about heterogeneity decline. Equality in turn encourages citizens to pool resources and form a European army or diplomatic corps. This strand of supranationalism likely explains why the standard story about international cooperation persists. The popular visions of an EU predicated on equality and democratic governance explain why we find robust correlations between European identification and support for security cooperation (Citrin and Sides, 2004; Schoen, 2008)—many citizens, though not all, likely have equality on the mind when they report their identification with Europe. Figure 1.2 summarizes my argument about equality, nationalism, and foreign policy attitudes.

Individual citizens perceive unity or equality as nationalist norms. Content represents an interaction between the individual and the group—not a dispositional trait—and two French citizens might ascribe different criteria to being French just as a single individual might ascribe different criteria to being French versus European. One American might view their country as a united family, whereas another thinks that being American means committing to equality. In other words, norms are properties of the group, but different people can view the same group as adhering to different norms. This characteristic animates debates within countries and continents, creating theoretically important variation among people who share nominal nationalisms.

---

42. See, e.g., Kupchan (2010) on reciprocity and *rapprochement*.

43. See McRoberts (1997) for a comprehensive discussion of Canadian federalism.

44. CBC News, 2016. "Majority of Quebecers believe question of independence is settled: Poll," 3 October. URL: https://www.cbc.ca/news/canada/montreal/quebec-angus-reid-canada-indepdence-1.3788110.

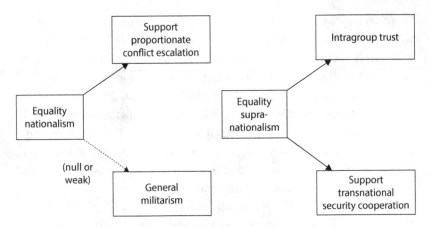

FIGURE 1.2. Equality mitigates support for nationalist conflict and promotes support for international cooperation.

Research design

To test my arguments about how unity- and equality-oriented nationalisms shape attitudes about international conflict and cooperation, I adopt a multi-method approach: I field original survey experiments to samples of the American public (chapters 3 and 4) and analyze survey data from citizens and elites across European Union member countries (chapter 5). Although I present a general theory, these American and European samples provide useful cases for my purposes. The United States is a frequent protagonist in militarized conflicts and foreign policy public opinion scholars disproportionately study the American public, leaving a long record that links nationalism to U.S. militarism. Moreover, extensive scholarly engagement with the "multiple traditions" that constitute American national identity—from commitment to the liberal American Creed to ethnoculturalism—facilitates crafting credible experimental treatments to target unity and equality.

A similar logic informs my choice to examine European supranationalism: The European Union endeavors to inculcate a transnational identity in the public, such that "European" supranationalisms have deeper institutional support compared to, for example, Arab or Southeast Asian supranationalisms. And the post-Maastricht Treaty period has witnessed a slow but sustained march toward foreign policy cooperation, making Europe a theoretically important case for testing my expectations about whether some supranationalisms might counter that trend.

Of course, focusing on Europe also risks elevating IR's Western dominance (Acharya, 2016a; Kang and Lin, 2019). More importantly, the field's overwhelming dependence on European supranationalism constitutes part of the puzzle itself. If our search for supranationalism and cooperation treats Europe as a benchmark (Acharya, 2014),[45] we might over-learn from this salient case or miss important patterns elsewhere in the international system.[46] For example, Barnett (1995) chronicles how Arab leaders like Jordan's King Hussein redefined Arab nationalism to require sovereign equality, not pan-Arab unification. These supranational norms, in turn, promoted regional order. And perhaps we underestimate the degree to which the Southeast Asia identity-building project contributes to support for cooperation and relative peace within the region (Kivimäki, 2010)—either because the "ASEAN Way" lacks the EU's legalism (Acharya, 2009), because we assume that ASEAN's heterogeneity and commitment to sovereign equality impedes supranational identification (Moorthy and Benny, 2013, 1044–45), or simply because surveys about ASEAN identity have only recently entered the field (Lee and Lim, 2020, 807; Moorthy and Benny, 2012, 2013). Questioning the nature of the relationship between supranationalisms and support for cooperation in Europe helps determine what we get right about supranationalisms—and what we get wrong—thereby setting the stage for rigorous comparative analyses in the future.

Plan of the Book

Why are some nationalists more belligerent than others? Moreover, why do some supranationalists—but not all—support transnational security cooperation? The remainder of this book combines theory, experiments, and survey analyses to answer these questions within a unified framework for research on nationalisms in international politics.

In chapter 2, I explain three things about nationalisms in international politics: (1) Nationalisms and supranationalisms represent different

---

45. See also Acharya (2016b) on the "EU-centrism" in research on regional institutions, and Börzel and Risse (2020, 32) on evidence that "Europe and the EU are not so special after all"— 62% of South American survey respondents felt close to their continent in 2003, for example (Roose, 2013, 287).

46. See Johnston (2012) for a discussion about how decisions to include or exclude East Asian cases have implications for IR theories, and Kang (2003) for a seminal argument about how IR scholars "[get] Asia wrong" to our detriment.

levels of categorization but share psychological foundations, and taking those foundations seriously requires accounting for content; (2) Unity and equality constitute two separate foundations for varieties of nationalisms; (3) Unity and equality have competing implications for attitudes about conflict and cooperation in international politics. After laying my theoretical groundwork, I review how history, institutions, rhetoric, and dispositions produce contestation between individuals about nationalist norms—thereby justifying my assumption that nationalisms vary within countries and transnational regions. I close the chapter by situating my framework vis-á-vis the civic/ethnic dichotomy that other scholars use to differentiate nationalisms in international politics.

In the next three chapters, I use a multi-method approach to test my *intergroup conflict* and *intragroup cooperation* hypotheses and triangulate evidence for my theoretical propositions. Experiments remain the gold standard for testing causality, but debates about nationalisms primarily rely on observational data. Accordingly, I use original survey experiments to investigate how unity and equality influence nationalist militarism in chapters 3 and 4. The experiment in chapter 3 manipulates the content of a fictional national identity—"Fredonia"—and measures responses to an escalating territorial conflict vignette. Building a fictional nationalism from scratch allows me to manipulate a country's norms while mitigating concerns that people will bring their pre-existing nationalist commitments to bear on the foreign policy crisis. Participants received instructions to imagine themselves as typical citizens of Fredonia, and read and wrote about how unity or equality prevail among the fictional Fredonians. The survey then asked them to report on Fredonia's national superiority—using the same scales for nationalism that scholars often equate with militarism—before eliciting responses to the foreign policy crisis. In the unity treatment, I find a positive relationship between nationalism and conflict escalation in the crisis and between nationalism and general militarism. Equality changes the story: Strong equality nationalists exhibit less hawkish attitudes compared to their counterparts in the unity group.

Chapter 3 introduces some evidence that content changes the relationship between nationalism and militarism and provides an important first test for my theory—but chapter 4 presents a second experiment that extends the results in two ways. First, I manipulate the content of American nationalisms to test the theory in a real-world context. Participants read fictional excerpts from an American history textbook, which described either unity or equality as foundations for American national identity.

A related writing task followed this excerpt. Like the Fredonia experiment, these treatments targeted content—what it means to be an American nationalist—using language and concepts that directly correspond to my theoretical framework. Second, I test the implications of unity and equality for general foreign policy militarism alongside concrete policy problems, like how the United States should respond to China and ISIS. In a national sample of Americans, I find evidence that both supports and extends my theory. Unity nationalism increases militant internationalism and hawkish China postures relative to equality, but both unity and equality drive nationalist support for conflict when an adversary has committed direct aggression against the United States or its allies.

In chapter 5, I shift from nationalisms to supranationalisms to test my intragroup cooperation hypothesis in Europe. I analyze data from surveys in 16 EU member-states, collected as part of the IntUne project on European identity (Cotta, Isernia and Bellucci, 2009), alongside Eurobarometer data from the complement of EU members (European Commission, 2018, 2020). These large-scale surveys bring important advantages in external validity: I test my hypothesis with data that spans multiple years (2007, 2009, 2014, and 2019), countries, and populations (public and elite). I first use a battery of items that tap what it means to be European to proxy equality and unity, and test the relationship between these supranationalisms and three attitudinal outcomes: intra-European trust, support for a single EU foreign policy, and support for military integration via a European army. These analyses account for alternative explanations by controlling for European identification, national attachment, generalized trust, political ideology, and other important traits like university education. If the conventional story suffices to explain attitudes about cooperation, the content-free measures for national and European identification should supplant any effects of unity or equality. Instead, the results provide clear and consistent evidence to support my expectation that equality promotes intra-European trust and support for EU security cooperation. Indeed, equality's effect on support for a single EU foreign policy is nearly five times the size of the effect associated with the one-dimensional measure for European identification in the IntUne mass public data. By contrast, unity decreases trust and drives opposition to foreign policy and military integration. Supplementing these analyses, I next show that my theory extends to attitudes about economic cooperation. Finally, I use data from the 2014 and 2019 Eurobarometer surveys—which include representative samples from all 28 member-states—to show that my core findings remain robust at different times and when I use a different strategy to measure commitments to unity and equality.

In chapter 6, I turn my attention to other important questions that my book invites and pave the way for future research. For example, who are the unity- and equality-oriented nationalists in the real world—where they do not have an experimental prompt to guide them? What does my theory imply about whether people support more aggressive action against some types of countries, like fellow democracies, compared to other types of countries? How could future research go beyond public opinion to examine the theory's implications for actual interstate conflict? Finally, I discuss the normative and policy implications that arise from my theory and results: Are there "good" and "bad" nationalisms? And what does my book imply about rising nationalism and prospects for enduring security cooperation in Europe?

2

Varieties of Nationalism and Attitudes about Conflict and Cooperation

How do nationalisms vary, and what do different nationalisms mean for foreign policy attitudes? In chapter 1, I explained that research on nationalisms and supranationalisms often misunderstands—or bypasses—important theoretical factors and empirical findings that undermine core claims about how nationalists navigate international politics. As a result, we lack answers to fundamental questions about nationalisms and foreign policy attitudes.

In this chapter, I introduce new theoretical architecture to conceptualize nationalisms and explain how unity- and equality-oriented nationalisms lead to competing attitudes about intergroup conflict and intragroup cooperation in international politics. I first leverage psychology's social identity approach to explain why scholars think that nationalist commitments implicate foreign policy attitudes in the first place: People categorize their social world, and group memberships shape attitudes toward both insiders and outsiders across the national and supranational levels of categorization. Next, I explain the missing piece in our current understanding of nationalisms in IR: Social identities have qualitatively different content (Abdelal et al., 2006). Individuals often hold markedly different ideas about what constitutes an "American" or "European" nationalist (Schildkraut, 2007;

Theiss-Morse, 2009; Prutsch, 2017). What it means to be part of the group, in turn, affects how nationalists respond to foreign policy problems (Citrin et al., 1994; Snyder, 2000; Schrock-Jacobson, 2012; Saideman and Ayres, 2008; Saideman, 2013).

Beliefs about the *content* of one's social group condition both intergroup and intragroup attitudes. Incorporating content allows me to make novel predictions about *which* nationalists support militarism, escalation, or security integration. After laying the groundwork, I present my framework for analyzing unity- and equality-oriented nationalisms in IR. Research on "relational models"—fundamental norms of human interaction (Fiske, 1991)—informs these two concepts and ensures that my theory starts from pre-political norms that apply across both the national and supranational categorization levels. Although relational models theory has a long scholarly record, to my knowledge this book is the first to apply the framework to both nationalisms and foreign policy attitudes.

I first detail how unity and equality constitute distinct nationalisms, before explaining the implications for attitudes about *intergroup conflict* and *intragroup cooperation*. A notable advancement, my theory encompasses both familiar and paradoxical patterns related to relationships between nationalisms and foreign policy attitudes at the country and regional levels: I chart the logic that connects unity-oriented nationalism (but not equality) to militarism and conflict escalation, and equality-oriented supranationalism (but not unity) to transnational trust and security cooperation. I next justify my assumption that countries and supranational regions feature *contestation* over nationalisms—individuals within the same group disagree about what it means to be a nationalist. Finally, I explain how my framework complements conceptual schemes that differentiate civic from ethnic nationalism, while also avoiding key limitations.

Before moving forward, I note two important conditions. First, my theory explains foreign policy attitudes. I am interested in whether and why only *some* nationalists support conflict escalation, for example, but not in ascribing a "national character" to whole populations or using that classification to analyze state-level variation and outcomes. People contest what it means to be part of a group. Widespread disagreement about identity content divides individuals within countries and regions—some American nationalists commit to unity, whereas others emphasize equality; some French citizens commit to European equality, whereas others emphasize unity and homogeneity. When we aggregate to the country level or higher, then, we obscure substantial individual-level variation,[1] ignore contestation, inappropriately elevate some nationalisms over others, and stymie our understanding of how nationalisms operate in the real world.[2] I therefore focus on people, not countries, in both my theory and analyses.

Second, this is a book about international politics. I test my theory in the foreign policy realm because nationalism plays a central role in international relations research on public opinion and conflict. Far from neglecting nationalism, IR scholars often take its implications for granted (Walt, 1996), making it essential that we understand nationalism properly. Moreover, the foreign policy domain allows me to simultaneously test my theory's implications for intergroup conflict *and* intragroup cooperation by bridging the national and transnational categorization levels. At the same time, I avoid concerns about whether people have domain specific belief systems that would complicate comparisons between nationalisms' effects on, for example, welfare attitudes versus a war with China (Hurwitz and Peffley, 1987; Liberman, 2006; Feldman and Zaller, 1992).[3] So although my psychological approach creates a framework that should generalize to subnational contexts,[4] I constrain my theoretical claims and empirical tests to the foreign policy realm.

Nationalisms as Social Identities

In 2001, Senator Snowe asserted that 9/11 was not just an attack on people at the Pentagon or World Trade Centers (individuals), but "an attack on

1. I thank an anonymous reviewer for pushing me on this point.

2. As Mercer (1995, 238) explains, we cannot reduce the influence of social groups to individual or interpersonal interactions. Instead, nationalisms are fundamentally *social*—we must understand the group, its norms, and the strength of identification to explain attitudes and behavior toward fellow group members and outsiders. Nationalisms reflect more than individual-level dispositions. For examples of research on nationalism in international politics that engages other units of analysis, see, e.g., Cronin (1999); Hopf and Allan (2016); Brown (1999); Greenfeld (1992); Lebow (2016).

3. Though cf. Rathbun (2007) or Goren et al. (2016) for theories that bridge the domestic and foreign policy divide.

4. For example, variation in content has implications for how people distribute resources to different communities within a country via disaster relief or the welfare state (Theiss-Morse, 2009; Wong, 2010; Wright and Reeskens, 2013), political participation (Raney and Berdahl, 2009), attitudes toward immigrants and immigration policy (Lindstam, Mader and Schoen, 2021), attitudes toward racial or religious minorities (Citrin, Wong and Duff, 2001; Collingwood, Lajevardi and Oskooii, 2018), and social cohesion within countries (Reeskens and Wright, 2013; Breidahl, Holtug and Kongshøj, 2018).

all Americans" (the group).[5] Her assertion resonated with regular citizens because categorization allows us to think and act as part of groups—interpersonal interactions become intergroup interactions.[6] Indeed, people are predisposed to see themselves in terms of groups and to feel connected to other members of their "imagined communities" (Anderson, 1983). We sort our social universe into men and women, Jews and Catholics, Republicans and Democrats (Greene, 1999; Huddy, Mason and Aarøe, 2015; Bankert, Huddy and Rosema, 2017), Ohio State Buckeyes and Michigan Wolverines, or French, Nigerian, Australian, East Asian or European.[7] Individuals choose to identify with some of these groups, and not others—for instance, a Catholic and Italian, but not a European. In turn, social categorization shifts our mindsets from "me or thee" to "we" (Dawes, Van De Kragt and Orbell, 1988, 83).

People exhibit remarkable flexibility in how they categorize themselves and others (McGuire et al., 1978; Turner, 1985; Hornsey and Hogg, 2000; Huddy, 2001), with identities often nested within one another like Russian Matryoshka dolls (Herrmann and Brewer, 2004).[8] We can belong to a national group, but also claim membership in a broader, encompassing group that exists at a higher level: Such "recategorization" brings separate "subgroups"—like French and German nationalists—together under a single "superordinate" umbrella group—like Europe (Gaertner and Dovidio,

5. Olympia Snowe, 2001. "September 11, 2001: Attack on America Congressional Record Senate—Terrorist Attacks Against the United States; September 12, 2001." Transcript available from *The Avalon Project*. URL: www.avalon.law.yale.edu/sept11/senate_proc_091201.asp.

6. The social identity approach combines social identity theory (Tajfel, 1981) and self-categorization theory (Turner, 1985). Whereas social identity theory primarily concerns what motivates people to join groups and the affective ties between group members, self-categorization theory stresses cognition. Self-categorization theory explains identification at different levels of categorization, from the personal to the global, and how people perceive the fit between themselves and prototypical group members. See Hornsey (2008) for a historical overview of these overlapping theories.

7. As Rosch (1975) writes, humans categorize our material and social worlds. Categorization reduces the cognitive effort required to navigate the world by helping us process information from the top down. If we can quickly differentiate whether a fluffy creature belongs to the class "dog" or "wolf," we can react appropriately, such as moving toward the former but backing away from the latter. If we relied instead on bottom-up processing, we would be more likely to make deadly mistakes.

8. See Risse (2010, 25) for a summary of other ways that scholars have thought about multiple social identities.

2000).[9] When Germans identify with Europe, they expand group boundaries to include previous outsiders like Italians, for example (Dovidio et al., 1997; Rousseau and Garcia-Retamero, 2007; Transue, 2007; Dovidio, Gaertner and Saguy, 2009). Notably, the same person can identify with groups at both levels of categorization. People can commit strongly to German and European (Mummendey and Waldzus, 2004), Canadian and North American, or Saudi and Arab (Telhami, 2013) identities. Nationalism at one level does not preclude commitment at the other level, a pattern borne out by research on dual identities (Dovidio, Gaertner and Saguy, 2009; Wenzel et al., 2003; Wenzel, Mummendey and Waldzus, 2007; Börzel and Risse, 2020).

The main difference between nationalism and "supranationalism" lies in the object of attachment or level of categorization—the country or region—but the central dynamics that political scientists use to explain their implications for foreign policy attitudes remain the same. At both levels, nationalisms are social identities.[10] Nationalisms entail 1) a cognitive awareness that one belongs to a group, defined by either national borders or a supranational collective, 2) an emotional attachment to that group, and 3) commitment to the group's superiority.[11] Nationalisms affect how we feel about and interact with "in-group" members, like co-nationals or fellow Westerners (Dumont et al., 2003), and "out-group" members, like citizens from foreign countries (Tajfel, 1982; Tajfel and Turner, 1986; Brown,

9. Notably, the common in-group identity model and related logic of categorization contradict research that treats national identities as objects of "terminal loyalty" (Cottam and Cottam, 2001).

10. A classic definition describes social identity as "that part of the individual's self-concept which derives from his knowledge of his membership of a social group (or groups) together with the value and emotional significance attached to that membership" (Tajfel, 1981, 255). For excellent work applying social identity theory to international relations, see, e.g., Mercer (1995); Larson and Shevchenko (2010); Risse (2010); Ward (2017); Snyder (2019). For reviews, see Hymans (2002), Monroe and McDermott (2010), Mols and Weber (2013); Kalin and Sambanis (2018); Brown (2020).

11. Notably, some political psychologists would disagree with my characterization of nationalisms as social identities, because many scholars separate nationalism from related constructs like patriotism or an ostensibly apolitical "national identification" (Schatz, Staub and Lavine, 1999; Huddy and Khatib, 2007; Huddy and Del Ponte, 2019; though see Mader et al., 2018; Bonikowski and DiMaggio, 2016). Such work often concludes that nationalism, wrapped up in notions of in-group superiority, must by definition entail "insidious" forms of out-group aggression (Bonikowski, 2016; Bonikowski and DiMaggio, 2016). But as I argued in chapter 1, such definitions risk conflating nationalism with the outcomes we expect it to explain. Moreover, readers who disagree with this conceptualization might nevertheless find value in my main theoretical contribution—that content matters for how nationalisms shape foreign policy attitudes.

2000). We hold a positive bias toward fellow group members and, often, a negative bias toward outsiders (Tajfel and Turner, 1979; Brewer, 1999).

The standard stories depend on the social identity approach

Treating nationalisms as social identities synthesizes two levels of categorization—national and supranational—that matter to foreign policy attitudes. Indeed, standard stories use insights from the social identity approach to explain the primary outcomes I examine in this book: militarism, escalation, and support for conflictual foreign policy on the one hand, and transnational trust and support for security integration on the other. Research emphasizes how nationalist "out-group hate" toward external adversaries manifests in hawkish intergroup competition, whereas supranationalist "in-group love" increases trust and cooperation within the transnational entity.

When scholars assert that separating "us" from "them" in national groups "provide[s] a fertile ground for conflict and hate" (Brewer, 1999, 435), they typically rely on three observations.[12] First, for "our" group to succeed in the international political arena, we need our country to maintain sovereignty, status, material assets, and/or moral and cultural superiority (Mercer, 1995; Wohlforth, 2009). Nationalists often adopt a competitive mindset whereby they forgo benefits to maximize relative gains for their country at the expense of outsiders (Mutz and Kim, 2017).[13]

Second, people perceive outsiders as more hostile, aggressive, and threatening than insiders (Schafer, 1999; Herrmann, Isernia and Segatti, 2009; Branscombe and Wann, 1994; Brewer, 1999; Monroe, 2008). Outsiders make dubious partners and pose potential threats, and nationalists treat single individuals as representatives for a larger group of "evil" others.[14] This dynamic explains why Americans who felt threatened by terrorism after the 9/11 attacks supported military action against Iraq

12. Although "in-group love" can arise independently from "out-group hate" (Brewer, 2001a)—national identification does *not* inexorably lead to conflict" (Gries, 2005, 237; see also Rathbun, 2015)—the chance for intergroup conflict increases when groups differ in status, compete, or are political entities. International politics meets these conditions.

13. This pattern mimics psychological research showing that strong identifiers adopt strategies that maximize the difference between rewards for their in-group members and rewards for relevant competitors, instead of strategies that maximize joint rewards (Hinkle and Brown, 1990).

14. Our tendency to see out-group members as all alike contributes to this phenomenon—psychologists chronicle the out-group homogeneity effect whereby "they" all look the same (Hogg and Abrams, 1988; Ostrom and Sedikides, 1992). See Horowitz (2001) for an example of how out-group homogeneity drives violent escalation in ethnic riots.

(Huddy et al., 2005). Iraqis bore no responsibility for the attacks, but to many Americans they served as representatives for the broader "terrorist" out-group.[15]

Third, external threats and out-group animosity reinforce each other. In one study, nationalists were more likely to derogate Russians when an experimental manipulation highlighted Russia as a geopolitical threat (Branscombe and Wann, 1994). Others find evidence for the reverse pattern—we inflate threats from outsiders, increasing our willingness to use force (Druckman, 1994, 2001; Federico, Golec and Dial, 2005; Herrmann, Isernia and Segatti, 2009; Ko, 2019).[16] And in part because our national identities are wrapped up in territory (Anderson, 1983; Gibler, Hutchison and Miller, 2012; Goemans, 2006), territorial disputes against rivals escalate to war more often than other types of disputes (Vasquez, 2009).

Although "the dark side of a strong national identity might . . . be a greater predisposition to conflict with other nations" (Sambanis and Shayo, 2013, 320), identifying with a transnational entity transfers "in-group love" and its cooperation-enhancing benefits across borders. Confirming the adage that "charity begins at home," people tend to support policies that benefit their in-group, like universal healthcare and domestic disaster relief (Johnston et al., 2010; Theiss-Morse, 2009; Wong, 2010).

"Home" encompasses a larger swath of territory when people think of themselves as Europeans and not just Belgian, Spanish, or Polish. But the same logic operates as the group's boundaries expand. In the words of Emmanuel Macron, "When we speak of our security, we are also speaking of Europe's security."[17] Identifying with a broader group increases people's willingness to forgive former adversaries (Cehajic, Brown and Castano,

15. Related, Huddy et al. (2005) also found that respondents who felt threatened by terrorism vilified Arab-Americans. Those respondents categorized Arab-Americans as violent and supported policies that restricted Arab-American rights. This finding focuses on subnational dynamics but mimics my earlier discussion of how some European supranationalists reject fellow Europeans they view as bad representatives for the group.

16. These patterns of out-group stereotyping and threat inflation have also been implicated in subnational conflicts, such as genocides and civil wars (Cederman, Wimmer and Min, 2010; Sambanis, 2001; Horowitz, 1985; Staub, 2000). For example, Horowitz (1985) presents a seminal application of insights from SIT to subnational, "ethnic," conflict. Although my book focuses on international politics rather than subnational politics, the theoretical claims could be applied to other levels of categorization.

17. Macron, Emmanuel, 2018. "Speech by President Emmanuel Macron—Ambassadors' Conference 2018," 27 August. Available at www.diplomatie.gouv.fr/en/the-ministry-and-its-network/events/ambassadors-week/ambassadors-week-edition-2018/article/speech-by-president-emmanuel-macron-ambassadors-conference-2018.

2008), provide moral and practical support to victims of terrorist attacks outside their own national borders (Dumont et al., 2003), and support security cooperation with neighboring countries (Beaton, Dovidio and Léger, 2008). We make sacrifices to help our group—a practice that has evolutionary advantages (Brewer and Caporael, 2006) and enhances the prospect for security cooperation.

We also trust in-group members more than outsiders (Brewer, 1999; Brown, 2000; Alesina and La Ferrara, 2002; Voci, 2006; Lyall, Shiraito and Imai, 2015), facilitating cooperation.[18] Trust and in-group solidarity mutually reinforce each other (Putnam, 1995; Reeskens and Wright, 2013; Robinson, 2016), such that supranationalism helps people overcome the mistrust that often tracks national borders and foments competition and conflict (Waltz, 1979; Mearsheimer, 2014; Rathbun, 2009).[19] Mutual trust opens the door for European policymakers to cede some foreign policy autonomy by implementing qualified majority voting rules on defense issues in the EU, for example. Such rules require politicians to trust that fellow Europeans will advance Europe's collective interests when they vote, and that the resulting policies will not compromise individual members' national security.[20]

In short, the conventional wisdom about nationalisms in international politics relies on psychology's social identity approach. When sovereign countries serve as the objects of identification, we expect hawkishness. When the object of identification shifts to a higher level of

18. Of course, particularistic trust—often reserved for in-group members—represents one aggregate tendency. Yet some people have trusting dispositions and place their faith in in-group and out-group members alike (Uslaner, 2002; Rathbun, 2011a). In their research on inter-ethnic trust in Russia, for example, Bahry et al. (2005) show that many Russians are "inclusionary" trusters who trust both in-group and out-group members equally, and others are "alienated" people who trust outsiders but not their own group members.

19. I focus on the relationship between identification and trust, though IR scholars also point to other paths to building cross-border trust. These include leaders who possess trusting dispositions (Rathbun, 2011a, 2012), unilateral vulnerability (Kupchan, 2010), gradual reciprocity and reassurance (Osgood, 1962; Hoffman, 2006), rational trust (Kydd, 2005), and interpersonal relationships (Wheeler, 2018).

20. See Balliet and Van Lange (2013) for more on the relationship between trust and cooperation in general, and Rathbun (2011a, 244) on why "transferring control over" security policy "is a trusting act." For Barnett and Adler (1998, 414), a security community—bound by a shared transnational identity—represents "unarguably the deepest expression of trust possible in the international arena." Though see Wheeler (2018) for a critique of how security community scholars theorize trust; he argues that trust cannot both cause community-building and emerge from identification.

categorization, we expect support for cooperation within the transnational in-group.

But at the same time that our current understanding of nationalisms in international politics *depends upon* the social identity approach, it also starts from an impoverished view of how identification shapes individual attitudes. If we accept that separating "us" from "them" has consequences for foreign policy attitudes, we must acknowledge that we are missing a fundamental aspect of the theory: Group norms have implications for how our identities manifest in attitudes and behavior (Turner, 1985; Hornsey, 2008). In that respect, we should understand the purported consequences of categorization and identification, for both intergroup conflict and intra-group cooperation, as contingent outcomes. Consequences that appear to be universal actually depend on what it means to be part of the group. Nationalisms vary.

Varieties of Nationalism: Content Matters

If a single continuous measure for nationalism sufficed to explain how peo-ple respond to international threats and regional partners, this book would be about nationalism—not nationalism*s*—in international politics. Nation-alisms include expectations about what it means to be part of the group.[21] We treat nationalism as one-dimensional when we limit our theory and analysis to whether a person agrees with abstract nationalist sentiments, like the notion that the world would be better off if more countries were like her own. Differences between strongly and weakly committed nation-alists matter, to be sure—a factor I return to later in the chapter. But what features does our hypothetical nationalist hope to export? Her country's dominant religious tradition? Parliamentary democracy? A culture that promotes gender equality? Answers to these questions have inescapable consequences for understanding *which* nationalisms correspond to greater support for using military force in a crisis or forming a supranational army.

WHY DOES CONTENT MATTER? WHO "WE" ARE SHAPES WHAT "WE" DO.

Social identities carry substantive meanings. Variation in *content*—"the meaning of a collective identity" (Abdelal et al., 2006, 696; Johnston, 2005)—provides the missing link to explain when nationalisms prompt

---

21. Like other social identities—see, e.g., Turner (1985); Raney and Berdahl (2009), and Huddy and Khatib (2007).

conflictual or cooperative foreign policy attitudes. People hold concrete mental representations of what differentiates their national or supranational group from outsiders, along with descriptive ideas about the values that group members hold and prescriptive expectations about how nationalists should behave (Turner, 1991; Hogg, Turner and Davidson, 1990; Hornsey, 2008).

Constitutive norms and relational comparisons comprise two aspects of identity content that divide nationalisms.[22] Constitutive norms provide informal rules for belonging within the group, whereas relational comparisons dictate how group members contrast "us" and "them."

First, constitutive norms define the rules of the road: how group members should behave, what they should believe, and how they should feel (Hogg and Abrams, 1988). People adjust their individual attitudes and behavior to match group-level norms. For instance, a group might prescribe dominance and aggression with respect to outsiders, a pattern that would lead to nationalist conflict. Norms can also prescribe diffuse reciprocity—sharing with others without expecting in-kind repayment—and thereby facilitate regional security cooperation. But they might just as easily advise out-group love via charitable giving (Catholics) or tolerance toward refugees (American Jews) (Reicher and Hopkins, 2001), rather than conflict, such that "predictions about group behavior will be wide of the mark if group norms are ignored" (Theiss-Morse, 2009, 68).

Differences in group norms produce contradictory—and sometimes counterintuitive—effects that we cannot explain with categorization alone. For example, some people assume that "collectivism" and "individualism"

---

22. Abdelal et al. (2006) outline four "nonmutually exclusive" dimensions for studying identity content: Constitutive norms, social purposes, relational comparisons, and cognitive models. My theory focuses on two of these dimensions, constitutive norms and relational comparisons. Social purposes refer to the goals that a group aspires to achieve (Abdelal et al., 2006, 22), and cognitive models refer to individuals' worldviews (Abdelal et al., 2006, 25). Social purposes likely provide important insights into the politics involved in promoting certain nationalisms—such as why countries adopt different citizenship laws or nation-building strategies. But I am interested in nationalisms as independent variables, not dependent variables, and a theory rooted in social purpose risks conflating cause and effect. Cognitive worldviews imply cross-cultural variation in how members of some groups reason, make causal attributions, or interpret and define their interests (Abdelal et al., 2006). Unpacking cognitive worldviews seems imperative for comparative research, where we can evaluate how group memberships shape people's beliefs. Some governments, for example, might encourage citizens to see the world as highly competitive, priming them for conflict. Aiming for a generalizable theory that can apply across identities and categorization levels, I incorporate the two dimensions—relational comparisons and constitutive norms—that correspond to a general and broadly applicable theory of social cognition from social psychology. See, e.g., Saideman (2013) for a similar approach.

represent two ends of an identification continuum (Triandis, McCusker and Hui, 1990; Markus and Kitayama, 1991; Hofstede, 1984). In that view, collectivists strongly identify with their group, elevate the group's interest, and believe that the group's success is more important than their personal goals. Individualists are weak identifiers who prioritize their own personal achievement over group success. But an illuminating experiment by Jetten, Postmes and McAuliffe (2002) illustrated the flaws in this reasoning: If we think about collectivism and individualism as distinct *norms*, strong identifiers in an individualist culture should be especially individualistic. If a person wants to adhere to their group's expectations in a collectivist culture (Tajfel and Turner, 1986; Hogg, Turner and Davidson, 1990; Turner, 1991), she will emphasize interdependence and cooperation ("we are all united"). By the same token, strong identification should lead people who belong to an individualist culture to act more like autonomous individuals ("we are all individuals") (Jetten, Postmes and McAuliffe, 2002, 190), *because* the group requires such behavior. And indeed, the authors find observational and experimental evidence to support their theory—Indonesians with strong national identities embraced collectivism, whereas Americans with strong national identities endorsed individualistic norms.[23] Notably, and a point I return to below, the pressure to conform to group norms depends on the strength of a person's connection to the group.[24] People who feel strong nationalist commitments will align their attitudes and behavior with the group (Terry and Hogg, 1996), whereas weak identifiers often will not.

Second, relational comparisons describe interactions between group members and outsiders (Abdelal et al., 2006, 697–98), thereby highlighting the fundamentally social nature of social identities. This dimension can encompass several features, including whether an identity implies exclusivity—whether an Ohio State fan can also root for Michigan; whether

23. For example, the authors compare Americans who report that they strongly identify with their nation to Indonesian participants with the same strong group identity, and find that committed Americans embrace individualist statements like, "If the group is slowing me down, it is better to leave it and work alone." By contrast, Indonesians endorsed collectivist norms like, "I would help within my means if a relative told me that he (she) is in financial difficulty" (Triandis, McCusker and Hui, 1990 qtd. in Jetten, Postmes and McAuliffe, 2002, 193).

24. In IR, some research on status-seeking behavior implicates norms, drawing a distinction between states like Norway that seek superiority via diplomacy, and those like Russia that instead seek dominance. See Wohlforth et al. (2018, 537) for a discussion about Norway's national identity discourse. They argue that in identifying as a peace-loving nation, Norway has pursued international status using social creativity—defining a new dimension on which they could gain esteem from international peers. See also Larson and Shevchenko (2010) and Gries (2005).

group members perceive outsiders as inherently hostile; and whether group membership requires homogeneity (Abdelal, Herrera, Johnson and McDermott, 2009; Saideman and Ayres, 2008; Risse, 2010, 24).

Existing research on nationalisms in international politics often incorporates explicit and implicit relational comparisons: Greenfeld (1992), for example, argues that a relational comparison to the West shaped Russian nationalism. Fueled by *ressentiment*, Russians defined themselves by who they were not; the West provided a relevant foil. According to Neumann (1999), European identity has also coalesced around a comparison to both Turkey and Russia as outsiders. Treating Turkey as a relevant other gives meaning to the European identity and poses a seemingly insurmountable barrier to entry for the predominantly Muslim state (Curley, 2009). Those relational comparisons stress the need to maintain intragroup homogeneity, and have consequences for how the group influences individual attitudes.

WHY DO WE NEED A NEW FRAMEWORK FOR NATIONALISMS IN IR?

Some IR scholars have brought important nuance to bear in nationalism research by incorporating content into their theories: Hymans (2006) shows that oppositional nationalists are more likely to "go nuclear" than their "sportsmanlike" counterparts; Snyder (2000) and Schrock-Jacobson (2012) show that "civic" nationalisms are less war-prone than "ethnic" or "revolutionary" varieties; Saideman and Ayres (2008) conclude that "intolerant" nationalists reject irredentism; and Risse (2010, 61) finds evidence for "two Europes" that divide public views about foreign policy.

These studies represent clear advancements in the movement to take identity content seriously in world politics (Chandra, 2006; Kalin and Sambanis, 2018), but they also highlight the problem of abundance. Nationalism alone can be "civic" or "ethnic" (Kohn, 1944; Reeskens and Wright, 2013; Greenfeld, 1992; Wright, Citrin and Wand, 2012; Reeskens and Hooghe, 2010), "revolutionary" or "counterrevolutionary" (Snyder, 2000; Schrock-Jacobson, 2012), "oppositional" or "sportsmanlike" (Hymans, 2006), "inclusive" or "exclusive" (Tudor and Slater, 2020), "malignant" or "benign" (Van Evera, 1994), "enlightened" (Jones, 2014), "gendered" (Deckman and Cassese, 2019), "nativist" or "antitraditionalist" or "pragmatist" (Zhao, 2000), "individualistic-libertarian" or "collectivistic-authoritarian" (Greenfeld, 1992), "disengaged," "ardent," "creedal," or "restrictive"

(Bonikowski and DiMaggio, 2016). Others separate nationalism from patriotism, attachment, and identification to blend content with dimensionality (Kosterman and Feshbach, 1989; De Figueiredo and Elkins, 2003; Huddy and Khatib, 2007; Gries et al., 2011), or differentiate "blind" from "constructive" and "constitutional" patriotism (Schafer, 1999; Blank and Schmitdt, 2003; Davidov, 2010) and "civic republicanism" from commitment to the American creed in the United States (Hartz, 1955; Schildkraut, 2007). Scholars describe European supranationalisms as "civic," "cultural" (Bruter, 2003, 2009; Börzel and Risse, 2007), "cosmopolitan" (Schlenker, 2013), "modern" or "nationalist" (Risse, 2010). It is no wonder that some readers either "conclude that identity is so elusive, slippery, and amorphous that it will never prove to be a useful variable" (Abdelal et al., 2006, 18) or "lump" all nationalisms together rather than select from the cornucopia of concepts (Mylonas and Kuo, 2017, 3).

I resolve this problem by developing a flexible theory of identity content rooted in fundamental norms of human interaction. General phenomena require a general framework, rather than ad hoc adaptations that widen the divide between research programs. I explain variation in nationalisms with variation in how people perceive the group-level norms that organize social interaction outside politics—using a theory that incorporates important ideas from past work, translates across levels of categorization, and makes clear predictions about relevant outcomes while putting conceptual distance between the psychological independent variables and political dependent variables. In the next section, I propose that fundamental structures of social interaction—relational models (Fiske, 1991)—produce at least two nationalisms, centered on unity or equality. With my framework in place for understanding what nationalism *means*, I explain how differentiating unity from equality produces novel expectations regarding the circumstances that lead nationalists to endorse militarism and supranationalists to promote or reject security cooperation.

SOCIAL RELATIONS CONSTITUTE SOCIAL IDENTITIES

Nationalisms vary, but how? Varieties of nationalism, like other group identities, depend on how people navigate their social worlds. If we want to create a generalizable typology for identity content, we should start from a general theory of social cognition. I adapt my framework from Fiske's

(1991) Relational Models Theory (RMT).[25] Of note, RMT asserts that people relate to one another based on a small, rudimentary set of norms that they adapt to different situations (Fiske, 2004, 3). These models include communal sharing (*unity*) and equality matching (*equality*) and serve as "the schemata people use to construct and construe relationships" (Fiske, 1992, 689).[26]

Each model represents a discrete structure—not two ends of a single continuum. Each structure shapes acceptable and expected behavior within a relationship and people's perceptions of other actors in the social world. In communal sharing relationships (*unity*), individuals abide by norms of diffuse reciprocity and parochial altruism. They view themselves as a unified whole comprised of homogeneous compatriots. In relationships based on equality matching (*equality*), people adhere to fairness and tit-for-tat reciprocity. They see each other as peers or equals.

The past thirty years have seen wide-ranging evidence that these relational models organize social life: Fiske (1991, 42-49) first found that relational schemata coordinate and explain behavior in politically important domains such as exchange, work, orientations toward land, decision-making, social identity, moral judgment, and aggression in his ethnographic analysis of Mossi people in Burkina Faso. Fiske, Haslam and Fiske (1991) show that when people make substitution errors—such as when they

25. Social identity theory is well-known within political science—reviews, applications, and extensions appear in top journals from the *American Journal of Political Science* (Transue, 2007) to *International Organization* (Mercer, 1995) and *Political Psychology* (Huddy, 2001). By contrast, political scientists have rarely engaged RMT directly, with Fiske and Tetlock's (1997) *Political Psychology* piece on taboo trade-offs a notable exception. Yet RMT has wide reach elsewhere in the social sciences including subfields of psychology (Haslam, 2004; Rai and Fiske, 2011; Vodosek, 2009), business (Blois and Ryan, 2012), marketing (Sheppard and Tuchinsky, 1996), anthropology (Nettle et al., 2011), and psychological work on political ideology (Simpson and Laham, 2015*a*). Moreover, it provides a theoretical foundation for Moral Foundations Theory, a theory of moral psychology that provides insights into ideology (Graham et al., 2011) and foreign policy attitudes (Kertzer et al., 2014). See also Bell and Kertzer (2018) for an argument linking RMT to the politics of NATO defense contributions.

26. The theory includes two other models, authority ranking and market pricing. Authority ranking relationships exist when there is a clear hierarchy among individuals—those at the top lead and subordinates follow, as in national militaries or Confucian families (Fiske, 1992, 2004; Fiske and Tetlock, 1997). I return to the possibility for hierarchy-based nationalisms and other types of content in the concluding chapter. Market pricing refers to a model of interaction built on proportionality; interactions are centered on cost-benefit calculations. This model dominates economic exchange and explains relations between merchants and customers (Fiske, 1991; Haslam and Fiske, 1999), but offers less guidance regarding nationalisms.

call someone by the incorrect name—they tend to identify someone who shares a similar relationship. My mother uses my sister's name when she refers to me more often than she uses a coworker's name, for example. Relational models predict such substitution errors better than other factors like race and gender. Survey research shows that moral judgments often depend on how people construe a relationship (Simpson and Laham, 2015*b*)—disobedience is wrong if the command comes from someone higher in a hierarchy, but not if it comes from an equal. Tendencies to construe relationships in terms of unity or equality also correlate with specific issue stances, like abortion, even when accounting for political ideology (Simpson and Laham, 2015*a*). Finally, RMT informs moral foundations theory (Haidt and Graham, 2007). On their search for a "common core" of cross-culturally valid moral models, Haidt and Joseph (2004, 58) engaged RMT and linked equality and unity to specific moral systems (Fiske, 1991).[27]

To my knowledge, I am the first to connect the relational models to nationalisms and foreign policy attitudes. I focus here on unity and equality for two reasons. First, each implies a distinct set of constitutive norms and relational comparisons that synthesize existing conversations about nationalisms. Respectively, unity-oriented relations emphasize group homogeneity and cohesion whereas equality-oriented relations stress fairness, individual rights, and responsibilities to the group.[28] Unity implicitly dominates most research on nationalism in IR: Scholars think that nationalism requires aggression and sacrifice because members want to protect the group at all costs. Equality, by contrast, provides a clear social and psychological foundation for so-called civic, tolerant, or individualistic nationalisms that researchers deploy across political science. But my theory builds from the bottom up, connecting foundational norms of social interaction to nationalism. This move avoids the conceptual debates and challenges that muddy top-down approaches that use abstract theory or political institutions to differentiate nationalisms.

27. Indeed, moral judgments are part and parcel of each relational model. The harm/care foundation pertains to the parochial altruism that manifests in unity-oriented groups, whereas the fairness/reciprocity foundation connects to expectations in equality-oriented groups. Though see Rai and Fiske (2011) for a relationship-based theory of moral psychology.

28. This distinction echoes Durkheim's (1933 [1893]) description of organic solidarity and mechanical solidarity. Like unity-oriented social relations, mechanical solidarity entails a fusion between similar individuals into a collective; it works best in small groups. But organic solidarity emerges when people perform separate, interdependent functions in society. Importantly, both create societal solidarity, despite their distinct foundations—much like equality and unity can each create nationalist commitments.

Second, the two models make divergent predictions about how nationalists will respond to external threats (intergroup conflict) and in-group heterogeneity (intragroup cooperation), thereby providing useful insights at both categorization levels. Comparing unity to equality facilitates theoretical synthesis with a tractable research design. Importantly, unity and equality norms do not exist on a continuum but are separate, unipolar factors (Haslam and Fiske, 1999; Fiske, 2004). While this means that unity- and equality-based nationalisms may not be mutually exclusive in practice—people might hold loose commitments to each but act on whichever is contextually salient, or rank order the two dueling commitments[29]—I treat them separately to understand their independent effects.

UNITY AND EQUALITY AS VARIETIES OF NATIONALISM AND SUPRANATIONALISM

In brief, I argue that when unity norms constitute nationalism, and when equality norms constitute supranationalism, the standard IR stories apply: unity-oriented nationalists promote militarism and conflict escalation, and equality-oriented supranationalists extend cross-border trust and support transnational security cooperation. Unity implies that "we" share a destiny and real or imagined common values, history, or other unifying bonds. Unity-oriented nationalists maintain solidarity in the face of threats, and support using force against enemies—like the 56% of Americans in January 2002 who supported a war in Iraq following a single terrorist attack that originated elsewhere (Foyle, 2004, 274). By contrast, equality-based nationalists support limited, proportionate escalation but not generalized militarism. Equality entails reciprocity-based social interactions common among peer groups and provides a strand of nationalism in which conationals view each other as friends, not family.

With respect to intragroup cooperation, equality facilitates support for transnational security integration. Transnational heterogeneity does not pose a threat when residents believe that group members embrace equality. But unity leads people to reject cooperation within diverse supranational groups, because differences hamper solidarity. European supranationalists committed to unity, for example, distrust "bad," non-prototypical

---

29. Similarly, Schwartz (1994) argues that people adhere to many personal values, but hold a rank order that helps them resolve trade-offs between competing values.

Europeans and prefer to maintain national control over their foreign and security policy.

Group norms like unity and equality are properties of the group, filtered through individual perceptions. People might perceive unity in their country but equality in their region, or vice versa, like colleagues who reciprocate in their department but emphasize unity within the university as a whole. Although individual attitudes such as political ideology likely play a role in which groups and norms appeal to individuals on average, a point I return to at the end of the chapter, unity and equality do not redound to individual differences. In turn, my theory explains how unity and equality operate within the national and supranational categorization levels separately, leaving questions about what happens when nationalisms across levels converge or diverge for future research.

In the rest of this section, I differentiate unity from equality by their constitutive norms and relational comparisons. Next, I explain the implications for attitudes about nationalist conflict and international cooperation. Table 2.1 summarizes the concepts and theory. The quotes in Table 2.1 and elsewhere in this book illustrate that prominent elites discuss national and supranational identities using language that taps unity and equality, though cannot tell us whether the speaker herself embraces one nationalism or the other.

Unity

Unity-oriented nationalisms carry expectations about the characteristics and values that group members share, and how they should behave— they help each other and protect the collective from threats. These social norms require cohesion, solidarity, consensus, group advancement, and group protection. People value each other equally. As Fiske (1991, 13–14) summarizes:

> What is salient is the superordinate group as such, membership in it, and the boundaries with contrasting outsiders. People have a sense of solidarity, unity, and belonging, and identify with the collectivity: they think of themselves as being all the same in some significant respect, not as individuals but as "we."

Unity requires that group members prioritize actions that contribute to the group's betterment even when they must pay individual costs. For instance, someone might give up a lucrative career to care for a sick family

TABLE 2.1. Varieties of Nationalism and Attitudes about Conflict and Cooperation

	Unity	Equality
Constitutive Norms	Diffuse reciprocity, unity, solidarity, consensus	Balance, specific reciprocity, fairness
Relational Comparison	Binary; insiders are all the same, outsiders all the same	Heterogeneity in the group; permeable with norm adherence
Group Identification	Members of a collective	Peers, a set of equals
Intergroup Conflict	Support use of force against threats, escalation	Support proportionate response to threats, incremental escalation
Illustrative Quote	"Today, we must stand united. United in our communities, united in our values and united in our determination to not let triumph those who would seek to divide us."[a]	"Canada figured out a long time ago that differences should be a source of strength . . . to define a country . . . on . . . openness, respect, compassion, a willingness to work hard."[b]
Intragroup Cooperation	Distrust within heterogeneous group, reject security cooperation	Trust within heterogeneous group, support security cooperation
Illustrative Quote	". . .we must change the European situation by uniting the Europeans. In this way we shall eliminate the menace which the division and weakness of Europe constitute for herself and others."[c]	"We are not the United States of Europe. . . . Europe is a cord of many strands."[d]

a. Jeremy Corbyn, 2017. "Jeremy Corbyn speech on terrorism and foreign policy: full text," *New Statesman*, 26 May.

b. Justin Trudeau, 2015. "'Differences should be a source of strength': Trudeau at G20," *CBC*, 15 November.

c. Jean Monnet, "To Make Europe is to Make Peace..." 17 May, 1953.

d. Jean-Claude Juncker, 2016. "Jean-Claude Juncker European Parliament speech in full," *Independent*, 14 September.

member. Such solidarity provides a powerful incentive to aid others—but expectations for altruism extend only to the group's boundaries. Unity encourages people to help fellow group members without expecting anything in return (diffuse reciprocity): For example, the Mossi people share food evenly regardless of who worked the field (Fiske, 1991). When someone in the group suffers, everyone suffers; solidarity requires empathy (Rai and Fiske, 2011). This logic corresponds to how IR scholars and policymakers describe integrated security communities. Each state member contributes to an ally's defense without concern for whether its assistance will be repaid in the future (Rai and Fiske, 2011; Deutsch, 1961; Cronin, 1999)—they act as one.

Unifying a social group requires glue to bind members together and create solidarity. Unity implies homogeneity. Any number of characteristics might provide the binding material: kinship/family ties, shared ethnicity, religion, culture, or a common national myth. These characteristics, alone or in combination, produce the "imagined communities" and "deep, horizontal comradeship" central to standard definitions of nationhood (Anderson, 1983, 7). To some, "the concept of the nation requires that all its members should form as it were only one individual" (Friedrich Schlegel qtd. in Greenfeld, 1992, 276). Each characteristic has the potential to produce "equivalence classes," within which comparisons across individuals do not exist—"we" are all the same, and "they" are different (Fiske and Tetlock, 1997; Brown, 2000).

Importantly, unity characterizes social relations beyond nuclear families and neighborhoods: People "may assert unity and solidarity at any level, however remote," including nations and larger regions like Europe (Fiske, 1991, 88). In the sixteenth century, for instance, nationalist themes emphasized continuity and kinship—"Mother France" unified Frenchmen who were "literally born of her" (Greenfeld, 1992, 107), for example. And in the 1990s, Syrian elites increasingly married across sectarian lines. This trend, alongside joint military service, contributed to increasingly homogeneous cultural values and, in turn, a nationalist identity that separated Syrians from their "corrupted" Lebanese neighbors (Sadowski, 2002, 150). Moving to the regional level, unity also appears in discussions about Arab and European identities. Many Arab citizens cite their shared history, religion, and language as sources of common ground (Zogby, 2010, 76). In Europe, left-wing Labour politician Jeremy Corbyn stressed national unity after the Manchester terror attack: "Today, we must stand united. United in our communities, united in our values, and united in our determination to not let triumph those who would seek to divide us."[30] Seventy years earlier, his fellow British statesman and Conservative Party leader Winston Churchill articulated similar ideas when he called for a "United States of Europe":

This noble continent, comprising on the whole the fairest and the most cultivated regions of the earth; enjoying a temperate and equable

---

30. Jeremy Corbyn, 2017. "Jeremy Corbyn speech on terrorism and foreign policy: Full text."

climate, is the home of all the great parent races of the western world. It is the fountain of Christian faith and Christian ethics. It is the origin of most of the culture, arts, philosophy and science both of ancient and modern times. If Europe were once united in the sharing of its common inheritance, there would be no limit to the happiness, to the prosperity and glory which its three or four hundred million people would enjoy.[31]

Common descent and culture, in Churchill's estimation, bound the European family.

Notably, Churchill described the European family as one that excluded Britain, later clarifying that he "meant it for them, not us" (qtd. in Fursdon, 1980, 77). This caveat highlights the second dimension of identity content—relational comparisons. Although unity entails caring for and protecting fellow group members, it does not carry an obligation to help outsiders. A stark categorical boundary divides "us" from "them." People make an explicit relational comparison between the in-group and out-group (Abdelal et al., 2006), a binary separation that distinguishes those inside the "family" from relevant and undifferentiated outsiders (Rai and Fiske, 2011; Fiske, 1991). Positive moral obligations extend to fellow group members, but not others—people view outsiders as homogeneous others at best, and as dehumanized "bugs, bushes, or stones" at worst (Fiske, 1991, 130).[32] Moreover, because the group requires homogeneity, nonconforming in-group members become as untrustworthy as out-group members. "They" do not represent the group. As Hamdullah Suphi insisted during the 1924 constitutional debates that followed the Armenian genocide, calling Armenian Christians in Turkey "Turks" would undermine national unity. He argued that they could be Turkish citizens, but their non-Muslim faith would separate them from fellow Turks (Bayar, 2016, 732). And despite their shared religious affiliation, many citizens in Arab countries exclude Turks who speak Turkish, and Farsi-speaking Iranians, from the Arab group (Zogby, 2010, 77). A 2009 poll, for example, found that citizens in Morocco, Egypt, Saudi Arabia, and UAE each listed "language" as the second-greatest source of common ground among Arabs (after political concerns) (ibid., 76).[33]

---

31. Winston Churchill, Zurich, 19 September 1946. Speech text accessed at http://www.churchill-society-london.org.uk/astonish.html.

32. See also Haslam (2006) on how unity-oriented relations relate to dehumanization.

33. In Lebanon and Jordan, citizens ranked language as the 4th and 5th most important source of Arab unity, respectively (Zogby, 2010, 76).

Binary comparisons play an especially important role in the context of intergroup conflict and violence. Political actors often pair unifying messages with binary rhetoric in the face of conflict. Hutu propaganda, for example, called for "unity and solidarity . . . [Hutus] must be firm and vigilant against their common Tutsi enemy" (Berry and Berry, 1999, quoted in Rai and Fiske, 2011, 61). Indeed, psychologists suggest that unity and stark intergroup comparisons reinforce each other: When people maximize the contrast between their in-group and out-group, they increase the degree to which they perceive both groups as homogeneous, coherent entities (Hamilton and Sherman, 1996)—a process that facilitates stereotyping, out-group devaluation, threat inflation, and sometimes intergroup violence. In an experiment with Hong Kong residents, for example, Lee and Chou (2020) manipulate perceptions of Chinese homogeneity. Those who read about China's historical unity held more negative attitudes toward migrants from the mainland.

Because unity requires solidarity and implies a binary comparison between insiders and outsiders, people view an attack from one out-group member as an attack by all out-group members. As Bush would state in his September 11 address to the nation, "We will make no distinction between the terrorists who committed these acts and those who harbor them."[34] He contrasted "civilized" people with "evildoers" (Krebs and Lobasz, 2007), drawing on binary rhetoric to create a narrative that " 'we' were attacked because of 'who we are' " (Krebs and Lobasz, 2007, 423), and emphasized that "in the face of all this evil," the United States would "remain strong and united."[35]

Unity norms and relational comparisons apply at both categorization levels. Indeed, unity-based nationalism fits comfortably with our intuition precisely because unity undergirds many theories about nationalism in international politics: From Anderson's (1983) imagined communities to Cronin's (1999, 4) references to a community of nations with a "shared sense of self," scholars invoke unity. Greenfeld (1992, 369), for instance, argues that German nationalism was predicated on the ideal of a unified German family. It stemmed from perceptions that Germans constituted a unique group, and required "the total submersion of the individual within

34. George W. Bush, 11 September 2001, "Statement by the President in His Address to the Nation."

35. George W. Bush, "National Day of Prayer and Remembrance for the Victims of the Terrorist Attacks on September 11, 2001." Available at www.georgewbush-whitehouse.archives.gov /news/releases/2001/09/20010913-7.html.

the collectivity." In this respect, nascent German nationalism revolved around unity.

At the supranational level, leaders like Jean Monnet (1952, 30) proposed that "if Europeans finally come to realize what qualities and abilities we have in common," they would be able to create a lasting peace—"a security which could not be achieved in any other way."[36] Constructivist IR scholars similarly contend that unity helps security organizations achieve peace (Deutsch, 1961; Adler and Barnett, 1998; Cronin, 1999; Hemmer and Katzenstein, 2002; Acharya and Johnston, 2007). Monnet's formal speeches fail to articulate what, precisely, unifies Europeans. But he notes that conflict stems from the fact that "divergent ways of life" more often come into contact in the modern world, and suggests that eliminating these divisions provides the path to progress (Monnet, 1952, 56).[37] Contemporary observers similarly use Europe's Christian heritage to draw a binary contrast with Turkey (Wimmel, 2006, 16). "We" form a family, that "their" EU membership would threaten by introducing religious differences.

Unity norms and comparisons also enrich our understanding of other typologies. Theoretical accounts that describe "ethnic" nationalism, for example, contain appeals to unity and homogeneity. Typical definitions posit that "natural" features tie group members together in ethnic nationalism (Hirschfeld, 2001; Brubaker, 2004; Smith, 1993a; Chandra, 2006). These connections might stem from actual blood ties or a national myth about common ancestry (Byman, 2000). But at the end of the day, these descriptions implicate the norms and relational comparisons that correspond to unity: members must meet certain ascriptive criteria (like race), maintain the group's solidarity in the face of creeping diversity, and protect one another. Other aspects of ethnic nationalisms also correspond to unity-oriented relationships. Ethnic nationalisms define the "nation" to include past and future generations, such that members must adhere to traditions and hand down a common culture to their heirs (Smith, 1993a), for example. Unity-oriented groups coincidentally demand a similar "continuity with the past" (Fiske, 1991, 70). But as I will explain later in the chapter, existing theories about ethnic nationalism face conceptual and normative scrutiny that leave scholars searching for alternatives (Brubaker, 2004; Hutchinson, 2017)—reorienting the focus to central norms like unity and binary relational comparisons resolves those issues.

---

36. Statement delivered to the Common Assembly, 16 June 1953.
37. Statement delivered at Columbia University, 2 June 1954.

Equality

Equality-oriented groups require fairness, reciprocity, and balance. These norms typically describe relationships among friends, colleagues, and peers. When people relate to one another on the basis of equality, members contribute equally to the group's success. Equality norms require evenness or balance between group members, including tit-for-tat interactions, in-kind reciprocity, and Hammurabi-style sanctions for offenses (Fiske, 2004). They imply specific rather than diffuse reciprocity, such that someone who receives assistance from a peer feels socially obligated to repay her in kind. For example, faculty members in a department might split course loads equally, or offer feedback on a colleague's paper with the expectation that they will receive feedback in the future. Congressional logrolling, where legislators exchange votes on each other's proposals, abides by equality norms (Fiske, 1992). Unlike the consensus-driven model of decision-making that unity demands, one-person, one-vote rules organize decision-making based on equality.

Equality provides the foundation for many social groups. Against conceptualizations that equate collectives with unity, "Balanced egalitarian relationships are significant in most parts of the world" (Fiske, 1992, 703). "We" can be equals, even at the level of national creeds. Some early Americans sought distance from the British conception of a nation as a unified collective, for example. Instead, they portrayed the United States as an association of "free and equal" citizens (Greenfeld, 1992, 449),[38] and the Federalist papers invoke John Locke to stress that Americans must be tolerant, respectful, and free (Sinopoli, 1996). Indeed, Thomas Jefferson claimed that American superiority rested on its commitment to equality. Similarly, the Canadian constitution contains a commitment to multicultural equality, such that institutionalized diversity and mutual respect define "Canadian exceptionalism" vis-à-vis other Western countries (Kymlicka, 2003).

People in equality-based groups build solidarity through reciprocity, not uniformity. But the group nevertheless exerts social influence:[39] Canadians who embrace the constitutional commitment to equality should trust one another to resolve problems via routine democratic deliberations. The

38. Of course, they often drew sharp boundaries around who counted as an equal—based on race and gender, for example—and thereby smuggled in a desire for unity and homogeneity. See Schildkraut (2005) for a discussion.

39. See, e.g., Cialdini and Goldstein (2004) for a review of social influence research.

constitutive norms require that everyone have the opportunity to participate in politics. Indeed, Kymlicka (2003, 384) lists several examples of
how intragroup identity politics from immigration laws to indigenous land
claims play out like "everyday democratic politics" in Canada. At the supranational level, Jean-Claude Juncker tapped equality norms in his September 2016 State of the European Union speech. He proclaimed that Europe is
"not the United States of Europe. . . . [it] is a cord of many strands. . . . Being
European also means being open and trading with our neighbors," offering
"a fair playing field," and inviting citizens and states alike to take responsibility for improving the EU.[40] If we are all equals and respect one another,
the norm dictates that we maintain reciprocity and jointly participate. For
Juncker, a good, committed European embraces equality, and some EU residents seem to have internalized this message. Asked to choose from a list of
which values best represent the EU in 2019, 13% of respondents from 27 EU
member-states selected "equality," and similar proportions chose related
values like tolerance (12%) and the reciprocity-oriented respect for other
cultures (15%).[41]

The relational comparison in equality groups does not lend itself to
the simple black-and-white division associated with unity—in part because
groups governed by reciprocity allow more flexibility in separating "us" and
"them." When equality constitutes a social identity group, members see
each other as peers, rather than a unified collective—"one of a set of equals
who reciprocate fairly" (Fiske, 1991, 89).

People still differentiate between insiders and outsiders in this setting. But when "all men are created equal" inside a group, it is easier
to construct a "friendly" narrative about the out-group because you see
them as individuals and not a homogeneous whole. Lind (2020, 8), for
example, describes how leaders can construct narratives about a conflict
that include expressions of empathy. The West German WWII narrative
acknowledged the German citizens *and* foreigners who suffered from past
German violence. This move opened the door to cooperation with victims
who might otherwise paint Germans as undifferentiated aggressors. Or
consider how U.S. President John F. Kennedy addressed the Soviets during

40. Jean-Claude Juncker, 2016. "Jean-Claude Juncker European Parliament speech in full,"
Independent, 14 September.

41. These data include EU-based respondents who completed the 2019 Eurobarometer surveys, adjusted for population weights (European Commission, 2020) (question qc7). The most
popular values from the list included peace (42%), democracy (34%), and human rights (32%).

his famously dovish speech at American University.[42] In 1963, during the bipolar struggle between the United States and Soviet Union, Kennedy called on Americans "not to see only a distorted and desperate view of the other side, not to see conflict as inevitable." He highlighted factors that made the United States and USSR similar—their commitment to science and economic growth, for instance—and called on both sides to recognize that peace does not require an idealistic community of nations, but merely "mutual tolerance."[43] If American nationalists could see one another as equals, they could extend that regard to the Soviets.[44]

Equality uniquely allows cooperation alongside heterogeneity. Members can differ on salient characteristics like religion, ethnicity, or other values as long as they accept each other as equals when it comes to "rights, opportunities, and benefits" (Simpson and Laham, 2015a, 217). Accordingly, national and supranational groups can persist despite diversity: Many majority-group Canadians count Canadian Muslims among their friends (Gravelle, 2018), perhaps because they believe that inclusion represents the Canadian way. And as Obama insisted in an Oval Office address, the United States was "founded upon a belief in human dignity—that no matter who you are or where you come from, or what you look like, or what religion you practice, you are equal in the eyes of God and equal in the eyes of the law."[45] As Wright (2011) describes in the context of immigration attitudes, some norms are more "achievable" than others—a newly arrived immigrant could integrate into an equality-oriented group if she upholds certain responsibilities like voting in regular elections. And while she cannot easily change her race or religion, that does not matter. Citizens can live and work together with reciprocity as their norm (Rai and Fiske, 2011; Haslam, 2004).

As with unity, focusing on equality helps bridge different research on varieties of nationalism: Equality norms often appear—by other names—in existing theories. For example, equality calibrates our understanding of

42. When she analyzes Cold War presidents' military assertiveness, for example, Yarhi-Milo (2018, 81–82) uses Kennedy's American University commencement speech as a "clear-cut example" and reference text for dovishness.

43. Kennedy, John F., 1963. "Commencement Address at American University, Washington, D.C.," *John F. Kennedy Presidential Library and Museum*, 10 June. Available at: www.jfklibrary.org/archives/other-resources/john-f-kennedy-speeches/american-university-19630610.

44. In this respect, my argument joins good company in contending that internal norms shape external foreign policy attitudes, like theories that connect domestic gender equality to a decline in war (Caprioli, 2005) or cultural variants of the democratic peace (Oneal and Russett, 2001).

45. Obama, Barack, 2015. "President Obama's address to the nation on the San Bernardino terror attack and the war on ISIS," 6 December.

research on "civic" nationalism and multiculturalism. Some theories turn to equality when defining civic nationalism as both more inclusive and less militaristic than other national identities (Greenfeld, 1992; Schildkraut, 2014). If ideas about justice through equal rights define civic nationalism (Snyder, 2000; Schrock-Jacobson, 2012), though, civic nationalism depends on equality.

Scholars also rely on equality-laden ideas to conceptualize muliticulturalism as a national identity. Multiculturalism implies that "all cultures [have] a reciprocal relationship—a healthy balance of give and take" (Davies, Steele and Markus, 2008, 309). For example, many Canadians see "multiculturalism . . . as an essential component of Canadian identity" (Ambrose and Mudde, 2015, 228)—in 2008, 39% of Canadians reported that they believe that immigration has a positive impact on their country, compared to less than 20% of Britons (ibid., 221)—and associate national pride with cultural equality (Citrin, Johnston and Wright, 2012). Per Justin Trudeau, "Canada figured out a long time ago that differences should be a source of strength . . . to define a country not based on . . . ethnicity or language or background, but on . . . openness, respect, compassion, a willingness to work hard."[46] Outside the Canadian context, experimental evidence shows that multicultural national identities predict international tolerance, not belligerence (Li and Brewer, 2004).

Research on transnational identities also engages equality to separate supranationalisms from each other. For example, the recent "practice turn" in constructivist IR contends that diplomatic practice undergirds cooperation in security communities. Pouliot (2007) details how Russia and the Transatlantic security community maintained post–Cold War rapprochement without unity. In a conclusion that hearkens back to Kennedy's speech, Pouliot argues that diplomatic practice facilitates cooperation without identification. But viewed in light of my framework, the Transatlantic relationship evokes equality: "We" are all separate states, committed to diplomatic exchange. Others similarly appeal to specific reciprocity-based norms to explain how enemies become friends. For Kupchan (2010), rapprochement begins when one state extends a hand, and the two sides build trust—Argentina and Brazil, for example, ended a bitter rivalry and joined forces via MERCOSUR without unity. Although both of these examples come from research arguing that cooperation does not require

46. Justin Trudeau, 2015. "'Differences should be a source of strength': Trudeau at G20," *CBC*, 15 November.

supranationalism, they implicitly equate identification with unity—but the factors that ultimately drive cooperation in the theories invoke equality.[47]

Finally, understanding unity and equality as different nationalisms illuminates existing evidence that relates European attachment to elite preferences regarding EU accession. Curley (2009) conducts a careful comparison between English, German, and French leaders to argue that their relative attachment to Europe shaped support for Turkey's bid to join the community. Leaders who identified more strongly with Europe harbored biases against Turkey, whereas leaders coded as "weak" European identifiers were more willing to support Turkey's accession so long as it could meet the basic membership criteria.[48] Yet his description of debates among German leaders suggests an alternate possibility—that some elites whom he codes as holding weak European identities may actually represent equality-oriented supranationalists. For example, leaders who identified as both European and German advocated for a deliberative process that would eventually integrate Turkey into the EU. If their nationalist commitments relied on a vision of Europe as a group of equals, Turkey would merely need to demonstrate its unequivocal commitment to EU norms as a condition of membership. Under this perspective, European supranationalism can accommodate rather than exclude.

Commitment: Strong and Weak Nationalists

Equality and unity represent two bases for nationalism. But my theory concerns how these norms manifest in foreign policy attitudes, and therefore must account for how *commitment* complements content. Nationalisms exist on a continuum, and commitment denotes how strongly a person connects to her group (Doosje, Ellemers and Spears, 1999; Huddy, 2001). Some weakly committed U.S. nationalists feel disconnected from their fellow Americans and, in turn, little pressure to conform to the group's norms. Conversely, strongly committed U.S. nationalists, those who view American superiority as core to their self-concept, conform to group expectations at greater rates—even though strong and weak nationalists belong

47. Institutionalist theories about cooperation eschew a role for identity and view reciprocity as the key to cooperation (Keohane, 1986). In this respect, my psychological argument reaches a similar conclusion about the role that reciprocal exchange plays in promoting security cooperation despite my distinct ontological claims.

48. See Mols and Weber (2013) for an additional discussion about Curley's (2009) assertion that attachment automatically arouses out-group biases.

to the same "American" category.[49] People also exhibit varying degrees of supranationalism despite sharing institutional or geographic ties: The 2009 IntUne data show that years before Brexit, 66% of UK citizens did not see themselves as European (Cotta, Isernia and Bellucci, 2009). And when Telhami polled citizens in six Arab countries in 2011 (Telhami, 2013, 28),[50] he found that just over half listed "Arab" as their primary or secondary identity.

Like other social identities, nationalisms' most profound effects on attitudes and behavior manifest among committed group members. If passport covers explained foreign policy attitudes, we would expect all residents in a country to be equally wary of outsiders, and all Europeans to embrace cooperation as soon as they joined the European Union and traded their lira and francs for euros. These dubious claims neglect commitment.

Instead, the patterns that scholars attribute to group membership primarily apply to those who feel strong connections to their group.[51] In fact, group membership often has little bearing on how weakly committed members behave (Perreault and Bourhis, 1999; Jackson and Smith, 1999; Van Vugt and Hart, 2004; Karasawa, 1991). When we create a continuous scale for nationalism and correlate it with militaristic policy preferences (Kosterman and Feshbach, 1989; Federico, Golec and Dial, 2005), or connect supranationalism to support for cooperation (Citrin and Sides, 2004, 174–76, Schoen, 2008), we correctly assume that strong and weak nationalists hold different attitudes.[52] Variation in commitment explains some paradoxical patterns, like the fact that Scots who believe that UK

---

49. See, for example, reviews in Huddy (2001) and Schildkraut (2014).

50. Egypt, Jordan, Lebanon, Morocco, Saudi Arabia, and United Arab Emirates.

51. I focus on individuals' subjective commitment—how strongly they agree that the world would be better off if other countries were more like the U.S., for example. But *context* also affects commitment by shaping salience (McGuire et al., 1978; Turner, 1985; Huddy, 2001). An Algerian immigrant living in France might use her Algerian identity to navigate her social world. But visiting family in Algeria, her French identity becomes more relevant. The situation shapes which identities influence her attitudes and behavior in a given circumstance—indeed, this logic informs experimental research that temporarily strengthens nationalism by "priming" it for participants (Kemmelmeier and Winter, 2008).

52. Of course, much of this research relies on observational data, like surveys, to test causal claims. This makes it harder to resolve the chicken-or-the-egg debate about whether strong commitments precede foreign policy attitudes. Although threats can increase nationalist commitments (Theiss-Morse, 2009), evidence shows that priming national identities increases support for conflict (Hassin et al., 2007; Althaus and Coe, 2011), and priming supranational identities increases support for transnational security cooperation (Beaton, Dovidio and Léger, 2008). In reality, the relationship probably moves in both directions—nationalism might be an independent and dependent variable in IR research.

membership undermines their culture only support separatism if they also strongly identify with Scotland (Sindic and Reicher, 2009).[53]

Crucially, strong identifiers conform to group norms to a greater extent than weak identifiers (Turner et al., 1987; Tankard and Paluck, 2016). We expect a die-hard Ohio State Buckeye to paint her face red and participate in group cheers, but expect less conformity from weakly committed alumni, just as strong (but not weak) partisans update their political attitudes to conform with polling results (Toff and Suhay, 2019).

Commitment correlates with self-reported conformity to group norms (Huddy and Khatib, 2007). In Canada, for example, an elite-led campaign pitched multiculturalism and tolerance as central norms—such that group conformity widely implied support for cultural diversity (Citrin, Johnston and Wright, 2012). And indeed, Citrin, Johnston and Wright (2012) find a strong association between Canadian pride and favorable immigration attitudes. People who expressed weaker commitments, by contrast, endorsed the anti-immigrant sentiments scholars often associate with nationalism. At the supranational level, financial policies designed to aid poorer EU countries garner more support among people who hold an inclusive, equality-based European identity *and* strongly identify as European (Bauhr and Charron, 2020*b*).

Research using experimental and quasi-experimental methods also shows that the effects of distinct norms manifest among people who express the strongest commitments to their group. Learning that fellow group members always recycle, for example, encourages environmentally friendly attitudes and behavioral intentions—but only for people committed to the group (Wellen, Hogg and Terry, 1998; Terry and Hogg, 1996; Terry, Hogg and White, 1999). Weak identifiers ignore the norms. Similarly, commitment conditions the effect of polling information on political attitudes—if a voter excludes her Democratic partisanship from her self-concept, she has little incentive to bandwagon with fellow Democrats to support the Trans-Pacific Partnership, for instance (Toff and Suhay, 2019). A weakly committed American nationalist easily brushes off accusations of "un-American" attitudes: For example, Collingwood, Lajevardi and Oskooii (2018) find that strong identifiers—but not weak identifiers—decreased their support

---

53. As McDermott (2009, 354) points out, the fact that strong identifiers remain committed to the group even when they might gain from leaving—or from staying in the UK in the case of Scotland—"makes sense from an evolutionary perspective, where individual motivation to join social groups is based on mutual goals of cooperation." See also Brewer and Caporael (2006) on an evolutionary approach to social identity.

for President Trump's 2017 "Muslim ban" after months of a popular narrative describing the policy's inegalitarian quality as anti-American. When the prescriptive norm changed, only people who felt connected to their American national identity adjusted their stance.

My theory and empirical tests account for both content and commitment. I emphasize strength and superiority as core components for nationalisms. Scholars often separate commitments—distinguishing "nationalism" from "attachment," "patriotism," and "identification" (Huddy and Khatib, 2007). But isolating "identification" as the degree to which people consider themselves typical of their group risks over-emphasizing the cognitive aspect of categorization relative to the affective component (Hornsey, 2008). Group superiority feels good, and nationalist ideas about superiority motivate attitudes toward out-groups. Moreover, schemes that separate these dimensions often mix content, commitment, and consequences to define and measure them as separate factors. For example, scholars describe nationalism as attachment's "evil twin" *because* people who score high on nationalism scales often hold hawkish and anti-immigrant attitudes (Bonikowski and DiMaggio, 2016, 952). But partisan and ideological pressures to endorse some survey items and reject others may confound these relationships and introduce superficial differences (Hanson and O'Dwyer, 2019). Moreover, commitment dimensions positively correlate with one another—even when scholars try to separate them (Huddy and Khatib, 2007; Herrmann, Isernia and Segatti, 2009; Parker, 2010; Ariely, 2016; Mader et al., 2018; Huddy and Del Ponte, 2019).[54] Context also appears to influence what these different dimensions of national identity mean to survey respondents and, in turn, how they affect political attitudes (Li and Brewer, 2004; Wolak and Dawkins, 2017; Mader et al., 2018).[55]

In light of these concerns and debates, I use a scale that incorporates ideas about national superiority ("national chauvinism") when I discuss nationalism and intergroup conflict in chapters 3 and 4, for two reasons. First, previous work specifically links national chauvinism—but not

54. See also Carter and Pérez (2016) on how race influences different shades of national identification.

55. See Bonikowski (2016) for a more thorough critique. Of course, some scholars will nevertheless disagree—see, for example, Huddy and Del Ponte (2019) for a thorough justification for why researchers should treat each version of commitment as a separate phenomenon. Those who disagree, in turn, could simply interpret my results in light of the specific nationalist commitments I measure.

other scales like attachment—to hostility and escalation. When I evaluate whether equality mitigates the relationship between nationalism and militarism, then, I'm taking the standard story on its own terms. Second, my theory about nationalism concerns how people respond to outsiders. Psychologists tend to agree that the intergroup context activates the moral superiority and status concerns that we tap with standard nationalism scales (Brewer, 1999), making this the most important aspect of a nationalist commitment for the foreign policy context. When I discuss supranationalism and support for intragroup cooperation in chapter 5, I infer commitment from respondent ratings about how important various norms are for being European. This measure implicitly taps moral superiority. Participants reported the norms that they associate with "good" Europeans, untethered from institutional ideas about geographic borders or EU membership. This measurement strategy also sidesteps issues with using standard attachment scales from observational data when content varies: Questions about whether someone "feels European" use abstract phrasing, but people respond with baked-in ideas about content—such that self-reported identification partly measures how well the respondent perceives herself to align with unobserved group norms. Content-free identification measures therefore mix second-order content perceptions with commitment (Huddy, 2001). My approach avoids concerns that nationalisms are endogenous to political ideology, for example (Huddy and Khatib, 2007), but incorporates both content and commitment into the empirical tests.

How Do Unity and Equality Shape Foreign Policy Attitudes?

Synthesizing research on nationalisms and supranationalisms in international politics, I argued that our theories about nationalist conflict and transnational cooperation share psychological foundations. One ramification of my position: Our theories about nationalisms must account for variation in *content* alongside phenomena associated with commitment and categorization. I contribute to this debate by offering a framework for classifying identity content grounded in fundamental models of human interaction—unity- and equality-oriented nationalisms. Those ideal types entail distinct constitutive norms and relational comparisons, and manifest by other names in past research on national and supranational identities. Here, I explain how unity and equality have different implications for foreign policy attitudes with respect to both *intergroup conflict*—nationalist militarism—and *intragroup cooperation*—support for supranational security integration.

UNITY, EQUALITY, AND NATIONALIST MILITARISM

Unity and equality have different implications for *intergroup conflict*. Internal norms shape how we respond to external conflict, and I expect that unity primes nationalists for militarism. The patterns that I expect from unity-oriented nationalists match the standard story about nationalist aggression. Unity encourages people to inflate threats, demand that enemies pay disproportionate costs, and treat any attack on co-nationals as an affront to the whole.

Unity-oriented nationalism rests on binary distinctions, which facilitate violence and escalatory aggression in response to real or perceived harm committed by an adversary. When "a clear delineation of the other" exists (Schrock-Jacobson, 2012, 829), nationalists paint the external threat as inherently evil, an enemy that threatens the community's existence. Indeed, Fiske and Rai (2015, 100) argue that virtue requires aggression against outsiders who threaten a unified group: "*we must all join* in the fight to protect *our* nation, indivisible, because it is *our* 'land.' "[56] Moreover, because "we" are united, an attack on one becomes an attack on all—and an attack *by* one out-group member becomes an attack by all who share similarities with the attacker.

Leaders often use unifying rhetoric and binary comparisons to justify or describe hawkish foreign policy choices. Despite the equality-oriented focus of his Democratic Party and domestic policy, U.S. President Franklin Delano Roosevelt drew sharp contrasts with WWII adversaries: Americans are "builders," whereas our enemies are "destroyers," "gangsters," and "criminal[s]" fighting a "dishonorable" and "dirty" war.[57] His Japanese internment policy in turn marked "every person of Japanese descent on the West Coast" as "a threat to national security" (Schildkraut, 2002, 521). Later, the United States and Soviet Union portrayed each other in the "enemy image" during the Cold War. Each was a united community struggling to protect itself against malicious outsiders (Herrmann, 1985).

---

56. Emphasis in original.

57. Roosevelt, Franklin Delano, 1941. "Fireside Chat 19: On the War with Japan," 9 December. Accessed via the University of Virginia Miller Center Presidential Speech archives. Available at: www.millercenter.org/the-presidency/presidential-speeches/december-9-1941-fireside -chat-19-war-japan.

And when Reagan justified the U.S. invasion of Grenada as an effort to limit Soviet influence, he appealed to unity—"We" Americans must band together against "them," the Communists and Communist sympathizers everywhere. Reagan bolstered his argument that Grenada was a "Soviet-Cuban colony being readied as a major military bastion to export terror and undermine democracy" with a binary comparison (Reagan, 1983). Hixson (2008) echoes these sentiments in his history of U.S. foreign policy, where he contends that cultural exceptionalism imbues American national identity. War helps "tightens the bonds of national unity" as the state maintains an interventionist stance against Communists, terrorists, and other enemies perceived to "undermine the American way of life" (ibid., 11, 279).

To illustrate these dynamics, consider how the Bush administration tied its rhetoric to binary distinctions and American unity in the lead-up to the war in Iraq. Following 9/11, Bush emphasized that the terrorist attacks were fundamentally attacks on all Americans. National unity themes appeared regularly in official government communication (Hutcheson et al., 2004).[58] As part of the binary rhetoric, the administration crafted a narrative that the attacks were not isolated but part of a broader war on America and Americans (Krebs and Lobasz, 2007). That narrative painted the war on terror as a battle between good and evil—Bush's references to the good and evil binary tripled after September 11 (Coe et al., 2004, 241)—and emphasized that "evil cannot be negotiated or reasoned with" (Krebs and Lobasz, 2007, 422). This reflected a naked appeal to unity-oriented nationalisms. Unity norms demand a severe response against actors who harm the group, without regard to proportionality. To protect the nation, we must respond with force. And because we see outsiders as a homogeneous mass, we hold them all responsible.

Public opinion data also support the notion that unity begets militarism. Public opinion surveys after 9/11, for example, found that some Americans became more likely to derogate Arabs and Muslims in the wake of the attack, and support for a war in Iraq grew despite the fact that neither Saddam Hussein nor Iraq perpetrated the attacks (Foyle, 2004; Liberman and Skitka, 2017). Indeed, insider accounts from the Bush administration suggest that their narrative frames constituted a deliberate strategy to justify the Iraq war to the American people (Butt, 2019; Woodward, 2012).

---

58. Although Bush made early nods to tolerance and equality in the immediate wake of the attack (Schildkraut, 2002), researchers have shown that binary rhetoric was heavily featured thereafter.

The administration's approach accords with the conclusions that Li and Brewer (2004) draw with experimental research. Those authors show that when citizens emphasize their country's membership in a unified, homogeneous group, a sense of superiority limits their tolerance of outsiders and encourages aggressive responses to threats (Li and Brewer, 2004).[59]

Equality carries different implications regarding nationalist attitudes about militarized conflict. Whereas unity-oriented nationalism promotes escalation—if all outsiders are the enemy, we must counteract attacks with strong shows of force—equality invites proportionate violence in response to other violence (Fiske, 1992). Nationalism based on equality means that nationalists commit to reciprocity, and they extend this norm to the foreign policy realm. Harm to one is *not* harm to all for a strong equality-oriented nationalist. People who commit to equality perceive greater heterogeneity within their group and among outsiders, lacking a binary relational comparison to bind them as a homogeneous whole and contrast themselves with outsiders. This produces a different type of reaction to an attack, because equality-oriented nationalists do not perceive the attack as targeting them or their families (Fiske, 1992). In an ambiguous crisis or low-level conflict, equality favors limited aggression. In turn, equality-oriented nationalists are less likely to succumb to inflated threat perceptions compared to their unity-oriented counterparts.

Returning to a reference that I discussed in chapter 1, recall that some IR scholars build from the social identity approach to argue that states use their internal commitments to equality and tolerance to build a reputation for greatness via moral esteem (Wohlforth et al., 2018). For example, the vast majority of Norwegians insist that tolerance and respect for other people constitute important values for children.[60] In particular, many Norwegians take pride in their commitment to gender equality (Skjelsbæk and Tryggestad, 2020). In 2017, 75.9% of Norwegians listed women having the same rights as men as an essential characteristic of a democracy.[61] With

59. Ginges et al. (2007) similarly find a relationship between nationalist unity and foreign policy aggression in a different context. They use a series of experiments to show that many Jewish Israelis—in their fervor to protect the homeland—feel a moral imperative to use violence rather than compromise sacred values.

60. In wave 7 of the World Values Survey, 90% of Norwegians rated this an important quality for children (Q12), compared to 71% of Americans, for example. Data available at http://www.worldvaluessurvey.org/WVSOnline.jsp.

61. Respondents rated this feature on a 10-point scale from "not an essential feature of democracy" to "an essential feature of democracy," and 76% selected the highest point on the scale, 10 (see Q249 on Wave 7 of the World Values Survey).

sex-based fairness and representation embedded in the culture and legal system since the 1980s, many Norwegians agree that these values set them apart—gender equality "has emerged as an identity marker of a core value that characterizes 'us'; gender equal is a descriptive term for the national identity" in Norway (Skjelsbæk and Tryggestad, 2020, 184). The commitment to fairness sits comfortably alongside high rates of out-group trust among Norwegian citizens. In the 2007 World Values Survey, for example, 83.4% of Norwegian respondents said that they would somewhat or completely trust people of another nationality.[62] Equality-oriented nationalists should trust outsiders at greater rates than other nationalists, since they do not frame all outsiders as potential threats. In turn, Norwegian nationalism prescribes promoting equality abroad and seeking diplomatic solutions to crises for many of the country's residents.

The dynamics associated with equality also explain the puzzling lack of monolithic nationalist support for foreign policy hawkishness that I discussed in chapter 1. Some portion of the population—equality-oriented nationalists—do not succumb to inflated threat perceptions. They potentially illustrate Jones's (2014) theory of "enlightened nationalism," which she built from evidence that study abroad experiences paradoxically deflate threat perceptions at the same time that they increase nationalist commitments. Her theory hinges in part on equality—she argues that some enlightened nationalists view other states and their citizens as different but equal international actors. Contact diminishes perceptions of out-group homogeneity and breaks down the binary relational comparison. In this dynamic, equality dampens public fervor for militarism while inspiring nationalism.

Similarly, the fact that "creedal" nationalists espouse less support for unilateral foreign policy conflict compared to some other nationalists appears less puzzling in my framework (Bonikowski and DiMaggio, 2016). In their study, Bonikowski and DiMaggio (2016) describe a subsample of Americans who cite their love of America's democratic principles, support for the rule of law, and equal treatment alongside nationalist pride. These respondents have clear nationalist beliefs about American superiority, but disagree with the proposition that the United States should

---

62. For comparison, this represents a greater proportion of out-group trust than other Western citizens, like American (72.5%) or French (77%) residents. Of course, many other factors shape out-group trust, and I include these data and comparisons only for illustration, not as a thorough test of my theory. See, for example, Dinesen, Schaeffer and Sønderskov (2020) for a meta-analysis that examines the relationship between ethnic diversity and social trust.

pursue its interests through conflict, consistent with my expectations regarding nationalism built on equality. "Creedal" nationalists likely think that American superiority depends on its commitment to equality.

As these two examples illustrate, equality changes how people respond to and think about foreign policy crises and provocations. Equality-based nationalism should attenuate the connection between nationalism and hawkish foreign policy thereby limiting escalatory behavior. But equality does not prescribe pacifism. Instead, my theory implies that equality-based nationalism encourages using proportionate force against identifiable adversaries. The commitment to reciprocity means that force must be repaid with equivalent force (Fiske and Rai, 2015).

For example, rather than support war in Iraq after 9/11 by holding all Arabs responsible, equality-based nationalists might have called for limited strikes against al Qaeda targets—like drone attacks and targeted air strikes alongside limited military incursions in al Qaeda territory. Dealing with ISIS later in the twenty-first century, Obama did just that: He used drone attacks against terrorist camps consistent with what he viewed as a proportionate response to ISIS beheading Western journalists or committing small-scale terrorist attacks on U.S. soil.

This logic suggests that equality and unity will sometimes prescribe similar foreign policy strategies. Nationalists committed to either set of norms will support hawkish foreign policy when the situation implicates both reciprocity and solidarity against an adversary viewed as implacably hostile. We should therefore find it unsurprising that 93% of Americans approved when the military killed Osama bin Laden in 2011: The mission could be construed as both reciprocity for 9/11 and vengeance against an inherently hostile outside group, in line with both equality- and unity-oriented nationalist prescriptions.[63]

This discussion leads to my *intergroup conflict* hypotheses. In chapters 3 and 4, I use experiments to test these propositions, bringing new and rigorous evidence to supplement the range of illustrative examples that I have synthesized to this point. The experiments provide an important advantage over previous work that measures nationalist commitments without content, because scales that measure nationalism on its own contain unobserved variation in how people interpret the group's norms. Combining

63. Newport, Frank, 2011. "Americans Back Bin Laden Mission; Credit Military, CIA Most," *Gallup*, 11 May. URL: www.news.gallup.com/poll/147395/americans-back-bin-laden-mission -credit-military-cia.aspx.

content and commitment, I expect that strong unity-oriented nationalists and strong equality-oriented nationalists will respond differently to foreign policy problems. Unity-oriented nationalism should prompt generalized hawkishness and escalation, whereas equality-based nationalism should not. Yet I expect that policy preferences will align when both reciprocity and solidarity norms dictate a response:

H1a: Unity-oriented nationalism will increase support for militarism and conflict escalation, whereas equality-oriented nationalism will not. The relationship between nationalism and conflict will be weaker for people in equality-oriented groups, compared to unity.

H1b: Unity-oriented nationalism and equality-oriented nationalism will be associated with similar foreign policy attitudes when reciprocity entails a conflictual response.

Moreover, my experiments manipulate identity content, and I anticipate that the effect of group norms will manifest among people who hold the strongest nationalist commitments. Equality should mitigate support for conflict among strong nationalists, but not weak nationalists who lack the motivation to adhere to group norms and sometimes rebel against what they think the group would want them to do (Terry, Hogg and White, 1999; Jetten, Postmes and McAuliffe, 2002; Citrin, Johnston and Wright, 2012; Collingwood, Lajevardi and Oskooii, 2018).

UNITY, EQUALITY, AND INTERNATIONAL COOPERATION

Shifting to the supranational level, I argue that unity and equality also carry distinct implications regarding *intragroup cooperation*. The differential capacity for unity- and equality-oriented groups to accommodate heterogeneity provides the key to understanding why equality-oriented supranationalism should drive trust and support for security cooperation in the international arena, whereas unity counteracts those trends.

A commitment to unity threatens intragroup cooperation in a heterogeneous group. Heterogeneity undermines unity (Rai and Fiske, 2011), such that identification is less likely to inspire widespread cooperation as the group grows in size and complexity. "We" cannot remain united if some members deviate from expectations about what binds the group together. In that respect, the same set of norms that serve a functional purpose at the national level—by mobilizing an aggressive response against outside threats—produce dysfunctional outcomes at the supranational level.

When European residents, for example, agree to open their borders, create a joint diplomatic corps, or establish a European army, they signal their expectation that group members can be trusted. We would expect European supranationalists to commit to such in-group altruism and particularistic trust so long as the group remains homogeneous and united. But heterogeneous groups necessarily include people who fail to conform to normative ideas about the prototypical member. We mistrust family deviants,[64] a notion that sits comfortably with the robust observation that ethnic diversity erodes social trust (Dinesen, Schaeffer and Sønderskov, 2020; Putnam, 2007; Alesina and La Ferrara, 2002).[65] And if people do not want to cooperate with others they perceive as poor representatives of Europe—the bad Europeans in the group—the self-assessed "good" Europeans will retreat from opportunities to join forces with neighbors and intertwine their national security with the supranational grouping. Public opinion data supports this expectation: Some Germans, for example, identify strongly with Europe but treat the continent as a united group that hews to Western and German ideals. Those individuals in turn disparage Europeans who they perceive as failing that test (Mummendey and Waldzus, 2004). Those Germans' commitment to unity precludes joining forces with Eastern Europeans who might not share essential characteristics required to unite the group.

Indeed, debates about the European Defence Community (EDC) and other precursors to the European Union reveal the heterogeneity-induced tension between unity and security integration. British reticence to adopt the Schuman proposal for European integration and join the EDC depended in part on the fact that policymakers saw themselves as separate from the European family. Churchill lauded European unity as a path to peace for *them*—the Europeans should unite, but keep Britain as a partner rather than a family member (Fursdon, 1980, 75–77). The British Labour

64. These ideas hearken to Walt's critique of constructivist prescriptions for identity as a path to cooperation—because "'family quarrels' are often especially bitter and difficult to resolve" (in Cumings et al., 1994, 118).

65. Though see Hooghe and Marks (2009) for research showing that country-level diversity in Europe does not correlate with lower levels of trust. My theory helps to bridge these contrasting perspectives, explaining how groups built on equality facilitate trust amid diversity. Diversity itself may only pose a barrier to social trust and cooperation insofar as groups privilege unity, a point similar to Putnam's (2007, 159–65) anecdotes about how various American institutions learned to embrace diversity.

Party described how Britain could not be European because they were too dissimilar from their continental partners, for example: "In every respect except distance we in Britain are closer to our kinsmen in Australia and New Zealand . . . than we are to Europe. We are closer in language and in origins, in social habits and institutions, in political outlook and economic interest" (qtd. in Monnet, 1978, 315). As Jean Monnet, Pleven, and others pushed behind the scenes for a truly united "European Community," down to details about how members of a European army should wear the same uniform (Monnet, 1978), their insistence on unity met resistance from their own French government who demanded that French soldiers maintain their distinct dress. The EDC dissolved before it began (Parsons, 2002; Fursdon, 1980). The EDC's trajectory comports with psychological research showing that people resist more inclusive, superordinate identities if they have to sacrifice their distinct subgroup identity (Brewer, 1991).

By contrast, equality facilitates cooperation and trust even in heterogeneous supranational groups because equality norms support interactions on the basis of equal status and contribution. The constitutive norms and relational comparisons that define equality allow group members to work together and tolerate differences, so long as all parties remain committed to fairness and reciprocity.[66] The bar that people must clear to represent a good group member entails a commitment to achievable norms like reciprocity and fairness. So long as I believe that my fellow Europeans, Arabs, or North Americans will reciprocate, I trust them to help advance my interests and come to my defense.

In turn, equality fosters the trust and cooperation that we typically associate with parochial unity. In one of the few experimental tests to compare the effects of equality and unity norms on cooperation, Grinberg, Hristova and Borisova (2012) manipulate the payoffs in a prisoners' dilemma game to conform to the distributional structure that each of the two models entails. In the unity condition, each player earns their dyad's full payoff ("all for one and one for all"), and for the equality condition, partners each earn an equal share of the total (Grinberg, Hristova and Borisova, 2012, 410). Both the equality and unity treatments increased levels of cooperation compared to the two other distribution treatments in the study. These findings are instructive because they demonstrate that equality encourages cooperation, too—tight-knit families do not hold a

66. At the subnational level, Tusicisny (2017) finds evidence that positive reciprocity can reduce ethnic discrimination and create virtuous cycles between Hindu and Muslim Indians.

monopoly on positive intragroup interactions. Yet my theory anticipates that if the group size ballooned to match the 700 million people who populate Europe, unity norms would decrease cooperation. Particularized trust, in which people hold an inherent faith in group members' trustworthiness, works best in homogeneous collectives (Uslaner, 2002; Rathbun, 2009). In a supranational group explicitly "united in diversity," like Europe, trust and cooperation require equality and reciprocity to thrive.

Although scholarly work often focuses on the positive relationship between supranationalism and support for security cooperation (Citrin and Sides, 2004; Schoen, 2008; Koenig-Archibugi, 2004; Schilde, Anderson and Garner, 2019), adding content to commitment suggests that equality-oriented supranationalists may bear responsibility for these correlations. Indeed, European Union institutions seem to recognize equality's cooperation-enhancing externalities. Committed to inculcating a sense of Europeanness among the citizenry, EU reports describe evidence about how unity can create a counterproductive internal "other" (European Commission, 2012, 22). Scholars and policymakers alike have sought insights for how to build a supranational identity in light of European heterogeneity (Cram, 2009), and associate "cosmopolitan" commitments—to a Europe defined by democracy and rule of law—with pro-integration views (Schoen, 2008). To the extent that people perceive European supranationalism as something rooted in the norms of tolerance and equality outlined in the Treaty of Lisbon (European Union, 2007), I expect them to endorse concrete efforts to deepen security cooperation—like support for the common foreign and security policy (CFSP) and a European army.

This logic leads to my *intragroup cooperation* hypotheses, which I test in chapter 5 by analyzing survey responses from both regular European citizens and elites. The primary surveys that I use contain lengthy scales that ask people to identify which characteristics are important for being European, and allow me to test whether content plays a role even when accounting for standard measures that tap abstract attachment to a European identity. When people commit to a heterogeneous supranational group, their support for security cooperation depends on the particular norms and relational comparisons that comprise their identity. Equality-oriented supranationalists will trust their co-regionals because they expect reciprocity, and the group's diversity poses little threat. By contrast, unity-oriented supranationalists will resist security cooperation. Although they can trust "good" group members, the breadth undercuts the group's unity.

In-group deviants cannot be trusted to maintain peace or advance "our" interests. Unity-oriented supranationalists, in turn, prefer to retain national sovereignty in foreign policy matters:

H2a: Unity-oriented supranationalism will be associated with less trust in fellow group members, less support for a common foreign policy, and less support for military integration.

H2b: Equality-based supranationalism will be associated with more trust in fellow group members, more support for a common foreign policy, and more support for military integration.

Because this book is about foreign policy attitudes, both my intergroup conflict and intragroup cooperation hypotheses refer to outcomes in that domain—international conflict on the one hand, and transnational cooperation on the other hand. But as I noted at the beginning of this chapter, the theory likely has different implications when we shift our lens to different levels. For example, I describe how supranational groups like Europe, sub-Saharan Africa, or Latin America feature heterogeneity that residents must confront. But national groups also contain substantial heterogeneity and salient subgroup cleavages, like the religious divide between Hindu and Muslim Indians. In turn, heterogeneity might also impede cooperation *within* states, whereby committed unity-oriented nationalists disparage co-nationals who threaten the group's solidarity. Although these dynamics merit further exploration, I expect them to bear little on the support for security cooperation addressed in this book due to variation in institutional consolidation: Compared to the foreign policy establishments associated with constituent EU member-states, the EU diplomatic corps and common foreign policy pillar are infants. Even if nationalist unity undermines trust across subnational groups in Italy, for instance, we would expect few modern "Italy-skeptics" to demand separate armies to protect Lombardy from Naples. In short, although the dynamics should be similar across levels, institutional structures likely condition the specific outcomes that stem from commitments to unity or equality.

Contestation: "We" Disagree about What Defines Us

People contest nationalisms. Contestation describes the degree to which individual group members agree or disagree about content (Abdelal,

Herrera, Johnson and McDermott, 2009, 19). Political scientists debate the extent to which we should expect contestation regarding nationalisms. On one extreme, some people view nationalisms as settled—once a national myth takes hold, it sticks (Smith, 1991; Bayar, 2016). For example, the French Revolution cemented the country's long-standing commitment to *laïcité*, and this norm retains a hallowed place in both the constitution and contemporary laws. Others criticize such claims as essentialist, and argue instead that nationalisms are subject to perpetual negotiation, debate, and refinement. In the European Union, these debates take place in public, where scholars and citizens accept that there is "no single imagining of the EU and no single understanding of what it means for an individual to identify with it" (Cram, 2012, 78). People constantly imagine and re-imagine Europeanness.

I assume that nationalisms remain subject to some contestation, a position between the two extremes. I reject strong claims that populations universally settle on one variety of nationalism. Some cases may feature little contestation: For example, the Indian National Congress defined Indian nationalism upon religious and linguistic inclusion—equality-style norms that helped cement democracy in the country and persisted for decades (Tudor and Slater, 2020). But this national narrative glosses over the fact that *some* Indian citizens have always been committed to the unity-oriented Hindu nationalism that contemporary observers associate with President Modi. And although the vast majority of Europeans might embrace values of tolerance, justice, and equality guaranteed by the Treaty of Lisbon, the treaty also calls for solidarity. Some Europeans, but not all, believe that Turkey's Muslim majority precludes its membership in a united Europe (Curley, 2009). Even when passionate debates about identity content constitute the norm rather than the exception, like the twenty-first-century American disagreement about whether Muslim immigrants threaten the group (unity) or mesh with the country's commitment to equality, people draw from a reservoir of reasonably stable narratives that they adapt to their needs.

Crucially, my theory requires the minimalist assumption that people contest nationalisms to some degree. And even if I assume that some narratives go uncontested, I would expect variation in how strongly people commit to the identity. People whose dispositions disincline them to adopt unity-oriented nationalism will be weakly committed nationalists if they do not have an alternative set of norms to embrace.

WHERE DO UNITY- AND EQUALITY-ORIENTED NATIONALISMS COME FROM?

Where do unity- and equality-oriented nationalisms come from, and why would people contest these identities? A dynamic relationship between competing national narratives, elite identity entrepreneurship, and individual dispositions drives nationalist commitments in the real world. The theory and empirical tests in this book probe how nationalisms (the independent variables) affect attitudes about conflict and cooperation (the dependent variables). A comprehensive theory about what drives contestation would change the *explanans* to *explanandum* and require an additional book (or several), but it is important to describe how the multiple foundations for nationalisms complement and inform my theory. Before moving forward, I therefore turn to existing research on nationalist narratives and institutions, leadership, and individual differences to briefly justify my assumption about contestation.[67] These competing influences also explain how people might come to embrace distinct national or supranational norms, and what factors may cause commitments to unity or equality to change over time.

First, institutions and national myths provide context and set the stage for content and contestation. Foundational moments allow elites to embed norms and definitions into constitutions, treaties, and historical narratives. Debates over Turkey's 1961 constitution, for example, featured demands for unity—some leaders wanted the constitution to reflect the fact that Turkish nationalism would require minorities to homogenize and assimilate (Bayar, 2016). This commitment to "national unity" made its way into the constitution's preamble. But foundational moments are also fraught with disagreement, such that alternative narratives remain available. To take the United States, for example, citizens can invoke the Federalist papers to assert that American nationalism requires respect and equality, or the anti-Federalist papers for evidence that American nationalism requires unity and homogeneity (Sinopoli, 1996). EU treaties, too, illustrate the delicate balance between unity and equality in commitments to preserve "Europe's cultural heritage" (Article I-3, Treaty of Lisbon) alongside egalitarianism and respect as core values (Articles I-2 and I-3).[68] Indeed, these

67. Tankard and Paluck (2016, 181) similarly describe how people use three "sources of information" to form subjective perceptions about the group's norms—others' behavior, aggregate information about the group, and cues from institutions.

68. See Risse (2010) for an extensive analysis of European identity contestation.

documents often reflect (sometimes explicit) efforts to compromise or paper over disagreements about national identity content.

Governments also weave ideas about identity content into domestic life through education, laws, and institutions. The French education system helped "turn peasants into Frenchmen" by indoctrinating core values (Weber, 1976), and the EU Parliament Committee on Culture and Education (the CULT committee) leverages educational exchanges and festivals to promote the EU's vision for Europeanness through practice (Prutsch, 2017; McNamara, 2015a). States and supranational groups also use citizenship laws, which enumerate specific criteria for group membership, to present an official perspective on identity content. Crucially, though, governments promote norms in a dynamic fashion; unity and equality can wax and wane in the prevailing discourse. A text analysis of American citizenship manuals, for example, reveals substantial variation: The U.S. government emphasizes certain strands of America's "multiple traditions" at different times (Goodman, 2021). In short, context and institutions set the stage. But they also point to pluralistic nationalisms and contestation, factors that preclude describing whole country or regional populations as universally committed to one flavor of nationalism.

Second, elites act as identity entrepreneurs. Powerful elites might force their vision through violent coercion (Kreuzer, 2006), but leaders also command attention and wield the power of words. Leaders and parties can draw from existing national narratives or present novel interpretations to advance ideas about who "we" are (Hooghe and Marks, 2009; Cram, 2012). Haslam, Reicher and Platow's (2011) "new psychology of leadership" draws from social identity research to explain that when followers view a leader as a good representative for the in-group, the leader can (re)define what constitutes a good American, German, or European. Just as Teddy Roosevelt used his bully pulpit to define "True Americanism" as a national identity that requires immigrant assimilation,[69] Barack Obama used his presidential campaign speeches to portray equality and justice as essential American norms (Augoustinos and De Garis, 2012). Committed followers, in turn, update their beliefs about national identity content to align with their leaders. Of course, individuals disagree about which elites merit their attention—Republicans in the United States would be unlikely to view Obama as a good representative for America and adopt his normative

---

69. See, e.g., Huntington (2004) for a contemporary assimilationist view of American national identity.

constructions—which returns us to my assumption that individuals exhibit substantial disagreement about nationalist content.

Third, individual differences matter even though nationalisms cannot be reduced to dispositional traits. Predispositions shape whether we are more likely to construe our identity in terms of unity or equality, which narratives animate us, which elites we respond to, how strongly we commit to one nationalist variety or the other—and, in turn, the degree to which the group's norms shape our attitudes and behavior. Scholars who study American and European nationalisms, for example, find substantial individual-level variation in the norms people perceive as constituting the group as a whole (Theiss-Morse, 2009; Schildkraut, 2007; Bruter, 2003; Cram, Patrikios and Mitchell, 2011). I expect that moral commitments, personal values, and personality traits like social dominance orientation and fixed or fluid worldviews explain average nationalist propensities at the individual level (Haidt and Graham, 2007; Schwartz, 1994; Pratto et al., 1994; Hetherington and Weiler, 2018). For example, people who adhere to "binding" moral values like loyalty and tradition—the same moral commitments that predict militarism in public opinion research (Kertzer et al., 2014)—likely exhibit a greater propensity to adopt and commit to unity-oriented nationalisms. Someone who values fairness and reciprocity, and whose personal moral systems demonstrate a preoccupation with equality, might instead commit to equality-oriented nationalism and bristle at elite cues that call for unity. Importantly, the fact that dispositions play a role does not mean that nationalisms are endogenous to values. Values shape political attitudes directly, to be sure, but also interact with social influence. Nationalist commitments create social pressures that exacerbate how we express group norms and our own values in intergroup contexts. Indeed, psychologists show that we are more likely to adopt group norms, and act on them, when we also personally favor them (Tankard and Paluck, 2016).

This book tests my theory about how content shapes the relationship between nationalisms and foreign policy attitudes, but does not present a comprehensive theory of contestation. The data in chapters 4 and 5 support my assumption that people contest nationalisms in both the United States and European contexts, though I find less contestation among European elites than among their counterparts in the mass public. I return to questions about the antecedents of unity- and equality-oriented nationalisms in chapter 6, with a more extensive discussion that paves the way for future research.

Nationalisms and the Limits of the Civic/Ethnic Debate

Nationalisms rooted in unity and equality carry different implications for foreign policy attitudes. Unity encourages nationalist aggression whereas equality fosters international cooperation. These constructs have psychological foundations, apply to nationalisms and supranationalisms alike, help resolve puzzling inconsistencies in the empirical record, and synthesize insights from existing research on identity content.

Yet readers familiar with the dominant civic/ethnic nationalism framework may take pause, and ask how my concepts improve upon this existing work. "Civic" nationalisms tie group membership to a set of beliefs and (typically democratic) institutions. "Ethnic" nationalisms rely on *jus sanguinis* rather than *jus soli* principles, and tie identification to common descent and kinship (Wright, Citrin and Wand, 2012; Brubaker, 2004). If the civic/ethnic dichotomy provides the disciplinary default (Kohn, 1944; Brubaker, 1992; Greenfeld, 1992; Snyder, 2000; Schrock-Jacobson, 2012; Wright, Citrin and Wand, 2012; Schildkraut, 2007, 2014; Citrin, Reingold and Green, 1990; Citrin and Sears, 2009; Reeskens and Hooghe, 2010; Lindstam, Mader and Schoen, 2021; Bruter, 2003; Citrin and Sides, 2008; Bruter, 2009; Wright, 2011; Risse, 2010),[70] why entertain unity and equality?[71] These concepts retain their hallowed place in nationalism research for a reason—they have informed careful historical analyses of national institutions, citizenship laws, democratization, and war (Smith, 1992; Snyder, 2000; Wright, Citrin and Wand, 2012; Schildkraut, 2014). My theory nevertheless overcomes three conceptual and theoretical challenges that hamper the inferences we can draw using the civic/ethnic framework alone.

First, scholars cannot agree on criteria for civic and ethnic nationalism. This problem presents challenges for theory, conceptualization, and measurement. Civic and ethnic nationalisms either represent discrete categories, ends of a spectrum, or something in between (Smith, 2000); ethnic nationalism sometimes denotes a biological connection, yet sometimes includes any cultural grouping; civic nationalism sometimes refers to a voluntary and universal association, but sometimes requires a

---

70. Some scholars add other dimensions: Kymlicka (2001) treats "cultural" identities separately from ethnic identities, and Snyder (2000) adds revolutionary and counterrevolutionary nationalisms to his typology.

71. Interested readers should turn elsewhere for comprehensive critiques (e.g., Nieguth, 1999; Kuzio, 2002; Brubaker, 2004; Kreuzer, 2006; Zimmer, 2003).

common historical memory and shared values; group membership by birth sometimes denotes civic nationalism (Snyder, 2000), but sometimes indicates ethnic identification (Theiss-Morse, 2009; Wright, Citrin and Wand, 2012). And when we treat civic nationalisms as uniquely predicated on sharing beliefs, we disregard the fact that "ethnic" nationalism implicates shared beliefs too—such as the notion that being part of a group requires that people share blood ties or a common religion.

These conceptual debates carry theoretical and empirical consequences. Measured at the individual level, civic and ethnic nationalism often point in the same direction (Janmaat, 2006): "*both* the ethno-cultural and the civic conceptions of national identity are associated with political conservativism and right-wing party affiliation, measures of both patriotism and chauvinism, and anti-immigrant attitudes" (Wright, Citrin and Wand, 2012, 471), lending credence to Wimmer's (2019) contention that civic identities are simply stand-ins for weak ethnic nationalism. If these existing concepts make indeterminate predictions regarding straightforward outcomes like immigration attitudes, we should doubt strong claims about what civic or ethnic nationalisms mean for more distant attitudes about conflict escalation and security communities.

Second, several prominent theories about civic nationalism prioritize laws and institutions over psychology. Such conceptualizations treat people who are loyal to a constitution or state institutions as civic nationalists irrespective of their connection to the group (Smith, 1991; Brubaker, 1992; Bruter, 2004). But social identities refer to groups, not objects: I might identify as American and view the prototypical American as someone committed to the constitution (Theiss-Morse, 2009). I nevertheless identify with fellow Americans, not a piece of paper.

When scholars instead define civic nationalism by the set of beliefs that group members commit to, they inevitably redound to norms like legal equality and other elements of liberal democracy (Snyder, 2000). Yet herein lies another problem that my framework overcomes by stipulating pre-political norms before institutions: There is nothing inherent in a civic institution that requires it to adopt liberal or inclusive values, promote cooperation, prioritize equality, or produce a less militarized foreign policy (Brown, 1999). Citizenship can be "an immensely powerful instrument for social closure," after all (Brubaker, 2004, 141). Examples from the French government's infamous face-covering ban in the name of *laïcité* to Denmark's restrictive immigration policies (Goodman, 2012, 676) and Indonesia violently imposing civic nationalism (Kreuzer, 2006) illustrate how nominal "civic" nationalism often masks commitments to unity. Similarly, ethnic nationalisms can be predicated on equality. Egalitarian norms partly explain why ethnic Quebecois nationalism has not turned violent in Canada, for example (Lange, 2013): Equals under the law, many Quebecers feel that the central government treats them fairly. "Ethnic" nationalism can also lead to isolationism if a state wants to maintain its peaceful way of life—Ireland stayed neutral in World War II, for example, preferring to take the moral high ground when it was not under attack despite the ethnic and religious character of Irish national identities (Hutchinson, 2017).

Third, unity and equality better synthesize the national and supranational categorization levels. If a civic European identity means that people are committed to "a political structure" like the European Union, citizens from Switzerland, Norway, and the UK lack a target for their civic commitment (Bruter, 2004, 26). Risse (2010, 52) elides the traditional nomenclature and instead differentiates between "modern" European identities marked by commitment to liberal democracy and human rights compared to exclusionary identities that "[transfer] nationalist values to the European level." His division closely matches what I term "unity" and "equality," but I provide the psychological foundations that make my typology adaptable across other regional contexts, and not bound to the European case.

My theory of identity content complements and refines the prominent civic/ethnic typology. I build my concepts on psychological foundations. In turn, I articulate distinct, discrete, pre-political norms that map onto groups that range in size from neighborhood associations to international coalitions. These norms illuminate the central elements that predict when "civic" nationalists will be less (or more) war-prone and "ethnic" nationalists less (or more) cooperative.

Conclusion

My theory of identity content substantially refines our understanding of nationalisms in IR. Although IR scholars independently research both nationalist support for conflict and supranationalist support for cooperation, scholarly advances tend to follow parallel tracks. Accordingly, I first synthesized the two levels to explain how nationalisms and supranationalisms occupy two sides of the same coin—they share psychological micro-foundations.

Second, I explained why content matters. Specifically, I argued that (1) someone's nationalist commitment provides an insufficient basis for understanding whether she prefers a bellicose foreign policy or a tit-for-tat response, and (2) supranationalism encourages cooperation when reciprocity prevails, but inhibits trust when group members demand unity in a heterogeneous coalition. Working from the ground up, I arrived at a theory of identity content rooted in fundamental norms of human interaction. I differentiated between equality and unity as foundations for nationalisms in international politics and explained how they relate to existing typologies. After deducing the theoretical implications that link unity and equality to different foreign policy postures, I introduced my intergroup conflict and intragroup cooperation hypotheses.

In the next three chapters, I evaluate these hypotheses using both novel experiments and observational survey data. The experiments (chapters 3 and 4) test the intergroup conflict hypothesis. They provide important causal leverage to show that unity-oriented nationalism promotes foreign policy aggression whereas equality-oriented nationalism corresponds to muted militarism but support for proportionate responses to aggression from adversaries. The European survey analyses (chapter 5) provide complementary observational evidence and external validity to show that Europeans who view themselves as part of a group of equals support deeper security integration, as compared to their unity-oriented counterparts. Throughout, I show that understanding why some nationalists support more external conflict—and why some supranationalists support more internal security cooperation—requires that we engage nationalisms' content and commitment dimensions.

3

Nationalisms, Support for Conflict Escalation, and Militarism

In 2019, analysts wrung their hands as Indian Prime Minister Narendra Modi's growing demands for nationalist unity gained traction—both in the media and among members of the mass public who enthusiastically voted him into office. Modi's brand of Hindu nationalism prioritizes unity and homogeneity: He and the BJP (Bharatiya Janata Party) set out to revise textbooks and National Day celebrations to eliminate alternative national narratives associated with religious diversity (Tudor and Slater, 2020). This nationalist fervor has threatened to stoke militarized conflict with China[1] and Pakistan.[2] Yet Mahatma Gandhi, known for his explicit commitment to nonviolence (Mantena, 2012a),[3] also embraced Indian nationalism in the

1. Ben Blanchard, 2017. "China-India border spat casts shadow ahead of BRICS summit," *Reuters*, 2 August. URL: www.reuters.com/article/us-china-india/china-india-border-spat-casts-shadow-ahead-of-brics-summit-iduSKBN1AJ08L.

2. Komireddi, Kapil, 2019. "The Kashmir Crisis isn't about Territory. It's about a Hindu Victory over Islam," *Washington Post*, 16 August. URL: www.washingtonpost.com/outlook/the-kashmir-crisis-isnt-about-territory-its-about-a-hindu-victory-over-islam/2019/08/16/ab84ffe2-bf79-11e9-a5c6-1e74f7ec4a93_story.html/. To be sure, the Hindu nationalism that Modi and the BJP endorse also has consequences for domestic politics, as they have used national unity to justify policies that degrade civil liberties for religious minorities (Tudor and Slater, 2020). Though I do not investigate subnational politics in this book, these policies correspond to my expectations regarding transnational intragroup relations—homogenizing identities reduce intragroup cooperation in heterogeneous groups.

3. See also Mantena (2012b) for a discussion about Gandhi's view of the state; Mantena (2012b) argues that Gandhi objected to states that enforced peace with violence—and that

struggle for independence from Britain. He wrote that "it is not nationalism that is evil" (Gandhi, 1925, 211), elsewhere adding that Indian nationalism would be inclusive and could serve humanity without harming outsiders (Gandhi, 1935). Equality underscored his nationalist vision for India.

In chapter 2, I argued that content, not commitment, separates Modi from Gandhi—it would be difficult to credibly argue that Gandhi's nonviolent approach stemmed from weak nationalism. Rather, these two leaders appear to rely on different nationalist norms. Modi's concern with maintaining unity in his multi-ethnic, multi-creedal state creates a sharp boundary between prototypical Indians (Hindus) and outsiders. Such nationalism facilitates threat inflation and militarism—evil adversaries bear collective responsibility in a dispute—and, in turn, encourages aggression and crisis escalation. Gandhi, by contrast, centered his description of Indian nationalism on norms of equality and reciprocity between Hindus and Muslims, an approach that the Indian National Congress adopted to build Indian democracy (Tudor and Slater, 2020). Gandhi and Modi undoubtedly differ in other ways, and we should be prudent before making claims about whether their nationalist orientations caused their distinct approaches to matters of war and peace. But the comparison illustrates that we miss important variation if we assume a co-constitutive relationship between nationalism and militarism; Gandhi seemed to experience little dissonance when he paired his nationalist vision with equality, fairness, and a desire to avoid escalating violence.

My theory is grounded in individual-level psychology, and I test my intergroup conflict hypothesis in a sample from the American public for both theoretical and empirical reasons. Theoretically, many of our claims about nationalist militarism depend on correlations in public opinion surveys, and macro-level theories that connect nationalism to war assume that the public plays a role—either as an instigator for conflict or as a permissive audience for hawkish elites. Empirically, my mass public focus allows me to test my expectations using experimental methods. Survey responses remain subject to confounding if participants bring prior, unobserved expectations to bear when they answer questions about national superiority. The experiment in this chapter manipulates the social relations

---

Indians could create and maintain a peaceful coexistence if they committed to individual freedom and the norm of nonviolence. Interestingly, Mantena (2012a) argues that Gandhi's beliefs stemmed from instrumental concerns about the tendency for violence to spiral out of control, rather than a moral belief.

and purported norms that prevail in a fictional country (Fredonia) and asks participants to imagine themselves to be Fredonian citizens and to respond to a fictional territorial dispute with a neighboring state.

The results show that the relationship between nationalism and (1) support for conflict escalation and (2) general militarism depends on content: equality weakens the positive association between nationalism and hawkishness. In the unity condition, nationalism corresponds to greater support for conflictual actions against a rival country (Rusburg) and more general militarism, compared to the equality treatment. Using a fictional scenario and country enables me to establish a baseline for how content and commitment interact to shape support for intergroup conflict, with minimal interference from an individual's pre-existing ideas about how they relate to real co-nationals or other facets of existing national identities. In subsequent chapters, I take up the challenge of testing my theory's implications in concrete, real identities via American nationalism (chapter 4) and European supranationalism (chapter 5).

The following discussion has four parts. I begin with a brief review of my theoretical expectations and intergroup conflict hypothesis before explaining why studying the public with experiments carries important advantages. Second, I describe the experimental design and methods. This section includes a thorough discussion about designing bundled treatments to manipulate identity content. Third, I present the results from the experiment. Fourth, I discuss the study's implications for my theory and for research on nationalism and public opinion more broadly.

Theoretical Expectations

Chapter 2 explained how unity and equality create distinct nationalisms, with implications for public attitudes about conflict escalation and generalized militarism. Strong unity-oriented nationalism inspires aggressive foreign policy attitudes among members of the public, while equality-oriented nationalism does not.

In chapter 2, I also discussed how content and commitment interact— people who commit to a group conform to the group's norms (Wellen, Hogg and Terry, 1998; Terry and Hogg, 1996; Terry, Hogg and White, 1999; Huddy, 2001; Jetten, Postmes and McAuliffe, 2002), whereas those with weak commitments do not. My expectations therefore concern the interaction between equality or unity and how strongly someone asserts her national superiority. I expect that equality's conflict-mitigating effects will manifest at high levels of nationalism, since weak identifiers typically ignore group expectations. Strong unity-oriented nationalism—like the German nationalism that consolidated the new state but helped spawn WWI—primes people for militarism and conflict escalation. By contrast, strong equality-oriented nationalism primes people to commit to norms of reciprocity and take a measured approach to crisis decisions.

But those expectations do not apply to people with weaker nationalist commitments, and for this reason I constrain my claims and empirical tests to differences in the *strength* of the relationship between nationalism and conflictual outcomes on one hand, and differences between *strong* equality- and unity-oriented nationalists on the other. Looking at average differences in militarism by equality and unity, for example, would mask theoretically important heterogeneity. Weakly committed nationalists typically ignore group norms and align their attitudes with individual dispositions. But they might also go further to react against what they believe the group expects them to do—if I do not feel like my group reflects me and my values, I will not see them as a legitimate authority to guide my behavior (Quick and Stephenson, 2007; Jetten, Postmes and McAuliffe, 2002). As one survey respondent wrote, "Being an American means being selfish, entitled, and capitalist. It is quite sad, also." By implication, she rejects the egoistic values she associates with the group and likely rebukes nationalist norms.

WHY THE PUBLIC?

This chapter tests my intergroup conflict hypothesis with a fictional national identity and foreign policy crisis. Building my theory from the ground up, from fundamental social cognition to expectations about nationalist foreign policy aggression, I focus on the public opinion samples that allow direct hypothesis tests. Of course, my theory might apply just as well to elites—a point I return to in chapter 5—but focusing on the public carries substantive and methodological advantages.

Correctly understanding the relationship between nationalism and militarism has implications for research on public opinion in general, but also for research on macro-level conflict. Public opinion plays a central role in theories that connect nationalism to foreign policy conflict in practice. Scholars propose direct and indirect bottom-up pathways that link nationalism to interstate conflict.

The direct pathway proposes that nationalist violence increases the chance of conflict. Events that increase mass nationalism then lead to direct aggression between rivals—violence between Salvadoran and Honduran football fans sparked a costly war in the 1960s when the two states faced off in the World Cup qualification round (Bertoli, 2017). Yet the Football War is salient in part because it is atypical; against Morgenthau's (1948) fears, research provides sparse evidence that conflict between nationalist civilians scales up to interstate wars that the respective states would otherwise avoid.[4] Even if confrontations between members of the public rarely move a dyad from stability to war, direct action from nationalist citizens might nevertheless heighten tensions between rivals and increase the probability of conflict. When Ukrainians protested outside the Russian embassy in 2014 by damaging property and tearing down flags, Russia issued a sharp condemnation—thereby stoking potential escalation (Gruffydd-Jones, 2017, 706).[5] Mass actions might require additional ingredients to move from a simmering dispute to fiery conflict, but publics who provoke adversaries with direct action can complicate a leader's diplomatic agenda. Indeed, leaders might see independence day celebrations or remembrance days as diplomatic risks given potential nationalist violence (Gruffydd-Jones, 2017).

The indirect bottom-up pathway suggests that public opinion informs elite decision-making. Nationalist publics might pressure elites to take action. Elites—especially those that helm democracies—pay close attention to their domestic audience because they fear backlash and electoral consequences.[6] Low approval ratings risk leaders' chances for re-election and stymie other elements of their political agendas (Gelpi and Grieco, 2015; Croco and Weeks, 2016). Although George W. Bush claimed that "he makes policy 'based upon principle and not polls and focus groups'" (Foyle, 2004, 269), he and his administration structured their post-9/11 plans to keep the American public on his side. They fretted about whether the angry and nationalist public would accept a measured response. Woodward (2012, 150) chronicles war cabinet meetings during the two weeks immediately after the attacks, during which elites wondered:

How long could they wait after September 11 before the U.S. started going "kinetic," as they often termed it, against al Qaeda in a visible way? The public was patient, at least it seemed patient, but everyone wanted

---

4. Indeed, while Bertoli (2017) lists 9 notable cases of international sports-driven nationalism and interstate conflict, only 2 cases were clearly driven by the public.

5. Marcus, Jonathan, 2014. "Ukraine Crisis: Russia Condemns Attack on Kiev Embassy," *BBC News*, 14 June. URL: www.bbc.com/news/world-europe-27853698.

6. On the relationship between public opinion and foreign policy in general, see, e.g., Aldrich et al. (2006) and Baum and Potter (2008). See Weeks (2014) on autocratic audience costs.

action. A full military operation—air and boots—would be the essential demonstration of seriousness—to bin Laden, America and the world.

Indeed, Colin Powell insisted that the administration should only pursue war if the American people would stand behind them. His assertions contributed to the administration's decision to move quickly against al Qaeda—a consensus target for nationalist retribution. And although scholars disagree about the extent to which leaders respond to public opinion in matters of war and peace, most members of the Israeli Knesset claim that they take public opinion into account when they are deciding whether to use military force (Tomz, Weeks and Yarhi-Milo, 2020). Their responses go beyond platitudes: public support increased Knesset members' willingness to use military strikes in an experimental scenario. And in budding democracies, Snyder (2000) posits that public nationalism creates inadvertent belligerence. Driven by their dual desire to gain public support for development but maintain power, elites in newly democratizing states use nationalist rhetoric to achieve their goals. When "nationalist mythmaking" dominates the popular discourse, it can provoke enmity and war (see also Mansfield and Snyder, 2007).[7] In non-democracies, leaders might escalate a conflict to appease nationalist protestors—when nationalist protests proliferated in Thailand in 2008, the government reversed course to take a hard-line stance against Cambodia in their dispute over a small piece of territory (Ciorciari and Weiss, 2016).

Finally, hawkish elites ostensibly use nationalism to their advantage. To the extent that nationalist publics demand military action—or at least, submit to an administration's decision to use force—nationalist surges create a window of opportunity to pursue a hawkish agenda. This top-down story proposes that public nationalism frees elites to initiate or escalate conflict without fearing punishment at the polls. Nationalist elites help determine whether a state goes to war (Snyder, 2000), but appeal to a preexisting identity in the process (O'Leary and Sambanis, 2018). Domestic interest groups map their own myopic agendas onto the "national interest" in part because doing so can consolidate support for an expansionist agenda (Snyder, 1991). Leaders who want to gin up support for confrontation or escalation can leverage national day celebrations to take a strong stand against an adversary (Gruffydd-Jones, 2017). For instance, the Chinese government often carries out military exercises around the disputed

---

7. Though see Narang and Nelson (2009).

Senkaku/Diaoyu Islands near the anniversary of Japan's 1931 Manchuria invasion, when nationalist sentiments run strong (Gruffydd-Jones, 2017). Or like Mussolini prior to Italy's invasion of Ethiopia, a leader might pair an aggressive agenda with concentrated efforts to foment nationalism and prepare the public to rally behind the intervention (Bertoli, 2017).

The mechanisms that connect public opinion to actual interstate conflict are complicated and sometimes contradictory, and I do not endeavor to adjudicate between them. Importantly, both the bottom-up story in which nationalist publics pressure their leaders to use force or escalate disputes and the top-down story in which elites take advantage of a nationalist surge to pursue pre-existing hawkish plans (or, like Mussolini, try to cause mass nationalism) share an assumption—that public nationalism arouses support for foreign policy aggression. Evidence to support this assumption relies on analyses of public opinion data that find robust associations between nationalism and militarism alongside support for a host of the aggressive, hard-line, or escalatory foreign policies that interest me (Hurwitz and Peffley, 1990; Druckman, 2001; Federico, Golec and Dial, 2005; Herrmann, Isernia and Segatti, 2009). Public opinion research provides the bedrock for arguments about nationalism's effects in international politics.

WHY EXPERIMENTS?

Members of the general public constitute an important population for substantive and theoretical reasons, but my focus on ordinary citizens also brings empirical benefits: I can test my intergroup conflict hypothesis with experiments.

Experiments offer two advantages. First, the logic of experiments maximizes internal validity and facilitates causal inference (McDermott, 2002b; Morton and Williams, 2010; McDermott, 2011; Mintz, Yang and McDermott, 2011). Although scholars have made advancements in measuring nationalism's various effects (Schildkraut, 2014; Huddy and Del Ponte, 2019), endogeneity concerns often plague observational data.[8] If we find a strong relationship between nationalism and Iraq war support on a survey, for example, we might ask whether supporting war caused people to cling to their national superiority rather than the reverse.[9]

8. For a thorough discussion of experiments in the context of political and social identities, see McDermott (2009).

9. See, for example, Kertzer and Powers (2020) for a discussion about how policy preferences can affect core beliefs.

Related, we might underestimate equality-oriented nationalism in observational data if respondents eschew a label that "is tainted by the worst horrors of the twentieth century" and evokes militarism (Rodrik in Tamir, 2019, ix). Like U.S. soccer's Megan Rapinoe submitted during the 2019 World Cup, survey respondents might feel "extremely American" and think that "we are a great country"—yet hesitate to call themselves nationalists because the term carries a negative connotation or because they believe that "the Western world . . . [has] outgrown nationalism" (Tamir, 2019, 5; Devos and Banaji, 2005).[10] If standard survey measures for nationalism smuggle in a respondent's interpretation about what *others* associate with nationalism, they frustrate attempts to disentangle commitment and content. Low scores on a survey-based nationalism scale could indicate weak nationalism from a respondent, or that she does not adhere to what she perceives as the dominant nationalist norms in her country and so she creates an artificial distance between herself and the group. Similarly, if we turn to large-n quantitative data and measure nationalism in part by whether the leader has recently used the military to protect the nation's distinct character (Schrock-Jacobson, 2012, 832), we cannot tell whether the military tension and elite rhetoric caused a certain type of public nationalism.

Manipulating constitutive norms allows me to assess whether differences in content alter the ostensibly inexorable link between nationalism and militarism. The experiment in this chapter maximizes control by manipulating a fictional national identity and presenting participants with a carefully controlled escalating crisis vignette. It enables me to establish a baseline causal argument for the intergroup conflict hypothesis before I manipulate American nationalisms in chapter 4 and use observational data to test my intragroup cooperation hypothesis in chapter 5.

Second, creating a purpose-built experimental instrument has important advantages for both conceptual clarity and for measurement. My theory borrows from relational models theory to specify sets of constitutive norms that describe unity- and equality-oriented nationalisms. Experimental methods allow me to craft treatment vignettes that encompass the norms contained within each complex model. Similarly, I can measure the key moderator and dependent variables, nationalism and militarism, using standard and well-validated scales. This provides an important advantage over the at-a-distance techniques typical of research on elites, where

10. Rapinoe, Megan qtd. in Fink, Jenni (2019). "Megan Rapinoe: America's a 'Great Country,' but We Can Still Improve," *Newsweek*, 13 July. URL: www.newsweek.com/megan-rapinoe-america-proud-great-patriotism-1447413.

speechwriters and a multiple audience problem confound the inferences we can make from public statements.[11] Finally, this experiment takes participants through a multi-stage crisis as it unfolds—making it possible to capture preferences for escalation.

The Sample

I conducted a survey experiment with a sample of 301 adult Americans recruited from Amazon.com's Mechanical Turk (MTurk) in 2014. Participants, 53.8% of whom identified as male and 77.4% as white/Caucasian, ranged in age from 18 to 68 (median age 32 years).[12] Mechanical Turk participants do not represent the American population, but provide useful samples for social science research[13]— both for ease of sample recruitment and for data quality. And the sample contains important demographic variation compared to college student participants: For example, 45.51% of participants in this sample have already obtained a bachelor's degree or higher, and 48.8% report a household income of greater than $40,000 per year.[14]

The Experiment

The between-group experiment contained four parts, summarized in Figure 3.1: (1) An experimental manipulation that exposed participants to a description of a fictional country's norms, (2) a series of questions

11. See Kertzer (2016) for a discussion, though see Renshon (2009) for evidence that a leader's public speeches can produce the same "operational code" profile as their private statements.

12. I recruited U.S. adults who had completed at least 100 Human Intelligence Tasks (HITs) with a 95% approval rating (Berinsky, Huber and Lenz, 2012). Participants received $1.00 to complete the survey.

13. MTurk samples have been used to replicate classic findings from research in political science and political psychology (Berinsky, Huber and Lenz, 2012), and results from MTurk studies have been replicated in nationally representative samples (Healy and Lenz, 2014; Weinberg, Freese and McElhattan, 2014; Mullinix et al., 2015). Experiments with MTurk samples have appeared in top political science journals—see Huber, Hill and Lenz (2012); Tomz and Weeks (2013); Chaudoin (2014); Healy and Lenz (2014); Renshon (2017); Huff and Kertzer (2018); Kertzer, Renshon and Yarhi-Milo (2021) and Nomikos and Sambanis (2019) for examples.

14. Sample composition could threaten internal validity if we expect a key demographic characteristic or predisposition to moderate the treatment: "When the target population differs on attributes that are *theoretically relevant* for a given study" (Renshon, 2017, 80). Renshon, for example, explains that regular citizens are more susceptible to status threat treatments than leaders. Leaders' high power provides an inoculation that reduces the treatment effect. My theory pertains to people in general, making a diverse sample of Americans appropriate.

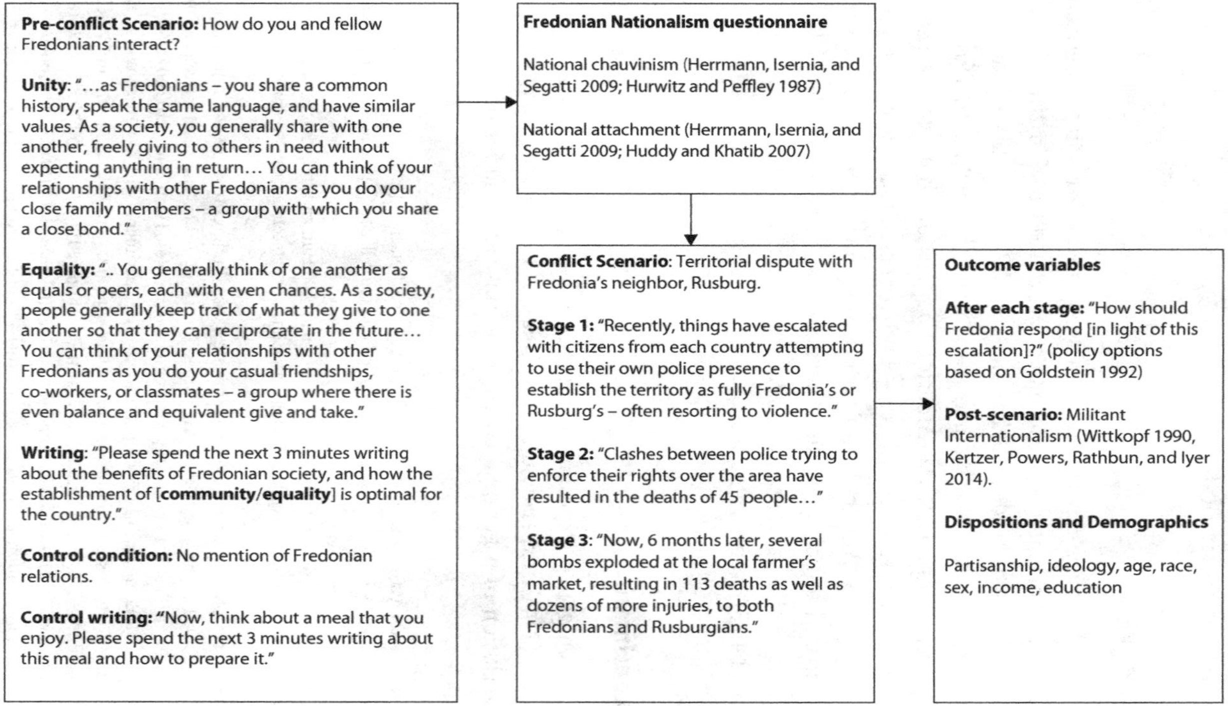

Pre-conflict Scenario: How do you and fellow Fredonians interact?

Unity: "...as Fredonians – you share a common history, speak the same language, and have similar values. As a society, you generally share with one another, freely giving to others in need without expecting anything in return.... You can think of your relationships with other Fredonians as you do your close family members – a group with which you share a close bond."

Equality: "... You generally think of one another as equals or peers, each with even chances. As a society, people generally keep track of what they give to one another so that they can reciprocate in the future.... You can think of your relationships with other Fredonians as you do your casual friendships, co-workers, or classmates – a group where there is even balance and equivalent give and take."

Writing: "Please spend the next 3 minutes writing about the benefits of Fredonian society, and how the establishment of [community/equality] is optimal for the country."

Control condition: No mention of Fredonian relations.

Control writing: "Now, think about a meal that you enjoy. Please spend the next 3 minutes writing about this meal and how to prepare it."

Fredonian Nationalism questionnaire

National chauvinism (Herrmann, Isernia, and Segatti 2009; Hurwitz and Peffley 1987)

National attachment (Herrmann, Isernia, and Segatti 2009; Huddy and Khatib 2007)

Conflict Scenario: Territorial dispute with Fredonia's neighbor, Rusburg.

Stage 1: "Recently, things have escalated with citizens from each country attempting to use their own police presence to establish the territory as fully Fredonia's or Rusburg's – often resorting to violence."

Stage 2: "Clashes between police trying to enforce their rights over the area have resulted in the deaths of 45 people..."

Stage 3: "Now, 6 months later, several bombs exploded at the local farmer's market, resulting in 113 deaths as well as dozens of more injuries, to both Fredonians and Rusburgians."

Outcome variables

After each stage: "How should Fredonia respond [in light of this escalation]?" (policy options based on Goldstein 1992)

Post-scenario: Militant Internationalism (Wittkopf 1990, Kertzer, Powers, Rathbun, and Iyer 2014).

Dispositions and Demographics

Partisanship, ideology, age, race, sex, income, education

FIGURE 3.1. Fredonia experiment structure.

that measured nationalism, (3) a multi-stage conflict scenario between Fredonia and a neighboring state (Rusburg) where participants made decisions about how to respond, and (4) a final questionnaire that contained questions about militarism, dispositions, and demographic characteristics.

IDENTITY CONTENT AND NATIONALISM

I designed novel experimental treatments to manipulate the *content* of a fictional, "Fredonian" national identity. Whereas past work either manipulates the strength of national identities but not content (Kemmelmeier and Winter, 2008; Gelpi, Roselle and Barnett, 2013), or approaches content as a measurement problem using observational survey data (Citrin et al., 1994; Wright, Citrin and Wand, 2012), these experimental treatments target the substance of someone's national identity—what it means to be Fredonian. Importantly, the treatments only describe relations between Fredonians. The treatments exclude any mention of outsiders or foreign policy that might implicitly guide participants to one set of responses, creating conceptual distance between the independent variables (content) and outcomes (foreign policy militarism).

Building an identity from the ground up requires participant attention and engagement. The scenario therefore incorporates a two-part manipulation designed to define Fredonian group norms and encourage participants to think about what it means to be a Fredonian. In step one, all participants imagined themselves as citizens of a fictional country—Fredonia—and received basic information about Fredonia's size and population.[15] In the control condition, participants read this brief description before navigating to a page that asked them to write about an unrelated topic (their favorite recipe). In the *unity* and *equality* conditions, participants learned that former Fredonians expressed animus toward one another. But now, they interact amicably on the basis of unity or equality norms within the country.

In the unity scenario, participants read that citizens of Fredonia have "unified as a community ... and have similar values.... You can think of your relationships with other Fredonians as you do your close family members—a group with which you share a close bond." The equality

15. 297,000 square miles and 34 million people, respectively—global means for country area and population.

TABLE 3.1. Manipulating Unity and Equality in Fredonia

	Unity	Equality
Central Theme	Unity	Equality
Constitution of Groups	Solidarity, shared kinship	Equals, peers
Reciprocal Exchange	Share freely	Expect reciprocity
Decision-making	Consensus	One person, one vote

scenario instead specifies that Fredonians "differ in many ways, but ... generally think of one another as equals. ... You can think of your relationships with other Fredonians as you do your casual friendships, co-workers, or classmates—a group where there is even balance and equivalent give and take." In both cases, the study instructed participants to consider themselves a typical citizen of Fredonia.[16]

I crafted the descriptive paragraphs to closely match each other in terms of structure, length, and themes. Unlike a typical experiment that manipulates a single word or phrase, these treatments bundle several aspects of unity- and equality-oriented relations to capture a holistic picture of each set of norms. Each discussed the central theme along with specific references to how unity and equality manifest in exchange, decision-making, and identity. To that end, the treatments use specific language from three sources: (1) Fiske's (1991) "master table," which shows how each relational model operates in various domains such as decision-making and social identity, (2) a confirmatory factor analysis of relational models survey items from Haslam and Fiske (1999), and (3) Fiske and Tetlock's (1997) experiments investigating taboo trade-offs using relational models theory. Each paragraph followed the same structure, and targeted the same bundle of concepts. Whereas the unity treatment noted that Fredonians make decisions by "reaching a consensus about what is best," the equality treatment pointed to a "voting procedure where each citizen gets one vote." Table 3.1 shows the dimensions included in each treatment.

After reading about Fredonia, participants completed the second stage of the treatment—they spent at least three minutes writing about the benefits of Fredonia's societal structure. The prompt asked them to discuss how the establishment of unity or equality is positive for the country (modified from Richeson and Nussbaum, 2004 and Wolsko et al., 2000). I designed this task to cement the norms identified in the vignette and

---

16. See the appendix for the full text of each treatment and directions for the writing task.

encourage participants to connect meaningfully with Fredonia, an especially important barrier to overcome in experiments that seek to maintain participant interest without sacrificing too much control (McDermott, 2002a).

Notably, these manipulations only contain descriptive information about Fredonia's size and population alongside the text describing in-group norms. The treatments do not mention the neighboring state that will serve as an adversary in the crisis vignette later in the survey. Nor do the treatments reference anything about foreign policy in even general terms. An alternative approach might tell participants directly that Fredonians adopt a reciprocity rule in foreign policy, for example, but my design allows me to create substantial conceptual distance between the independent variable I manipulate and the outcomes that I measure. To the extent that the treatments affect the relationship between nationalism and foreign policy attitudes, I can attribute the differences to how participants apply in-group norms to their interactions with adversaries—a rigorous test for my hypothesis.

Manipulation check

Did participants understand the treatments and complete the writing task? One way to check that participants focused on the correct set of Fredonian norms is to analyze text from the open-ended responses. I used automated text analysis to explore whether the different treatment paragraphs encourage participants to write about systematically different concepts.

Structural topic models (STM) implement a method for unsupervised, automated text analysis. "Unsupervised" means that the algorithm induces the topics from the data itself, rather than relying on the researcher to supply a topic and relevant target words (Roberts et al., 2014). These models allow researchers to evaluate group-based differences in the prevalence of each topic by combining the topics with metadata. In this case, I incorporate data on whether a participant received either the equality or unity treatment. I omit the control group participants from this analysis, because they wrote about food rather than Fredonia.

I examined the extent to which two clearly distinct topics emerge from the data, whether they connect to the targeted models, and whether the topics systematically vary with the treatments. I estimate a structural topic model with two topics using the *stm* package in R (Roberts, Stewart and Tingley, 2014).[17] The highest probability words in Topic 1—labelled

---

17. The number of topics selected depends on exclusivity, semantic coherence, and researcher discretion. While relying on the exclusivity/coherence "frontier" could yield a model

Manipulation check

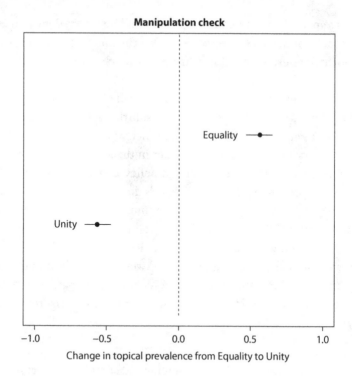

FIGURE 3.2. Structrual topic model.
Note: Figure shows the difference in topic prevalence moving from the equality to unity treatment with 95% confidence intervals. The results show that participants in the equality and unity treatment groups wrote about distinct topics, labeled "equality" and "unity," respectively.

"Equality"—include "equal," "everyon," "peopl," "societi," "one," "differ," and "group." Topic 2—"Unity"—contains word stems like "societi," 'countri," "peopl," "like," "one," "comuniti," and "fredonian." Among words that have high values on frequency and exclusivity—the likelihood that they appear in one topic but not the other—the top word is "equal" for Topic 1 and "communiti" for Topic 2. The words in each topic correspond to the two treatments.

Figure 3.2 displays the changes in topic prevalence between the equality and unity conditions. The results illustrate a clear, significant difference in the prevalence of each topic between the two treatment groups. The difference in the proportion of people in the equality treatment who discuss

with 8-10 topics, the topics that differ across the treatment conditions overlap enough to threaten interpretability. To facilitate appropriate topic labels, I present results based on two topics.

"Equality," compared to their unity counterparts, is 0.56. As one respondent offered, highlighting decision-making: "you each get a vote so that makes everyone equal in terms of running the government." Another representative respondent wrote about reciprocity: "one of the biggest benefits of this society is that it is fair when you give something you can trust that you'll receive something else in return."

The difference in topic proportion for Topic 2 (unity) is comparably large at 0.56. Representative responses for the unity topic again emphasize the unity norms targeted in the treatment. One respondent underscored the family analogue when they wrote that "fredonians hold to the idea that we are all family and watch out for each other all the time." Another highlights the unity-oriented approach to decision-making, noting that "when something needs to be decided a consensus is sought." The same respondent concisely reiterates the central theme for unity: "like a large family group, if one is threatened then all are threatened."

In sum, the treatments targeted the complex set of norms that underlie unity and equality, as reflected in respondents' open-ended writing task. To test hypothesis 1, though, I require a measure of nationalism—to what degree do participants embrace Fredonia's greatness?

Nationalism

To measure nationalism, I adapt a widely used scale for "national chauvinism" from Herrmann, Isernia and Segatti (2009), and replace references to America/Italy with Fredonia.[18] Participants received four questions about their commitment to Fredonian nationalism: "How superior do you think Fredonia is compared to other nations?"; "How many things about Fredonia make you feel ashamed?"; "How much better would the world be if people from other countries were more like Fredonians?"; and do you agree that "Patriots should support Fredonia even if it is in the wrong?" I used scores for each item to create an additive scale for Fredonian nationalism. As discussed in chapter 2, research from social psychology and political science agrees that strong identifiers conform to group norms at greater rates than weak identifiers (Jetten, Postmes and McAuliffe, 2002; Hogg, Turner and Davidson, 1990). In measuring national commitments post-treatment, the experiment asks participants to report their commitment to the Fredonian identity they read and wrote about.

18. Though my interest here lies in nationalism, the survey also includes questions about attachment and culturalism from Herrmann, Isernia, and Segatti (2009).

Using this scale also allows me to compare my findings to past work that associates individual-level nationalism with hawkish foreign policy preferences. When Kosterman and Feshbach (1989) conclude that nationalists— but not patriots—promote an aggressive nuclear posture or when Herrmann, Isernia and Segatti (2009, 742) write that "it is chauvinism that is positively related to militarist dispositions," they posit a role for nationalism that separates nationalist superiority from national attachment, patriotism, or other measures of identification (Huddy and Khatib, 2007; Schildkraut, 2014). Insofar as I find evidence for less belligerence among people who believe the world would be better off if more countries were like Fredonia, I am taking nationalism on its own terms.

Importantly, I argue that the equality and unity treatments change what it means to be a Fredonian nationalist. Random assignment determines who populates each treatment group. But if one group expressed stronger nationalism than the other, it would be hard to attribute effects to the interaction between norms and nationalism rather than to Fredonian nationalism on its own. If the unity treatment provoked more nationalism, for example, it would undermine my assertion that superiority can be built on the back of equality. I test this possibility in two ways.

First, I calculate the difference in mean nationalism scores between the equality, unity, and control groups. Nationalism should be higher in both treatment groups compared to the control since those in the latter group had limited exposure to Fredonia. Yet I should find similar average nationalist commitments in the unity and equality groups if my treatments succeeded in targeting content rather than commitment. Indeed, I find near-identical means for the nationalism measure in the equality and unity treatment groups. The additive nationalism scale ranges from 0 to 1, and reveals a non-significant 0.007 difference between the two treatment groups ($mean_{unity} = 0.554$, $mean_{equality} = 0.546$, $t = 0.28$).

Second, I test the full probability distributions against each other, since measures of central tendency sometimes mislead. Using a bootstrapped Kolmogorov-Smirnov test (Sekhon, 2011), I find results that confirm the difference of means test and mitigate concerns that nationalists overwhelmingly populate one treatment group or the other. Figure 3.3 plots these distributions. The results show statistically indistinguishable distributions between the equality and unity groups ($D = 0.04$, $p = 0.97$). The only significant differences occur between the control and each treatment group (for equality, $D = 0.38$, $p < 0.001$, for unity $D = 0.36$ and $p < 0.001$). Participants in both treatments expressed more nationalism than the baseline

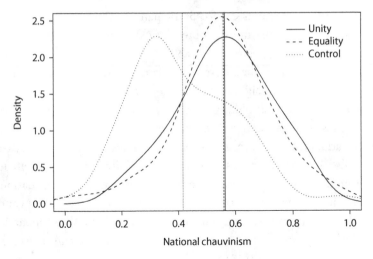

FIGURE 3.3. Unity and equality groups are equally nationalisitic.
Note: Vertical bars show the mean nationalism scores within each treatment group. Curves plot kernel density estimates that show the distribution on the nationalism scale within each treatment group. Bootstrapped Kolmogorov-Smirnov tests show that the distribution of nationalism does not differ significantly between the equality and unity groups (conducted using the Matching package in R; Sekhon, 2011). Both the equality and unity treatments produce stronger nationalism than the control group.

control group—unsurprising given the nature of the task—but unity and equality produced similar commitments to Fredonian nationalism.

Still, another concern pertains to *which* participants express strong nationalism, and whether different types of people commit to Fredonian equality or unity. If pre-treatment characteristics correlate with who ends up on the more committed end of the nationalism scale, it would weaken my ability to claim that differences in content cause differences between strong nationalists on the outcome variables. To evaluate the relationship between pre-treatment characteristics and nationalism, I created a subsample of the dataset that includes participants who assigned to either unity or equality, but excludes control group participants. I then regressed the nationalism scale on (1) a set of demographic characteristics—age, race, gender, university education, political knowledge, party identification, and whether the participant has ever taken a political science class;[19] (2) a

19. I measured each of these items at the end of the study. The treatments do not likely affect these stable individual differences, with the possible exception of party identification. Party identification is an increasingly important social identity for U.S. citizens, which in turn contains its own meaning and norms. Measuring party identification pre-treatment therefore risked contaminating the study by priming people to think about that social group (Klar, 2013; Klar, Leeper and

dichotomous variable coded 1 for participants in the equality group and 0 for participants in the unity group; and (3) interactions between each characteristic and the treatment variable.

The coefficients on the interaction terms constitute the quantities of interest. A positive and significant interaction coefficient on age, for example, would indicate that older participants assigned to the equality treatment express stronger nationalism than older participants assigned to the unity treatment. Instead, results reveal no significant differences between nationalists in the two groups. The only statistically significant coefficient in the model suggests that men score lower on the Fredonian nationalism scale in the unity group ($b = -0.07$, $p = 0.07$). But, crucially, I cannot reject the null hypothesis that gender has the same relationship with nationalism in both groups—the interaction between equality and male is not significant ($b = 0.06$, $p = 0.25$).[20]

I find demographic and partisan similarity between equality- and unity-oriented nationalists, increasing my confidence that the treatments target content and mitigating concerns that a pre-treatment covariate shapes the variable at the center of this chapter and my theory. Of course, this analysis cannot account for the possibility that an unknown and unmeasured factor confounds the results. Indeed, my chapter 2 discussion about where identity content comes from suggests that people have different inclinations toward unity- or equality-oriented nationalisms. Such an unmeasured confounder would weaken causal identification but nevertheless align with my broader framework—if people commit to nationalisms when they believe that the group matches their personal values, for example, and in turn conform to the group's norms in foreign policy crises, my evidence would show that unity and equality correspond to different foreign policy postures.

SCENARIO

Next, participants completed a 3-stage foreign policy crisis vignette, inspired by what Gartner (2008) and Kertzer (2016) call a panel experiment but with different inferential goals. The multi-stage design allows me to

---

Robison, 2020), and I therefore included it at the end alongside other demographic variables. Removing party identification from the models does not change the results of the analysis, and the benefits of accounting for partisanship outweigh the costs because the relationship between partisanship and a variety of dispositional traits increases the chance that I can capture potential unmeasured confounders.

20. See the appendix for results.

assess whether participants choose to escalate the conflict over time while keeping the consequences (military stakes) sufficiently low, and antagonists sufficiently ambiguous, for military strikes to represent an escalatory response.

The scenario description explains that Fredonia has a long-standing territorial dispute with Rusburg. A territorial dispute provides the ideal crisis to motivate the vignette, because it poses a hard test for my theory: citizens tie their national identities to the soil (Anderson, 1983), and territorial conflicts escalate to greater levels of intensity and severity compared to other issues (Vasquez, 2009; Gibler, Hutchison and Miller, 2012). From China and Japan trading blows over the Senkaku/Diaoyu Islands to the 4.6km^2 parcel that kicked off disputes between Thailand and Cambodia (Ciorciari and Weiss, 2016), territory implicates the nationalist desire to protect the homeland. Evidence that equality ameliorates nationalist escalation with respect to territory would therefore provide an important modification to our expectations about nationalist aggression in general.

In the vignette, citizens from each country occupy a swath of territory that lies between them, and both countries claim ownership over this territory. In the first stage, participants receive this information about the conflict and learn that as both Rusburgians and Fredonians vie to establish a police presence in the territory, violence has been on the rise. After a break where participants reported attitudes about Rusburgians, they proceeded to stage 2. Described as 2 weeks following the recent outbreak of violence, they read that 45 people had been killed in clashes between police forces. Both Rusburgians and Fredonians are included in the deaths, and the description does not attribute blame to either side. In Stage 3, 6 months have passed and now several bombs have detonated in the local market. This time, 113 people die but "there is no evidence to say who planted the bombs." In short, while the hypothetical stakes grow more dire at each time point in the story, the vignettes do not ascribe sole blame to Rusburg for the attacks, nor do they immediately implicate a muscular response. Controlling these aspects of the situation makes it possible for thoughtful, reasonable participants to choose from an array of options. Unlike a direct, identifiable attack on the homeland or a low-level fishing dispute, the scenario belies a "correct" or obvious foreign policy response.

The survey asks participants how Fredonia should respond to the situation after each stage. Participants choose from 8 (at stage 1) or 9 options (in stages 2 and 3, where escalating a declared war is an option), ranging from least to most conflictual. On the dovish end, participants can choose to welcome Rusburgians and craft an agreement to share the space—against their stated goals—while on the higher end they can opt to launch a targeted strike or start/escalate a full-scale war. I tailored these items to suit the vignette, but took inspiration from Goldstein's (1992) scale for cooperative and conflictual foreign policy events. This widely used scale provides support for my assumption that the options appear in the correct order from cooperative to conflictual, making them amenable to analysis with statistical models that rely on an ordered dependent variable.[21]

Finally, I elicit general militarism with a standard militant internationalism scale. Widely used in public opinion research and based on Wittkopf's (1990) influential theory of foreign policy orientations, this series of questions asks participants whether they agree or disagree that countries should use their military power to pursue foreign policy goals.[22] Militant internationalism constitutes my final dependent variable.

Results

I present the results in two stages. First, I examine responses to the vignette: How do unity and equality interact with nationalism to shape policy choices and escalation in the crisis? In the second section, I analyze the effect of the treatments on the relationship between nationalism and general militarism.

FOREIGN POLICY CRISIS: RESPONSES TO THE RUSBURGIAN CONFLICT

The fictional crisis includes 3 outcomes of interest—policy preference at stages 2 and 3 and the total escalation between stages 1 and 3. Stage 1 introduced participants to the conflict, but this description involved minimal violence and no deaths. It set the stage with miniscule stakes—police from each country were attempting to enforce the territory as either Fredonia's or Rusburg's—making it an unlikely candidate to animate nationalist aggression. Indeed, participants' policy preferences displayed limited

---

21. See the appendix for the full text of policy options.

22. See the appendix; the scale has high reliability ($\alpha = 0.88$), consistent with its use in other work, (Kertzer et al., 2014), and cross-national research on the structure of foreign policy attitudes (Bjereld and Ekengren, 1999; Reifler, Scotto and Clarke, 2011; Gravelle, Reifler and Scotto, 2017).

variation. Across conditions, 79% of the sample chose options 1 or 2: welcoming Rusburgians to a shared space or negotiating a peaceful partition of the territory. I present the results from stage 1 in column 1 of Table 3.2, with a dichotomous dependent variable coded 0 if respondents chose the most cooperative option and 1 if they instead chose the 2nd level or greater. Consistent with its stage-setting function, neither the treatment nor nationalisms affected responses at stage 1.

Columns 2–4 in Table 3.2 present results from OLS models predicting participants' preferred foreign policy options at each stage and the total escalation between stages 1 and 3. Total escalation denotes how much a participant moved up the ladder of conflict between stage 1 and stage 3, the highest point of the crisis. This variable thus incorporates participants' own baseline preferences in the conflict to treat escalation as contingent on their initial choices. The analysis treats each response as a separate outcome. Participants had the opportunity to choose from among the full array of options at each stage, which allowed them to escalate, de-escalate, or stay the course. Each stage presented new information to participants without reminding them about their previous choice. Still, the outcome variables clearly correlate and so I estimate a seemingly unrelated regression (SUR) model to account for the relationship between the error terms across each equation.[23]

To facilitate interpreting the results and effect sizes, I rescaled the dependent variables at each stage and nationalism to range from 0 to 1. Prior to rescaling, total escalation ranges from -5 to 8 due to the small number of participants who chose less conflictual policies as the crisis progressed. These analyses test my hypothesis by comparing equality to unity because participants in the Fredonian control group express limited nationalism; the results in Table 3.2 omit the control group and include a dummy variable coded 1 for participants assigned to the equality treatment, and 0 for those exposed to the unity treatment.[24]

23. Estimating separate models without the efficiency gains from SUR produces near-identical results.

24. The control group served primarily to check that the manipulations succeeded in creating Fredonian nationalisms in the treatment groups. The control group contained little information for participants to engage while they considered Fredonian nationalism—offering only Fredonia's area and population size. Indeed, I found that both treatment groups score higher on nationalism than participants in the control group. Supplementary analyses in the online appendix incorporate the control condition and show significant interactions between equality and nationalism, compared to the control group, for stages 2 and 3 and militant internationalism. Because the

Each model includes nationalism, the treatment indicator, and the interaction between nationalism and the treatment. The interaction coefficient provides the key test for my hypothesis, which proposes a strong and positive relationship between unity-oriented nationalism and conflictual foreign policy preferences—an upward-sloping line—but that equality will flatten that slope. Because I am interested in differences in slopes rather than overall means, I first examine the extent to which the treatment moderates the relationship between nationalism and conflictual foreign policy preferences. After I discuss the slopes, I concentrate on differences between unity and equality at the high end of the nationalism scale. Strong nationalism corresponds to group conformity, whereas weak nationalism does not, such that I expect to find more support for conflictual policy options and greater escalation among strong nationalists in the unity condition compared to strong nationalists in the equality condition.

Model 2 shows that neither the treatments nor national chauvinism had statistically significant effects on policy preferences at stage 2, though the negative sign on the interaction term suggests that nationalism may have a stronger positive effect in the unity condition. At stage 2, participants learned that about 45 people (from both countries) died in clashes between police enforcing their claims over the land since the starting point, a relatively low stakes outcome. By the time the conflict escalates to stage 3, though, the results show clear differences.

Models 3 and 4 from Table 3.2—which estimate policy choice at stage 3 and total escalation, respectively—draw attention to the fact that although both nationalism and the equality treatment appear to have a positive effect on conflictual policy choices, these coefficients belie significant interactions between the equality and nationalism ($b_{stage3} = -0.519$, $p = 0.053$; $b_{escalation} = -0.323$, $p < 0.05$). The association between nationalism and each outcome variable differs based on whether a participant commits to Fredonian superiority on the basis of unity versus equality. Recall that I measured nationalism as a person's belief that the world would be a better place if other nations were more like her own. Those who wrote about equality, then, should have been responding to questions about their degree of nationalism based on the terms provided by the prompt: nationalism here refers to a strong preference for equal, peer-like relations in Fredonia. Strong nationalism indicates a commitment to these norms; Fredonian

---

lower nationalism scores in the control group confound those results, however, I focus on the comparison between unity and equality.

TABLE 3.2. Equality Moderates the Relationship between Nationalism and Conflict

	Stage 1 (binary) (1)	Stage 2 (2)	Stage 3 (3)	Total Escalation (4)
Equality	0.166	0.164	0.323**	0.188**
	(0.234)	(0.130)	(0.155)	(0.092)
Nationalism	0.190	0.203	0.405**	0.272**
	(0.295)	(0.163)	(0.194)	(0.116)
Equality × Nationalism	−0.378	−0.233	−0.519*	−0.323**
	(0.407)	(0.225)	(0.269)	(0.160)
Constant	0.569	0.173*	0.235**	0.443***
	(0.170)	(0.094)	(0.112)	(0.067)
N	190	190	190	190
R^2	0.007	0.013	0.028	0.030

*p < .1; **p < .05; ***p < .01

Note: Main entries are OLS coefficients from a seemingly unrelated regression. The reference group for equality is the unity condition. All other variables are rescaled from 0 to 1.

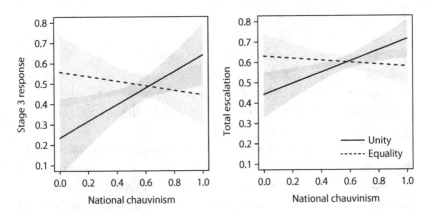

FIGURE 3.4. The relationship between nationalism and militarism depends on content.
Note: Variables are rescaled from 0 to 1. Shaded areas depict simulated 90% confidence bands.

superiority rests on equality. By contrast, nationalism in the unity group means something else—it considers Fredonian culture and unity in comparison to other countries. Nationalism has a conceptually distinct meaning if a person responds from the perspective of a group that exemplifies unity or equality.

Figure 3.4 plots these interactions. The conventional story leads us to expect that as commitment to nationalism increases, conflictual policy preferences rise in tandem. This expectation holds in the unity group—for both the response at stage 3 and total escalation between stages 1 and 3. But among participants in the equality condition, the relationship reverses. Stronger nationalism corresponds to *less* conflictual policy choices at stage 3 and less escalation throughout the scenario. The weakly negative relationship between equality-oriented nationalism and hawkish policy choices contradicts the standard story. Even as violence in stage 3 reached a bomb that killed more than 100 people, participants who committed to Fredonian nationalism and lauded its equality-based relational structure expressed less support for aggression and escalation.

Figure 3.4 presents compelling patterns—despite wide confidence intervals—given the subtlety of the manipulations.[25] The statistically significant interaction shows that the change from low to high levels of nationalism in the unity group corresponds to a meaningful positive change in both the stage 3 response and total escalation. At the minimum level of nationalism, the predicted response for participants in the unity condition is 0.24 [0.05, 0.42] (simulated 90% confidence interval in brackets)— just shy of requesting that Rusburg withdraw their claim to the territory. At the maximum, the model predicts a value of 0.64 [0.48, 0.80] on the policy preference dependent variable. This indicates a 0.40-unit change on the 0–1 scale, equivalent to moving up roughly three steps on the scale— from the request to withdraw to launching a targeted strike against Rusburg, a substantively significant jump. Movement over the same range in the equality condition instead predicts a 0.11-unit *decrease* along the cooperative-conflictual policy scale.

Figure 3.5 visualizes the marginal effect of the equality treatment, relative to unity, across the range of the nationalism scale. My theory predicts that differences between equality and unity should manifest among people who express the strongest commitment to Fredonian nationalism. Yet creating strong commitments to a fictional identity presents challenges, in that only a small proportion of participants express the fervent belief in Fredonian superiority that we might expect in real-world nationalisms. When a theoretically important range of the moderator contains fewer

---

25. Moreover, Krupnikov and Levine (2014, 77) show that experiments on Mechanical Turk samples that require substantial "buy-in" from participants—such as those that involve reading a long article or trusting information from the experimenter—tend to produce weaker effects than those observed in laboratory samples. While my analysis of the writing selections suggests that most participants understood the manipulations and took the task seriously, it is possible that the nature of my sample accounts for wider variance.

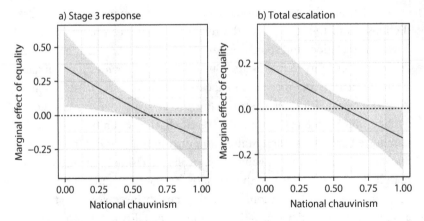

FIGURE 3.5. Equality mitigates conflictual attitudes among strong nationalists.
Note: Dependent variables and nationalism range from 0 to 1. Bands depict bootstrapped 90% confidence intervals implemented using the interflex package in R (Hainmueller, Mummolo and Xu, 2019).

observations, marginal effect estimates could be biased. I therefore estimate the marginal effects of equality, relative to unity, using a procedure that estimates a series of local effects across the range of nationalism and introduces more uncertainty—depicted with wider confidence bands—when data are sparse (Hainmueller, Mummolo and Xu, 2019).

Panels (a) and (b) plot the marginal effect of equality, compared to unity, on both the stage 3 response and total escalation outcomes. A negative value indicates that participants in the equality group have lower scores on the dependent variable than their counterparts in the unity treatment at that point along the nationalism scale. Grey bands depict bootstrapped 90% confidence intervals. The results provide tentative support for my hypothesis: Higher values on the nationalism scale correspond to negative marginal effects. Unity-oriented nationalists express more aggression at stage 3 and escalate more throughout the crisis, compared to nationalists in the equality group. These results suggest that strong equality-oriented nationalists take a more measured approach to escalating conflict. Stoking nationalism might cement support for a military campaign among unity-oriented nationalists, but less so for equality-oriented nationalists. At the same time, the results introduce meaningful uncertainty into these conclusions because the confidence intervals contain 0 for the strong nationalists that my theory pertains to, who score in at least the top quintile for nationalism (> 0.67). In chapter 4, I address this concern using a salient real-life nationalism and a larger sample to enhance the statistical power I have to detect effects among strong nationalists.

What about the weak nationalists? My theory generates concrete predictions about the strength of the relationship between nationalism and hawkish escalation, and about differences between strong nationalists who commit to equality versus unity. But my theory provides less guidance about what type of attitudes to expect from weak nationalists in either group. When political scientists test the interaction between group norms and identification measures in other research, they often find that weakly committed group members simply do not respond to group norms (Toff and Suhay, 2019; Collingwood, Lajevardi and Oskooii, 2018). But the marginal effect estimates on the left side of panels (a) and (b) reveal that at the lower ends of the nationalism scale, equality increases militarism relative to unity. Indeed, weak nationalists in the equality condition appear to approach conflicts much like strong unity-oriented nationalists.

Unlike strong identifiers, weak identifiers give little credence to the group's norms (Wellen, Hogg and Terry, 1998; Ellemers, Spears and Doosje, 2002; Theiss-Morse, 2009; Huddy and Del Ponte, 2019), and dispositional traits usurp social influence for weak identifiers (Terry, Hogg and White, 1999). Yet here I find evidence of something closer to reactance rather than indifference—the weak nationalists exhibited behavior that contradicted the group's norms. Indeed, psychological reactance theory explains that people often rebel against perceived constraints on their choices—especially illegitimate constraints—by doing the opposite of what someone else expects them to do (Brehm, 1966; Miron and Brehm, 2006). If we think about weak nationalists as participants who reject their membership in the Fredonian group, then they might resist the group's influence via rebellion: If Fredonians favor reciprocity, but I do not think that Fredonians hold any moral superiority, I will do the opposite of what my hypothetical comrades prefer. Previous research hints at similar effects. For example, Jetten, Postmes and McAuliffe (2002) conduct an experiment to test whether strong nationalists display individualist behaviors when individualism, rather than collectivism, constitutes the group. The authors find some evidence that weak identifiers preferred to buck the trend and "react against group norms that are imposed upon them by acting in opposition to the group norm (ibid., 192)." Similarly, although not their analytic focus, Citrin, Johnston and Wright (2012) show that Canadians with the least national pride hold the strongest anti-immigrant sentiments, contrary to the prevailing multicultural norms.

Although I did not anticipate this backlash effect among weak nationalists, the results suggest that weak nationalists in the equality treatment reject reciprocity and opt for escalatory aggression. And weak nationalists in the unity group reject the impulse to destroy their adversary and adopt a relatively measured approach to the crisis. These findings are speculative but inject a degree of caution into conclusions about how foreign policy elites could mobilize support for their hawkish or dovish agenda by appealing to nationalist norms. Obama reminded his "fellow Americans" that "you are equal in the eyes of God and equal in the eyes of the law" while he appealed to them to support his strategic restraint following the 2015 San Bernardino attack,[26] for instance. His appeal may have convinced some Americans to endorse his call to maintain the status quo, but it may have hardened support for escalation among others. Yet I do not find evidence for backlash effects among weak nationalists in chapter 4. Together, these contrasting results imply that determining the conditions under which weak nationalism encourages rebellion against national norms requires new studies explicitly designed to test hypotheses about weak nationalists.

MILITANT INTERNATIONALISM

I next test my intergroup conflict hypothesis using general militarism as the dependent variable (Wittkopf, 1990; Kertzer et al., 2014). The results displayed in panels (a) and (b) in Figure 3.6 show that equality mitigates the relationship between nationalism and militarism—outside the hypothetical vignette.[27]

Nationalism corresponds to higher militant internationalism scores in the unity group, but a significant interaction shows that the equality treatment substantially mitigates this relationship. Panels (a) and (b) in Figure 3.6 visualize this interaction. Consistent with the theory, the relationship between nationalism and militant internationalism depends on the treatment assignment. Panel (b) shows the marginal effect of equality on militarism across the nationalism moderator and provides the clearest evidence yet for the effect of equality, relative to unity, among strong nationalists. For participants who score in the top quintile on the nationalism scale (scores greater than 0.67), equality significantly reduces militant internationalism ($p<0.01$)—producing a 9.1 percentage point decrease at

26. Obama, Barack, 2016. "Transcript: President Obama's address to the nation on the San Bernardino attack and the war on ISIS," available from CNN.com, 6 December.

27. See the online appendix for regression results.

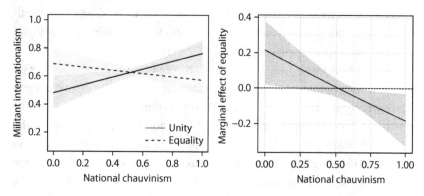

FIGURE 3.6. Nationalism and militant internationalism.
Note: Dependent variable and nationalism range from 0 to 1. Shaded bands depict (a) simulated 90% confidence intervals, and (b) 90% bootstrapped confidence intervals using the kernel estimation procedure from Hainmueller, Mummolo and Xu (2019).

the 90th percentile, for example. The same people who seemed to commit to less conflictual strategies during the Rusburg crisis also reject hawkish approaches to unspecified threats at greater rates than committed nationalists in the unity group.

Finally, I conducted several supplementary analyses to probe the robustness of these experimental results and account for alternative explanations. First, the results remain robust to including a panel of control variables.[28] Second, I find similar results if I measure nationalism by extracting factor scores from a factor analysis of the constituent items—indeed, these analyses in the online appendix also a show significant negative interaction between nationalism and equality at stage 2 ($b = -0.36, p = 0.046$). Third, I analyze participants' separate policy choices during stages 2 and 3 in the Rusburg crisis because (1) I am interested in differences in the specific choices that people make at each stage during the crisis and designed the study to allow participants to choose from the full range of policy options at each point; and (2) I can account for their initial choices using the total escalation variable, which allows me to evaluate escalation relative to participants' baseline preferences. But if I wanted to evaluate stage-by-stage escalation, I could include the outcome from the prior stage as a covariate in the regression equation—in other words, use participants' stage 1 response as an independent variable in the equation for stage 2 and their stage 2 response as an independent variable for stage 3. This adjustment produces

28. See Table A.1 in the appendix.

minor changes to the coefficient estimates and p-values on the interactions at stage 2 ($b = -0.24$, $p = 0.21$) and stage 3 ($b = -0.34$, $p = 0.095$), though the direction of the effects remains consistent with my expectations and with the results in Table 3.2.[29]

Fourth, readers might worry that the treatments represent general primes rather than foundations for nationalist conformity. Although that proposition would lead me to expect average differences between the two groups—which I do not find—rather than the interactions and effects among strong nationalists that I theorized, it also raises questions about whether the results are an artifact of some other confounding moderator. To test these possibilities, I replace the nationalism scale with several alternative variables and estimate new models that include the treatments, these alternative moderators, and interaction terms. Akin to a series of placebo tests, I find that neither partisanship, ideology, nor political knowledge moderate the equality treatment, relative to unity. And if nationalism reflects a general propensity to comply with the treatment rather than expressed commitment to Fredonian superiority, I should find negative interactions between the treatments and a scale for national attachment that taps whether people report feeling close to Fredonia. Null results alleviate that concern and show that the interaction effects I find for nationalism do not transfer to other operationalizations for Fredonian identification. This finding underscores my contribution, because I show that equality ameliorates the relationship between nationalist commitments and conflict using the same scale that other scholars treat as synonymous with militarism.[30]

Conclusion

In this chapter, I used experimental methods to manipulate fictional national identity content as a first test of my intergroup conflict hypothesis. Whereas many IR scholars posit a relationship between nationalism and both conflict escalation and militarism among members of the public, existing research primarily relies on observational data to assert that nationalism inevitably causes foreign policy aggression.

The experimental results produce four main findings. First, I find *conditional* evidence that nationalist commitments increase conflict escalation

29. See the online appendix for these results.
30. See Figure A.1 in the appendix.

and militarism. I find a strong positive relationship between nationalism and hawkishness in the unity group, but not in the equality group. Nationalism and militarism have a contingent relationship—not an automatic relationship. This finding hints at a possible middle ground between nationalisms as risk factors for crisis escalation versus foundations for measured, reciprocal responses. Yet the apparent reactance against group norms from weak nationalists suggests that we need to know more about average contestation in a country before we claim that equality-oriented nationalism might dampen public bellicosity in a crisis.

Second, the results provide suggestive evidence that strong nationalist commitments condition the effect of content. Random assignment to the equality group has a negative marginal effect on aggression at higher scores on the nationalism scale. The effects clearly manifest for militant internationalism, but skim the traditional frontier between statistically significant and non-significant for the Rusburgian crisis outcomes. Of course, the hypothetical identity-building exercise may bear responsibility for relatively weak treatment effects, and contribute to the meaningful uncertainty around my estimates for strong nationalists. In chapter 4, I use a stronger content treatment and measure real-world nationalisms with a larger sample to triangulate the results.

Third, and related, the contingent relationship between nationalism and militarism extends to individuals' broader foreign policy postures. Unity-oriented nationalists were more likely to agree that states sometimes must use the military to advance their interests compared to equality-based nationalists. Fourth, weak nationalists seemed to have approached the crisis by rejecting their group's norms. People who did not commit to an equality-based Fredonian identity were more militaristic than their nationalist counterparts, opting for an escalatory approach to their adversary rather than accommodation.

The results in this chapter suggest that creating unity and solidarity—the process of binding competing groups into a unified "we"—may have dangerous implications for foreign policy attitudes. But also that "nationalism" sometimes fails to stoke the embers of international competition. The connection between nationalism and foreign policy conflict depends on the norms that underlie the nationalist commitment. Citizens who hold a unity-oriented understanding of their identity will temper their outward militarism so long as nationalism remains low. Of course because public nationalism will likely rise in the face of threats or security competition, we should hesitate to place too much weight on the possibility that weak unity-oriented nationalism will dampen public demands for war. By contrast, the strongest equality-oriented nationalists reject the sharp distinction between their own nation and the enemy and passionately commit to norms of reciprocity. Violence, for them, must occur only in proportion to that inflicted upon their group.

Recognizing that one experiment is not a panacea, this Fredonian experiment provides a foundation for the study that follows in chapter 4. First, using a hypothetical country and conflict allowed for a remarkable degree of control over content and raised fewer concerns about confounding than if I targeted a pre-existing identity. The hypothetical study therefore has important leverage when it comes to both internal validity and construct validity. Yet evidence that unity and equality matter for real-life nationalisms and contemporary foreign policy problems would lend external validity and illustrate my theory's relevance to nationalism research and international politics in practice. Second, the crisis vignette presented a territorial dispute that directly implicated Fredonian national interests. And the scenario presented ambiguous information about the actor at fault for the conflict and casualties. These design features made it possible to draw inferences about which policy preferences entailed Fredonian aggression versus which did not. But real-world adversaries introduce higher stakes and often blur the lines between proportionate responses and aggressive escalation. Third, the smaller sample size and hypothetical identity introduced uncertainty into my estimates for equality's effects among strong nationalists. Thus, chapter 4 picks up where this chapter leaves off and introduces a second experiment that 1) manipulates American national identity content, 2) includes a panel of policy issues and scenarios that vary according to whether they involve American national security and whether reciprocity entails military force, and 3) includes a larger sample with greater statistical power to detect treatment effects among strong nationalists.

4

American Nationalisms and Support for Conflict

Nationalism runs strong in the United States. In 2013, for example, 70% of respondents to the International Social Survey Program (ISSP) National Identity Survey agreed that "generally, America is better than other countries."[1] But just as Americans disagree about whether and when U.S. foreign policy should feature military force (Wittkopf, 1990; Holsti, 2004), they contest American nationalisms (Smith, 1997; Schildkraut, 2007). Some founders like John Jay asserted that Americans should be a united group (Park, 2018, 25), whereas others like Thomas Jefferson appealed to egalitarian values as the bedrock of American superiority. Contemporary public opinion data reveal similar discord (Schildkraut, 2014). American nationalisms are unexceptional with respect to contestation.[2] What do dueling nationalisms mean for the relationship between nationalism and militarism, and for public opinion regarding contemporary conflicts with China, Russia, and ISIS?

1. Among U.S. respondents, 25.35% and 44.51% strongly agreed or agreed with the statement, respectively. See variable V20 in ISSP Research Group (2013). See also Bonikowski and DiMaggio (2016) for similar data from the 2004 General Social Survey.

2. See also Mead (1999) and Lieven (2016), and see Lepore (2019) for an accessible overview of American historical narratives. Trautsch (2016) reviews the historiography of American nationalism studies, including past historians' treatment of American nationalism as a unique liberal foil for "European" nationalisms—and the contemporary correctives that examine the illiberal strains in American nationalisms.

Chapter 3 presented evidence that equality-oriented nationalism decreases hawkishness compared to its unity-oriented counterpart. In a hypothetical foreign policy crisis marked by limited violence and ambiguous perpetrators, nationalists in the unity treatment opted for escalation—they supported more punitive policies compared to people who received the equality treatment, and became more aggressive as the crisis wore on. The design prioritized internal and construct validity. The treatments targeted the key concepts, and the scenario depicted a realistic crisis whereby reasonable respondents could choose from policies that ranged from accommodation to war. Unity-oriented nationalism increased general militarism and support for using force to avenge 113 civilian deaths and retain a small piece of territory. Equality-oriented nationalism did not. Although the results largely supported my intergroup conflict hypothesis, the small sample of Fredonian nationalists limited how precisely I could estimate the marginal effect of equality on policy preferences among strong nationalists.

This chapter presents a second experiment that replicates and extends the Fredonia study for four reasons. First, although Mechanical Turk workers constitute a diverse sample of American residents who can provide key insights into questions about nationalism and foreign policy attitudes, my theory implicates people in general and would therefore benefit from testing on a wider cross-section of the U.S. population.[3] Second, an additional experiment enhances external validity, or "the extent to which . . . conclusions can generalize" when we replicate a study with different populations, at different times, in different situations, and with different measurement scales (McDermott, 2011, 28). External validity, in other words, requires replication (ibid., 34). This study introduces a modified content manipulation that targets varieties of American nationalism while maintaining key strengths from the treatments in chapter 3. Moreover, this experiment includes a panel of dependent variables that range from general hawkishness to support for specific strategies in the battle against ISIS in Syria and

---

3. Of course, the theory is not just about Americans—a notoriously WEIRD population (Western, Educated, Industrialized, Rich, and Democratic)—such that even inferences drawn from a representative probability sample of the American public could not offer global generalizations (Henrich, Heine and Norenzayan, 2010). Some IR experiments find consistent treatment effects in cross-national samples, like similar reputation effects on support for war in Israeli and American samples (Yarhi-Milo, 2018). But the cross-cultural variance in relational model implementation rules posited by Fiske (1991) and others (e.g., Thomsen, 2010) suggests that future research must be tested outside WEIRD samples to better capture heterogeneity in the human population.

Iraq. If I find similar results with novel treatments and operationalizations for my dependent variables, and in a different sample, I gain confidence in my theory that unity and equality have different implications for foreign policy attitudes. Third, and related, this American nationalism experiment uses a larger sample to increase the statistical power relative to experiment 1 and enable more precise estimates for the treatment effect among strong nationalists.

Fourth, this setup allows me to assess the conditions under which unity- and equality-oriented nationalists align. As I explained in chapter 2, equality sometimes manifests in support for force. Equality-oriented nationalism mitigates generalized militarism and support for hawkish postures toward adversaries who have not yet committed aggressive acts against the United States. But equality does not redound to pacifism. Equality-oriented nationalism should prompt reciprocal violence in response to aggression. Faced with a clear, identifiable adversary and the option to respond with proportionate force, equality-oriented nationalists may support conflict. By contrast, unity-oriented nationalism should drive people to assume aggressive postures across situations, considering their tendency to inflate external threats and commitment to protecting the group from any harm. In turn, they join equality-oriented nationalists to support conflict against identifiable adversaries. Yet unity *also* prescribes generalized hawkishness and support for disproportionate escalation, such as sending ground troops to fight ISIS. To unpack these expectations, I include two dependent variables that implicate unity, but not equality: militant internationalism and support for a tough stance against China. Two additional dependent variables—which measure support for using various foreign policy tools to repel a Russian incursion in the Baltics or to combat ISIS—implicate both varieties of nationalism because they entail proportionate responses to aggression against the United States and its allies.

As in chapter 3, I analyze the *strength* of the relationship between nationalism and support for conflict and the treatment effects among strong nationalists. And indeed, the results show that unity-oriented nationalism creates general hawks: I find a strong, positive relationship between nationalism and all four dependent variables in the unity condition. But the equality treatment substantially weakens the effect of nationalism on militant internationalism and hawkish China postures, a finding that provides important evidence that converges with the results from the Fredonia experiment and adds external validity to the research. At the same time, the scenarios with identifiable perpetrators show that contextual factors sometimes push equality- and unity-oriented nationalists toward the same foreign policy agenda. In a hypothetical Russian invasion of the Baltics, both fairness and solidarity prescribe a resolute response from the United States. Similarly, unity- and equality-oriented nationalists agree that in dealing with ISIS, the United States should conduct air strikes, refuse to negotiate, and impose a no-fly zone. But when it comes to sending ground troops to Syria—an act that would entail substantial escalation by the United States—equality- and unity-oriented nationalisms once again diverge. Unity-oriented nationalism drives significantly more support for sending ground troops to the region. Collectively, the results show that content matters for understanding whether nationalism drives conflict, but also that equality and unity can converge.

In the remainder of this chapter, I explain why the U.S. public provides a useful sample for testing the theory and justify my claim that American nationalism is contested. Next, I describe the experiment and discuss the results, starting with the generalized hawkishness outcomes before turning to the Russia and ISIS scenarios.

Why the United States?

I assume that citizens from the same country contest nationalisms. Although existing research suggests that this assumption travels cross-nationally—my argument could apply to people in France, Argentina, or Canada—I focus this experiment on the U.S. population and American nationalisms for two interrelated reasons. First, decades of research by public opinion scholars and historians demonstrates that Americans contest the norms that constitute American nationalism. Moreover, the lines of contestation implicitly tap unity and equality by other names. Demonstrable contestation bolsters my assumption but also facilitates experimental manipulation, because I am able to craft credible treatments that draw on the dueling narratives that divide contemporary Americans. Stories about "American exceptionalism" and the liberal American Creed pervade U.S. history lessons and presidential addresses (Gilmore and Rowling, 2018). But a prominent, unity-oriented discourse features in constitutional debates, presidential proclamations and public opinion surveys—making American nationalisms ripe for experimental prompts. Second, U.S. power projection and global influence make the country a frequent protagonist in military conflicts. This allows me to measure respondents' support for military force across a range of hypothetical and real scenarios and thereby maximize my ability to test the conditions under which unity and equality lead to convergent prescriptions for U.S. foreign policy. The potent combination of contestation and foreign involvement make the United States an ideal case.

AMERICAN NATIONALISMS

Americans disagree about what it means to be an American (Citrin, Reingold and Green, 1990; Schildkraut, 2007).[4] The Treaty of Paris brought independence in 1783, but left revolutionaries with a similar problem to the one that manifests in modern debates about European supranationalism: How do you create unity from diversity (Park, 2018, 32)? Eighteenth-century answers planted the seeds for ideas that animate twenty-first century Americans. American nationalism contains shades of equality and shades of unity.

One strand of American nationalism centers on the belief that the polity holds a collective commitment to equality. Nationalism requires Americans to accept a set of liberal, egalitarian principles similar to the ideals espoused in the Federalist papers and by later observers of the American project (Hartz, 1955; Citrin et al., 1994; Sinopoli, 1996; Huntington, 1997). Liberal philosophical commitments allow for a diverse society, one where people with heterogeneous beliefs, appearances, and practices comfortably create a group. "Good" Americans, in turn, tolerate one another and recognize their mutual equality under the law (Schildkraut, 2007). Sometimes associated with the "American Creed," scholars use adjectives like "civic," "liberal," or "inclusive" to modify this nationalism but equality provides a central organizing theme. A majority of Americans agree that things like respect for the law and tolerating diversity represent important norms for their compatriots (Schildkraut, 2007; Theiss-Morse, 2009; Wright, Citrin and Wand, 2012; Sides, Tesler and Vavreck, 2019). U.S. presidents, too, pepper proclamations with references to equality. In respective statements to recognize Loyalty Day, Nixon declared that loyal Americans embraced national values like "individual freedom under the law" and "equality of opportunity,"[5] Carter called for "dedication to our democratic

4. See Schildkraut (2014) for a recent review that examines identity content in the American public, and Park (2018) for a historical look at subnational variation in post-revolutionary American nationalisms.

5. Nixon, Richard, 1969. "Proclamation 3904—Loyalty Day, 1969," 26 March. Available at www.presidency.ucsb.edu/documents/proclamation-3904-loyalty-day-1969.

traditions of liberty and justice,"[6] and Obama described loyal Americans as people committed to "core values of liberty, equality, and justice for all."[7] Equality-oriented nationalists contend that American superiority lies in "our" commitment to fairness and ability to accommodate heterogeneity, akin to the constitutive norms and relational comparisons that comprise equality-oriented nationalism.[8]

But unity also pervades American nationalist discourse. Indeed, the notion that American nationalism comes in more than one flavor presents one of the clearest points of interdisciplinary agreement.[9] John Jay famously wrote that the new United States belonged "to one united people—a people descended from the same ancestors, speaking the same language, professing the same religion, attached to the same principles of government, very similar in their manners and customs" (Hamilton, Madison and Jay, 2009 [1788], 12).[10] In short, he saw Americans as unified. And although "it is not fashionable today to think of the American nation as a folk community bound together by deep cultural and ethnic ties" (Mead, 1999, 9), contemporary Americans take up Jay's mantle when they call for assimilation (Huntington, 2004),[11] or like former Ohio governor John

6. Carter, Jimmy, 1979. "Proclamation 4657—Loyalty Day, 1979," 11 April. Available at www.presidency.ucsb.edu/documents/proclamation-4657-loyalty-day-1979.

7. Obama, Barack, 2011. "Proclamation 8666—Loyalty Day, 2011," 29 April. Available at www.presidency.ucsb.edu/documents/proclamation-8666-loyalty-day-2011.

8. Leaders sometimes talk about equality-oriented nationalism in terms of "American exceptionalism" rather than nationalism because the word nationalism carries a negative connotation. But as Lieven (2016, 11) writes, "American exceptionalism" is just another way of saying American civic nationalism without using the word nationalism."

9. For example, historians once classified the American commitment to equality and pluralism as part of its "exceptional" national character (Trautsch, 2016)—an assertion that treated American nationalism as *sui generis* and normatively superior to its European counterparts. But the dominant perspective in modern historiography accepts that American nationalism is neither unique nor singular, similar to dominant perspectives in political science and sociology (Schildkraut, 2014; Smith, 1993a; Bonikowski and DiMaggio, 2016).

10. The anti-federalists, too, promoted unity—though in their case, they argued that the importance of homogeneity to good governance meant that the new country should place more power in local units (Sinopoli, 1996).

11. People who are motivated to maintain the group's solidarity often inflate the threat posed by foreigners. This book explains how this dynamic creates support for military aggression and conflict escalation, but it also implies that unity-oriented nationalists will reject immigration. And indeed, research on the relationship between national identities and anti-immigrant sentiment has substantially advanced our understanding of contestation among Americans (e.g., Citrin, Reingold and Green, 1990; Schildkraut, 2005). But like Kinder and Kam (2010) argue with respect to ethnocentrism's influence on a wide range of political attitudes, this book shows that unity has implications for foreign policy beyond immigration.

Kasich assert that "at the base of America is a Jewish and Christian tradition that says that we must realize that we are all brothers and sisters."[12] Kasich's description hearkens to unity-oriented nationalism with its emphasis on kinship, tradition, and religious homogeneity.

Variously captured by research on "ethnocultural," "ethnic," "ascriptive," or "Christian" nationalisms (Citrin, Reingold and Green, 1990; Wright, Citrin and Wand, 2012; McDaniel, Nooruddin and Shortle, 2016; Whitehead and Perry, 2020), unity constitutes another core theme in public opinion. Theiss-Morse (2009, 88) finds that 60% of survey respondents who moderately identify with the nation say that being Christian is important for being American, for example,[13] and many citizens embrace "English only" laws that promote linguistic homogeneity (Schildkraut, 2005). Moreover, existing research likely underestimates the unity-oriented strand of American nationalism: Americans implicitly associate national symbols with white faces (Devos and Banaji, 2005), reflecting their intuitive desire for cohesion even as they reject explicit calls for unity in favor of more socially acceptable equality-laden norms.

American nationalism features both historic and contemporary contestation. As a result, members of the public can construct two distinct and sometimes overlapping national narratives that correspond to unity and equality. Public opinion research suggests that older, more conservative Americans point to unity-oriented norms more often than their younger, liberal counterparts (Theiss-Morse, 2009; Schildkraut, 2014). But the fact that both nationalisms exist in the American consciousness make them susceptible to manipulation, in an experimental setting or in the real world where entrepreneurial leaders might promote one narrative to serve their political interests (Haslam, Reicher and Platow, 2011)—like the binary rhetoric that helped keep the public on Bush's side as he prepared the country for two wars. Unity and equality each constitute a potential foundation for American greatness (Levendusky, 2018).

The United States provides a useful case for my experiment because the scholarly evidence points to ample contestation, such that both equality and unity have the potential to resonate with members of the public. Yet

12. Kasich, John (@JohnKasich). "At the base of America is a Jewish and Christian tradition that says that we must realize that we are all brothers and sisters. Rhetoric like the President's works against that foundation of our country and all that we teach our children." 15 July 2019, 11:40 am. Tweet.

13. See also McDaniel, Nooruddin and Shortle (2011); Wong (2010); Schildkraut (2011); Wright, Citrin and Wand (2012); and McDaniel, Nooruddin and Shortle (2016).

readers might nevertheless be concerned that my theoretical framework presents a mismatch for real attitudes among Americans—after all, the fact that measures from past work constitute imperfect proxies for equality and unity partially motivated my experiments.

To address concerns about whether my concepts resonate with everyday Americans, I included a single question on a survey fielded to a diverse sample of 1,509 undergraduates.[14] The sample does not represent the American public—participants are both younger and more educated than the population of U.S. adults—but varies on key characteristics: 34.5% identified as non-white, 38% as Republicans, and participants attended colleges in the South, Midwest, and Northeast. This heterogeneity makes it a useful sample to explore whether unity and equality animate Americans, linking my theoretical framework to the real world.

I included a short prompt—"Which of the following most closely matches your view on what it means to be an American?"—followed by four options: "Americans are a group of equals, like peers who treat each other fairly and reciprocate" (equality); "Americans are members of the same community, a close and unified group" (unity); "both of these match my view on what it means to be an American" (both); or "neither of these match my view on what it means to be an American" (neither). Figure 4.1 shows that among the 1,509 citizens who answered the question, the plurality chose "both." Independently, unity and equality had many adherents—with 24.52% selecting equality and 15.11% selecting unity.

Interestingly, among the 21.14% of participants who chose "neither," many nevertheless pointed out that unity and equality represent American norms. But to their mind, Americans had failed to live up to these ideals. As a consequence, many participants who selected neither appear to have weak nationalist commitments—they see the United States or Americans as morally inferior, not superior, because they have failed to live up to the group's promise. One respondent noted that "sometimes the above options are true, but not currently," while another reported that

14. Together with other researchers, I fielded the survey online to students at 10 different universities across the United States. The universities varied by size, ranging from small liberal arts colleges to branch campuses for state public university systems and large public flagships. The survey was part of a larger, collaborative project and was approved by IRBs at Illinois State and the University of Georgia. For excellent research on diversity in student subject pools, see Lupton (2019). The total sample included 1,698 participants, 1,596 of whom reported that they are American citizens. Of the American citizens, 1,509 responded to my query about American nationalisms—which appeared at the end of a long questionnaire.

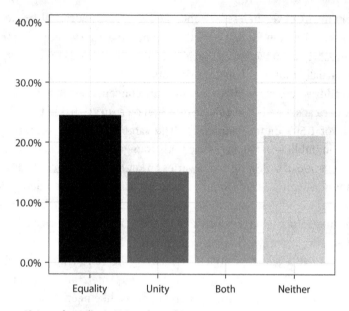

FIGURE 4.1. Unity and equality in U.S. undergraduates.
Note: N=1,509. Bars show the percentage of respondents who selected the category when asked what it means to be an American.

"these reflect my view on what it SHOULD mean to be an American." Other respondents emphasized existing racial and economic inequality in the country, alluding to the notion that being American means embracing these negative characteristics. Far from national superiority, these respondents seem to think about their American identity as something that confers low status and therefore want to distance themselves from the group. For example, one respondent wrote simply that "being american means facing discrimination," and another explained that "we pretend the above statements are true, but being an american means being highly unequal." Others referenced racism and other divisions but saw potential in unity or equality. As one respondent wrote, "To me the second option [unity] is a solid ideal"—leaving the door open for unity-oriented nationalism if that participant updates their beliefs about what the group represents in practice.

Collectively, these data support my assumption that Americans contest nationalist norms, and that the dual unity- and equality-oriented narratives open the door to manipulating the content of American nationalism. And crucially, the responses show that my theoretical framework captures norms that a diverse group of Americans select as the foundations for their national identity content. This survey item thereby lends validity to my concepts as I move from Fredonia to the real world.

DIVIDED VIEWS ON AMERICAN FOREIGN POLICY

The United States faced a growing threat from ISIS in December 2015. The Syrian civil war had intensified over 4 years, providing additional latitude for the terrorist organization to establish bases and fight back. Meanwhile, ISIS was expanding their reach in the Western world. In 2015 alone, they claimed responsibility for attacks in Belgium and Germany, while ISIS-inspired individuals opened fire against Parisians at Charlie Hebdo and killed 14 people in the December 2015 San Bernardino shooting.[15] After these high-profile incidents, the year culminated in calls for President Obama to ramp up the U.S. war on terror. Republican opponents like Senator Ted Cruz called for the United States to "utterly destroy" ISIS so that "every militant on the face of the earth will know" that if you fight America, "you are signing your death warrant,"[16] while 35% of Democrats in the public worried that Obama's foreign policy stance was not "tough enough" (Pew Research Center, 2015). The President disagreed, telling NPR's Steve Inskeep that he wanted to react "appropriately" and "in a way that is consistent with American values." For Obama, that meant staying the course—with limited, targeted strikes against verified ISIS assets, because "it is important not just to shoot but to aim."[17] Public opinion evenly divided on the question of ground troops at the time, with 47% of Americans in support and 47% opposed (Pew Research Center, 2015).

A notable aspect of these divisions over how to respond to ISIS: Each represented a realistic possibility for the United States, a country that was simultaneously dealing with the continued fallout from Russia's 2014 Crimea annexation and concerns about China's rapidly growing defense budget (Bitzinger, 2015). To capture the relationship between unity- and equality-oriented nationalism and support for force, the survey must

15. Of course, these attacks in Western Europe and North America supplemented regular, deadly operations in Libya, Egypt, Syria, and Iraq. For an overview of ISIS and ISIS-inspired attacks in 2015, see data collected by journalists from the *New York Times*: Yourish, Keren, Derek Watkins, and Tom Giratikanon, 2016. "Where ISIS Has Directed and Inspired Attacks Around the World," *New York Times*, 22 March. URL: www.nytimes.com/interactive/2015/06/17/world/middleeast/map-isis-attacks-around-the-world.html.

16. Ted Cruz qtd. in Rucker, Philip, 2015. www.washingtonpost.com/news/post-politics/wp/2015/12/05/ted-cruz-vows-to-utterly-destroy-isis-and-carpet-bomb-terrorists/

17. See Inskeep (2015) for the interview transcript.

include outcome variables that invite reasonable participants to take a hawkish approach, opt for measured, proportionate aggression, or choose to stay out. The second rationale for testing my hypotheses in the U.S. case hinges on the observation that the United States has options. The United States has unmatched military capabilities, global interests, and a favorable geographic position (Wohlforth, 1999; Brooks and Wohlforth, 2016)—granting the government remarkable flexibility in how it responds to adversaries.

In turn, members of the public may conclude that using force abroad or taking a tough stance against great power rivals constitutes a realistic option, whether the United States acts alone or with a partner. But staying home, conducting limited strikes, or even extending a hand to negotiate also constitute options for Americans who have little to fear from homeland attacks. The United States has latitude regarding whether or not to use force—and how much force to use—when given the opportunity.[18] American foreign policy options allow me to include a range of concrete, contemporary issues—like how the country should respond to the threat that ISIS poses in Syria or to China's military rise—alongside hypothetical scenarios like another Russian incursion in Eastern Europe and general militarism. And like the ambiguous crisis in chapter 3, each issue creates room for variation on the dependent variable without demanding additional information that would complicate measurement. For example, citizens from other NATO allies might only support substantial force against Russia or ISIS if they know that the United States will be involved, and must consider additional constraints when deciding whether they could fight wars on multiple fronts. Demonstrated contestation over American nationalism combines with the country's foreign policy flexibility to make the United States an ideal case for testing my intergroup conflict hypothesis.

The Sample

I administered this survey experiment to a sample of 632 Americans recruited through Survey Sampling International in autumn 2016.[19] I implemented quota sampling targets based on U.S. population parameters

---

18. See, for example, Meernik (2004), Howell, Howell and Pevehouse (2007), and Gallagher and Allen (2014) for research on domestic and leader-level factors that influence whether the U.S. uses military force when opportunities arise.

19. SSI is now called Dynata. Dynata panels contain participants who opt-in to complete surveys in exchange for modest compensation, charitable donations, or gift cards.

for age, gender, census region, and race to capture a broad cross-section of the U.S. population. Quota sampling does not produce a national probability sample, but participants exhibit substantial diversity compared to Mechanical Turk participants (Berinsky, Margolis and Sances, 2014).[20] The panel features a lower percentage of non-Hispanic whites (64%), for example, compared to the 77.4% of white Mechanical Turk participants in the Fredonia experiment, and a smaller proportion of male respondents (46%). The sample contains fewer college-educated Americans (40%) compared to the Mechanical Turk sample (45.5%), and skews older due to the targeted sampling procedure (median age range 45–54 compared to 32 years).

The Experiment

The between-subjects experiment proceeded in five steps, summarized in Figure 4.2: (1) Participants responded to a demographic questionnaire to monitor the quota sampling by age, gender, race, and residence; (2) random assignment to a three-stage experimental treatment in which participants i) read a control statement or a fictional textbook selection highlighting norms of equality or unity, ii) listed the benefits of these norms, and iii) selected similar statements about benefits from a list provided to them; (3) the nationalism questionnaire; (4) a series of foreign policy questions; and (5) a final questionnaire that contained a knowledge quiz, questions about respondents' political preferences, and additional demographic questions on education, income, and military service.

After responding to a short demographic questionnaire to monitor sample quotas (age, sex, location, and race), participants read an introductory statement. This page instructed them to think about relationship norms: "People relate to one another in different ways, with various norms or guidelines for how to behave. Think about how your relationships with close family members, supervisors, friends, or merchants, for example, are distinct." The instructions then advised that the next part of the survey would entail reading about how such norms inform what it means to be an American.

Like the Fredonia experiment, I randomly assigned participants to a multi-step treatment designed to manipulate the content (unity or equality), or to a control condition that contained innocuous information about

---

20. Samples from similar panels feature in other experimental international relations research (e.g., Quek, 2017; Brutger and Kertzer, 2018).

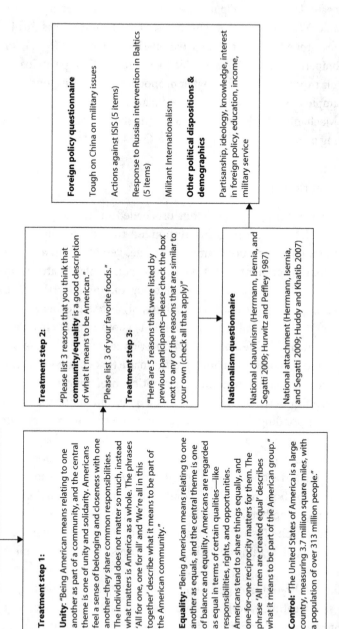

Demographic questionnaire (age, gender, race, residence)

Treatment step 1:

Unity: "Being American means relating to one another as part of a community, and the central theme is one of unity and solidarity. Americans feel a sense of belonging and closeness with one another—they share common responsibilities. The individual does not matter so much, instead what matters is America as a whole. The phrases 'All for one, one for all' and 'We're all in this together' describe what it means to be part of the American community."

Equality: "Being American means relating to one another as equals, and the central theme is one of balance and equality. Americans are regarded as equal in terms of certain qualities—like responsibilities, rights, and opportunities. Americans tend to share things equally, and one-for-one reciprocity matters for them. The phrase 'All men are created equal' describes what it means to be part of the American group."

Control: "The United States of America is a large country, measuring 3.7 million square miles, with a population of over 313 million people."

Treatment step 2:

"Please list 3 reasons that you think that **community/equality** is a good description of what it means to be American."

"Please list 3 of your favorite foods."

Treatment step 3:

"Here are 5 reasons that were listed by previous participants—please check the box next to any of the reasons that are similar to your own (check all that apply)"

Nationalism questionnaire

National chauvinism (Herrmann, Isernia, and Segatti 2009; Hurwitz and Peffley 1987)

National attachment (Herrmann, Isernia, and Segatti 2009; Huddy and Khatib 2007)

Foreign policy questionnaire

Tough on China on military issues

Actions against ISIS (5 items)

Response to Russian intervention in Baltics (5 items)

Militant Internationalism

Other political dispositions & demographics

Partisanship, ideology, knowledge, interest in foreign policy, education, income, military service

FIGURE 4.2. American nationalisms experiment structure.

the country's size and population. And I again designed these treatments to target national identity content and in-group norms but left them devoid of either foreign policy information or any references to outside groups. This feature helps ensure that any effects on foreign policy stem from how participants themselves interpret and enact the group norms, a rigorous test for my theory.

But this experimental treatment differed from the Fredonian version in four ways. First, rather than build a new identity from the ground up, the treatments targeted the content of participants' American national identities. I implemented a three-step manipulation designed to reinforce the information about identity content and overcome people's pre-existing ideas about what it means to be an American nationalist (Theiss-Morse, 2009; Schildkraut, 2007). Responses from the student survey confirmed that many Americans already hold ideas about these dueling nationalist norms in their minds—the stronger three-step treatment adjusts to this context.[21] In addition, the survey attributed the text selection to a reputable authority—an American history textbook called *A Concise History of the American People* by Alan Brinkley—to lend credibility to the description.[22]

Second, these treatments targeted the same relational norms but added a few key phrases to highlight the central themes in unity- and equality-oriented relationships. I drew these phrases from the summaries and instructions developed for Simpson and Laham's (2015a, 217) work on the relationship between relational models and political ideologies.[23] For unity, those phrases included "All for one and one for all" and "We're all in this together." After an opening paragraph that detailed the land area and population of the United States,[24] participants in the unity condition read that:

> Being American means relating to one another as part of a community, and the central theme is one of unity and solidarity. Americans feel a sense of belonging and closeness with one another—they share common

21. I adapted my treatments from previous work on multiculturalism (Wolsko et al., 2000; Verkuyten, 2009), where scholars engaged similar multi-step procedures to "encourage participants' agreement with the . . . perspective provided in the prompt" (Richeson and Nussbaum, 2004, 419).

22. For this attribution, I used a truncated version of the title to Brinkley's (2014) survey textbook *The Unfinished Nation: A Concise History of the American People*. A debriefing statement informed participants about the false attribution.

23. See also Simpson and Laham (2015b).

24. See the appendix for the full treatment text.

responsibilities. The individual does not matter so much, instead what matters is America as a whole. The phrases "All for one, one for all" and "We're all in this together" describe what it means to be part of the American community.

Americans experience a sense of solidarity, communality, and compassion toward each other. Americans share a common history and language, making them similar in important respects. When Americans make a decision, they can do so by consensus and act in solidarity as a group.

By contrast, the equality treatment summarized the central theme with "All men are created equal," and participants read about specific reciprocity and fairness:[25]

Being American means relating to one another as equals, and the central theme is one of balance and equality. Americans are regarded as equal in terms of certain qualities—like responsibilities, rights, and opportunities. Americans tend to share things equally, and one-for-one reciprocity matters for them. The phrase "All men are created equal" describes what it means to be part of the American group.

Americans experience a sense of fairness, reciprocity, and balance with each other. Americans may speak various languages or have distinct histories, making them different in important respects but equals as Americans. When Americans make a decision, they do so with one-person one-vote rules.

Third, the instructions directed participants to "list three reasons why [community/equality] is a good description of what it means to be an American," rather than complete an unstructured writing task like participants in the Fredonia experiment. In the control condition, the instructions asked participants to list their three favorite foods. Fourth, this manipulation included an additional stage. After listing their own reactions to unity and equality in the United States, participants read a list of five statements from past respondents. The survey instructed them to select any statements similar to the reasons that they listed in the previous step, providing another opportunity to encourage participant understanding of the key concepts and to ensure that the participants received the treatment

25. Simpson and Laham (2015a) conducted a thorough review of the central concepts, themes, and summary quotes, including consultations with Alan Fiske, to ensure that they corresponded to the underlying relational models and remained accessible to research participants.

(Verkuyten, 2009).[26] For example, the equality list includes an item stating that "citizens are fair in their treatment of each other and have a reciprocal method of helping each other and being good neighbors" while a unity item comparably indicates that "Americans hold to the idea that 'we are all family' and watch out for each other all the time." In both groups, participants selected anywhere from 0 to 5 statements, and majorities selected 2 or more of the listed reasons.

Participants then completed a factual manipulation check asking whether their assigned passage indicated that equality or unity was important for being American. They could also select "neither." I included this item immediately after the treatment tasks in order to assess participant attentiveness. I used a factual manipulation check because it has an objectively correct response but also varies across treatment groups (Kane and Barabas, 2019).[27] In the unity group, 63.9% of people correctly recalled that they read about unity-oriented relations in the United States, and 74.5% of participants who received the equality prompt selected equality. These passage rates compare favorably to factual manipulation checks in other online panels (Kane and Barabas, 2019). In the control condition, however, only 40.7% of respondents correctly reported that they read about neither unity nor equality. Of the remainder, 39% selected equality, and 20.3% selected unity. To the extent that reading even a dry statement about the size of the American population encouraged control participants to think about equality or unity in the United States—even in the abstract—it might have introduced noise into the control condition. Moreover, it may signal other challenges associated with manipulating content in real nationalisms if control group participants enter the study steeped in ideas about American nationalism. In that sense, the direction of deviations from the control group—whether unity exacerbates nationalist hawkishness and/or equality mitigates it—provide a helpful signal regarding which norms predominate at baseline.

26. I drew the statements from the open-ended comments provided by participants in the Fredonia experiment, and edited them to i) reference the U.S. rather than Fredonia and ii) correct grammar and syntax.

27. While some scholars suggest that manipulation checks should be placed at the end of an experiment to avoid calling attention to the treatment (Mutz, 2011; Berinsky, Margolis and Sances, 2014), Kane and Barabas (2019) find "only modest (but inconsistent) evidence that placing an FMC before (vs. after) an outcome measure produces significantly different treatment effects, suggesting that manipulation check placement is largely inconsequential for treatment effects" (247). See Mutz and Pemantle (2015) for a discussion about the importance of manipulation checks in experimental research.

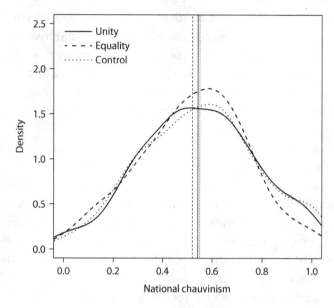

FIGURE 4.3. Average nationalism scores by treatment group.
Note: Vertical bars show average nationalism scores within each treatment group; unity mean=0.54, equality mean=0.52, control mean=0.55. Curves plot kernel density estimates showing distributions on the national chauvinism scale within each treatment group. Bootstrapped Kolmogorov-Smirnov tests, estimated using the Matching package in R (Sekhon, 2011), reveal no significant differences in the distributions.

Next, participants completed the same nationalism scale from chapter 3 (Herrmann, Isernia and Segatti, 2009), though this time the items referenced America. I created an additive three-item scale for nationalism ($\alpha = 0.65$).[28] Before moving forward, I again compare nationalism levels across the three treatment conditions to show that the treatments target content, not commitment. Unlike the Fredonia experiment, where the limited information meant that control group participants had little to go on when evaluating their commitment to Fredonian superiority, all participants in this study have access to pre-existing ideas about American nationalism. In turn, I should find similar nationalist commitments among control and treatment participants.

Figure 4.3 plots mean nationalism scores (vertical lines) and density curves for participants in the unity, equality, and control groups.

28. An item analysis revealed that the scale reliability would improve from 0.62 to 0.65 without the fourth item, "How many things about America make you feel ashamed?" Moreover, while a subsequent factor analysis revealed that the four nationalism scale components constitute a single dimension, the shame item only weakly correlates with the latent favor (0.27). I therefore removed this item from the scale for analysis.

Average nationalism appears marginally higher in the control (*mean* = 0.55) and unity groups (*mean* = 0.54) compared to equality (*mean* = 0.52), but an analysis of variance reveals that the between-group variation does not approach standard thresholds for statistical significance ($F = 0.91$, $p = 0.403$). I also use a bootstrapped Kolmogorov-Smirnov test to test for meaningful differences between the distributions (Sekhon, 2011), and find no statistically significant differences between the control and equality groups ($p = 0.395$), the control and unity groups ($p = 0.996$), or the unity and equality groups ($p = 0.388$). These findings increase my confidence that I can attribute any differences between the treatment groups to content, rather than a more intensely nationalistic unity group.

Figure 4.3 also shows that this sample contains more strong nationalists compared to the sample from chapter 3. Since content should matter the most among committed nationalists inclined to conform to group norms, the sample allows me to estimate more precise treatment effects in this key subgroup.

Before moving forward, I also evaluate whether treatment assignment moderates the relationship between pre-treatment characteristics and nationalism. I assess whether the three groups contain similar compositions of committed nationalists by regressing nationalism scores on a panel of demographic covariates—sex, age, race, education, income, political knowledge, and partisanship[29]—and interacting each of these variables with treatment assignment. The results reveal remarkable similarity. Republican partisanship corresponds to higher scores on nationalism ($b = 0.17, p < 0.01$) in the control group, but, crucially, neither the unity ($b = 0.04$, $p = 0.6$) nor equality ($b = -0.03$, $p = 0.65$) treatments moderate that relationship. Indeed, out of 30 interaction coefficients in the model, only 3 have p-values below 0.1. People in the 35–44 ($b = -0.17$, $p < 0.07$) and 55–64 ($b = -0.17$, $p = 0.07$) age categories exhibited slightly less nationalism in the equality group, compared to 18–24 year-olds in the control group, and white Americans reported slightly lower nationalism scores in the unity group ($b = -0.11$, $p = 0.05$). All remaining

---

29. I measured party identification at the end of the survey to avoid the possibility that answering questions about partisanship would prime certain nationalist norms. In this case, the risks associated with priming outweigh the minimal risk that the treatments caused people to change their party preference and induced posttreatment bias in this supplementary analysis (see Klar, Leeper and Robison, 2020, 58 for a discussion). I have no reason to expect that the treatments affect political knowledge, but removing party identification and knowledge from the models does not change the results.

interaction coefficients have small magnitudes and correspondingly large p-values.[30]

This overwhelming *absence* of evidence that demographic covariates systematically differentiate nationalists in the unity, equality, and control groups—coupled with the unsurprising observation that Republican partisanship correlates with nationalism—provides additional assurance that the nationalism scale serves as an appropriate metric for commitment, not content. As with chapter 3, I cannot fully rule out the possibility that an unmeasured confounder affects susceptibility to experimental manipulations that manifests in nationalism scores. These analyses—and the fact that nationalism levels tend to be relatively stable (Huddy and Del Ponte, 2019)—nevertheless provide substantial confidence in the assertion that the scale taps nationalism's commitment dimension.

DEPENDENT VARIABLES

The dependent variables measure attitudes about American foreign policy. I included two sets of questions to test the effects of unity- and equality-oriented nationalism on i) general hawkishness and ii) support for conflict after direct aggression from an adversary. Within each of these categories, I included one hypothetical situation—militant internationalism on the one hand, and how the United States should respond to a future Russian incursion in the Baltics on the other—alongside one concrete issue facing the United States at the time of the study—China's military rise and the campaign against ISIS in Syria. Including multiple issues allows me to explore the conditions under which unity- and equality-oriented nationalisms correspond to similar policy preferences, providing a more complete test of the theoretical implications that I outlined in chapter 2.

---

30. See the online appendix for results. To further eliminate the possibility that the results could be an artifact of identity salience, the experiment also randomly presented participants with an American flag prime. Some scholars argue that national symbols remind people about their American identity, for example (Kemmelmeier and Winter, 2008), and that salience in turn leads people to view the world from the perspective of their group membership and U.S. dominance (though see Gelpi, Roselle, and Barnett 2013). By that logic, simply priming an intergroup context could drive people toward hawkish foreign policies irrespective of norms and nationalist commitments. Crucially, I find that this flag prime has no effect on nationalism ($b = 0.019$, $p = 0.3$), nor any of the dependent variables ($p > 0.2$ for coefficient on flag in each model). The analyses in this chapter therefore pool across the flag prime. Models in the online appendix show that controlling for the flag produces nearly identical results.

Pairing hypothetical issues or postures with actual problems that feature in newspaper headlines provides a practical advantage over the fictional crisis that dominated my analysis in chapter 3. I can evaluate whether the theory travels outside the realm of imagination. Moreover, the dependent variable questions mimic those that average Americans might encounter in their daily lives, either when they answer calls from pollsters or read the news. These questions therefore increase the experiment's "mundane realism," or "the extent to which events occurring in the research setting are likely to occur in the normal course of the subjects' lives, that is, in the 'real world'" (Aronson, Brewer and Carlsmith, 1985, 485).[31] The survey platform presented the question sets in randomly ordered blocks to guard against question-order effects (McFarland, 1981; Krosnick and Alwin, 1987; Krosnick, 2018).[32]

To measure hawkish aggression in the absence of a clear, identifiable adversary that has harmed the United States or its allies, I measured militant internationalism in general, and attitudes about how the United States should respond to China in particular. A five item militant internationalism scale asked participants whether they agree or disagree with different statements about whether U.S. foreign policy should feature demonstrations of military strength, such as whether the United States should "strike at the heart of an opponent's power" ($\alpha = 0.815$) (Wittkopf, 1990; Kertzer et al., 2014). Participants who score high on militant internationalism embrace the "deterrence model" and believe that dominance (Jervis, 1976), even via conflict escalation, represents the best route to promote U.S. interests. To measure attitudes toward China, I included a question asking participants whether they think that it is important to be tough on China regarding military issues. This question taps hawkishness regarding a specific adversary—one that, at the time, had not mustered their military resources to directly threaten the United States.

Two additional sets of questions asked about how the United States should respond to two contemporary adversaries, Russia and ISIS. I chose these adversaries because, in addition to China, they represented salient

31. See also McDermott (2002*b*); Morton and Williams (2008); and Druckman and Kam (2011). Notably, many scholars argue that researchers should prioritize experimental realism—the degree to which participants are invested in the task—over mundane realism given that absence of the latter does not threaten our primary causal inferences.

32. See the appendix for measurement scales. The survey also included questions about international economic policy and cooperative foreign policy issues as part of a broader study.

U.S. competitors at the time of the survey. The hypothetical scenario gauged support for a series of conflictual actions that the United States might consider if Russia continued its recent expansionism and invaded Latvia and Estonia. After reading the prompt, individual items asked participants whether they would support or oppose sanctions, increasing NATO troop presence, targeted strikes in Russia, sending American ground troops, and declaring war against Russia. High scores on the additive scale ($\alpha = 0.82$) indicate greater overall support for countering Russia with conflictual policies.

Next, participants received introductory information about ISIS, including the fact that the United States had previously conducted airstrikes against ISIS in Iraq and Syria.[33] Participants then indicated whether they would support or oppose a series of potential foreign policy actions against ISIS forces, which included continuing air strikes, using unmanned aircraft to target militants, imposing a "no fly zone" in Syria, and sending ground troops. An additive scale ($\alpha = 0.773$) represents general support for using the U.S. military to combat ISIS.

Notably, both the ISIS and Russia questions tackle issues in which the real or hypothetical American adversary had perpetrated some clear violation or wrongdoing that might command reciprocal violence on behalf of the group. After high-profile ISIS attacks against Western targets and growing reservations about whether the United States was losing the war against terrorism, both equality and unity prescribe a conflictual response.[34] Similarly, the options for dealing with Russia represent standard tools in the foreign policy toolkit when the United States considers how to repel an invader and protect NATO allies. Unlike the hypothetical and ambiguous crisis vignette from chapter 3, and the generalized aggression captured by militant internationalism and China postures, these two policy issues implicate both unity- and equality-oriented nationalisms.

33. See the 2015 CNN/ORC International Poll conducted via telephone in December 2015. Details and topline results available at http://i2.cdn.turner.com/cnn/2015/images/12/25/terrorpoll.pdf, page 9. An additional policy option—whether the U.S. should negotiate with ISIS—reduced the scale reliability ($\alpha = 0.67$) and loaded on a separate factor in an exploratory factory analysis. I therefore exclude it from the additive scale and analyze it individually later in this chapter.

34. Schleifer, Theodore and Agiesta, Jennifer, 2015. "CNN/ORC poll: More Americans say terrorists are winning than ever before," *CNN*, 28 December. URL: www.cnn.com/2015/12/28/politics/american-terrorists-poll-winning-cnn-orc.

Results

I present the results from this study in two phases. First, I test whether unity and equality shape the strength of the relationship between nationalism and i) militarism and ii) support for taking a tough stand against China on military issues. My theory expects more hawkishness among unity-oriented nationalists compared to their equality-oriented counterparts. Second, I probe the limits to these differences between unity and equality by analyzing support for conflictual responses to iii) ISIS and iv) the prospective Russian invasion in Eastern Europe.

NATIONALISMS AND MILITARISM

Table 4.1 presents results from four OLS regressions that model support for conflictual foreign policy preferences as a function of nationalisms. Each model regresses the dependent variable (recoded to range from 0 to 1) on the treatments, nationalism (recoded to range from 0 to 1), and the interaction between the treatments and nationalism. The control condition provides the reference category, such that the coefficient on nationalism represents its effect on each outcome for participants in the control group. Models 1 and 3 display the results for the full sample, while Models 2 and 4 restrict the sample to participants who passed a conservative compliance threshold by entering at least 1 response that pointed to unity or equality norms during the writing task.[35] Higher values of the dependent variables indicate a more militant foreign policy orientation (Models 1 and 2) or support for taking a tough stance against China (Models 3 and 4).

The results in Table 4.1—and substantive effects plotted in Figure 4.4—suggest three important points with respect to my intergroup conflict hypothesis. First, the equality treatment displays the same conflict-mitigating effect that it did in the first experiment. Models 1 and 2 show that national chauvinism has a strong, positive effect on militant internationalism in the control group ($b = 0.342, p < 0.01$). But the negative coefficient on the interaction between equality and chauvinism shows that equality weakens nationalist aggression. The same pattern appears in Models 3 and 4, where the dependent variable measures militant stances toward

---

35. A research assistant coded the open-ended responses based on a conservative criterion for treatment take-up: Did the participant enter any responses that touched on the constructs defined in the experimental prompts? Non-compliers did not complete the task or stated explicit disagreement. Under this coding scheme, 13.23% and 15.08% of the unity and equality groups, respectively, counted as non-compliers. See the online appendix for additional discussion.

TABLE 4.1. Equality Reduces the Effect of Nationalism on Militarism

| | Militant Internationalism | | Tough on China | |
	(1)	(2)	(3)	(4)
Equality	0.069*	0.082**	0.070	0.105*
	(0.038)	(0.040)	(0.051)	(0.054)
Unity	−0.010	−0.019	0.013	0.021
	(0.039)	(0.040)	(0.052)	(0.054)
Nationalism	0.342***	0.342***	0.388***	0.388***
	(0.043)	(0.042)	(0.057)	(0.057)
Equality x Nationalism	−0.142**	−0.129*	−0.199**	−0.216**
	(0.066)	(0.069)	(0.089)	(0.093)
Unity x Nationalism	0.012	0.032	−0.078	−0.084
	(0.065)	(0.067)	(0.087)	(0.090)
Constant	0.519***	0.519***	0.516***	0.516***
	(0.026)	(0.025)	(0.034)	(0.034)
N	632	574	632	574
R^2	0.174	0.189	0.115	0.113

$^*p < .1; ^{**}p < .05; ^{***}p < .01$

Note: Main entries are OLS coefficients. The reference group is the control condition. Continuous variables are rescaled from 0 to 1. Models 2 and 4 remove non-compliers from the sample.

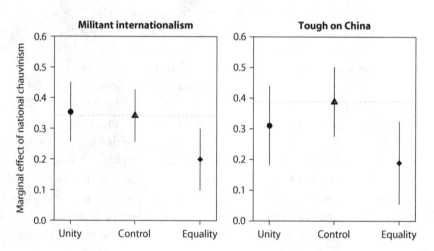

FIGURE 4.4. Marginal effect of nationalism by treatment.
Note: Variables are rescaled from 0 to 1. Vertical bands depict 95% confidence intervals. The plots show the marginal effect of national chauvinism in each treatment group. The effect of nationalism is weaker in the equality group, compared to both the control and unity groups.

a specific adversary, China. Figure 4.4 displays this striking pattern of results by plotting nationalism's marginal effect in each treatment group (lines depict 95% confidence intervals). Equality causes a 41.5% decrease in the size of nationalism's effect on militant internationalism relative to the control group—reading and writing about American equality substantially weakened nationalism's conflict-promoting tendencies.

Second, nationalism increases militarism in both the unity and control groups. The small and non-significant coefficient on the interaction between unity and nationalism shows that when American nationalism requires group solidarity, or when people answer questions about nationalism without prompts about content from experimental treatments, commitments produce militarism. The interaction coefficients in Models 3 and 4 reveal the same pattern with respect to hawkish China postures—nationalists committed to protecting their united group are more likely to draw a hard line against this great power competitor compared to weak nationalists. American greatness demands military dominance when a stark line divides "us" from other, threatening, out-groups.

Third, participants in the control group seem to act like unity-oriented nationalists. Indeed, the plots of marginal effects in Figure 4.4 display remarkable similarity between the unity and control groups. Unity does not enhance nationalism's effect relative to the control, an intriguing finding that opens the door for additional research on "default" nationalisms in the American public. If most Americans respond to survey questions about nationalism as if it requires unity, our surveys may mis-characterize equality-oriented nationalists as weakly committed to the group.

To further unpack these results, I follow the same procedure from chapter 3 to estimate the marginal effects of the treatment along the range of the nationalism scale. Separate panels in Figure 4.5 display the conditional effect of (a-b) equality and (c-d) unity, relative to the control group, on the two dependent variables. To prevent extreme values on the moderating variable from influencing the estimates, I again estimate a string of local effects across the range of nationalism (on the x-axis) (Hainmueller, Mummolo and Xu 2019). These conditional effect estimates have wider confidence intervals when the data contain few observations for values of the moderator variable—depicting an appropriately wide range of uncertainty for outlying nationalism values.

The results in panel (a) confirm that strong nationalists in the equality group express less hawkish attitudes than their control group counterparts. Adjusting their attitudes to the group norms, these committed nationalists take a less militaristic stance in foreign policy. At the 75th percentile on

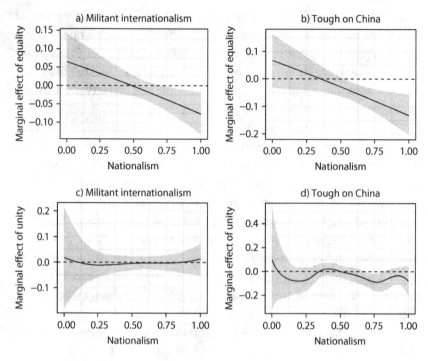

FIGURE 4.5. Equality decreases militarism among strong nationalists.
Note: Nationalism and dependent variables rescaled from 0 to 1. Shaded bands depict 90% bootstrapped confidence intervals, generated using the interflex package in R (Hainmueller, Mummolo and Xu, 2019).

the nationalism scale (0.694), equality produces a statistically significant ($p < 0.1$) 3 percentage point decrease in militant internationalism. This effect grows to negative 5 percentage points at the 90th percentile and 7 percentage points at the 95th percentile, a shift that constitutes about two steps down on the militant internationalism scale. Panel (b) reveals even starker effects. Equality decreases support for taking a tough stance against China by 7 percentage points at the 75th percentile on the nationalism scale and 12 percentage points at the 95th percentile. This effect represents about one half of a standard deviation for scores on the dependent variable, or one step down on the seven-point scale. Although these treatment effects may seem small in size, they are statistically significant and substantively striking insofar as scholars tend to think about hawkish postures as orientations that resist change (e.g., Holsti, 1979; Wittkopf, 1990; Bjereld and Ekengren, 1999; Gravelle et al., 2014; Gravelle, Reifler and Scotto, 2017).[36]

---

36. Though see Kertzer and Powers (2020) for evidence that issue positions can influence foreign policy orientations.

By contrast, weak nationalists in the equality treatment do not differ from weak nationalists in the control group on militant internationalism or China attitudes. Unlike the backlash phenomenon that I observed in chapter 3—whereby weak equality-oriented nationalists exhibited surprising bellicosity—the results in panels (a) and (b) show that the treatment has no effect on militarism on the lower end of the nationalism scale. This finding underscores why our theories and empirical tests must account for commitment alongside content—people adopt the group's norms when they are connected to the group, but otherwise ignore them (or perhaps rebel against them).

Turning to unity, the results in panels (c) and (d) of Figure 4.5 largely confirm my expectations. Unity has no effect on militant internationalism for any value on the nationalism scale, relative to the control group. And although the plot in panel (d) reveals a surprising negative and statistically significant effect on China stances for values around the 75th percentile on the nationalism scale, the nonlinear marginal effect estimates and nonsignificant differences at the higher ends of the nationalism scale prohibit concluding that unity reduces hawkish China attitudes among nationalists. Unity's negative local effect could indicate that unity-oriented nationalism has a paradoxically pacifying effect on attitudes toward China for people around the 75th percentile on nationalism, that strong nationalists in the control group implicitly associated nationalism with unity to a greater extent than they did in the unity treatment, or perhaps that the single-item dependent variable requires refinement to better capture attitudes. In the online appendix, I split the sample into high and low terciles on the nationalism scale to further examine this finding. I find that unity decreases scores on the China measure among strong nationalists, relative to the control group. But, crucially, comparing unity to equality reveals that equality has a stronger pull against hawkish China postures relative to unity (bootstrapped $p = 0.06$). In general, these considerations suggest caution in over-interpreting this result as evidence that unity-oriented nationalism softens stances on China. Consistent with the null coefficient on the interaction between unity and national chauvinism, the small and fickle marginal effects for unity suggest that nationalists in the control group may implicitly rely on unity norms.

In that sense, the data support my expectations about equality's conflict-mitigating effects but also illustrate the challenges associated with comparing equality and unity to a control group comprised of people who hold prior but unobserved perceptions regarding the group norms. Indeed, this challenge resembles the problem that survey researchers face when they draw inferences about nationalism's effects without data on content. More importantly, the results provide consistent support—across both outcomes—for my expectation that equality mitigates the relationship between nationalism and hawkishness.

Robustness

I carried out several supplementary analyses. First, results in the online appendix show that including a panel of demographic control variables in the models does not change the results. Second, I follow the logic I laid out in chapter 3 to test whether a key placebo moderator—an additive scale for national attachment—produces the same results. If the nationalism scale proxies an unobserved propensity to comply with the treatment, switching from nationalism to feelings of closeness to the group should produce the same effect. Instead, supplementary analyses in the appendix show largely null interactions between unity, equality, and national attachment or other placebo moderators. Third, I account for treatment compliance more directly in the online appendix by estimating the complier average causal effects (CACE) for unity and equality in strong (N=229) and weak (N=207) nationalism subgroups. I find consistent results—equality reduces hawkish attitudes among strong nationalists relative to the control and unity groups—and the CACE estimates closely match intent-to-treat estimates that do not account for participant engagement.

UNITY, EQUALITY, AND RECIPROCAL CONFLICT

Thus far the experiments in this book have stressed differences in the foreign policies prescribed by unity versus equality. One of the striking features of the results: Equality's consistent conflict-mitigating effects. Equality-oriented nationalists were more willing to extend a hand to Rusburg during a complex and ambiguous conflict, choosing more measured approaches over the course of the crisis rather than elect dangerous escalation. Equality-oriented nationalists exhibit less militaristic stances in general, and toward potential adversaries who have not posed a direct threat to Americans.

But the opportunity to include additional outcome measures that feature different contextual elements constitutes a chief advantage of moving to the American foreign policy realm. What foreign policy issues might implicate each of these dueling nationalisms? Under what conditions will both unity- and equality-oriented nationalists support military force?

Equality demands reciprocity, and if an adversary fails to practice mutual tolerance—if they do attack the United States or its interests—the threat becomes real. Unity-oriented nationalists in the public might hold inflated threat perceptions regarding ISIS if they believe that isolated attacks represent an existential threat to the group, like Senator Cruz implied after San Bernardino. In that understanding, an attack on any American means an attack on all, and merits a response that musters the full force of the U.S. military. At the same time, equality-oriented nationalism implies that the United States should respond in kind to direct threats. The notion that "when terrorists attack Americans, the American military strikes back at the terrorists" entails a commitment to tit-for-tat reciprocity (Fiske and Rai, 2015, 20). Following Obama's logic that "this is not an organization that can destroy the United States . . . But they can hurt us"[37]—and have hurt Americans—airstrikes against ISIS targets, drone attacks on militants, and even a "no fly zone" constitute reciprocal responses. Equality then prescribes conflict.

Similarly, if Russia invaded NATO allies in the Baltics, public demands for some form of retaliation would not depend on inflated perceptions about Putin's expansionist aims. Those aims would be on full display, and both solidarity and fairness demand U.S. involvement. Steps like imposing economic sanctions, increasing NATO troop presence, and even targeted strikes against Russian military bases constitute in-kind responses to international aggression. Policies that we categorize as hawkish or conflictual constitute efforts to protect American solidarity against creeping Russian power (unity) and entail proportionate responses to a concrete aggressive act (equality). Equality does not denote pacifism, an important implication that helps separate my argument from dispositional theories that cast people who value fairness as reflexively cooperative (Kertzer et al., 2014).

Table 4.2 presents the results, where I model the effects of the experimental treatments, nationalism, and the interactions on support for conflictual policies against ISIS and a hypothetical Russian incursion in Eastern Europe. The striking *absence* of statistically significant interaction coefficients emerges as the primary takeaway from these models. Nationalism has a strong, positive effect across all three treatment groups. Committed nationalists support conflictual policies vis-à-vis both ISIS and an expansionist Russia, irrespective of treatment assignment.

37. See Inskeep (2015) for interview transcript.

TABLE 4.2. Equality and Unity Align in Response to Direct Attacks

	ISIS		Russia	
	(1)	(2)	(3)	(4)
Equality	−0.031	−0.034	0.064	0.064
	(0.048)	(0.050)	(0.048)	(0.051)
Unity	−0.093*	−0.098*	−0.001	0.001
	(0.048)	(0.050)	(0.048)	(0.051)
Nationalism	0.262***	0.262***	0.265***	0.265***
	(0.054)	(0.053)	(0.054)	(0.054)
Equality x Nationalism	0.018	0.036	−0.083	−0.076
	(0.083)	(0.087)	(0.083)	(0.088)
Unity x Nationalism	0.111	0.132	0.017	0.010
	(0.081)	(0.084)	(0.081)	(0.085)
Constant	0.569***	0.569***	0.367***	0.367***
	(0.032)	(0.032)	(0.032)	(0.032)
N	632	574	632	574
R^2	0.119	0.126	0.080	0.081

*p < .1; **p < .05; ***p < .01

Note: Main entries are OLS coefficients. The reference group is the control condition. Continuous variables are rescaled from 0 to 1. Models 2 and 4 remove non-compliers from the sample.

These results suggest that equality- and unity-oriented nationalists align when both sets of norms prescribe hawkish foreign policies. To conform with the U.S. commitment to reciprocity, equality-oriented nationalists support targeted strikes against ISIS and taking a firm stand against Russian aggression. Figure 4.6 depicts the limited variation in nationalism's marginal effects across the treatment groups. Especially stark in the Russia scenario, nationalism exerts a positive effect on conflict in all three groups. Point estimates suggest that nationalism may have a slightly weaker effect in the equality group, compared to unity, in both scenarios. But the confidence intervals indicate the absence of statistically significant differences and prevent me from concluding that the treatments changed nationalism's relationship with foreign policy attitudes.

At the same time, these foreign policy scenarios may simply leave me unable to distinguish real differences between unity and equality, and other operationalizations of the dependent variable might have produced a different set of results. Indeed, the fact that I observe a negative

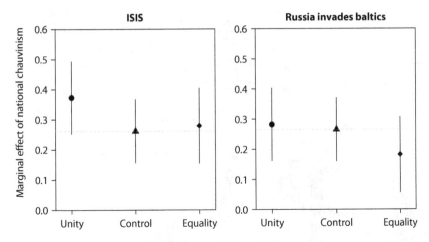

FIGURE 4.6. Nationalism increases support for conflict against ISIS and Russia.
Note: Variables are rescaled from 0 to 1. Vertical bands depict 95% confidence intervals. The plots show the marginal effect of nationalism in each treatment group.

shift in the marginal effect of nationalism between unity and equality in Figure 4.6—albeit differences that just miss statistical significance (bootstrapped $p = 0.13$ for ISIS attitudes, $p = 0.12$ for Russia)—could indicate that equality-oriented nationalists remain slightly less hawkish than their unity-oriented counterparts even when the United States faces a direct threat. Although I chose these two policy issues for their practical and theoretical value, future research could examine a broader range of scenarios or experimentally manipulate features of the situation to further refine our understanding of nationalisms in international politics.

To leverage the current experimental data and subject the second half of my intergroup conflict hypothesis to an additional test, I break down the multi-item scale measuring support for conflict against ISIS into its component parts. Although the first three items in this scale measure support for proportionate retaliation in line with the Obama administration's approach, and opposition to negotiating taps cooperative inclinations, the last component item asked about support for sending U.S. ground troops into combat operations against ISIS forces. Putting American boots on the ground would represent clear escalation, turning limited operations into something with the potential for a large-scale war. As Obama explained, few of even his staunchest opponents called for the United States to take this step because "when you start looking at an Iraq-type deployment of large numbers of troops," the United States creates an indefinite commitment that

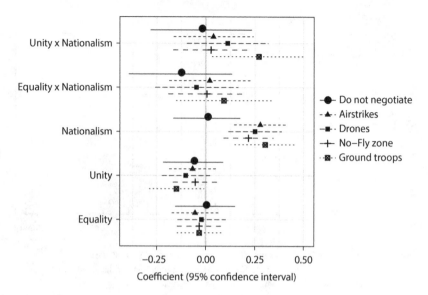

FIGURE 4.7. Unity-oriented nationalism increases support for ground troops.
Note: Nationalism and dependent variables are rescaled from 0 to 1. Points represent regression coefficients, and horizontal bands depict 95% confidence intervals, for each individual item in the ISIS scale.

moves beyond just "going door to door in places like Mosul and Raqqa."[38] Per my theory, I should find null interaction coefficients for the more limited responses, but significant differences between unity and equality on support for ground troops.

To test this possibility, I estimate separate regression models for constituent items from the ISIS scale. Figure 4.7 presents the results, displaying coefficient estimates and 95% confidence intervals for each of the 5 outcomes.[39] Overall, the results suggest that members of the public advocate action against ISIS and that nationalism has a consistent positive effect on support for countering ISIS in the control group.[40]

And, for the most part, the results reveal the weak and non-significant interaction terms we would expect from the null findings for the full additive scale. However, Figure 4.7 plots one notable exception. Whereas unity- and equality-oriented nationalisms both increased support for limited

38. See Inskeep (2015) for transcript interview.

39. See the online appendix for regression table.

40. The null effects for the "do not negotiate" item likely stem from the skewed distribution on this outcome; in line with standard counter-terrorism doctrines in the Western world, most participants oppose negotiating with ISIS.

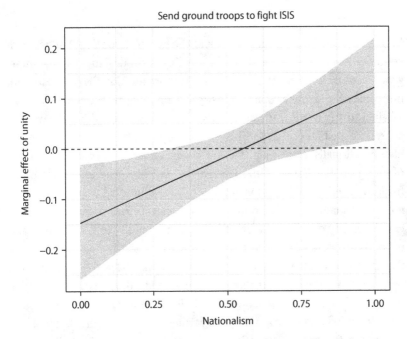

FIGURE 4.8. Unity-oriented nationalism increases support for ground troops in Iraq and Syria. *Note*: Nationalism and support for ground troops rescaled from 0 to 1. Horizontal bands depict 90% bootstrapped confidence intervals, generated using the interflex package in R (Hainmueller, Mummolo and Xu, 2019).

forms of involvement, unity-oriented nationalism dramatically increases support for ground troops—compared to both the control and equality groups.[41] Figure 4.8 plots unity's marginal effect across the nationalism scale, and reveals that unity increases support for ground troops among stronger nationalists. Unity-oriented nationalists appear to favor taking any step that might help the United States destroy enemies abroad. But the paucity of serious ISIS attacks against Americans leads equality-oriented nationalists to adopt a less aggressive approach mimicking their tendency to reject generalized militarism. They oppose sending ground troops that could lead to a conflict that spirals out of control.[42]

41. Although nationalism has a positive marginal effect in both the unity and equality groups, unity-oriented nationalism has a stronger positive effect compared to equality-oriented nationalism (bootstrapped $p = 0.067$).

42. Of course, we cannot use the fact that the interaction coefficient for ground troops meets statistical significance thresholds, but others do not, to compare the strength of the interaction nor marginal effects of nationalisms across outcomes. Bootstrapped tests show that the marginal effect of unity-oriented nationalism on support for ground troops is larger than its effect on support for refusing to negotiate, airstrikes, drone strikes, and a no-fly zone (all $p < 0.05$).

Conclusion

In this chapter, I took a second look at the complex relationship between content, commitment, and foreign policy attitudes to test my intergroup conflict hypothesis. I first justified my assumption that contestation, not consensus, defines American nationalisms and presented data from an original survey to show that equality and unity resonate with ordinary citizens. Like the Fredonia experiment from chapter 3, this experiment manipulated nationalist norms and measured participants' responses to a series of foreign policy issues. Although much about this experiment borrowed from the Fredonia study—for example, using a bundled multi-stage treatment and standard scales to measure nationalism and militarism—it also contained key differences that added external validity to the research and tested both parts of my intergroup conflict hypothesis. Namely, I fielded the study to a national sample, increased the statistical power, manipulated real-world American nationalisms, and included a diverse panel of foreign policy attitudes for my dependent variables. The foreign policy questionnaire included two issue areas that described adversaries engaged in direct aggression against the United States and its allies. Comparable to the results reported in chapter 3, strong equality-based nationalists expressed a less militaristic posture in general and toward China. In a different population, with a different manipulation, and different measures, I reach the same conclusion that varieties of nationalism often have distinct implications for foreign policy attitudes.

At the same time, equality- and unity-oriented nationalists converged to support conflict against ISIS and Russian expansionism. This agreement represents a sharp departure from the previous results, and an important rejoinder to those who might hasten to label some nationalisms "benign" in the foreign policy realm (Brown, 1999). Fairness demands retaliation, though equality-oriented nationalists are more likely to stop short of unprovoked war. Equality-based nationalists may not demand war if China injured a member of the U.S. military during a freedom of navigation operation in the South China Sea for example, but could join their unity-oriented counterparts to support in-kind retaliation for a military strike on an American base.

Both experiments complicate the standard story about nationalism and foreign policy attitudes. Nationalism sometimes prescribes foreign policy aggression, but not always. Liberal nationalists tout the virtues of a strong national identity for in-group loyalty (Kymlicka, 1998), but IR scholars caution that strong national identities create negative international externalities (Mercer, 1995; Herrmann, Isernia and Segatti, 2009; Schrock-Jacobson, 2012; Bertoli, 2017). My theory and results introduce contingency into these claims, potentially offering a viable middle ground between nationalisms as causes of war or peace.

Methodologically, the innovative research design in this chapter illustrates new pathways for experimental research on varieties of real-world nationalisms. Researchers tend to measure content rather than manipulate it (Wright, Citrin and Wand, 2012; Schildkraut, 2007), but experimental data are better suited to testing causal claims. Moreover, political scientists tend to tautologically treat nationalism as a commitment defined by its conflict orientation, making it harder to study nationalisms in the plural. But when survey respondents report whether they think the United States is better than other countries, they smuggle their own ideas about content into the answers. The results from the control group in this experiment suggest that in the U.S. case, unity may represent the baseline perceptions about content for many Americans—but researchers should test this assumption directly or risk missing consequential variation in nationalism's effects.

The results in this chapter confirm that experimentally targeting content rather than commitment advances how we understand the connection between nationalisms and foreign policy attitudes. At the same time, the rates of non-compliance coupled with participants' pre-existing views on content, implied by the effects of nationalism in the control group, reveal limits to these experimental treatments. Other experimental designs could combat this issue. For instance, future researchers might use pre-selection—a design that groups people according to their pre-existing beliefs about unity and equality and then randomly assigns treatments within those blocks. But we should also embrace the fruits of multi-method research designs with well-designed surveys that specifically probe identity content. Armed with the knowledge that content has causal effects in the intergroup context, I next use large-scale observational evidence to examine the relationship between content and intragroup cooperation in chapter 5.

If I were only interested in intergroup dynamics, these nationalism experiments would fulfill this book's goals. But as I argued in chapter 2, nationalisms and supranationalisms refer to different levels of categorization but represent two sides of the same coin. At the national level, commitment and content shape how members of the public respond to *out-group* members, like foreign adversaries. But research at the supranational level primarily deals with intragroup dynamics to make claims about how supranationalists perceive *in-group* members and in turn, whether transnational communities can bypass nationalist strife to advance security cooperation.

Indeed, even though my theory and experimental results might temper our worst fears that nationalism's twenty-first century rise will spark World War III, citizens and policymakers might nevertheless want to hedge their bets by promoting and embracing supranationalisms: If unity-oriented nationalism creates a hawkish impulse that increases the risk for conflict, and supranationalism (of any variety) overrides this impulse, broader identities create an opportunity. Moving our commitments up one categorization level replaces out-group hate with in-group love. But that assertion relies on heroic assumptions about intragroup dynamics in large, heterogeneous groups. As I argued in chapters 1 and 2, turning Italians and Frenchmen into Europeans does make regional identities relevant for attitudes about international cooperation, but we would be misguided to conclude that supranationalism has universally cooperation-enhancing effects. Supranationalisms vary by content—like their nationalist counterparts—and I expect that equality (but not unity) promotes security cooperation within the group. Thus, the next chapter shifts from the national to the supranational and tests the second prong of my theory by examining equality and unity among Europeans. Having used experiments to demonstrate the theory's causal currency, I build on these foundations to study supranationalisms using several sources of observational data that maximize external validity.

5

Supranationalisms and Support for Security Cooperation in Europe

In his memoirs, Jean Monnet (1978, 357–59) recalls a notable 1951 exchange with U.S. President Dwight Eisenhower. After nationalism ravaged the continent in the last half-century, representatives for six European parties had just signed the treaty establishing the European Coal and Steel Community (ECSC). The ECSC would integrate national economies to create "*de facto* solidarity" and provide "the basis for a broader and deeper community among peoples long divided by bloody conflict."[1] Meanwhile, the fate of the proposed European Defence Community (EDC) and European army remained uncertain—but to Monnet, essential. He explained to Eisenhower that "without unity, . . . everyone will go on seeking power for himself. . . . The strength of the West does not depend on how many divisions it has, but on its unity and common will." Both Monnet and Eisenhower had little patience for haggling over technical details regarding the size of each army unit. They instead operated from the premise that European unity provides the linchpin for success. As Eisenhower summarized, "The strength of the divisions is one aspect of things, but the real problem's a human one. What Monnet's proposing is to organize relations between people, and I'm all for it."

---

1. Preamble to the treaty establishing the European Coal and Steel Community qtd. in Monnet (1978, 357).

Monnet and the other policymakers envisioned an intimate relationship between unity and peace—an impression shared by modern-day leaders, like Emmanuel Macron, and academic scholars who study transnational identities and cooperation (Cronin, 1999; Adler and Barnett, 1998; Koenig-Archibugi, 2004; Beaton, Dovidio and Léger, 2008; Schoen, 2008; Lee and Lim, 2020). In chapters 3 and 4, I identified some flaws in the assumption that nationalism necessarily inspires warmongering and conflict escalation. Yet even equality does not denote pacifism, and people might seek supranationalism if it bypasses nationalism's destructive effects.

In chapter 2, I explained how supranationalism complements nationalism by shifting commitments to a higher level of categorization. Whereas "territorial fences" ostensibly "promote mistrust and suspicion" and inhibit security cooperation,[2] the conventional story suggests that supranationalism overrides these tendencies. And from the 1957 Treaty of Rome that aimed to establish "an ever-closer union among the European peoples"[3] to the repeated mentions of "solidarity" in the 2007 Treaty of Lisbon,[4] official EU documents allude to continental unity. Practically speaking, supranational identification "is an issue of perennial concern for the EU institutions" (European Commission, 2012, 7), with programs that range from the EURO-ARTS festival to transnational television programming and educational exchanges designed to promote Europeanness (European Commission, 2012; McNamara, 2015b).

Does the widespread support for security integration, among both members of the public and elites (Müller, Jenny and Ecker, 2012; Schilde, Anderson and Garner, 2019), illustrate an achievement in the move to replace nationalism with supranational unity? I argue that this simple story neglects two factors. First, the pressure to maintain unity when a group contains substantial heterogeneity undermines the cooperation-enhancing benefits from "in-group love" (Mummendey and Waldzus, 2004). Contrary to Monnet's insistence that "a lasting peace" requires that we "unit[e] the Europeans,"[5] I expect that unity-oriented supranationalists hesitate to entrust their security to fellow Europeans, many of whom represent "bad" in-group members in their eyes. Second, European identities are contested (Risse, 2010). The same treaties that tout solidarity paradoxically

---

2. Dwight D. Eisenhower, Speech at the English-Speaking Union, London, 3 July 1951, qtd. in Monnet (1978, 359–60).

3. Preamble to the Treaty of Rome (European Union, 1957).

4. See, for example, Articles 1a, 2, 10a, and 16 in the Treaty of Lisbon 2007.

5. Jean Monnet, "To Make Europe is to Make Peace . . .," 17 May 1953.

profess that Europeanness requires a commitment to tolerance and equality.[6] Equality opens the door for trust and cooperation in heterogeneous groups, whereas unity often closes it.

In this chapter, I test my *intragroup cooperation* hypothesis and show that content still matters at the supranational level—equality and unity have competing implications for attitudes about international cooperation. In the following sections, I first explain why Europe presents an ideal case for testing my theory before describing the connection between public opinion, elites, and security cooperation.

Next, I analyze data from the 2007 and 2009 waves of the IntUne project survey on European identity (Cotta, Isernia and Bellucci, 2009) and the 2014 and 2019 Eurobarometer surveys. The IntUne survey data include representative mass public samples from 16 EU member-states alongside targeted elite samples, and the Eurobarometer data contain representative public samples from countries throughout the EU. These observational analyses complement the experiments from chapters 3 and 4. Single-country experiments suited my intergroup conflict hypothesis and helped establish causality, but testing the intragroup cooperation hypothesis requires a broader cross-national panel to protect against one country's dominant supranationalism driving the results. Moreover, although the experiments used carefully targeted treatments to manipulate unity and equality, I use common survey items to measure content in this chapter. But when I rely on proxies to operationalize the core constructs, I do so bolstered by the experimental findings.

Finally, mass publics and elites each play important roles in theories about nationalist aggression and regional cooperation. Experiments with elites require atypical access and often depend on small samples (Bayram, 2017; Renshon, 2017; Hafner-Burton, LeVeck and Victor, 2017; Tomz, Weeks and Yarhi-Milo, 2020). But the IntUne project fielded a near-identical survey instrument to the public and nearly 4,000 political and business elites, allowing me to assess whether my theory applies to the public who elect politicians and to the elites with policy-making or agenda-setting powers. In short, these observational analyses have key advantages for testing whether the argument generalizes to different populations, categorization levels, and operationalizations for the independent variables (McDermott, 2011)—rounding out this book's multi-method approach.

---

6. See, for example, the preamble to the Treaty of Lisbon (2007) as well as Article 1a, which both refer to equality as one of the EU's core values.

I begin my analyses with the IntUne mass public surveys. After explaining my measurement strategy and exploring contestation in the European public, I show that equality-based European identities correspond to greater intra-European trust, support for foreign policy cooperation, and support for a European army to replace national forces. By contrast, respondents who see Europe as a united family express more intragroup *dis*trust and oppose security cooperation. I examine the data to show that commitment alone cannot explain these relationships, and explore the potential interaction between unity and equality to find that they have separate and opposite effects on support for European cooperation. I then turn to the elite data to show that European elites likewise contest European supranationalism, and that equality corresponds to support for security cooperation whereas unity does not.

I close with several analyses that increase this chapter's external validity by examining my theory's implications for other forms of cooperation and by supplementing the IntUne surveys with data from two waves of the Eurobarometer public opinion surveys. The results corroborate my findings and reveal that equality—but not unity—increases support for security integration and for aiding fellow members in a financial crisis. I adopt a distinct measurement strategy to gauge unity and equality on the Eurobarometer surveys, and the results extend this chapter's empirical reach to new time periods, countries, and issues.

Why Europe?

"As you know I am obsessed by unity."[7] This concise statement opened President Donald Tusk's remarks to the 2017 European Council meeting, where he emphasized European solidarity against threats to the Union like Brexit. He asked his colleagues to commit to funding the PESCO (Permanent Structured Cooperation on defence) to protect encroaching threats to "our" European territory, using language familiar to IR scholars who connect collective identities to security cooperation (Acharya, 2001; Wendt, 1992, 1999; Cronin, 1999). Tusk's speech illustrates how far European security cooperation has advanced and the ease with which Europeans

---

7. Donald Tusk, 2017. "Report by President Donald Tusk to the European Parliament on October European Council meetings and presentation of the Leaders' Agenda." Transcript available at https://www.consilium.europa.eu/en/press/press-releases/2017/10/24/tusk -report-european-parliament-strasbourg/, 24 October.

discuss supranational identities—features that make Europe an ideal case for testing my intragroup cooperation hypothesis.

First, the European Union project provides the most advanced contemporary example of interstate security integration. Although detractors warn that homogenization pressures could threaten the fate of the Union (Delanty, 1995), elite discourse and political science scholarship both conclude that identification begets trust and cooperation on the continent. For example, scholars treat Europe as an exemplar for collective identification in security communities (Cronin, 1999; Acharya and Johnston, 2007). Other regions serve as foils: The absence of supranational identification helps explain why there is no NATO in East Asia (Hemmer and Katzenstein, 2002; Collins, 2007) nor a robust pan-Arab League (Barnett and Solingen, 2007). Other regional projects like ASEAN have gained ground in the past two decades, but both scholars and policymakers use Europe as a benchmark (Moorthy and Benny, 2012, 2013; Lee and Lim, 2020). Getting Europe right provides an important step in understanding other supranationalisms.

Research that connects individual supranationalism to cooperation predominantly relies on commitment. A formidable body of work examines both whether citizens feel attached to Europe (see, e.g., Duchesne, 2008; Citrin and Sides, 2004; Marks and Hooghe, 2003; Stoeckel, 2016) and how actors like the EU can contribute to the "Europeanization" of political identities (Börzel and Risse, 2007; Cram, Patrikios and Mitchell, 2011; Cram, 2012; Bruter, 2003, 2009; Herrmann and Brewer, 2004; Checkel and Katzenstein, 2009; Risse, 2004; Smith, 1992). This line of research overwhelmingly starts from the premise that European identification promotes cooperation (Koenig-Archibugi, 2004). And indeed, strong European identifiers hold favorable views of the common defense policy (Citrin and Sides, 2004; Schoen, 2008), promote the monetary union (Marks and Hooghe, 2003; Hooghe and Marks, 2004), support deeper integration (Hooghe and Marks, 2005; Risse, 2010), and will absorb national costs to comply with EU law (Bayram, 2017). Research in other regions follows suit to treat citizens' identification with ASEAN, for example, as *indicative of* successful integration (Lee and Lim, 2020)—making Europe an important test case for my theory of identity content.

Second, Europe's advanced integration process makes it a practical choice for analysis: Debates about "Europeanness" dominate the modern zeitgeist. Testing the *intragroup cooperation* hypothesis requires cross-national, individual-level data that measures identity content (the independent variable) alongside trust and support for security cooperation (the dependent variables). What Laffan (1996, 82) surmised a generation ago—that "the *politics of identity* have enormous salience in the new Europe"—holds true in the twenty-first century.[8] Europeans remain enthralled by supranationalism. Outside Europe, few regions feature widespread conversations about supranationalisms.[9] Surveys rarely ask Argentinians what it means to be South American, for example. And although questions about supranational identification now appear on polls in Southeast Asia,[10] the current agenda prioritizes commitment over content. European survey respondents, by contrast, regularly grapple with questions about what it means to be European.

Support for deeper security cooperation also resonates with everyday Europeans. EU member-states signed and implemented the Lisbon Treaty while the IntUne surveys were in the field (2007 and 2009), and the foreign policy pillar featured prominently in debates. In turn, many citizens have formed opinions about everything from a shared foreign policy platform to a European army. Questions about cooperation remained atop the agenda during the Eurozone financial crisis and post-Brexit, allowing me to test the theory using Eurobarometer surveys from 2014 and 2019. By contrast, posing analogous questions to Americans about whether to unite the U.S., Mexican, and Canadian armies may not measure meaningful policy preferences.[11] The European case provides a theoretically important and practical setting to measure my independent and dependent variables.

Theoretical Expectations

In chapter 2, I argued that content shapes whether supranationalism increases support for security cooperation. People who commit to European unity distrust fellow Europeans who threaten the group's homo-

8. Emphasis in original.

9. See, for example, Moorthy and Benny (2013) and Lee and Lim (2020) on Southeast Asian identities, and Zogby (2010) and Telhami (2013) on Arab nationalism.

10. The Asian barometer surveys introduced a question asking residents in ASEAN member-states how close they feel to ASEAN in 2014–15. Core questionnaire available at http://www.asianbarometer.org/data/core-questionnaire.

11. Many citizens in Arab countries endorse Arab nationalism (Telhami, 2013), but surveys about foreign policy tend to elicit attitudes about external interference in the region rather than specific forms of intra-Arab cooperation. See, for example, waves 4 and 5 of the Arab Barometer surveys, available at https://www.arabbarometer.org/survey-data/#surveys-grid.

geneity, and express less support for security integration compared to those who view fellow Europeans as equals who reciprocate. This section provides a brief review of my *intragroup cooperation* hypotheses with respect to intra-European trust and support for security cooperation.

First, I argue that equality-oriented supranationalism increases European trust, whereas unity-oriented supranationalism decreases it. Theories about transnational cooperation place trust at the center—trust facilitates qualitative multilateralism in general (Kupchan and Kupchan, 1991; Ruggie, 1992; Barnett and Adler, 1998; Rathbun, 2009, 2011*a*), and European integration in particular (Deutsch, 1957; Verhaegen, Hooghe and Quintelier, 2017; Mitchell, 2015). Unity-oriented supranationalists trust people who represent the group's normative ideal, but tighten their circle of trust in a pattern that hearkens to nationalist parochialism (Rathbun, 2009). By contrast, equality norms accommodate heterogeneity, allowing people to trust fellow Europeans across the continent; reciprocity takes hold without unity.

Second, I expect similar patterns in support for policies that entail a concrete merger between the national interest and the supranational entity. Equality-oriented supranationalists will support a common foreign and security policy for the EU, and military integration via a European army. They anticipate reciprocity from group members because being European means committing to fairness and equality. They can rely on fellow Europeans to look out for their security. Unity-oriented supranationalists, by contrast, will prioritize national autonomy rather than rely on potentially perfidious partners in matters of war and peace.

Which Europeans Matter?

In chapters 3 and 4, I focused exclusively on members of the public to test my intergroup conflict hypothesis. In this chapter, I examine elites alongside regular citizens—two separate populations implicated in the relationship between supranationalism and foreign policy integration (Koenig-Archibugi, 2004, 146–47).

A direct line connects elite identification to security cooperation. Simply put, European elites can promote policies that enhance regional interdependence or national independence (Bayram, 2017). In that respect, we can think about transnational security cooperation as a product of sincere supranationalist commitments among elites who hold political power in the policymaking process.

Public opinion also has important implications for security integration, both because citizens determine which leaders hold positions of power and because elites have incentives to respond to their constituents. The public plays a role in selecting leaders whose sincere preferences reflect their own desire for cooperation or disintegration. Understanding the public then calibrates what we should expect from politicians who later serve in office.

Moreover, elites sometimes adjust their behavior to match public preferences. Motivated either by their desire to win re-election or to act as public stewards (Tomz, Weeks and Yarhi-Milo, 2020), responsive politicians might promote pro-integration policies when the public demands. Of course, the relationship between European elites and the mass public most likely has recursive elements: Elites shape public identities and policy preferences by cueing the public with their own policy beliefs, which in turn affects the elites who remain in power (Koenig-Archibugi, 2004; Risse, 2001).

I take an agnostic stance about which specific mechanisms connect supranationalisms to policy outcomes and when. Nevertheless, testing the theory in paired populations has important implications for future research on European security policy. If the expected relationships between content and attitudes toward security cooperation hold for members of the public but not elites (or vice versa), scholars who advance elite-driven theories of policy change might question whether identity content matters in the European security coalition.

The IntUne Public Surveys

Testing my theory requires data that probe supranational identity content alongside attitudes about trust and foreign policy cooperation. In turn, I analyze data from the 2007 and 2009 waves of the "Integrated and United. The Quest for Citizenship in an Ever Closer Europe, 2005–2009" (IntUne) surveys (Cotta, Isernia and Bellucci, 2009).[12] These cross-national public opinion surveys collected representative samples in 16 EU member-states,[13] and include items that measure European trust and

12. The extensive survey instrument is useful for my purpose because it includes reasonable proxies for individuals' understandings of the social relations that underlie European identity alongside items that tap trust and support for European security integration. Other publicly available data such as the International Social Survey Programme or European Social Survey contain items that comprise the independent variable or outcomes of interest, but not both.

13. Countries include France, Belgium, Denmark, Germany, Greece, Spain, Italy, Portugal, United Kingdom, Estonia, Hungary, Poland, Slovakia, Slovenia, Bulgaria, and Austria. The

support for security cooperation. To my knowledge, no large, cross-national surveys measure relational models directly.[14] But the IntUne surveys ask respondents about what it means to "be European," joining a broader political and academic trend in attempting to measure components of European identity (Bruter, 2003; Cram, Patrikios and Mitchell, 2011; Smith, 1992; Herrmann and Brewer, 2004; Fligstein, 2008; Checkel and Katzenstein, 2009).

DEPENDENT MEASURES

I expect that equality-based European supranationalism correlates with intra-European trust and support for foreign policy cooperation, and use three dependent variables to test this proposition. First, I assess intra-European trust. Participants rated how much they personally trust people from other European countries on an 11-point scale that ranges from I "do not trust the group at all" to I "have complete trust" in them (Cotta, Isernia and Bellucci, 2009, 77). Like other continuous variables in the data, I rescaled this item to range from 0 to 1.[15]

The second and third dependent variables assess participant support for security cooperation within the EU. One item asks participants whether, "in the next ten years or so," they favor a single foreign policy toward outside countries for the European Union (5-point scale from "Strongly against" to "Strongly in favour") (Cotta, Isernia and Bellucci, 2009).[16] In general, respondents seem happy to relinquish the foreign policy sphere to the EU—across both survey waves, 70.5% of respondents report that they at least somewhat favor the CFSP. Support varies—only 49.3% of UK respondents favor the CFSP—but large majorities in other countries remain positively disposed (Müller, Jenny and Ecker, 2012). In Germany, for example, 78.8% of respondents would like to craft a common EU defense.[17]

2007 data includes a sample from Turkey, and both waves sampled the Serbian population. I exclude these non-member states from my analyses because my theoretical interests lie in intra-European foreign policy cooperation. Details about the sampling procedures are available in the study documentation uploaded to the ICPSR database (ICPSR 34421 and ICPSR 34272).

14. Recent work by Simpson and Laham (2015a) surveys individuals to assess the relationship between social relations, political ideology, and policy positions, but the survey includes a limited scope and scale by design.

15. Mean intra-European trust is 0.54, and the standard deviation is 0.21.

16. The mean of this variable is 0.67, and the standard deviation is 0.31. I recoded "don't know" responses to the scale midpoint.

17. Descriptive statistics and subsequent analyses account for population weights.

The CFSP requires cooperation among member-states—primary policy areas include peacekeeping, trade, and diplomacy. These substantive domains entail trade-offs between national autonomy and transnational coordination. Yet European citizens would escape relatively unscathed if they wrongly assumed that the EU would advance their country's interests during the EU's 2006 mission in the Democratic Republic of the Congo. I include a third dependent variable, support for a European army, as a harder test. Participants responded to the following question: "Some say that we should have a single European Union Army. Others say every country should keep its own national army. What is your opinion?" (Cotta, Isernia and Bellucci, 2009, 15) by choosing a European army only, a national army only, or both.[18]

This item offers a particularly strong indicator of support for lasting transnational security cooperation. Systemic pressures push states to retain sovereign control over decisions related to war and peace (Waltz, 1979). A person who advocates a regional army, especially at the expense of an independent national military apparatus, signals that she expects peaceful, reciprocal dispute resolution in the region. Establishing a joint military indicates a willingness to turn over responsibility for her state's defense— deep integration by the standards of research on security communities (Barnett and Adler, 1998). Although 34.3% of respondents chose to maintain the status quo, where each country would continue to host an independent national army, the remainder endorsed establishing an EU army either to supplement (45.5%) or replace (20.2%) their country's army. Average support varies cross-nationally, of course—only 6.6% of UK respondents support a European army to replace their national defense, for example, compared to 33.7% of their Belgian counterparts.

INDEPENDENT VARIABLES: UNITY AND EQUALITY

Eight survey items probed participant ideas about what it means to be European, and I use these responses to construct scales for unity and equality. My analyses include all of the target items included on the survey instrument, which follow the prompt, "People differ in what they think it means to be European. [For] being European, how important do you think each of the following is?" Participants responded to each characteristic on

---

18. Analysis and following descriptive statistics exclude those who spontaneously refused to answer, didn't know, or preferred no army of any kind.

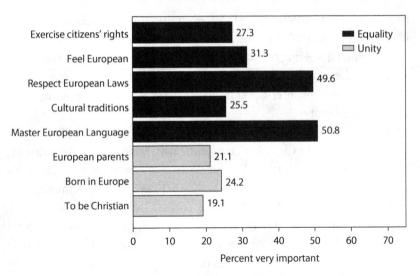

FIGURE 5.1. How important is each of the following for being European?
Note: Figure displays the percent of respondents who rate the criterion "very important," adjusted for population weights and pooled across countries and survey waves. Data exclude respondents who did not answer. I recoded spontaneous "Don't Know" responses to the scale midpoint. Darker bars represent features associated with equality norms, and lighter bars represent unity norms.
Note: The percent of respondents who stated that they don't know ranges from 1.6% for "Master any European Language" to 3.1% for "Exercise citizens' rights."

a 4-point scale from "Not at all important" to "Very important." Figure 5.1 displays the percentage of respondents who rate each dimension "very important" for European identity. Roughly half of European respondents prioritize language skills and respect for European laws and institutions, whereas just 19.1% of respondents think that Europeans must be Christian.

These questions cover a range of norms well-suited to capture the multi-faceted nature of equality- and unity-oriented supranationalisms. To create the independent variables, I deductively classify each target item, guided by concepts from relational models theory (Fiske, 1991, 1992, 2004), before using exploratory factor analysis (EFA) to extract latent factors.

Unity requires individuals to bind together—something makes group members "all the same in some significant respect" (Fiske, 1991, 14) and differentiates insiders from outsiders. Binding material varies, but many communities entail "membership in a natural kind" and the belief that group members share "a common nature, an 'innate' common substance" (Fiske, 1991, 44, 14). The binding material might include blood ties as in extended kin networks or other signals that create a clear binary between "us" and "them" (Fiske, 1991, 46). Moreover, unity-oriented "relationships are idealized as eternal" (Fiske, 1991, 44), such that "continuity is the essence of the Communal Sharing orientation toward time: past, present, and future should be the same" (Fiske, 1991, 71). Europeans who emphasize biological connections or inter-generational ties express their commitment to supranational unity.

Three survey items, represented by the light grey bars in Figure 5.1, proxy unity. "To be a Christian" highlights shared religion as a condition for belonging. For some citizens, Europe's historical connection to "Christendom" separates it from other countries like Turkey and its Muslim-majority population (Risse, 2010), or from EU citizens who practice Judaism or Islam. Respondents who declare that to be European means to be Christian suggest that although citizens may adhere to many faiths, the group's historical commitment to Christianity unites prototypical, "good" Europeans (Mummendey and Wenzel, 1999). Two other items, having European parents and/or being born in Europe, highlight kinship and continuity. Agreeing with either item suggests heritable group membership, with Europeanness passed down from parents to offspring or conferred upon infants at birth. Like nationalisms that emphasize extended kinship (Smith, 1993a), some people insist that blood and soil unite transnational groups.[19]

Reciprocity and fairness constitute equality. Equality implies that members have "equal starting points" (Fiske, 2004, 5) and aim for even balance. Because specific reciprocity maintains the group, individuals must each contribute equally to work that benefits the whole. All members get an equal voice in decisions or elections. And members should help maintain the group: When it comes to participation, "people expect and require it of each other and consider its functions for the social structure" (Fiske, 1992, 704). A good measure of equality should emphasize features that are "achievable" as opposed to "ascriptive," since genetics have no bearing on citizens' ability to contribute to civil society (Wright, 2011).

The dark grey bars in Figure 5.1 plot the five characteristics that correspond to equality-based supranationalisms.[20] The first item asks about

19. Elsewhere, scholars have used similar items to test the relationship between cultural concepts of European identity and anti-immigrant sentiment. Such findings complement my theory. If a citizen believes that Europe requires unity, she will reject the additional cultural or religious heterogeneity created by new arrivals. See, for example, Sides and Citrin (2007) and Risse (2010).

20. Collectively, the equality items are similar to Bruter's (2003; 2009) notion of civic European identities, which tap the idea that citizens may identify with their political system

respecting European laws and institutions. To the extent that the law of the land ought to apply equally across Europeans, laws and institutions provide "equal starting points" as a baseline, consistent with what equality-oriented groups require. The second item asks about the importance of *feeling* European for *being* European, which on its own carries an egalitarian connotation. Some respondents may assert that only some types of people can *truly* feel European. But in principle, everyone has a fair and co-equal opportunity to feel European by embracing the group's social norms.[21] Third, individuals who expect political engagement from their fellow citizens emphasize that group members must contribute their fair share—a sentiment that hearkens to debates about "civic republicanism" in American identities (Schildkraut, 2007). People who avoid political activities choose not to participate as full, equal members. Participants who ascribe importance to this item reinforce equality norms about shared work and decision-making.

The final two items refer to respecting European cultural traditions and mastering any European language. Although each could theoretically tap unity-oriented supranationalism via concerns about historical continuity (Fiske, 1991), the question wording evokes equality. To master *any* European language allows for meaningful heterogeneity—good Europeans can speak Czech or French. It also implies a low cost of entry that embraces equality for different spoken languages. Indeed, when the European Union discusses linguistic competence for migrants, they use the rhetoric of exchange rather than heritage. They strive to create opportunities for new Europeans to develop language skills, and hope that lifelong residents will become proficient in a second language. Linguistic variety facilitates "the free movement of employees/employers" because it breaks down barriers and allows Europeans to compete for jobs across the continent (European Commission, 2012, 21). In short, although scholars often use national language assimilation as a marker for "ethnic" nationalism because it creates a boundary against outsiders (Schildkraut, 2005), speaking any European language is more akin to equality in a supranational context. Finally, individuals who share in European cultural traditions enact the participatory

---

even absent a sense of unity. Per the discussion in chapter 2, my theory of identity content complements this work but provides a psychological foundation for the distinction.

21. In his research on the relationship between nationalism and immigration attitudes, for example, Wright (2011, 839) similarly argues that the importance of feeling like a national implies inclusion because it is "easily 'achievable' the moment an immigrant arrives on new shores," and Bruter (2004) uses this indicator to measure civic Europeanness.

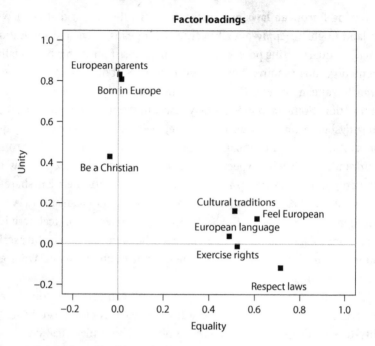

FIGURE 5.2. Unity and equality as latent factors.
Note: Figure displays rotated (oblimin) factor loadings from a principal axis factor analysis.
N = 31,726.

norms that prevail in equality groups. Everyone should be an equal and active citizen.

My theory assumes that unity and equality form distinct, unidimensional constructs—not two ends of a spectrum. To examine whether these items correspond to separate unity and equality scales, I conducted an exploratory factor analysis (EFA). This approach has two advantages. First, it allows me to determine how many latent constructs explain the variance in the data, and how each item contributes to the different constructs (Fabrigar et al., 1999). If Europeanness comprises only a single dimension, EFA should reveal a single-factor solution. Second, this process also allows me to test, not assume, whether the items fit together as my theory describes. EFA offers an empirical test of my theoretically derived concepts.

Figure 5.2 displays the results from a principal axis factor analysis with an oblimin rotation.[22] Higher values indicate a stronger correlation

22. Parallel analysis and inspection of the scree plot suggest that a two-factor solution is appropriate for the data. See Table A.4 in the appendix for estimates from a three-factor solution that places "To be Christian" on a separate, third factor. I suspect that this item might

between the individual item and the underlying factors. The five equality items have significant, positive coefficients for the first factor (equality) and load only weakly on the second factor (unity). The three unity items correlate with the second factor. Fit statistics indicate that this measurement model provides a good fit for the data ($TLI = 0.962, RMSEA = 0.051[0.049, 0.054]$). The two factors moderately correlate with each other ($r = 0.51$), but nevertheless remain distinct. I extract factor scores for each dimension and rescale them to range from 0 to 1 to create independent variables for the subsequent analyses, which I label unity and equality.

I depend on theory and empirics to create scales that cohere with my concepts as closely as possible. Of course, the results from factor analyses depend on interpretation: The researcher must use theory to draw inferences about what each factor represents, and readers might worry that any one of these scale items actually maps onto the opposing construct. Although the current data lack open-ended questions or opportunities to interview participants to probe how they understood the scale components,[23] I conducted a series of supplementary analyses to show that my primary results hold when I drop each item in turn and regress the new factor scores (based on each combination of 7 items) onto the dependent variables, and present these results in the appendix.[24]

CONTESTATION IN THE EUROPEAN PUBLIC

Before I analyze the relationship between unity, equality, and European cooperation, Figure 5.3 presents a snapshot of supranationalist contestation in the mass public. Each panel displays the distribution of factor scores for equality (dark grey) and unity (light grey) for each country in the sample. Dashed and dotted lines mark the country level means for equality and unity, respectively, to illustrate the size of the gap. Larger gaps suggest less contestation at the country level, insofar as they suggest that members of the public have converged on stronger support for one set of norms over the other. French respondents show remarkable

---

tap individual-level religiosity in addition to European identity content, and although the fit marginally improves with a three-factor solution, I retain the theoretically motivated two-factor solution for analysis. Supplementary analyses showed that my results remain robust if I use the first two factors from the three-factor solution to represent unity and equality.

23. Though see Bruter (2003) for research on European identities that relies on focus group discussions rather than deduction.

24. See Figure A.3.

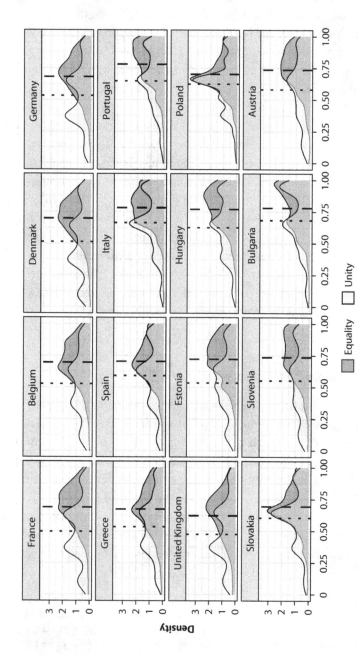

FIGURE 5.3. Contestation in the mass public.

Note: Figure displays kernel density estimates for the distribution of equality and unity in the mass public, by country (adjusted for population weights, pooled across survey years). The x-axis represents factor scores, which have been rescaled to range from 0 to 1 for both dimensions. Dashed and dotted vertical lines represent the means for equality and unity, respectively.

consensus around equality at the expense of unity, for example, whereas both supranationalisms maintain broad support in Poland.[25]

The plots reveal two interesting patterns. First, citizens in the mass public contest European nationalisms. Although respondents endorsed equality at higher rates than unity in every country—perhaps due to social desirability pressures that push respondents to emphasize equality—unity clearly captures the way that many European citizens perceive supranationalist commitments. Second, the results counter simplistic notions that unity dominates the East or that Western Europeans exclusively commit to equality. Indeed, the plots show that substantial portions of the populations in the four "original 6" EU countries in the sample (Belgium, France, Italy, and Germany) embrace European unity, and depict right-skewed equality distributions in newer member-states like Poland, Hungary, and Estonia. Together, these patterns illustrate the value in examining supranationalisms at the individual level—aggregating content to entire countries or regions glosses over important variation.

CONTROL VARIABLES

My analyses include several additional independent variables that I expect to explain some of the variation in the dependent variables. First, I control for the respondent's sex (coded 1 for male) and age (6 categories for age cohort). I expect younger people to trust their fellow Europeans more and express greater support for regional security integration, having spent more of their lives under the EU umbrella. Previous research finds more "Euroskeptics" among older Europeans—who, for example, oppose bailout packages for European states in fiscal crises at greater rates (Hakhverdian et al., 2013; Kuhn and Stoeckel, 2014)—and that younger people adopt supranational identities at higher rates (Jung, 2008). Second, I control for ideology with an item that asks participants where they fall on a left-right ideological spectrum (rescaled from 0 to 1, higher values indicate more right-wing). Left-wing ideologies correlate with greater cosmopolitanism (Bayram, 2015), which in turn likely relates to my dependent variables, and many right-wing citizens oppose additional government regulation layers (Hooghe, Marks and Wilson, 2002; Brinegar and Jolly, 2005). Yet greater reticence about using force on the left—and support for defense spending

---

25. The difference in average support for equality minus unity in France is 0.19, compared to 0.08 in Poland.

on the right—could counteract these preferences. For example, left-wing Europeans often oppose establishing a European army (Hofmann, 2013; De Vries, 2020).[26] Third, I control for university education because less educated Europeans are more skeptical of EU membership (Hakhverdian et al., 2013), and likely to oppose specific cooperative policies like the CFSP.[27]

Fourth, I include a measure of travel within Europe. The contact hypothesis predicts that interacting with Europeans in other countries fosters supranationalism, trust, and support for cooperation (Hewstone and Brown, 1986). Stoeckel (2016) finds that social interaction through study abroad programs fosters collective identity in Europe, for example. Respondents reported how many times they had visited another EU country within the past year, from 0 to "5 or more" (median=0; 57% of respondents had not visited another EU country in the past year).[28]

26. Controlling for ideology introduces two potential concerns related to cross-national variation and posttreatment bias. First, variation in the meaning of left and right ideologies across parts of Europe makes this control variable difficult to interpret (Aspelund, Lindeman and Verkasalo, 2013). Second, if commitments to unity and equality theoretically cause individual left-right ideology, controlling for ideology could induce a type of posttreatment bias that has unpredictable effects on regression estimates (King and Zeng, 2007), and changes the quantity of interest from the average effect of unity and equality to the direct effects "net the posttreatment variable" (Montgomery, Nyhan and Torres, 2018, 514). One possible remedy for both issues entails simply removing ideology from the models. Although doing so mitigates concerns about posttreatment bias, it re-introduces the omitted variable bias that control variables ideally address (King and Zeng, 2007, 148). From a theoretical standpoint, the question of whether supranationalisms cause ideology, or vice versa, remains unsettled—and engages the broader question of what causes nationalisms in the first place. In chapters 2 and 6, I explain how various traits that we associate with ideology, such as moral and personal values, likely play a role in which norms individuals commit to even though nationalisms cannot be reduced to ideology. Indeed, ideology appears to be a stable disposition that precedes even core moral values in the causal chain (Hatemi, Crabtree and Smith, 2019). If that theoretical model holds, ideology constitutes a "pre-treatment" variable and we can include it on the right-hand side of the regression. Of course, I cannot test these assumptions with cross-sectional data. Notably, removing ideology from the models has no effect on the substantive or statistical significance of the estimated coefficients for unity and equality, thereby mitigating concerns that ideology inflates the importance of equality and unity for my dependent variables. See the online appendix for results.

27. I would expect a similar pattern with regard to higher income; however, the survey instrument did not collect income data from participants and I therefore could not include it.

28. Like ideology, if supranationalisms cause EU travel, including it in the regression models would introduce posttreatment bias that could affect the estimated coefficients on unity and equality. Given the dynamic relationship between contact and supranational identities revealed in previous work—whereby identification predicts who travels more *and* contact from travel affects identification—theoretical concerns about omitted variable bias lead me to include this

Fifth, I account for individuals' trusting dispositions using a measure for generalized trust. Respondents indicated on a scale from 0 to 10 whether, generally speaking, they think that most people can be trusted (rescaled from 0 to 1 for analysis). Higher generalized trust should correlate with trust toward Europeans and support for cooperation, consistent with evidence that trusting individuals support international institutions that limit their country's autonomy (Rathbun 2011a; 2011b; 2012). Sixth, each model includes country fixed effects to account for stable cross-national differences, and a dummy variable for survey year to account for general time trends. For example, the survey year dummies would capture a uniform decline in intra-European trust between 2007 and 2009. Seventh, I control for national attachment with an item that asks participants to report the extent to which they feel attached to their country on a 4-point scale. National identification does not preclude European identification, but previous research finds that national attachment predicts lower support for EU membership (Carey, 2002).[29]

Finally, my theory posits an important role for European commitment— those who most strongly commit to a group and embrace its moral superiority conform to the group's norms—but the survey structure merges commitment and content. Those most committed to their equality-based European identity will be more likely to list those criteria as "very important" to being European. A positive coefficient on equality in the models would therefore indicate that people most strongly committed to equality norms support cooperation.

At the same time, I must address the possibility that a standard measure for European commitment might account for any observed relationships between unity, equality, and support for European cooperation to demonstrate my theory's added explanatory value beyond the standard story. Scholars often address concerns like this by including an additional control variable in the analysis. In this case, one item asks participants to report

---

control variable. Nevertheless, I also estimate the primary models without European travel and show that removing this variable has no effect on the statistical or substantive significance for unity and equality.

29. Immigration status could also play an important role in explaining intra-European trust and support for cooperation, but the surveys almost exclusively sampled native born Europeans. Across the two waves, 97.1% of respondents reported that they were born in the country that they currently live in, another EU member-state, or another European country. Although future research should investigate how immigrants conceptualize their European identity—and its implications for security cooperation—these data lack sufficient numbers to draw meaningful inferences about immigrant supranationalisms.

the extent to which they identify with Europe by reporting how much being European has to do with how they feel about themselves (4-point scale from "not at all" to "a great deal") (Huddy and Khatib, 2007). I include this variable in the analyses to account for variance from commitment independent of content, but also to estimate whether identification interacts with unity or equality. At the same time, this approach poses inferential challenges if a person's reported distance from her supranational identity is in part a *consequence* of her belief about what constitutes being European. The measure of identification would then be "post-treatment," and estimating the effects of content while including a separate control for European attachment could bias the results (King and Zeng, 2007). I nevertheless include these analyses for interested readers, and to forestall concerns that my findings can be explained by commitment alone.

Results: Who Wants to Cooperate with Their Fellow Europeans?

To test my hypotheses regarding supranationalisms and support for European cooperation, I first analyze the relationship between unity, equality, and (1) intra-European trust and (2) support for a common foreign and security policy. Figures 5.4 and 5.5 present results from OLS models. The triangles display estimates from models that regress the dependent variables on only equality and unity, whereas circles display estimates from models that include a panel of controls. I rescaled the variables to range from 0 to 1. All models include country and survey wave fixed effects— France and the 2007 wave are the reference categories—and cluster standard errors by country.

The results provide clear and consistent support for my intragroup cooperation hypotheses. Turning first to the models without control variables, those who hold equality-based conceptions of European identity report greater trust in other Europeans ($b = 0.314$, $p < 0.01$) and more strongly favor formal foreign policy cooperation ($b = 0.451$, $p < 0.01$). Unity-oriented supranationalists, by contrast, report less trust in fellow Europeans ($b = -0.110$, $p < 0.01$), and a weaker inclination to support a common EU foreign policy ($b = -0.118$, $p < 0.01$).

The associations between equality, unity and both intra-European trust and support for the CFSP are statistically significant and substantively meaningful when I include the panel of controls. A two standard deviation (SD) increase in equality corresponds to an 8.3 percentage point increase in European trust, whereas the analogous two-SD increase in

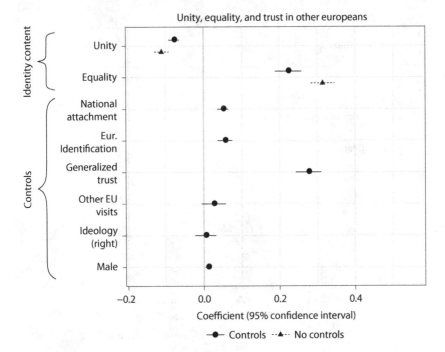

FIGURE 5.4. Equality increases intra-European trust.
Note: Points display OLS coefficient estimates from models with (circles) and without (triangles) additional control variables, with 95% confidence intervals (standard errors clustered by country). The dependent variable and continuous independent variables have been rescaled from 0 to 1. All models incorporate population weights, control for university education, and include survey wave and country fixed effects (France is the reference category), omitted for presentation.

unity produces a 3.9 percentage point *decrease* in the intragroup trust that underlies cooperation.

To put those values in perspective, a two standard deviation (SD) change in equality corresponds to more than twice the 3.7 percentage point increase associated with a two-SD shift in European identification, and more than half the 14.3 percentage point increase predicted by a two-SD increase in generalized trust. The comparison to generalized trust confirms that equality has a powerful substantive effect. Dispositional trust should play a dominant role in driving particularized intragroup trust—we should not be surprised to learn that people who trust other people in general also trust fellow Europeans.

Similarly, higher scores on equality generate greater support for a common European foreign policy. A two-SD change in equality increases CFSP support by 14.3 percentage points—nearly five times the effect of a two-SD

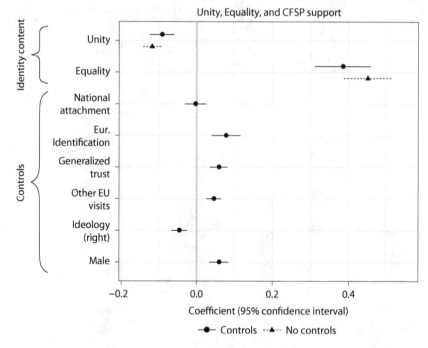

FIGURE 5.5. Equality increases support for foreign policy cooperation.
Note: Points display OLS coefficient estimates from models with (circles) and without (triangles) additional control variables, with 95% confidence intervals (standard errors clustered by country). The dependent variable and continuous independent variables have been rescaled from 0 to 1. All models incorporate population weights, control for university education, and include survey wave and country fixed effects (France is the reference category), omitted for presentation.

increase in generalized trust. Moving from the minimum to maximum on equality corresponds to nearly two rungs on the 5-point scale measuring support for a common security policy ($b = 0.384$, $p < 0.01$)—enough to shift a participant from being "somewhat against" the CFSP to "somewhat in favour." Unity, by contrast, decreases trust ($b = -0.078$, $p < 0.01$) and support for a common European foreign policy ($b = -0.093$, $p < 0.01$), even after the models account for potential confounders. These substantively smaller effects—a two-SD increase in unity decreases trust and CFSP support by 3.9 and 4.7 percentage points, respectively—nevertheless support my intragroup cooperation hypothesis. Unity-oriented supranationalists trust fellow group members less, and resist ceding foreign policy control to a supranational authority. Content shapes mass public attitudes about cooperation.

I include control variables for identification with Europe to show that commitments to equality and unity drive support for European cooperation—or opposition to it—even accounting for the degree to which respondents value their European identity. Concerns about posttreatment bias outlined in the preceding section make this analysis problematic, but the consistency across models increases my confidence in the role played by content. Omitted variables that correlate with both content and the dependent variables do not appear to drive unity's and equality's effects, nor does a content-free measure for supranationalism.

Coefficients on control variables largely comport with findings from past work. The positive coefficient on visits to other EU countries suggests that travel and contact correlate with support for foreign policy cooperation ($b = 0.045$, $p < 0.01$), though the coefficient remains small and nonsignificant for trust. Younger participants trust Europeans more compared to the oldest group, but age has little bearing on support for the CFSP. Men report marginally greater trust ($b = 0.011$, $p < 0.01$) and favor a common foreign policy more than women ($b = 0.059$, $p < 0.01$). Right-wing ideology decreases support for the common foreign and security policy ($b = -0.046$, $p < 0.01$), though I find no statistically significant association between right/left-wing ideology and trust. American politics research suggests that right-wing ideologies correspond to lower social trust because conservatives view their environment as more threatening (Feldman and Stenner, 1997). The somewhat surprising null coefficient in these European data, however, could stem from two sources. First, the generalized trust measure likely captures ideological variation in trust. Second, cross-national variation in how people perceive the ideological spectrum suggests caution in interpreting the average effect of ideology in a cross-national sample (Aspelund, Lindeman and Verkasalo, 2013; DeBell and Morgan, 2015)— researchers interested in ideology should adopt a multi-level modeling approach to capture country-level variation in the slope.

The effects of unity and equality do not depend on content-free identification

The scales for equality and unity account for commitment and content together. A higher score on equality implies a stronger commitment to that version of a respondent's European identity, for example, compared to a respondent who views equality as unimportant for supranationalism. Yet another approach to modeling commitment entails following the model from chapters 3 and 4 to test the interaction between content and how strongly participants identify as Europeans.

On one hand, the continuous independent variables already account for commitment, such that an interactive analysis may be moot. Indeed, respondents always bring ideas about content to bear on ambiguous questions about identification—self-categorization theory tells us that people compare themselves to the prototypical group member to calibrate their identification (Turner, 1985). In that respect, measures for "European identification" depend on unobserved ideas about the content of that identity.[30]

But on the other hand, modeling an interaction helps rule out the possibility that weak identifiers drive my findings. Perhaps content has a null effect among strong European identifiers, such that content becomes irrelevant with supranational commitment. Such a finding could cast doubt on my claim that content drives mass attitudes about security cooperation, and instead provide additional fodder for the standard story. If I instead find that equality and unity have stable or increasing effects on trust and CFSP support as abstract European identification increases, it would bolster this book's claim that content provides an essential ingredient for understanding attitudes about security cooperation.

I estimate the marginal effect of unity and equality on trust and CFSP support across levels of European identification to rule out the possibility that identification accounts for my results. I again use the kernel estimation procedure to create a smoothed estimate for the marginal effect of unity and equality across European identification (Hainmueller, Mummolo and Xu, 2019).[31]

Panels (a)–(d) in Figure 5.6 display the results, revealing two important findings. First, marginal effects for unity and equality remain consistently negative or positive across values for identification. Neither the estimated effects nor confidence intervals ever cross zero. Second, the results provide little evidence to suggest that content-free European identification independently explains the effects of unity and equality. Panels (a) and (c) show that equality has a relatively constant positive effect, and panel (d) shows a similar pattern for the effect of unity on CFSP support. Panel (b)

---

30. Though, notably, I use the degree to which participants report that they "identify with" Europe precisely because it mitigates this concern to some degree. See, for example, Huddy and Khatib's (2007) analysis of identification compared to attachment in the U.S.

31. None of the linear interaction coefficients reach statistical significance—see the online appendix—but I use the kernel estimator to account for possible nonlinear effects.

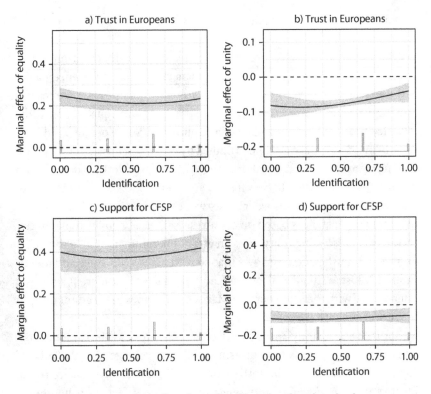

FIGURE 5.6. Unity's and equality's effects do not depend on identification in the abstract. *Note:* Lines display the estimated marginal effect of the independent variable on (a)–(b) intra-European trust and (c)–(d) support for the CFSP, across values of European identification. Models control for the full set of covariates specified above, incorporate population weights, and include robust standard errors clustered by country. Bands depict 95% bootstrapped confidence intervals, and the histograms display the distribution for the moderator.

displays the one exception, where the negative marginal effect of unity appears slightly weaker among the strongest identifiers. To summarize, the results from a series of interaction tests support my expectation that content underlies European trust and cooperation.

Equality does not constrain unity

Throughout this book, I treat unity and equality as distinct concepts—two separable nationalisms. The experiments in chapters 3 and 4 used manipulations that targeted one set of norms, dividing people into two groups. My survey analyses include separate scales for unity and equality to capture their distinct effects. These strategies serve my theory-building goals, because demonstrating the importance of accounting for content requires evidence that unity and equality have distinct effects on foreign policy attitudes.

Moreover, my theory contends that unity and equality constitute separate, unipolar dimensions. As the survey data in chapter 4 showed, equality and unity do not form opposite ends of a continuum—many American undergraduates reported believing that *both* unity and equality constitute American nationalism. One plausible implication: Some people hold both ideas in mind—they see Europe as unified by common ancestry and by their commitment to fair and equal exchange. Indeed, the IntUne data show a positive 0.51 correlation between unity and equality. "Mixed" supranationalists either implicitly rank order these two sets of norms or activate them in different circumstances based on contextual salience or environmental factors, perhaps stressing unity after an attack on continental neighbors, for example. Robust evidence shows that context affects identities and identification,[32] just as situational factors lead people to apply different scripts to interactions with the same person: Married colleagues likely adopt unity at home and equality at work.[33]

Yet measuring unity and equality on a survey poses three unique challenges that may lead us to over-estimate the percentage of truly "mixed" supranationalists. First, the IntUne surveys deploy "ratings" scales to tap identity content. Respondents separately rate each factor on its importance for being European, dodging any difficult trade-offs (Wright, Citrin and Wand, 2012). As a result, many respondents report equally strong commitments to *both* unity and equality. Second, people use different reference points when rating importance—one person's "very important" may be another's "somewhat important," which introduces potential measurement error.

Third, the ratings approach may induce biases if unity-oriented Europeans report their commitment to equality because the scale items echo EU rhetoric. EU documents and institutions describe liberal democracy

---

32. For reviews, see Hornsey (2008) and Huddy (2001).

33. Methodologically, the separate regression coefficients estimate the direct effect of each variable on the outcome measures net other factors in the model—holding all else constant, including scores on the other identity content variable. Although the OLS estimates remain unbiased, including correlated independent variables in a regression model can risk problematic multicollinearity that produces unstable coefficient estimates and inflates standard errors. Though the large sample size mitigates these concerns, I calculate the variance inflation factors (VIF) for each model. VIF scores measure the degree to which multicollinearity inflates the variance for each coefficient. All VIFs fall well below widely accepted thresholds for concern (all <2; VIFs of 5 or greater merit further examination).

as a core tenet of Europeanness, stressing equality. People committed to unity alone—who reject equality as a foundation for European supranationalism—might nevertheless rate equality norms "important" because disagreement reflects undesirable or bad behavior even on an anonymous survey. If so, the data capture superficial commitments to equality for many "mixed" supranationalists.

I tackle this suite of considerations about the independent scales for unity and equality in two ways. First, I examine the interaction between unity and equality. Do people who strongly commit to both unity and equality exhibit more support for cooperation compared to those who commit to equality or unity alone? Put differently, can equality-based identification ameliorate unity's cooperation-threatening properties? Because more Europeans adhere to equality than unity, testing the interaction can tell us whether efforts to "[strengthen] a European sense of belonging" (Prutsch, 2017, 1) might meet policymakers' goals *in spite of* the many Europeans who also value homogeneity. On average, unity makes citizens wary about entrusting their nation's security to neighbors. But perhaps a dual commitment to equality increases their tolerance for cooperation. Conversely, if unity-oriented supranationalism weakens equality's positive effects on attitudes toward cooperation, it would suggest that unity and diversity work at cross-purposes. Second, I adopt an alternative measurement strategy that turns ratings scales into implicit relative rankings to better capture which norms matter the most to respondents (Wright, Citrin and Wand, 2012).

To test the proposition that unity constrains the effect of equality (or that equality weakens the negative effect of unity), I estimate the marginal effects of each content variable on trust and CFSP support across levels of the other. Panels (a) and (c) in Figure 5.7 display the marginal effect of unity at different values of equality. The results provide unambiguous evidence that unity's negative effect persists even as people strongly endorse equality. Panels (b) and (d) show that the marginal effect of equality remains positive across values of unity, with an important caveat: the marginal effect of equality slightly decreases when people also commit to European unity. Unity appears to usurp equality when people embrace both.

Why might equality's marginal effect decrease at higher levels of unity, but not the converse? I propose two complementary possibilities. First, unity's emphasis on protecting the group from danger might provide a stronger motivation when unity and equality clash. Imagine someone who believes that Europeans should commit to equality in principle, but also believes that some rogue Europeans threaten the group from inside. Even

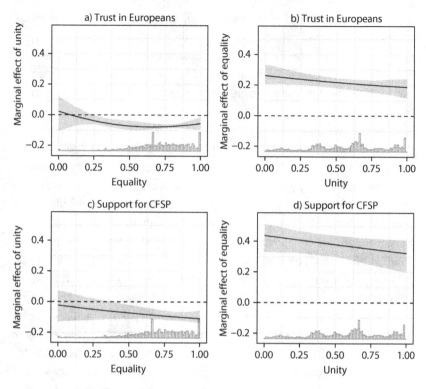

FIGURE 5.7. Interaction between unity and equality.
Note: Lines display the estimated marginal effect of the independent variable on (a)–(b) intra-European trust and (c)–(d) support for the CFSP, across values of the moderators. Models control for the full set of covariates specified above, incorporate population weights, and include robust standard errors clustered by country. Bands depict 95% bootstrapped confidence intervals, and the histograms display the distribution of the moderator.

if that person stipulates that a coordinated EU foreign policy could bring benefits, those benefits may not outweigh the potential costs to national security from allowing "bad Europeans" to coordinate and influence foreign policy. They might prefer to play it safe by leaving security issues to their national government.

Second, these findings are consistent with the possibility that social desirability inflates reported commitments to equality. If strong commitments to unity better represent respondents' true beliefs even when they also express regard for equality, it would explain the fact that unity moderates the effect of equality on CFSP support.

I further explore this possibility in my second approach to assessing "mixed" supranationalists: I use the raw importance ratings to generate information about respondents' relative *rankings* for unity and equality.

I classify respondents based on whether they consistently rate unity or equality more important relative to their own personal reference point, using a procedure adapted from Wright, Citrin and Wand's (2012) research on American national identities. For example, a respondent who rates each equality item as "somewhat important" and each unity item "somewhat unimportant" expresses a consistent preference for equality relative to unity. Of course, with 5 items that constitute the equality scale and 3 for unity, the combinations quickly become unwieldy: A "pure" equality-oriented supranationalist would have to satisfy 15 conditions whereby they rate each of the 5 equality items higher than each of the 3 unity items. To make the classification scheme tractable, I focus on two items that correlate most strongly with each respective factor—feeling European and following European laws and institutions for equality, and being born in Europe and having European parents for unity.

I generated a dummy variable for equality that I coded 1 for anyone who rated each equality item more important than each unity item. This procedure classified 24.6% of respondents as equality-oriented supranationalists. Next, I classified unity-oriented and mixed respondents using two different specifications. I first mirrored the approach I used to code equality and classified participants as unity-oriented if they rated both unity items as more important than both equality items. Only 3.5% of respondents qualify as unequivocally unity-oriented supranationalists by this strict definition, and the remaining 71.9% comprise a mixed category. To better account for the possibility that social desirability inflates participant ratings of equality items to the scale's ceiling, an alternate coding scheme includes people who rated the unity items as greater than *or tied with* the equality items. In this version, the unity group comprises 38.4% of respondents and the mixed category contains the remaining 36.9% of respondents.[34]

I then regress the two outcomes—support for the CFSP and intra-European trust—on these indicators for equality and unity (rather than the factor scores) and the panel of control variables. Figure 5.8 displays the predicated value on each dependent variable for the three resulting respondent groups, based on estimates from the OLS models.

The results reveal three important findings. First, I again find that equality-oriented supranationalists report more support for the CFSP and

---

34. The choice to include ties for unity follows Wright, Citrin and Wand (2012), who argued that capturing the relative importance of what they call "ascriptive" dimensions of American identity required additional adjustments for social desirability concerns. Percentages adjust for population weights.

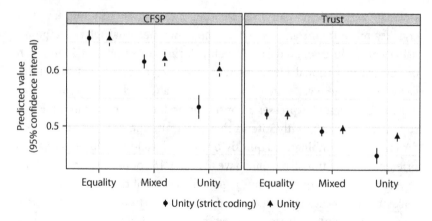

FIGURE 5.8. Relative rankings and support for cooperation.
Note: Points display the predicted value for CFSP support and European trust from OLS models that include dummy variables for each class of supranationalists and the panel of controls, robust standard errors clustered by country. Continuous control variables indexed at their means, and dichotomous control variables indexed at median values. Country set to France and survey year 2009. Circles represent values from models that use a strict cutoff for unity-oriented supranationalists (n=904) whereas triangles represent estimates from models that include ties for unity to capture a wider range of respondents (n=12,152).

greater intra-European trust compared to their unity-oriented counter-parts. Second, the strictest coding for unity-oriented supranationalists—those who consistently rank homogenizing European ancestry *above* equality—yields the lowest predicted values on both outcome variables. Unity undermines support for regional cooperation. Third, predicted values for "mixed" respondents—who do not consistently rank equality or unity above the other—fall between unity and equality. I would expect this pattern if the ratings scales and social desirability mean that the mixed group contains many masked unity-oriented supranationalists.[35]

UNITY, EQUALITY, AND SUPPORT FOR A EUROPEAN ARMY

Results from the preceding sections support my argument that unity-oriented supranationalism diminishes intragroup trust and decreases

---

35. In their study of national identity content and immigration attitudes in the U.S., Wright, Citrin and Wand (2012) similarly conclude that people who appear to have unstructured views of identity content are actually "quasi-ascriptives" in disguise. I suspect that the category entails more heterogeneity than such a description implies, but also that the ratings procedure inflates the number of people who truly endorse both equality and unity supranationalism.

support for a common foreign and security policy—two essential components of security cooperation—whereas equality produces the opposite effects. Unity creates Euroskeptics. But security cooperation takes many forms—from contingent, ad hoc agreements to tightly integrated security communities (Koremenos, Lipson and Snidal, 2001; Cronin, 1999). Shifting even partial military control to a supranational authority reflects an especially strong form of what Ruggie (1992) calls "qualitative multilateralism": If states dismantle their national militaries to create a European force, they signal their commitment to peaceful intragroup dispute resolution and long-term trust that any threats will come from outside the continent (Barnett and Adler, 1998). This section tests my intragroup cooperation hypothesis with respect to supranational military integration by asking how unity and equality shape support for a European army.

To analyze the relationship between unity, equality, and support for a European army, I estimate a multinomial logit model that predicts whether respondents support maintaining separate national armies, replacing national armies with a European army, or adding a European army to supplement national forces. I use multinomial logistic regression because the response options are not ordered along a single dimension.

To summarize, the results support my second intragroup cooperation hypothesis. Unity-oriented supranational commitments correspond to decreases in the odds that an individual prefers a European army alone, or both European and national armies, relative to maintaining the military status quo. Equality-based identities, by contrast, correspond with an increase in the likelihood that participants prefer some degree of explicit supranational military integration. Ready to give up some degree of national autonomy when it comes to decisions about war and peace, equality-oriented European nationalists support a European army. I present the substantive effects here, and include complete regression results in the online appendix.

Figure 5.9 plots changes in the predicted probability that a participant chooses each of the three categorical outcomes as equality (panel a) or unity (panel b) moves from the minimum to the maximum. To estimate these predicted probabilities,[36] I set index values for other variables in the model at appropriate values: the median or mode on each control variable, and the 5th percentile value on the alternative content variable.

The plots illustrate a substantively and statistically significant association between supranational identity content and support for European

---

36. See the appendix for coefficient estimates.

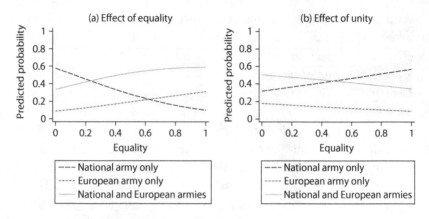

FIGURE 5.9. Predicted probability of support for European army.
Note: Lines show predicted probabilities generated from a multinomial logit model, and shaded areas display 95% confidence intervals. I use median values to index European identification, generalized trust, other EU visits, and ideology, and modal values for gender (male), age (65 and over), and university (no degree). Country is set to France, and survey year to 2009. I set identity content variables to their 5th percentile values when fixed—unity at 0.11 in panel (a) and equality at 0.38 in panel (b).

security integration. The lines in panel (a) show that moving from the minimum to the maximum on equality leads to a substantial decrease in the predicted probability that respondents prefer national armies only— from a 57.7% to 9.9% chance. Equality instead increases the chance that a respondent supports dismantling national militaries in favor of a single EU army from 8.7% among weak equality-oriented supranationalists to 31.1% for strong equality-oriented supranationalists. Years before leaders like Macron and Merkel gave a unified military prime billing on the European agenda, equality-based supranationalists were ready to transfer their security to a transnational authority.

By contrast, panel (b) shows that support for European military integration drops precipitously with unity-oriented supranationalism. Moving from the minimum to the maximum on unity corresponds to a large increase in the chance that an individual prefers to keep their national army in lieu of any unified EU force—from 31.8% to 56.7%. At the same time, the predicted probability that a participant chooses a joint European force declines, whether that European army would replace or supplement national armies. Support for a single European army to replace national militaries decreases from 17.8% at the minimum to 8.9% at the maximum score on unity. In a heterogeneous transnational region, unity imposes barriers to costly security cooperation.

The IntUne Elite Surveys

Equality and unity have countervailing effects on foreign policy cooperation among members of the European public, but do these relationships hold among the elites better poised to influence EU security policy? Members of the public serve as an important population for understanding European identity content and the micro-foundations of supranational cooperation. Maintaining a security community requires buy-in from democratic governments accountable to their constituents, and supranationalisms should percolate to the masses even if they emerge among technocrats or political elites (Deutsch, 1961). Yet elites play a direct role in deciding whether to implement specific foreign and security policies, and this section analyzes evidence from elite surveys collected concurrent with the public surveys. Finding support for my intragroup hypotheses in an elite sample would further suggest that my theory has implications for real foreign policy outcomes.

The IntUne project collected responses from a diverse sample of 4,238 European elites. In 2007, the elite sample included 1,901 respondents across 17 EU member-states; 1,972 elites from 16 EU member-states comprise the 2009 sample.[37] For the purpose of the study and sampling procedure, "elites were defined as 'groups of people who are able to personally have a significant influence on nation-wide reproduction processes'" (Lengyel and Jahr, 2012, 242). This definition included members of parliament who ranged in age, party affiliation, and status as senior "frontbenchers," like former ministers, or "backbenchers" lower in the party's hierarchy. These political elites account for 62% of the respondents included in my analyses. The remaining 38% include a mix of business leaders, members of the media, trade union leaders, and bureaucrats.[38] The latter group may not participate in high-level policy debates, but they serve as opinion leaders with agenda-setting powers (Koenig-Archibugi, 2004).

37. The 2007 wave included respondents from Austria, Belgium, Bulgaria, Denmark, Estonia, France, Germany, Greece, Hungary, Italy, Poland, Portugal, Slovakia, Spain, United Kingdom, Czech Republic, and Lithuania. The 2009 wave excluded Estonia. I removed respondents located in non-EU member-states for analysis—240 Serbian and 125 Turkish elites in 2007 and 2009, respectively.

38. See Lengyel and Jahr's (2012) survey methodology appendix in Best, Lengyel and Verzichelli's 2012 edited volume *The Europe of Elites* for details on the sampling procedure, fieldwork, and descriptive statistics.

DEPENDENT VARIABLES

The elite questionnaires closely matched the mass public versions, but they excluded questions about trust—such as the intra-European trust item I used as a dependent variable in the public surveys. I cannot evaluate the first prong of my intragroup cooperation hypothesis in the elite sample, because the respondents did not report whether they trust fellow Europeans.

The elite questionnaire did include identical questions to gauge support for the CFSP and a European army. I therefore turn my attention to the second prong of my intragroup cooperation hypothesis. These two dependent variables exactly match their mass survey counterparts: Participants reported on a 5-point scale whether they support a single EU foreign policy (rescaled from 0 to 1) and whether they would support a single European army to supplement or complement national armies.

UNITY AND EQUALITY IN EUROPEAN ELITES

I use seven items that probe the constitutive norms that underlie what it means to be European to measure unity and equality. As in the mass surveys, participants individually rated seven characteristics as unimportant or important for being European on a 4-point scale.[39] The items matched those that the public received, with one exception: The surveys did not ask elites whether or not exercising citizens' rights was important. I start with all 7 items that appeared on both waves of the elite surveys.[40]

Figure 5.10 displays the percentage of respondents who report that each dimension is very important to being European. European elites stress unity less frequently than members of the public; very few rate Christianity, birth, or parentage very important. Large majorities instead emphasize feeling European, respecting European laws, and mastering a European language. This suggests that on average, equality-based identities predominate among policymakers moreso than in their citizenries.

39. I recoded "Don't Know" responses to the scale midpoint.

40. In 2009, the questionnaire also included an eighth and ninth item that asked respondents to evaluate 1) whether they believed that it was important to participate in the European Parliament elections, and 2) to *benefit* citizens' rights by being active in EU policy. To create comparable scales to use in a pooled analysis, I only incorporate items common to both waves. Supplementary analyses that included only wave 2 data and use all 9 items revealed no substantive differences.

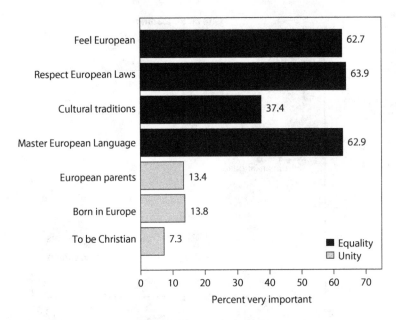

FIGURE 5.10. How important is each of the following for being European?
Note: Figure displays the percent of respondents who rate the criterion "very important" on a four-point scale, pooling across countries and survey waves. Data exclude respondents who did not answer, and I recoded spontaneous "Don't Know" to the scale midpoint.

To generate scales for equality and unity, I conducted an exploratory factor analysis using principal axis factoring and an oblique (oblimin) rotation. With all seven content items in the model, the parallel analysis suggested that a 3-factor solution best fit the data. The estimated solution placed "cultural traditions" on its own factor.[41] Although fit statistics suggest that the 3-factor solution fits the data well,[42] latent factors with a single strongly loading item produce unstable results (Fabrigar et al., 1999). I follow Osborne and Costello's (2009, 3) advice to drop "freestanding" items and remove the cultural traditions item to create a clean, interpretable, and good-fitting model of elite identity content.[43]

41. The cultural traditions factor moderately correlates with both unity and equality (correlation between culture dimension and unity $r = 0.35$; with equality $r = 0.44$).

42. $RMSEA = 0.01(0, 0.031)$, $TLI = 0.998$.

43. A two-factor solution using all 7 items provides a reasonable, parsimonious, and interpretable fit for the data with items that load on the factors expected by the theory and mass-level analyses (on the importance of interpretability as a criterion, see Osborne and Costello, 2009). Yet fit statistics do not reach conventional levels of acceptability: The RMSEA value of 0.073

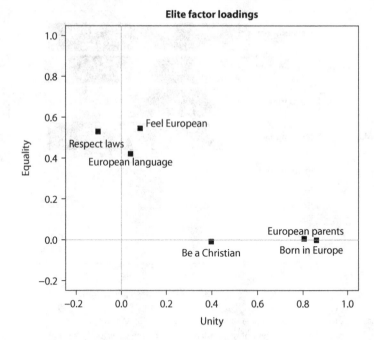

FIGURE 5.11. Unity and equality among European elites.
Note: Figure displays rotated (oblimin) factor loadings from a principal axis factor analysis. N=3, 873. Fit statistics: $RMSEA = 0.009$; $TLI = 0.999$; $BIC = -27.73$. Correlation between the two factors is 0.23.

Figure 5.11 displays the results of this analysis, which produces a factor structure similar to what I observed among members of the public. Three items correlate with the equality factor (respect laws, European language, and feel European) while three items correlate with the unity factor (be a Christian, born in Europe, European parents).

I derived factor scores from the EFA model depicted in Figure 5.11 to create scales for unity and equality and rescaled them to range from 0 to 1. Figure 5.12 plots the distributions of commitment to unity (light grey) and equality (dark grey) among European elites by country.

The plots suggest that European elites exhibit less contestation over European supranationalisms compared to the mass public. Like the public samples, European elites commit more strongly to equality on average ($mean = 0.82$, $sd = 0.15$) than to unity norms like European ancestry

---

(0.064, 0.082) exceeds the suggested 0.05 bound, and the TLI value of 0.908 falls below the recommended lower bound of 0.95 (Fabrigar et al., 1999). Importantly, the substantive results remain the same if I use factor scores extracted from this model.

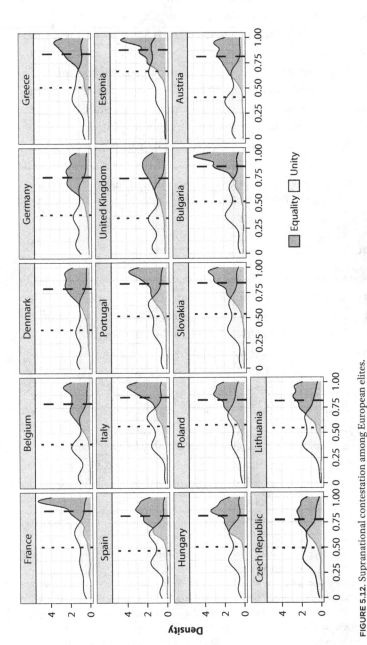

FIGURE 5.12. Supranational contestation among European elites.

Note: Figure displays kernel density estimates for the distributions of equality and unity among European elites by country (pooled across survey years). The x-axis represents factor scores rescaled to range from 0 to 1. Dashed and dotted vertical lines depict the means for equality and unity, respectively.

($mean = 0.49$, $sd = 0.25$). But the elite participants display remarkable consensus. Large gaps between mean commitment to equality and unity in each country suggest that most European elites agree that supranational superiority rests on equality, not unity. Figure 5.11 shows that this sizable gap varies in magnitude, from 0.41 in Denmark to only 0.21 in Estonia, but even the smallest differences between the distributions outstrip those I observed in the public data. These data suggest that the elite sample contains relatively few strong unity-oriented supranationalists or weak equality-oriented supranationalists—perhaps due to demographic differences between elites and masses (Kertzer, 2020). This pattern could have implications for the subsequent data analysis if the skewed distributions limit effect sizes, though the sample contains enough variation to proceed in testing my intragroup cooperation hypothesis.

CONTROL VARIABLES

I again control for other variables that might be correlated with unity or equality and affect support for European security cooperation. First, all models include country and survey year fixed effects to account for stable spatial and temporal trends. For example, consistent with Koenig-Archibugi's (2004) analysis showing that the UK delegation opposed any revisions to the EU that would further integrate member-states' foreign policies, support for the CFSP is lowest among UK elites (0.37 compared to 0.81 in the overall sample). Italian elites were especially enthusiastic—over 80% strongly favored establishing a common foreign and security policy.[44] My analyses account for this variation with country fixed effects.

Second, I control for national and European attachment (4-point scales, rescaled from 0 to 1) to account for the degree to which elites report connecting to both group identities[45]—though the same caveats from the public opinion analysis also apply here. To account for how frequently

---

44. See Müller, Jenny and Ecker (2012) for a detailed discussion about cross-national variation in support for the CFSP among European elites.

45. To measure European attachment, I used the following question: "People feel different degrees of attachment to their town/village, to their region, to their country and to Europe. What about you? Are you very attached, somewhat attached, not very attached, to (Nation/Europe)?" The elite survey did not ask about how much being European has to do with how the respondent feels about themselves like the mass survey identification measure. These attachment items carry a bigger risk for posttreatment bias due to the potential conflation with content, but I include them to ensure that my results hold when I account for variables associated with the standard story.

respondents interact with Europeans from outside their home country (Mitchell, 2015; Stoeckel, 2016), I include a variable that measures how often the respondent reported being in contact with EU actors and institutions in a one-year period (a 5-point scale ranging from "no contacts last year" to "at least once a week").[46] Finally, I include variables for whether the survey classifies the respondent as a political elite (1) or not (0), gender (coded 1 for male), and a continuous measure for left-right political ideology. Elites tend to have more coherent political ideologies than members of the mass public, such that it remains an important control variable.[47]

RESULTS

Figure 5.13 displays estimates from two OLS regressions that model support for a common foreign and security policy. Triangles represent results from a model that includes the two independent variables—factor scores for unity- and equality-oriented supranationalisms—alongside country and survey year fixed effects. Circles represent estimates from a model with controls. Lines display robust 95% confidence intervals, clustered by country.

The results displayed in Figure 5.13 support my intragroup cooperation hypothesis: unity decreases support for foreign policy cooperation. By contrast, equality correlates with greater CFSP support. European elites generally favor the prospect of a CFSP—all else equal, most elites at least "somewhat favor" a single European foreign policy (intercept $b = 0.67$). But the strongest support comes from those committed to equality. Moving from the minimum to the maximum on equality predicts a 0.31-unit increase in the dependent variable. Substantively, this means that a French elite surveyed in 2007 would "somewhat" support a single foreign policy if she scored the minimum on the equality scale, but "strongly" support the CFSP if she were a maximally committed equality-oriented supranationalist. By contrast, the weakly negative coefficient on unity shows that moving

46. The elite questionnaire did not include the mass public item that asked respondents how often they visited other countries, and so I use this measure of contact with EU institutions as an alternative.

47. Like the mass public surveys, I conclude that the costs of omitted variable bias outweigh concerns about the possibility that ideology is posttreatment to supranationalisms. See the online appendix for evidence that the results remain robust when dropping ideology and EU contacts from the models. The survey researchers kept age and birth year anonymous for the elite participants, and therefore the models do not control for age.

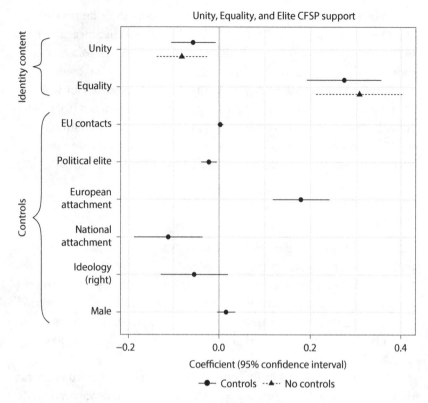

FIGURE 5.13. Equality increases CFSP support among elites.
Note: Points display OLS coefficient estimates from models with (circles) and without (triangles) additional control variables, with 95% confidence intervals (standard errors clustered by country). The dependent variable and continuous independent variables have been rescaled from 0 to 1. All models include survey wave and country fixed effects (France is the reference category), omitted for presentation.

from the minimum to the maximum corresponds to a 0.08-unit decrease in CFSP support.

These relationships hold when I account for theoretically relevant controls—the coefficients on equality and unity remain positive or negative, respectively, and statistically significant. Moreover, the coefficient on equality suggests a substantively large effect. Regarding the controls, European attachment correlates with CFSP support ($b = 0.18$, $p < 0.01$) whereas national attachment correlates with opposition ($b = -0.11, p < 0.01$). Frequent professional contacts with EU institutions have no statistically significant relationship with attitudes about the CFSP. Political elites express marginally lower support for the CFSP compared to other elites in the sample, and right-wing ideology correlates with weaker

CFSP support though the effect is not statistically significant ($b = -0.054$, $p = 0.15$).

These results support my core proposition, that content and commitment together explain the relationship between supranationalisms and support for security cooperation among European elites.[48] Equality increases support whereas unity undermines it. Moreover, with the methodological caveats noted previously, the results remain robust when I control for both European and national attachment—two variables that previous scholars treat as the key ingredients driving attitudes about supranational cooperation.

Elite support for a European army

In this section, I evaluate my second measure of support for security cooperation: whether equality-oriented elites support "a real, true European army" like the one that Merkel and Macron recently elevated on the EU agenda.[49] Respondents reported whether European states should maintain their own national militaries, have a joint European army, or have both European and national armies, and I use a multinomial logistic regression to estimate the predicted probability that respondents chose each of the three categories.

Figure 5.14 displays the results.[50] Panel (a) shows that commitment to equality increases the probability that a respondent wants some kind of multi-state force. Moving from a 0.5 on the equality scale to the maximum (1) produces an 8.6 percentage point increase in the chance that the participant selects a single European military to supplement national forces, and a smaller 2.3 percentage point increase in selecting a single European army to usurp national forces. The same change corresponds to a commensurate 10.8 percentage point decrease in the chance of electing to maintain national armies. Many of these political elites bear responsibility for representing their state's interests, yet most want deeper security integration on the continent.

---

48. Supplementary analyses in the online appendix show that the effects of unity and equality persist after splitting the sample between people who express an attachment to Europe and those who do not, though the strong average CFSP support among "attached" elites has consequences for the observed effect size. I also test the interaction between equality and unity and find that neither constrains the other.

49. Rankin, Jennifer, 2018. "Merkel joins Macron in calling for a 'real, true European army,'" *Guardian*, 13 November. URL: www.theguardian.com/world/2018/nov/13/merkel -joins-macron-in-calling-for-a-real-true-european-army.

50. See the appendix for coefficient estimates.

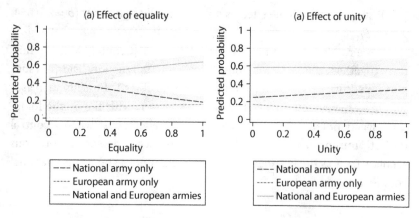

FIGURE 5.14. Predicted probability of support for a European army (elites).
Note: Lines show predicted probabilities based on the multinomial logit model, and shaded areas display 95% confidence intervals. Independent variables indexed at France, 2009, political elites, median values for attachment, contact with other EU actors, and ideology. I set identity content variables to their 5th percentile values when fixed—unity at 0.054 in panel (a) and equality at 0.54 in panel (b).

By contrast, unity-oriented supranationalism increases support for a state-centric security model and opposition to a European army. Moving from a 0.05 on unity to the maximum (1) predicts a 9.4 percentage point increase in the chance of selecting "national army only," and an 8.4 percentage point decrease in the chance that they want to cede national forces to create a single European army. The results reveal a small, 1 percentage point decrease in the chance that unity-oriented supranationalists support a dual system whereby countries add a European army to supplement national forces. This small effect seems less surprising considering the dual system's overwhelming popularity—43.51% of respondents said that they would like both national and European armies.

Extensions

Using survey data from representative mass samples in 16 EU countries and a large sample of European elites, I find that unity-oriented supranationalism consistently undermines support for security cooperation. Equality-oriented supranationalism, by contrast, increases intra-European trust, support for a common foreign and security policy, and support for a European army. My findings suggest that the patterns scholars tend to attribute to supranationalism instead depend on equality-oriented identities and norms.

These analyses nevertheless invite questions about whether the results generalize to other times, operationalizations of the independent variables, and issues. Perhaps the buzz around the Treaty of Lisbon aroused competing concerns about supranationalisms or unusual enthusiasm for deepening security integration when the IntUne surveys entered the field. Or perhaps later shocks to the EU integration process—like the Eurozone crisis or 2016 Brexit vote—changed perceptions about European supranationalisms or their implications for foreign policy attitudes. And do unity and equality exert competing pressures on other types of cooperation, like financial assistance within the EU or forming a confederation of states?

This section includes two contributions that supplement and extend the previous analyses. First, I supplement the IntUne analyses with data from two waves of the Eurobarometer surveys. These additional surveys expand the temporal and cross-national scope of my analysis and introduce alternative measures for unity and equality. The surveys entered the field 5 and 10 years after the second wave of the IntUne surveys, capturing public attitudes 3 years after the UK's Brexit vote (2019) and during the sovereign debt crisis (2014). They also include representative samples from each EU member-state. Second, I test whether unity and equality explain other forms of supranational cooperation—expanding my theory's explanatory scope to probe support for helping fellow EU countries through economic challenges.

To the extent that I recover the same general patterns in these analyses, it should increase readers' confidence in my findings. Of course, I centered this chapter on the IntUne surveys for a reason—they offered useful and theoretically sound proxies for unity- and equality-oriented European supranationalism alongside specific questions about security cooperation. Alternative large-scale surveys are significantly less ideal for testing my intragroup cooperation hypothesis, because recent waves lack questions about what it means to be a European. Moreover, these surveys tend to prioritize questions related to EU governance, monetary policy, or other issues that bear little resemblace to the attitudes about international security cooperation that I target in this book.[51] In short: These supplementary

---

51. Outside Europe, cross-national surveys only rarely ask about supranational identities. When they do—like the 2013–15 Asian barometer wave or Telhami's (2013) sweeping polls in the Arab world—to my knowledge, they lack questions about content. Because my theoretical contribution centers on content, I continue to focus on the European case to test my intragroup cooperation hypothesis.

analyses use data that are not purpose-built for testing my theory, but offer a useful if limited perspective on my argument's generalizability.

THE EUROBAROMETER SURVEYS

This section includes data from two waves of the Eurobarometer surveys: Eurobarometer 92.3 fielded in November–December 2019 (European Commission, 2020), and Eurobarometer 81.4 fielded in May–June 2014 (European Commission, 2018). The European Commission regularly surveys its citizens to capture trends in public opinion.[52] I selected these two waves first because they contain questions that probe ideas about what subjects "create a feeling of community" among Europeans alongside questions about cooperation on either defense issues or economic transfers—a surprisingly rare convergence on Eurobarometer instruments. Second, both years correspond to significant times in EU integration. Hand-wringing about post-Brexit prospects for cooperation provided the backdrop in late 2019. And a destabilizing financial crisis brought economic cooperation to the top of the 2014 agenda, as citizens grappled with whether wealthy members should provide material support to fellow Europeans outside their national borders.

UNITY, EQUALITY, AND SUPPORT FOR SECURITY COOPERATION IN 2019

To what extent do my conclusions about unity and equality extend to support for security cooperation in 2019? This analysis uses new measures to test this chapter's core argument in public opinion data from all 28 EU member-states.[53] Two questions about security cooperation serve as dependent variables: support for "A common defence and security policy among EU Member States" (CDP) and for "A common foreign policy of the 28 Member States of the EU" (CFP). On the surveys, participants

52. Importantly, these cross-sectional surveys track aggregate trends but do not survey the same individuals over time. See https://ec.europa.eu/commfrontoffice/publicopinion/index .cfm for more information.

53. This wave includes separate samples from Eastern and Western Germany, and the models include separate fixed effects for each. I exclude citizens from non-EU countries: Turkey, North Macedonia, Montenegro, Serbia, and Albania. I also exclude the additional Turkish Cypriot Community.

reported whether they were "for or against" each policy.[54] I created two dichotomous variables, coded 1 for favoring and 0 for opposing the policy.[55]

These items closely match outcome measures from my IntUne analyses, but I adopt a distinct approach to measure unity and equality. The survey asks respondents which subjects "most create a feeling of community among EU citizens." Response options span topics from familiar ideas like history and values to other aspects of European life like healthcare and sports.[56] Respondents could select up to 3 subjects. These choices capture individual perceptions about descriptive European norms. If someone declares that history creates a feeling of community, for example, she implies that a shared historical narrative unites good Europeans.

I created dichotomous variables for unity and equality using the four items from this list that most closely correspond to my concepts and scales from the IntUne surveys: history and religion for unity, and the rule of law and values for equality.[57] History and religion implicate the unifying bonds and temporal continuity associated with unity-oriented supranationalism. In the EU context, the rule of law implies equality under the law. And although "values" constitutes an overtly ambiguous topic, citizens tend to associate equality with European values, perhaps due to successful top-down efforts to inculcate this norm among members of the public. Indeed, a separate survey question asked participants which values "best represent the European Union" (not necessarily the European people). Top choices included democracy (34%), human rights (32%), and the rule

54. These items appeared in a longer list of different integration policies including common EU policies for trade, migration, and energy, alongside support for enlarging the EU and the free movement of EU citizens to "live, work, study, and do business" throughout the region. See QB5 on Eurobarometer 92.3.

55. I excluded people who refused to respond or stated "don't know" from the analysis. For the common foreign policy, 2.2% of respondents refused to respond and 8.4% chose don't know. For the common defense and security policy, 1.7% refused to respond and 6.0% chose don't know. Analyses in the online appendix show similar results when I recode these responses to the scale midpoint.

56. The survey offers 14 topics: history; religion; values; geography; languages; the rule of law; sports; inventions, science and technology; economy; healthcare and pensions; solidarity with poorer regions; culture; education; and care for the environment. Some participants offered spontaneous alternatives, reported that no such feeling of community exists, or stated that they don't know or that none of the subjects apply. See QC4 on Eurobarometer 92.3.

57. Of course, the full list of subjects contains many items that bear little resemblance to unity or equality, either because they reference orthogonal topics like science and technology or because they refer to ambiguous constructs like "culture."

of law (22%).[58] Respect for other cultures, equality, and tolerance also received frequent mentions—15%, 13% and 12%, respectively—whereas only 4% of respondents listed religion. These responses increase my confidence that participants who reported that "values" bind the European community most likely had ideas about equality in mind.

I adapt the procedure that I applied earlier in this chapter to create dichotomous independent variables that categorize respondents based on the relative importance they place on unity or equality as binding material for Europeans (Wright, Citrin and Wand, 2012). Participants coded as a 1 for unity satisfied two conditions: (1) They selected *either* history or religion; and (2) they *did not* select either the rule of law or values. I completed this procedure in reverse for equality, recording a 1 for participants who (1) selected either the rule of law or values and (2) selected neither history nor religion. This scheme defines 18.6% and 26.4% of the sample as committed to European unity and equality, respectively. A separate "no bonds" variable captures the 9.9% of participants who selected nothing from the list or said they don't know. The remaining 45.1% of respondents form a heterogeneous mixed group of people who failed to meet the criteria for unity, equality, or no bonds.

Before proceeding, I note two caveats about these variables. First, these items constitute weak measures of my core constructs. The question only tangentially references supranationalism. And because participants select from a list rather than explicitly rank order or rate the subjects, the items limit inferences about commitment. Second, people fairly criticize the Eurobarometer surveys for painting a rosy picture about public attitudes toward the EU with selective response options (Nissen, 2014; Höpner and Jurczyk, 2015). The question about which values represent the EU, for example, offers peace, democracy, and tolerance—but not Western hegemony. These concerns raise the specter of biased responding.

Still, asking what binds Europeans somewhat mitigates these social desirability concerns. Participants have several neutral options to choose from—if they do not want to say that religion binds Europeans or that Europeans do not share values, they can turn to sports or technology. In turn, I have more confidence that the items I associate with unity and equality

58. Percentages restricted to the sample of EU member-states and incorporate population weights. Participants mentioned "peace" more often than any other single value—42% of respondents selected this value.

reflect honest perceptions about the group. Although this limits my ability to draw inferences about the mixed group—nearly half the sample—my main interest lies in comparing equality to unity. Regarding the dependent variables, the survey included balanced response options that lessen concerns about question framing inflating support for the CFP and CDP (Höpner and Jurczyk, 2015).

All models include a panel of control variables: an 11-point scale for left-right ideology (rescaled to range from 0 to 1), gender (coded 1 for man, 0 for woman), and age (dummy indicators for four age groups). I again control for national and European attachment to account for the possibility that identification alone, rather than content, suffices to explain effects I observe. The models also include country fixed effects and incorporate population weights.

Results

I estimate two logistic regression models that regress whether respondents favor the CFP or CDP on the independent variables. Rather than present coefficient estimates,[59] Figure 5.15 plots substantive results for each outcome. The plot displays the change in the predicted probability that a participant supports the CFP (triangles) or CDP (circles) associated with switching from a 0 to 1 on each content variable. The "mixed" group serves as the reference category. Positive values indicate that a change in the independent variable increases the probability of support for the dependent variable, and lines represent 95% bootstrapped confidence intervals.

The results illustrate three important findings. First, people who endorse equality favor security cooperation at greater rates than their unity-oriented counterparts. The likelihood that someone supports the CFP and the CDP increases by 2.8 and 2.5 percentage points for participants who believe that equality binds Europeans, relative to the mixed reference group. By contrast, people who selected history or religion as binding material for the European community, but not the rule of law or values, report similar levels of support for security cooperation as their mixed group counterparts. Moving from a 0 to 1 on unity does not meaningfully change the probability that someone supports the CFP or CDP relative to that mixed group. And—crucially—comparing unity to equality reveals

---

59. Figure A.4 in the appendix displays average marginal effects for unity and equality alongside the control variables.

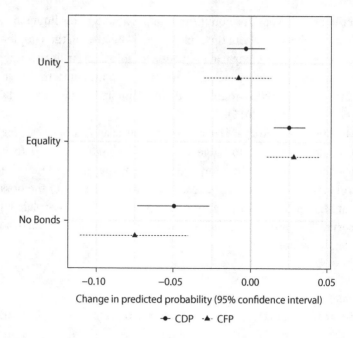

FIGURE 5.15. Equality increases the probability of favoring the common foreign and defense policies.

Note: Figure displays the change in the predicted probability that a participant supports either the common EU foreign policy (CFP) or common EU defense and security policy (CDP). Models include controls and country fixed effects and incorporate population weights. The reference category for the identity content measures is the mixed group. The index values used to calculate the change in predicted probabilities include overall means for European attachment, national attachment, and ideology; female, aged 65 and over, and France. Lines represent 95% confidence intervals based on 1,000 bootstraps. N=21,022 for CFP and 21,530 for CDP.

that equality increases the probability of supporting each form of security cooperation (both $p < 0.01$).

Second, people who chose not to answer the question—or who said that nothing binds Europeans—rejected security cooperation at greater rates than even their unity-oriented counterparts. Switching from a 0 to 1 on this indicator corresponds to a 7.5 percentage point decrease in the chance that someone supports the CFP and a similar 4.9 percentage point decrease in the chance that they support the CDP. This result suggests at least two possibilities. On one hand, we might view people who dismiss European bonds as individuals with low commitment—feeling completely disconnected from the group, they reject deeper integration. On the other hand, social desirability biases might manifest in some unity-oriented supranationalists choosing nothing rather than contradicting the European Commission. In that sense, the group could include a mix of weak supranationalists and committed but self-censored unity-oriented supranationalists.

Third, these effects are statistically significant but substantively small. The quantities in Figure 5.15 represent changes in predicted probabilities using a specific set of index values. But to compare unity and equality to other variables in the model, I estimate the average marginal effects (AMEs). AMEs represent the discrete change in the probability that someone supports the CFP or CDP averaged across values for other variables in the model. Here, control variables from the standard story perform relatively well: The 0.026 ($p < 0.01$) average marginal effect for equality on support for the CFP is similar in size to national attachment ($AME = 0.0242$, $p < 0.26$), but constitutes about 1/10 the AME associated with European attachment, for example ($AME = 0.264$, $p < 0.01$). Support for the CDP follows the same pattern—equality plays a slightly larger role ($AME = 0.037$, $p < 0.01$), but remains weak relative to content-free European attachment (0.199, $p < 0.01$). These results clash with the IntUne analyses, where equality's effect consistently outstripped content-free attachment measures. I suspect that measurement shortcomings account for these differences. These indicators for unity and equality lack precision and information about commitment, such that "European attachment" likely captures ideas about content that I cannot empirically evaluate with these data. Still, even these rough proxies add value—wald tests show that including the content variables significantly improves the model fit for both CFP ($F = 8.15$, $p < 0.01$) and CDP ($F = 12.64$, $p < 0.01$).

Given the constraints imposed by using a survey instrument without purpose-built measures for my key concepts, it is especially striking that the results largely support my intragroup cooperation hypothesis. Using data collected a decade after the IntUne surveys, I find that equality increases support for the CFP and CDP, relative to unity.

UNITY, EQUALITY, AND OTHER FORMS OF INTRAGROUP COOPERATION

I developed my intragroup cooperation hypothesis to test a theory about supranationalisms and support for security cooperation. But unity and equality might also explain attitudes about a broader suite of policies that implicate transnational cooperation. In this section, I first return to the IntUne surveys to show that unity and equality increase support for economic solidarity. Then, I replicate these results in the 2014 Eurobarometer surveys to show that equality and unity correlated with support for economic cooperation and U.S.-style confederation during the debt crisis.[60]

Like research on attitudes about security cooperation, the notion that identification increases support for fiscal solidarity constitutes a practical truism in previous work. For example, European identification increased German citizens' support for bailouts and debt relief to the embattled Greek government (Rathbun, Powers and Anders, 2019).[61] Yet as Bauhr and Charron (2020*b*) point out, the degree to which people support international redistribution likely depends on both content and commitment. And when those authors separate "religious" from "secular" Europeans, they find that those two supranationalisms have opposing effects on support for regional redistribution.

In turn, I expect that equality will increase support for regional economic assistance. Equality-oriented supranationalism prescribes that citizens mitigate economic duress for fellow Europeans, expecting future reciprocity. By contrast, the same logic that connects unity to reticence about security integration will reduce citizens' relative desire to join forces against financial threats.

On the IntUne surveys, participants responded to a prompt asking them whether, in the next 10 years or so, they favor "more help for EU regions in economic or social difficulties." Response options ranged on a 5-point scale from "strongly against" to "strongly in favour," just like the item that probed support for the CFSP. I recoded responses to range from 0 to 1, and then regressed this variable on unity, equality, and the controls.[62]

Figure 5.16 presents the results and shows that equality increases support for economic cooperation, whereas unity has the opposite effect. Equality-oriented supranationalists reported stronger support for helping their fellow EU members through economic and social challenges ($b = 0.355$, $p < 0.01$), whereas their unity-oriented counterparts expressed less

60. I again limit my analyses to the 28 current EU member-states and exclude candidate countries.

61. See Hobolt and De Vries (2016) for a review of research on public support for European integration in general. For more on the relationship between identification and economic integration see, for example, Kuhn and Stoeckel (2014) and Hooghe and Marks (2004). Of course, several other material, non-material, and contextual factors also influence attitudes about international economic cooperation—see Kleider and Stoeckel (2019) for excellent work on how social class, cultural orientations, and ideology combine to shape public opinion about fiscal transfers in the EU and Bauhr and Charron (2020*a*) on the role played by domestic corruption.

62. I recoded "don't know" responses to the scale midpoint.

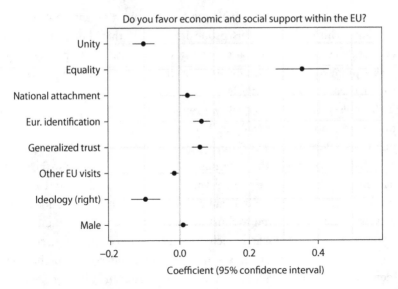

FIGURE 5.16. Equality, unity, and economic support in the IntUne surveys.
Note: Figure displays coefficient estimates and 95% confidence intervals from OLS models that regress whether participants favor providing economic and social support to other EU countries on the independent variables. Models include country and survey year fixed effects (France is the reference country), omitted for presentation, and incorporate population weights. N=29,940.

appetite for such economic cooperation ($b = -0.10$, $p < 0.01$). Again, I find that content shapes support for a type of intragroup cooperation that scholars often attribute to commitment alone. And as with security cooperation on the IntUne surveys, the content variables swamp content-free attachment measures.

The IntUne surveys entered the field as the global financial crisis that produced the Great Recession (2007) began, and just before the Greek deficit that would portend the wider continental debt crisis. These analyses therefore support my expectations about economic cooperation during a relatively tumultuous time for the European economy. Still, the full weight of the debt crisis and its consequences had yet to take shape. I therefore turn to the 2014 Eurobarometer surveys to test my theory's implications for economic cooperation after the dust began to settle and questions about bailouts captivated the public.

I measure support for financial cooperation using a survey item that asks participants whether "EU Member States should work together more in tackling the financial and economic crisis." Although this question does not mention specific policies like bailouts, debt relief, or redistribution, it provides a good financial analogue to a common defense policy: Participants who agree with this proposition imply that the region should cooperate against threats that affect any single member. Responses range on a 4-point scale from "totally disagree" to "totally agree," which I rescale to range from 0 to 1 for analysis.[63]

To measure unity and equality, I replicated the coding procedure from my 2019 Eurobarometer analysis. This process yields a similar distribution on the 4 content groups: 19% qualify as unity-oriented, 21.5% as equality-oriented, 14% populate the no bonds group, and 45.7% comprise the residual "mixed" group.[64] For control variables, I include ideology (rescaled from 0 to 1, higher values indicate right-wing), gender, age cohorts, and country fixed effects. And to illustrate again that the effects of unity and equality remain robust when I include items that tap content-free commitment, I control for respondents' self-reported identification: whether they identify as their nationality and European, European and their nationality, or European only. "Nationality only" serves as the reference category. This imperfect measure contradicts what we know from psychology—that people often have strong commitments to identities across categorization levels—by requiring participants to rank order their multiple social selves. But the survey instrument lacks alternative measures for commitment. Because I primarily include these controls to confirm that the effects of unity and equality persist when I account for variables associated with the standard story, I include them in my analyses.

Panel (a) in Figure 5.17 displays results from an OLS model that regresses the dependent variable—support for working together in a financial crisis—on unity, equality, and the controls.[65] Positive coefficients indicate that higher scores on the independent variable correspond to greater agreement that EU members should work together in financial crises, relative to the reference categories.

Like the 2019 Eurobarometer analysis, the most important test for my intragroup cooperation hypothesis entails comparing the effects of

63. I removed participants who chose "don't know" or refused to respond for the primary analysis. Supplementary analyses show that recoding these responses to the scale midpoint yields nearly identical results.

64. Percentages adjusted for population weights.

65. The model also includes country fixed effects and incorporates population weights. Like the 2019 Eurobarometer, these surveys include separate samples for Eastern and Western Germany, and this 2014 wave also includes separate samples for Great Britain and Northern Ireland. I incorporate individual fixed effects for each.

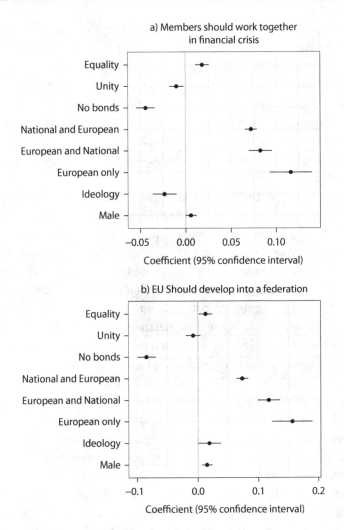

FIGURE 5.17. Equality, unity, and support for other forms of supranational cooperation.
Note: Figure displays coefficient estimates and 95% confidence intervals from OLS models that regress whether participants agree that European states should cooperate in financial crises (N=21,729) or further develop into a federation (N=18,331) on the independent variables. Models include country fixed effects (France is the reference country), omitted for presentation, and incorporate population weights. The reference category for the identity content measures is the mixed group, the reference category for age is 65 and older.

equality to unity. And again, I find small but significant differences. Equality correlates with a 1.8 percentage point increase in support for regional cooperation in the financial crisis, whereas unity leads to a 0.9 percentage point decrease, relative to the mixed group. The 2.8 percentage point difference between unity and equality constitutes 12% of one standard deviation on the dependent variable ($sd = 0.23$). The largest effects on support for economic cooperation come from the content-free measures for identification included as control variables, though these results are hard to interpret without data on what content participants have in mind when they describe themselves as "European and Bulgarian" rather than "Bulgarian only." And most importantly for my purposes, including the content measures again improves the model fit ($\chi^2 = 42.61$, $p < 0.01$)—demonstrating that content adds explanatory value even after accounting for abstract notions of commitment.

Finally, I estimate the same models using a strong form of cooperation as my dependent variable: The degree to which respondents agree that the EU should "develop further into a federation of nation states." Support for confederation combines economic with security cooperation as participants consider whether they want the EU to resemble a "United States of Europe." Although truly amalgamated security communities rarely arise in practice (Deutsch, 1957), support for confederation implies support for concentrating substantial authority in a supranational body. European residents must trust each other, and the centralized authority, to make decisions that benefit the group if they endorse developing a federation.

Panel (b) in Figure 5.17 presents the results of an OLS model that regresses whether people agree that the EU should develop into a federation (4-point scale, rescaled from 0 to 1) on the independent variables and panel of controls. The positive coefficient on equality shows that people who think that equality binds Europeans express more ardent pro-federation sentiment compared to both the mixed group ($b = 0.13$, $p < 0.05$) and their unity-oriented counterparts ($b = 0.02$, $p < 0.01$). And once more, these content measures have important explanatory power relative to a model that only includes the content-free identification variables and demographic controls ($\chi^2 = 46.18$, $p < 0.01$).

These wide-ranging supplementary analyses test my intragroup cooperation hypothesis with different approaches to measuring unity and equality, in 4 survey years that span a 12-year period from 2007–2019, and across multiple issue areas. The results enhance my book's external validity by testing whether my theory and concepts generalize across time and with samples from all 28 EU member-states. Importantly, each analysis tells a similar story about the relationships between unity, equality, and support for regional cooperation. The results from the Eurobarometer surveys posed new challenges to interpreting the evidence—imperfect proxies for unity and equality do not account for commitment, for example. And the

Eurobarometer results provide some equivocal support for the standard story, because coefficients on unity and equality fail to match other identification measures in magnitude even as they add explanatory value. But in each model, the findings underscore my core claim: Content creates meaningful variation in support for European cooperation that we cannot account for with commitment alone.

Conclusion

In this chapter, I tested my theory's implications for intragroup security cooperation: Content explains whether supranational commitments facilitate or undermine cooperation. Equality drives support for European cooperation, unity does not.

People who conceive of their European identity in terms of equality—those who see Europeans as peers who abide by democratic norms and who tolerate heterogeneity—trust their fellow citizens and support security integration. I find consistent evidence for this proposition in representative samples from the mass public. In the IntUne analyses, equality has a large effect on each indicator for intragroup cooperation. In the Eurobarometer data, I find smaller but significant effects using different measures. These equality-minded citizens play an important role in "bottom-up" models of supranational cooperation (Fligstein, 2008). They provide policymakers with room to negotiate over forming a European army and working collectively to combat threats that affect Europeans.

The ultimate fate of binding multilateral commitments may rest on the shoulders of voters in the long term if they elect candidates who favor security integration over those who do not. But vote choices depend on a host of factors; foreign policy preferences may give way to partisanship, ideology, domestic politics, or economic strife. Yet the elite results demonstrate that my theory also carries currency among policymakers. The elite sample includes a diverse collection of parliamentarians with direct policy influence alongside business and media elites with agenda-setting power. Elites tend to exhibit less contestation over European supranationalism—favoring equality over unity—but stronger equality-oriented commitments correlate with stronger support for security integration.

Unity-oriented supranationalism produces less clear-cut patterns in these survey data. In the IntUne analyses, unity always has a negative effect on the cooperative outcomes. And in the supplementary Eurobarometer analyses, unity corresponds to weaker support for cooperation relative to equality. But the weak pull against cooperation from unity compares poorly to the countervailing push toward trust and deeper integration from equality, a pattern most starkly on display in the elite results for European army support.

Why do the results for European elites differ slightly from the mass public? At least two possibilities merit consideration. First, differences in sample composition distinguish the elite sample from the mass public. Figures 5.12 and 5.3 showed greater contestation over European identity among regular citizens compared to their elite counterparts, who coalesced around stronger commitments to equality and weak unity commitments. This difference highlights how observable traits divide average elites from mass publics. If people with certain characteristics have a greater propensity to select into political and business leadership positions, sample composition differences could skew results (Dynes et al., 2021; Kertzer, 2020). And indeed, comparing the paired samples reveals stark differences: Men constitute 78.6% of the elite sample, compared to 48.1% of the mass sample. Meanwhile, of the elites who reported their education level, 86.3% completed a university degree—a factor positively correlated with each of the dependent variables in the mass public[66]—compared to just 24.5% of the mass sample. Elite respondents were also more ideological. Although mean ideology scores hover near 0.5 in both groups,[67] the mean belies a remarkable disparity: A full 42.8% of the mass public sample chose the midpoint—"neither left nor right." By contrast, elites distributed themselves more evenly across the ideological realm, with 39.8% and 43.1% describing themselves as left or right of center, respectively. In short: the elites in these surveys differ from their fellow citizens on several observed traits, a pattern almost certainly matched by unobserved characteristics.[68] Such differences could explain both the overwhelming support for cooperation among elites and the relative differences in contestation between the mass public and elites.

66. See online appendix.

67. Mean ideology in the mass public is 0.5, compared to 0.51 in the elite samples, pooled by country and survey wave.

68. For example, differences in dispositional perspective-taking, the ability to adopt another person's viewpoint (Davis, 1983), might facilitate the political ambition necessary to launch a campaign (Clifford, Kirkland and Simas, 2019). Perspective-taking, in turn, might decrease the stereotyping behavior associated with viewing heterogeneity as a threat to the group and amplify the existing cooperative relationships that constitute other aspects of EU policy (see Paluck and Green, 2009 for a review).

The second explanation for greater elite consensus over both European identity content and security cooperation lies in differences between mass and elite psychology. Whether from domain-specific expertise that they acquire with experience or because elites with certain cognitive styles rise to power, elites may reach different conclusions about the best future for European security integration. Thinking "down the game tree" (Hafner-Burton, Hughes and Victor, 2013; Hafner-Burton et al., 2014), for example, they may adopt a rational outlook about the strategic gains from reciprocity. Elites' domain-specific expertise may also increase their propensity to adopt the EU's formal positions on both supranationalisms and the foreign policy pillar.

What do this chapter's findings mean for research on supranationalisms and security cooperation in general? Constructivist theories argue that lasting security cooperation depends on creating international *communities* (Deutsch, 1957; Acharya and Johnston, 2007; Wendt, 1999; Cronin, 1999). Although some scholars contend that their macro-arguments cannot depend on micro-foundations, others use social identity to claim that identification cements cooperation (Cronin, 1999). Moreover, those macro-theories do not need to employ the state-is-a-person assumption to justify individual-level tests. Elites and ordinary citizens comprise the state,[69] meaning that people contribute to policy processes. And indeed, Kupchan (2010) treats social integration as a step along the way to stable peace, and both Risse (2010) and Cronin (1999) turn to European elites to seek evidence for transnational unity, for example.

My results suggest that when scholars conclude that "shared identities, values, and meanings" matter for international cooperation (Adler and Barnett, 1998, 33), they get the story partly right. But my theory recognizes a further, consequential dimension: We need to know *which* values underlie supranationalism to determine whether someone supports cooperation. As a consequence, efforts to create unity might work against cooperative integration. Indeed, unity's negative effect on intra-European trust suggests that unity likely relates to Euro-skepticism across a range of cooperative outcomes from the financial cooperation scenario assessed in this chapter to attitudes about intra-European immigration or the European Court of Justice. Equality, however, enables people to maintain dependable expectations of peaceful dispute resolution. In this respect, my results provide a

---

69. On the state as a person in IR theory, see Wendt (2004).

via media between constructivist scholarship steeped in collective identification and institutionalist arguments about how organizations like the EU build trust through reciprocity. Testing the micro-foundations of security cooperation, I find that equality and reciprocity provide a better conduit for supranational cooperation than unity.

6

Conclusions

I began this book with Emmanuel Macron's confident pronouncements that nationalist passions presage war, whereas supranational unity stands poised to sustain peaceful cooperation. But I end this book after introducing substantial qualifications to those ubiquitous claims. Despite the intuitive appeal of the standard stories, I argued that both gloss over important contradictions and build on incomplete conceptual foundations. Asking whether nationalisms influence attitudes about conflict and cooperation—or simply assuming their effects—diverts our attention away from a key component: what it means to be part of the national or supranational group.

Stepping back from the conventional stories, I developed a theoretical framework to explain how nationalisms vary, and which nationalist commitments generate support for international conflict and cooperation. I used concepts and tools from social psychology to develop—and test—my theory of identity content. In the broadest sense, I showed that when we separate equality- from unity-oriented nationalisms, we reach new and surprising conclusions about group dynamics on issues of perennial concern to scholars who study war and peace.

This book thereby advances theories about nationalisms in international politics in three ways. First, it synthesizes research on nationalisms and supranationalisms to capture both levels of categorization in one theory. Second, my theory accounts for the trail of evidence that links nationalism to conflict and supranationalism to in-group cooperation, *but also for* puzzling inconsistencies in the theoretical and empirical record.

Third, I provide a generalizable typology for differentiating nationalisms, grounded in fundamental norms of human interaction.

Chapters 3, 4, and 5 present reasonably consistent evidence that distinguishing unity from equality creates theoretical and empirical consequences for understanding how nationalisms relate to foreign policy attitudes. In chapters 3 and 4, I presented results from two survey experiments to demonstrate that unity- and equality-oriented nationalisms have distinct implications for militarism and conflict escalation. On one hand, unity-oriented nationalism creates hawks. In both the fictional Fredonian scenario and an experiment that targeted American nationalism, unity-oriented nationalism provoked militarism and tough stances against key adversaries. Committed unity-oriented nationalists also endorsed disproportionate conflict escalation when they called for strikes against Rusburg in the simmering but ambiguous territorial dispute, and when they expressed support for sending ground troops to fight ISIS—thereby escalating U.S. involvement in the Middle East. On the other hand, equality-oriented nationalists followed unconventional patterns. The equality-oriented nationalists in my experiments were not doves—they supported using force to combat Russian aggression in the Baltics and limited strikes against ISIS in chapter 4. But they adopted less militaristic orientations in general, and when they took a more patient approach to the conflict with Rusburg or opposed sending ground troops into Syria and Iraq. Although unity- and equality-oriented nationalisms sometimes inspire complementary foreign policy attitudes, the differences fundamentally challenge existing theories that equate nationalism with military aggression.

I moved to the regional level in chapter 5 to evaluate whether unity and equality shape attitudes about cooperation, having established their implications for conflict. The European surveys offered the chance to test my intragroup cooperation hypothesis while sticking to foreign policy. There, I introduced large-scale surveys to test my theory in a new context and with different operationalizations for the independent variables. With data from surveys fielded in four different years, with representative samples from countries throughout the EU and a targeted sample of European elites, I added important external validity to this book's claims and found robust support for my theory. Equality increased trust, support for security integration, and support for helping fellow Europeans through economic crises—fodder for research that links supranational identities to intragroup cooperation. But my results also showed that pressures for unity and solidarity counteract efforts to increase cooperation in heterogeneous regions like Europe. To the extent that our theories about the relationship between supranationalism and cooperation depend on fomenting intragroup trust, it is especially telling that the unity-oriented supranationalists in the IntUne surveys expressed more suspicion toward their fellow Europeans. Though unity had relatively small negative effects on the dependent variables, the results underscore the fact that unity creates surprising barriers to durable cooperation.

Collectively, the theory and evidence have implications for several prominent research programs in IR. First, I uncovered significant, consequential variation in nationalism's effects on conflictual attitudes, while taking nationalism on its own terms. Rather than pivot to alternative concepts like patriotism or attachment as the "good" sides of national identification, I showed that national superiority can rest on equality. Equality, in turn, produces relatively diplomatic foreign policy orientations compared to unity. Against research that treats nationalism as a monolithic impediment to peace (Federico, Golec and Dial, 2005; Herrmann, Isernia and Segatti, 2009)—or as an insurmountable antecedent to war in the international system (Mercer, 1995)—I showed that nationalism's so-called dark side depends on content. Theories that hinge on commitment, intensity, or extremism to explain nationalism's effects without equal regard for content lead us astray. At the same time, my theory complements new approaches to studying status in international politics. Some states seek status through war (Renshon, 2017), whereas others promote humanitarian aid to gain recognition as paragons of virtue (Wohlforth et al., 2018). Nationalist norms likely play a role in determining the status-seeking strategies that states pursue—and that their citizens support.

Second, my theory and results challenge the constructivist orthodoxy about supranationalisms in international politics. Past scholarship relies on psychological micro-foundations to proclaim that transnational unity begets peace (Adler and Barnett, 1998; Cronin, 1999; Hemmer and Katzenstein, 2002). Even those scholars who flip the causal arrow to argue that cooperation creates identification imply that the new umbrella identity, in turn, dissolves borders and cements cooperation in the long run (Deutsch, 1961). Constitutive arguments similarly conceive of supranationalism as inextricably linked to cooperation via security communities (Adler and Barnett, 1998). Like the research that conflates cause and effect by defining nationalism in terms of its aggressive tendencies, these arguments risk tautology when they treat evidence for multilateral decision-making and unfortified borders as evidence for supranational identities (Pouliot, 2007).

And these assertions clash with our knowledge of human psychology—pressures to adopt an "all for one, one for all" orientation work well for small groups but often backfire at broader levels of categorization like the regional and global groups that occupy IR scholars.[1] Case in point, demands for unity in the European Union create an in-group caste system that breeds mistrust and inward-looking security preferences (Mummendey and Waldzus, 2004). Regional unity might doom security integration rather than bolster it. But if equality nevertheless prompts intragroup trust and willingness to forge a common foreign policy, my research suggests that scholars go too far if they reject the notion that supranational identities contribute to international cooperation. When group norms implicate fairness and reciprocity, supranationalism supplements dispositional or dyadic theories about what drives cooperation (Rathbun, 2012, 201–5; Wheeler, 2018).

Indeed, constructivists might be right that identity plays an important role in European support for security integration, but for the wrong reasons: Steady progress on the European security project may be linked to equality's relative dominance on the continent, compared to unity, a pattern conspicuously on display among the elite survey respondents in chapter 5. These lessons suggest that scholars must consider content before exporting theories about European supranationalisms to other parts of the world. Rather than assume that identification signals support for integration—or that weak supranationalism signals opposition—research should first examine the group norms. To evaluate how identity shapes public support for cooperation in ASEAN member-states (Lee and Lim, 2020), for example, we should assess content alongside commitment.

Third, this book reasserts that classifying nationalisms in international politics benefits from psychological foundations. Some previous IR scholars have incorporated content into their theories, refining how we understand the relationship between nationalisms and foreign policy in both public opinion and in practice (Snyder, 2000; Schrock-Jacobson, 2012; Risse, 2010). But in chapter 2 I noted that one of the most striking features of this work is the sheer volume of typologies. Even the well-known civic/ethnic framework contains enough conceptual challenges and indeterminate causal mechanisms that many contemporary nationalism scholars have abandoned it (Saideman, 2013; Hutchinson, 2017). More

---

1. On the potential for a "world state" to create a global collective identity and reduce war, see Wendt (2003).

importantly, the laudable proliferation of nationalisms creates a disconnect between human psychology and scholarly concepts. As Schildkraut (2007, 611) points out in her research on the multiple strands of American national identification, concepts derived from political theory may not map cleanly onto citizens who "have not read their Louis Hartz, their Michael Walzer, or their Rogers Smith." I developed a framework that resolves conceptual challenges from past work at the same time that it informs them—providing insights into when and why, for example, "civic" *or* "ethnic" nationalisms correspond to external conflict. Building a theory about nationalisms from the ground up, in turn, avoids concerns about developing our frameworks to suit the data post hoc and hews closer to what we know about how humans navigate their social worlds.

In the rest of this chapter, I turn to several open questions, qualifications, and avenues for additional research on nationalisms in international politics. First, I tackle the normative questions raised by my theory and speculate about whether my framework distinguishes "good" from "bad" nationalisms. Second, I turn to the limitations imposed by my conceptual scheme and case selection. I consider how scholars might think about other varieties of nationalism, and how my theory travels to other countries and regions. Next, I consider my theory's implications for dyadic interactions and macro-level patterns of war and peace in international politics. I subsequently revisit my discussion about where nationalisms come from in chapter 2, and suggest specific strategies for how scholars could examine the effects of context, elite cues, and dispositional traits on nationalisms. I conclude by discussing what this book implies about salient policy debates.

Are There Good and Bad Nationalisms?

At its core, this book makes the case that some nationalist commitments encourage hawkishness, but others do not. And that supranationalism either promotes or undermines international cooperation, depending on the content. I did not embark on this research program to mount a campaign for one variety of nationalism or another. Rather, I wondered whether nationalisms and supranationalisms truly created countervailing forces in world politics, and whether IR theories about nationalisms squared with decades of psychological research on the importance of group norms to identification and social influence. Despite my positive, empirical goals, the research raises important normative concerns. To echo a question that David Brown posed in 1999, does my argument insinuate that there are good and bad nationalisms?

Nationalism certainly has a bad reputation. It is "one of those words that evokes a knee-jerk, invariably negative response in polite company" (Rodrik in Tamir, 2019, ix). Even American presidents largely treat nationalism as a taboo, despite the cloud of superiority that surrounds rhetoric about American exceptionalism. As President Trump put it in 2018, "We're not supposed to use that word."[2] My theory and the evidence in chapters 3 and 4 caution against our modern tendency to equate nationalism with its most pernicious foreign policy consequences. But it would be equally misguided to cast the conflict-mitigating equality-oriented nationalism as a "good" foil for "bad" unity-oriented nationalism. Each variety of nationalism entails trade-offs that could prove advantageous, depending on the situation. There are shades of good and bad to each.

Unity positions nationalists to protect their group against a hostile adversary, motivating domestic sacrifice. The human predisposition to form coalitions and coordinate group behavior has evolutionary advantages (Lopez, McDermott and Petersen, 2011)—our desire to protect kin helps to ensure the group's survival by motivating sacrifice and enabling coordinated action during conflict (Posen, 1993). As a consequence, most cultures include unity and loyalty as virtues (Haidt and Graham, 2007).

The domestic solidarity associated with unity creates international costs, of course. Unity encourages nationalists to support wars of aggression or to escalate a crisis beyond what may suffice to resolve the dispute—like the resounding public support for war in Iraq that followed 9/11 (Foyle, 2004). By contrast, we know from chapters 3 and 4 that equality drives nationalists to take a relatively measured approach to international conflicts. Support for deliberate, proportionate, crisis responses could buy time for diplomacy and prevent spirals of self-defeating escalation (Jervis, 1976), potentially saving lives and conserving resources. Like Kennedy and Khrushchev's reciprocal agreement to re-position ballistic missiles that ended the Cuban missile crisis, fairness allows tensions to simmer rather than boil over. In this way, committing to equality could stave off a long and deadly war.

---

2. Donald J. Trump quoted in Baker, Peter. 2018. "'Use That Word!': Trump Embraces the 'Nationalist' Label," *New York Times*, 23 October. URL: www.nytimes.com/2018/10/23/us/politics/nationalist-president-trump.html.

Yet if surging unity-oriented nationalism signals resolve and defuses the conflict by coercing an adversary to back down (Weiss, 2014), unity appears normatively superior. The proportionate escalation and reciprocal exchange associated with equality could exacerbate conflicts or cause endless tit-for-tat violence. When a large show of force would swiftly end a bloody conflict, the policies implicated by unity could reduce long-term damage: Limited air strikes often fail to communicate a country's resolve and in turn fail to prevent future aggression or protect civilian lives (Lupton, 2020). Indeed, many U.S. military veterans favor using greater levels of force—once the United States initiates a dispute (Gelpi and Feaver, 2002)—as the quickest potential route to ending the conflict.

Although unity and equality also create trade-offs regarding regional cooperation, my evidence suggests that the normative balance tilts toward equality. On one hand, equality seems to create the very possibility for supranational conformity that fosters cooperation. As I showed in chapter 5, ideas about European unity undermine trust and cooperation. In that respect, equality provides the more viable path to peace. On the other hand, equality could produce unintended problems if strong expectations regarding intragroup reciprocity blind people to free-riding behavior. If some EU member-states fail to pull their weight in the European army, for example, other countries will bear unfair burdens to protect the group. If that imbalance were to foster resentment, it could endanger the community's very existence. European security integration might grind to a halt if citizens conclude that the disproportionate costs for collective security unfairly outweigh the benefits (Dorussen, Kirchner and Sperling, 2009, 806). That said, such concerns may be unwarranted. Humans have evolved a unique capacity to detect and punish cheaters (Cosmides, 1989). With a keen eye for fairness violations, supranationalists committed to equality could halt free-riding before it threatens long-term cooperation.[3]

Moreover, I argued in chapters 1 and 2 that unity might quickly fade at the supranational scale. Pressures to homogenize in a large, inclusive group often encourage people to retreat to their national identities rather than conform: French demands to keep their own military uniforms proved a sticking point in the first negotiations to create a European army

3. And indeed, when Dorussen, Kirchner and Sperling (2009) account for the multiple dimensions of collective security in the European Union, they find little evidence for chronic free-riding problems in the region.

(Monnet, 1978; Fursdon, 1980). Yet if policymakers could find a psychologically tractable way to foment European unity, perhaps through dual identification campaigns that pair national distinction with supranational solidarity (Dovidio, Gaertner and Saguy, 2009; Curtis, 2014)—and without creating an image of a prototypical European that links back to individual national identities (Mummendey and Wenzel, 1999)—it could engender parochial altruism that surpasses equality in its benefits. A truly united Europe would meet challenges like the debt crisis or COVID-19 pandemic by transferring resources wherever needed, without expectations for debt repayment (Rathbun, Powers and Anders, 2019). Unity creates obligations to group members (Wong, 2010). But given the psychological constraints that make this implausible to sustain in practice, equality creates more promise for transnational cooperation.

Limitations, Extensions, and Open Questions

This book presents a general theory for how nationalisms shape attitudes about conflict and cooperation, but the focus on two nationalisms and samples from the United States and Europe limit the scope.

First, my framework proposes two nationalisms, based on unity and equality. This typology has several advantages: It builds from a general theory of social cognition, provides a bridge to other work on nationalisms in political science, generates a priori expectations about foreign policy attitudes, and maintains conceptual distance between the independent and dependent variables. Yet this framework is not exhaustive.

In particular, some nationalisms might depend on hierarchy—what Fiske (1991) calls "authority ranking" social relations. If the group's central norms require people to follow the government's rules or defer to a central power within a regional entity, nationalism should invite and exacerbate actions that enforce the hierarchy. IR scholars point out that the East Asian international order depends on hierarchy (Kang, 2020), for example, a description that clashes with Eurocentric ideas about sovereign equality as the foundation for order. Future studies might therefore turn to Taiwan, for one, to probe the theory's generalizability and test the implications of hierarchy-oriented nationalism. Taiwan has one foot in Western-style democracy but remains embedded in a system dominated by Mainland China. Taiwanese nationalists who accept the legitimacy of that hierarchy might take a softer stance against the Mainland than fellow citizens who reject it.

Of course, some readers might agree with my conclusion that content matters, but disagree with my focus on unity and equality or relational models theory in general. On one hand, I welcome the prospect that future scholars could use my theoretical architecture to build new schemes for studying nationalisms in international politics. Renewed attention to content and commitment could bring additional conceptual and theoretical insights to bear on lingering questions about nationalisms and foreign policy.

But on the other hand, I advanced unity and equality in part to whittle the unwieldy list of "adjectival" nationalisms and thereby nudge the field toward synthesis. In that respect, I encourage scholars to consider treating my framework as "thin" scaffolding for other, targeted norms.[4] I hint at this possibility when I discuss civic and ethnic nationalisms in chapter 2, where I note that the "civic" or "ethnic" quality of a particular identity may matter less for the outcomes that concern political scientists than the norms that underlie it.

Going forward, we could apply the same logic to a broader class of nationalisms. For example, Whitehead and Perry (2020, 10–11) describe how "Christian nationalism" in the United States is "as ethnic and political as it is religious" and "rarely concerned with instituting explicitly 'Christlike' policies." Its core features seem to unite Americans around a common culture, reinforce binary boundaries, and promote authoritarian control over outsiders and internal deviants. In turn, we could understand Christian nationalism as a manifestation of unity—and possibly hierarchy—and link it to the Jewish nationalism popular among many Israeli citizens, the Christian tradition in European identification (Risse, 2010, 51-52), the Muslim core of some Arab nationalisms (Zogby, 2010; Telhami, 2013), and a broader range of ethnic or exclusive nationalisms that demand homogeneity. Similarly, the core norms that bind existing characterizations of "inclusive" and multicultural nationalisms redound to equality. These identities afford all citizens "equal political rights" (Tudor and Slater, 2020, 2)

---

4. By analogy, consider Mudde's (2007) canonical conceptualization of "populism" as a "thin-centered ideology" (see also Mudde and Kaltwasser, 2013). Populism contains several necessary and sufficient attributes (Sartori, 1970)—the belief that ordinary people are good and competent whereas elites are untrustworthy, and that policy should reflect the will of the people. Political actors then combine other ideologies with these core features to create specific manifestations of populism. Right-wing populists are more likely to embrace nativism in defining "the people," whereas left-wing populists advance socialism to push back against the corrupt business interests of elites. Both remain tied to one populist core.

or require that group members commit to egalitarian values (Collingwood, Lajevardi and Oskooii, 2018). The multicultural prescription—that states should grant equal space to diverse cultural traditions rather than promote assimilation (Citrin, Johnston and Wright, 2012)—taps equality. Articulating these core norms facilitates synthesis, and promotes theoretical and conceptual rigor: The exercise encourages scholars to clarify which theoretical expectations stem from central norms like unity and equality versus which depend on the specific character of the unity- or equality-oriented nationalism.

Second, and related, this book tests the theory in two important contexts, the United States and Europe. The populations considered in chapters 3, 4, and 5 provide the bedrock for the conventional wisdom and constitute important and hard tests for my theory. Scholars often test theories about nationalist militarism in the United States, the country best poised to channel a bellicose public into conflictual foreign policy. The European Union similarly represents the foremost testing ground for research on how supranationalisms percolate to the public and reinforce security cooperation. But by rooting my individual-level theory in fundamental patterns of human social behavior—patterns with demonstrated cross-cultural validity (Fiske, 1992)—I provide a path for testing nationalisms elsewhere. Indeed, preliminary data from Argentina suggest that the constructs travel: In a national sample of Argentinians, 43.5% of respondents agreed or strongly agreed that their nationality requires reciprocity, whereas about 43% think of fellow Argentinians like family members.[5] But because those Argentinians do not share the United States' relative power advantage, even unity-oriented nationalists might be reticent to escalate militarized disputes and instead seek to protect their group through isolationism. Additional comparative research will help to unpack similarities and potential differences.

My framework and empirical tests further invite at least two additional areas for future research. This book established the typology and examined implications for foreign policy attitudes. Future work could build on it to evaluate dyadic interactions and second-order perceptions at the individual level, or patterns of conflict and cooperation in macro-level international politics.

---

5. Two separate questions asked participants to rate how strongly they agreed on a 5-point scale that "I owe duties to my fellow Argentinians because they owe duties to me" (equality) and "I owe duties to my fellow Argentinians just as I owe duties to my family." The two scales correlated at 0.39. Thank you to Hein Goemans for generously sharing these data with me.

INTERACTING NATIONALISMS

This book presents a monadic view of both nationalistic foreign policy and supranational cooperation. This approach follows both recent quantitative work on nationalism and war (Schrock-Jacobson, 2012; Bertoli, 2017) and psychological evidence that in-group perceptions predict the degree of external prejudice (Effron and Knowles, 2015). But it also raises questions about dyadic interactions and clashing identities. The experiment in chapter 3, for example, holds descriptions about the adversary's society and actions constant to maintain a tractable design. The observational data in chapter 5 contain information about how respondents view Europe, but not their second-order beliefs about how fellow citizens view the group. If I sought to examine nationalisms in an interactive context, I could extend the research in at least two ways.

First, I could amend the experiment in chapter 3 to manipulate Fredonia's partner or change the design to mimic a behavioral economics-style experiment. The first approach would be relatively straightforward: I could manipulate descriptions of Rusburg to emphasize either unity or equality in the adversary. We know from research on the democratic peace that citizens in democracies adopt different strategies when confronting a crisis with a fellow democracy versus an autocracy (Tomz and Weeks, 2013), and perceptions about national norms might moderate the effects of unity- and equality-oriented nationalisms. Equality-oriented nationalists might be especially conciliatory when facing an adversary whose population shares similar national norms if that knowledge reinforces the expectation that the partner will reciprocate rather than escalate. If so, the experiment in chapter 3 represents a conservative test for equality's mitigating effects on nationalist militarism, given that the brief description of Rusburg alluded to unity. Alternatively, I could opt for an approach that places participants in a strategic interaction game against a live partner. Randomly assigning each person to a description of her partner's equality- or unity-oriented nationalism—and incorporating real payoffs in a stylized crisis simulation[6]—could reveal how people use information about their partner's identity to structure their strategies.

Second, supranationalisms' effects on support for security cooperation raise questions about the interaction between a person's own regional commitment and second-order perceptions about how her group members view the supranational entity. What happens when someone commits to

6. See, for example, McDermott and Cowden (2001).

equality, but believes that her fellow citizens desire unity? Answering this question would require additional survey or experimental data on second-order perceptions, data outside this book's scope. But it is worthwhile to speculate about the implications for both European supranationalisms and other cases. A European committed to equality might hesitate to join forces with her neighbors if she thinks that they desire unity, for example. Indeed, Britain's early hesitation to join the burgeoning EU institutions—and later decision to leave—reflects a plausibly consequential mismatch. If some British citizens perceive their continental neighbors as friends not family, *and* believe that other Europeans think about themselves as part of a unified family, they might retrench despite holding supranational commitments.

The relationship between Taiwan and China presents a similar and enticing opportunity to probe the theory's implications in a non-Western context: Whereas Mainland China insists that Taiwan and China are part of "one family," whose "closeness" is "rooted in our blood, our history, and culture" (Xi, 2014, 260), many Taiwanese people view themselves as equals vis-à-vis the Mainland, and will only cooperate if China "handle[s] cross-strait differences peacefully, on the basis of equality."[7] This rhetoric suggests a content mismatch between the two sides. If that mismatch hardens Taiwanese resistance to economic integration or other forms of exchange and cooperation, it could provide a novel identity-based approach to understanding why Taiwanese attitudes toward economic cooperation often counteract their material interests.[8]

FROM MICRO TO MACRO

IR scholars use nationalisms to explain macro-level phenomena. And they often bring psychological insights to bear on those arguments, using the social identity approach to assume that nationalism causes war by inflating threat perceptions and encouraging hawkish escalation, or that supranationalism fosters in-group love that cements trust and redefines states' interests. But our macro-level theories require refinement if some nationalisms counteract those cooperative or conflictual tendencies. I propose

7. Tsai Ing-Wen, 2019. "President Tsai issues statement on China's President Xi's 'Message to Compatriots in Taiwan.'" Transcript available at the Office of the President of the Republic of China (Taiwan). 2 January. URL: https://english.president.gov.tw/News/5621.

8. I thank Dalton Lin for spotting my theory's potential implications for Taiwanese identities, and for his collaboration as we subject this speculation to empirical tests.

several options for future work to examine whether varieties of nationalism shape conflict and cooperation in practice.

Research could deploy proxies for aggregate trends in unity and equality paired with exogenous nationalist surges to explain militarized interstate disputes, for example. The most challenging step would be to classify states by their "average" aggregate nationalist norms. Existing theories about varieties of nationalism and international conflict either turn to in-depth case analyses that limit the scope of potential claims (Snyder, 2000), or employ discrete measures that may miss important variation by capturing only explicit, elite-driven nationalist ideas (Schrock-Jacobson, 2012).[9] Measuring cross-national variation in unity and equality requires careful validation, though population-level trends in personal values offer one possibility. Cross-cultural psychologists examine value distributions at the country level to determine how groups respond to challenges (Schwartz, 1999; Hofstede and Bond, 1984; Knafo, Roccas and Sagiv, 2011), and research could build from this premise to assess average and relative commitments to values associated with unity and equality across countries. In IR, for example, Stein (2019) compares country-level retribution values to show that vengeful democracies initiate militarized interstate disputes at higher rates than others.

Research should account for exogenous forces that stoke nationalist commitments, too, like World Cup qualification (Bertoli, 2017) or national day celebrations (Gruffydd-Jones, 2017). I expect that unity- and equality-oriented nationalisms will diverge when it comes to conflict initiation and escalation, but converge with respect to reciprocity. A thorough investigation should therefore include dependent variables that measure dispute escalation alongside initiation and severity.[10]

Alternatively, scholars could use discourse analysis to capture nationalist identity content at specific points in time (Hopf and Allan, 2016).

9. To my knowledge Schrock-Jacobson (2012) has produced the most comprehensive large-n dataset on varieties of nationalism. Setting aside that my framework differs from the civic, ethnic, revolutionary, and counterrevolutionary typology that she advances, the data are nevertheless limited in their scope. For example, they contain only 12 cases of American nationalism between 1821 and 1991, all coded as "civic," a coding that clashes with how historians depict the various strands of American nationalism rooted in hereditary rights and unifying republicanism (Sinopoli, 1996; Trautsch, 2016; Park, 2018). Although the dataset represents a major advance in understanding nationalisms in international conflict, a measure of content that applies to each year could make tests more precise and increase the number of observations in the data.

10. See Senese (1996) for one approach to measuring escalation with conflict data, for example.

This method entails deeply reading text and requires extensive contextual knowledge. But the inductive process alleviates concerns about assigning categorical identities to countries from "above"—problems that plague previous work on country-level nationalisms in IR. Moreover, an inductive and purpose-built analysis helps ensure that scholars capture group-level norms without reducing nationalisms to dispositional traits (Hopf and Allan, 2016, 13, 20). It could lead to rigorous case study research, for example.

Scholars might apply a similar logic to testing whether cross-national variation in supranationalisms corresponds to government decisions regarding security cooperation. For example, which EU member-states support concrete efforts to craft a common foreign and security policy, and when? In chapter 5, my survey analyses revealed evidence for contestation both within and between EU member-states. Although I focused on individual attitudes, the national balance between equality and unity provides one reasonable proxy for which views carry the day within each European country. I would expect to find more moves toward an integrated foreign policy from countries where citizens have coalesced around equality, building on past research that shows a relationship between European identification and a state's support for integration policies (Risse, 2001; Koenig-Archibugi, 2004). Researchers pursuing this route will need to overcome the absence of panel data on European nationalisms, perhaps by examining cross-sectional variation during consequential deliberations (Koenig-Archibugi, 2004). The 2007 Intergovernmental Council (IGC) that preceded the Lisbon Treaty, for example, recommended specific changes to the Common Foreign and Security Policy. Evidence that average supranationalist commitments within a country explain variation in government support for foreign policy integration at the IGC would comport with my theory's macro-level implications.

Nationalisms also appear in elite rhetoric, which invites tests of elite-driven theories of nationalist conflict. Nationalist elites stand at the helm and bear ultimate responsibility for a state's foreign policy behavior. Prominent traditions in foreign policy analysis implicate nationalism as a characteristic that drives conflict (Hermann, 1980; Walker, Schafer and Young, 1999; Renshon, 2009), but separating elites committed to equality from those committed to unity could refine these frameworks.[11] Most leaders

---

11. Moreover, research on nationalisms at the leader level would supplement the renaissance of individual-level IR research showing that belief systems (Saunders, 2011), dispositions (Yarhi-Milo, 2018; Gallagher and Allen, 2014; Cuhadar et al., 2017), and other traits shape decisions about war and peace (Chiozza and Goemans, 2004; Horowitz, Stam and Ellis, 2015).

likely endorse nationalism even if they reject the label: Per Obama, "There's no American politician, much less American President, who's not going to say that we're not the greatest country on earth."[12] Advancements that allow researchers to efficiently gather and analyze speeches, for example, facilitate our ability to comb public-facing discourse for commitments to national unity or equality. Developing a corpus of speeches would require attention to concerns about strategic rhetoric and endogeneity with respect to ongoing crises, of course. But limiting the collection to regularly scheduled declarations and speeches associated with annual celebrations ameliorates these concerns somewhat. In the United States, congressional statute requires presidents to issue an annual proclamation that recognizes Loyalty Day on May 1. These official statements—which began in 1959— typically include references to American values that may provide insights into the president's own commitments. Independence Day speeches and State of the Union–type addresses to legislative bodies have similarly desirable qualities if leaders deliver them regardless of external circumstances. Alternatively, speeches delivered on the campaign trail could provide a lens into a leader's nationalist commitments before they face foreign policy crises (Augoustinos and De Garis, 2012; Saunders, 2011). Comparing leaders within a country, researchers could determine whether relative commitments to unity and equality correlate with involvement in militarized interstate disputes (MIDs), MID escalation, or the probability that a leader uses force when presented with an opportunity (Yarhi-Milo, 2018; Gallagher and Allen, 2014).

In short, future research could enrich our understanding of nationalisms in international politics by subjecting my micro-level theory to macro-level tests. Experiments and surveys have significant advantages for testing new theoretical and conceptual frameworks, both for causal identification purposes and because they facilitate more fine-grained measurement. Having used those methods to test the theory in this book, I hope that additional studies can test the macro-level implications that follow.

Where Do Nationalisms Come From?

In the sections above, I described several limitations and extensions related to this book's primary objective—assessing whether and how nationalisms shape attitudes toward conflict and cooperation. This book analyzes

12. Barack Obama, 2013. "Remarks by the President at a DNC Event—New York, NY", 13 May. Obama White House Archives.

nationalisms as independent variables rather than dependent variables—as *explanans* and not *explanandum*. In turn, the theory and empirical tests presented in chapters 2–5 evaluate whether nationalisms carry distinct implications for attitudes toward foreign policy conflict and cooperation. My approach generated new insights and resolved several problems with past work: Although decades of research has coalesced around the idea that nationalism causes support for conflict and foreign policy aggression—and that supranationalism prompts public support for intra-European trust and security cooperation—my theory explains how those relationships depend on content.

This book therefore provides an important rejoinder to the conventional wisdom, but also raises questions about the independent variable: Who are the unity- and equality-based nationalists? What factors shape contestation, content, and commitment outside the context of a scientific questionnaire? This limitation differs from those that I identified above because it precedes the book's core questions, and therefore calls for a more extensive discussion.

As I previewed in chapter 2, I expect that variation in nationalism stems from at least three sources: Historical narratives and institutions, elite messaging, and dispositional traits.[13] Although I discuss each element in turn and suggest fruitful avenues for future research, I expect dynamic and reciprocal relationships between dispositions, leaders, context, and nationalisms. Social structures have downward effects on identity content, for example, but also change in response to individual actions and practice just as cognitive factors shape which identities people commit to and when.[14]

CONTEXT: INSTITUTIONS AND NATIONAL MYTHS

Nationalisms are made and learned, not born from the soil (Anderson, 1983; McNamara, 2015a). Historical narratives, constitutions, and institutions embed norms in an entity's collective memory. Historical events produce social structures and narratives that fuel the nationalisms most

13. Of course, these do not exhaust the set of potentially relevant inputs. For example, a rich tradition in cross-cultural psychology examines the complex relationship between cultural paradigms and everything from how people express their identities to personality and fundamental neurological responses (Triandis and Brislin, 1984; Heine and Buchtel, 2009; Kitayama and Uskul, 2011). In political science, Snyder (2000, 342–52) details how international factors like trade, military competition, and the transnational marketplace of ideas can shape domestic institutions and in turn, nationalisms, whereas scholars like McNamara and Musgrave (2020) point to democratic practices.

14. See, for example, McNamara and Musgrave (2020) for a discussion.

likely to captivate the contemporary population. In one respect, a discussion about historical and social context brings us full circle—back to scholarship from political scientists, sociologists, and historians who divide the world into "civic" and "ethnic" nationalisms with richly detailed case studies, but who pay less attention to contestation within countries or regions (Kohn, 1944; Greenfeld, 1992; Snyder, 2000; Park, 2018; Tudor and Slater, 2020). I agree that founding narratives and explicit efforts to craft nationalisms each play an important role in shaping perceptions. Yet myths and institutions reflect "multiple traditions" that remain subject to renegotiation over time (Smith, 1997; Kymlicka, 2003; Schildkraut, 2005; Tudor and Slater, 2020). Context shapes identity content, but also sets the stage for enduring contestation.

Creating nation-states and regional organizations entails more than marking borders and writing laws; founders also set group boundaries and standards for current and future residents to follow. Debates about governance are debates about identity—nation-building "is a powerful and complex process of socialization and ideological engineering" (Lee and Chou, 2020, 924). The exchange between Monnet and Eisenhower that kicked off chapter 5 illustrates this process. Both leaders recognized that mustering enthusiasm for the ultimately ill-fated European Defence Community required inculcating ideas about Europeanness in the population (Fursdon, 1980, 118). Monnet (1978, 10) repeated this sentiment in the epigraph for his memoirs, where he wrote that "we are not forming coalitions between States, but union among people."

Actors adopt several methods to create enduring nationalist norms. One method involves laws or other coercive tools. Governments often use national language policies to create unity within heterogeneous populations: Atatürk imposed a common vernacular on the Turkish people in his effort to develop productive national pride (Emerson, 1960), for example, and the Tanzanian government used the shared Kiswahili language to create a unifying bond and stymie the cycle of intrastate violence (Sambanis and Shayo, 2013). The postcolonial government in India leveraged the education system to facilitate communication between heterogeneous communities and foster nationalism (Tudor and Slater, 2020): Although all Indians begin learning in their local dialect, they would eventually learn Hindi and English (Emerson, 1960, 144). To be Indian was to be multilingual.

Conversations among politicians, intellectuals, religious leaders, and literary figures similarly give rise to nationalisms. Being French meant speaking French, according to elites, long before a constitution recognized the official language (Greenfeld, 1992, 102). Participation and self-governance dominated the discussions when English nationalism emerged in the 1600s (Greenfeld, 1992, 45), such that English nationalism centered on the idea that the polity retained individual liberties. Early English nationalists provided a liberal narrative for many modern Britons to embrace in articulating their Englishness.

Constitutions and constitutional debates provide a more formal venue for elites to define nationalisms. Canada's constitutionalized commitment to diversity and multiculturalism, for example, represents an effort to enshrine equality norms into law and thereby shape popular perceptions (Kymlicka, 2003). In the United States, the Federalist and Anti-Federalist papers revealed competing visions for the new nation. The Anti-Federalists advanced ideas akin to unity: "In a republic, the manners, sentiments, and interests of the people should be similar" (Brutus qtd. in Sinopoli, 1996, 38). Small, homogeneous communities would promote the common good. The Federalist papers, by contrast, contained language and commitments steeped in liberal norms that hearken to equality (Sinopoli, 1996, 6). Founders like Thomas Jefferson stressed that people owe each other respect and freedom to live as equals. This contestation persisted beyond the constitutional conventions (Park, 2018; McNamara and Musgrave, 2020). For example, Mead (1999) describes the "Jacksonian" tradition as a culture-bound, homogeneous, unified American nationalism—incidentally, one that promotes using overwhelming force, especially against "dishonorable" enemies.[15] Although the Jeffersonian tradition intended for equality to exclude women and non-white Americans (Trautsch, 2016, 300), the "American Creed" retains a hallowed place in the mythos and drives nationalist commitments to equality today (Smith, 1993b; Theiss-Morse, 2009, 18).

National governments and EU institutions commit copious resources to other top-down efforts to craft nationalisms through laws and education (Cram, 2012). These efforts target identity content in different ways. Citizenship laws at the national level, or accession criteria at the regional level, delineate official norms for new immigrants or member-states. Laws and procedures often require immigrants to demonstrate proficiency in the national language (such as Austria), identify local holidays and customs (the Netherlands), prove to an interviewer that they can assimilate (France) (Goodman, 2012, 666–67), or identify their constitutional rights (the United States). The EU's Copenhagen criteria apply analogous tests

---

15. See also Mead (2002).

to candidate states, setting expectations for aspiring EU citizens. Beyond explicit legal requirements, governments also convey nationalist norms through civic education materials—the early twentieth century American-ization movement created orientation programs to teach immigrants about national norms (Goodman, 2021, 1478), for example. Of course, govern-ments also seek to inculcate values and norms in native citizens, often using the public education system (Weber, 1976). For instance, Nasser mustered state-controlled media, political organizations, and schools in his ultimately failed push for Arab nationalism in Egypt (Karawan, 2002, 158). Native citizens and new arrivals receive similar information albeit via distinct routes.

ELITES, LEADERSHIP, AND IDENTITY CONTENT

Historic debates, social context, and legal frameworks define the menu. But members of the public rely on elite recommendations and individual dispositions to make their selection. On the campaign trail and in office, national and regional leaders pitch themselves as good representatives for the group (Augoustinos and De Garis, 2012), and use implicit and explicit appeals to advance their ideas about national identity content (Schildkraut, 2002).[16] We embrace leaders who we view as "one of us"—so-called "proto-typical" Americans, Scots, or Europeans (Hogg, 2001)—and reward them with our loyalty and support. Standing at the "bully pulpit," elites become identity entrepreneurs—who use oratorical opportunities to elevate certain group norms (Fielding and Hogg, 1997; Hogg, 2001; Reicher, Haslam and Hopkins, 2005; Reicher, Haslam and Platow, 2007; Haslam, Reicher and Platow, 2011).[17] Nationalist cues and constructions, in turn, could mobilize support for elite foreign policy agendas.

Constitutions contain many principles. Elites choose which to priori-tize, and in turn can redefine nationalisms to advance their own principles and priorities as group norms. Although leaders sometimes use coercive

16. See, for example, Mendelberg (2001) for a similar argument regarding the interaction between normative context and elite cues in American politics. The book demonstrates that elites can use implicit racial appeals to prime voters, but do so against a backdrop of changing racial equality norms. As the U.S. embraced a norm of racial equality, elites shifted away from explicitly racist campaigns to use more subtle cues.

17. See Steffens et al. (2015) for a review of leadership psychology and research on leaders as identity entrepreneurs, and Haslam, Reicher and Platow (2011) for a book-length treatment of the "new psychology of leadership." For a recent study that uses interviews to examine national identity construction in Sudan, see Moss (2017).

tools to impose group norms (Kreuzer, 2006; Moss, 2017), they also rely on the power of charisma: U.S. President Lincoln used his Gettysburg address to anoint equality as the "touchstone of American identity" in the minds of his eager audience, for example (Reicher, Haslam and Platow, 2007, 28; Wills, 1992). National and EU elites alike sprinkle political platforms and major speeches with references to who "we" are: When then-candidate Ursula von der Leyen laid out her vision "for a Union of equality, tolerance and social fairness" in 2019,[18] or when President Nixon explained that patriotic Americans must "make personal sacrifices when our Nation is challenged,"[19] each provided information about the qualities that bind Europeans or Americans. And research suggests that these appeals work. People adjust their understanding of the group's values, boundaries, and norms to the vision laid out by respected leaders. Leaders can then persuade followers to make sacrifices, support political violence (Kunst, Dovidio and Thomsen, 2019), or embrace political tolerance based on their shared identification (Reicher, Haslam and Rath, 2008).

This sequence reveals how an elite could foment unity- or equality-oriented nationalism to advance her foreign policy agenda. Research on American foreign policy public opinion provides ample evidence that citizens respond to elite cues to inform their attitudes about specific policies.[20] Extending this logic implies that elites could use the language of nationhood and identity to connect group ideals to political actions (Reicher, Spears and Postmes, 1995; Reicher and Hopkins, 2001). National leaders might stress unity to mobilize support for war: If *we* Americans are united as Nixon claimed, then *we* must be prepared to use force to protect our homeland against threats. Similarly, if citizens become more committed to European equality after Ursula van der Leyen's description, my theory implies stronger public support for the "genuine European Defence Union" that she proposes.[21]

18. Ursula von der Leyen, 2019. "A Union that strives for more: My Agenda for Europe," *Political Guidelines for the Next European Commission 2019-2024*, p. 14. URL: https://ec.europa.eu/info/sites/default/files/political-guidelines-next-commission_en_0.pdf.

19. Nixon, Richard, 1974. "Proclamation 4277–Loyalty Day, 1974," 25 March. Available at https://www.presidency.ucsb.edu/documents/proclamation-4277-loyalty-day-1974.

20. See, for example, Berinsky (2009); Althaus and Coe (2011); and Guisinger and Saunders (2017) for research on the relationship between elite cues and foreign policy attitudes (though cf. Kertzer and Zeitzoff, 2017).

21. Ursula von der Leyen, 2019. "A Union that strives for more: My Agenda for Europe," *Political Guidelines for the Next European Commission 2019-2024*, p. 19.

What might mobilization based on identity content look like in practice? Consider how two U.S. presidents responded to homeland attacks. FDR ascended to the presidency promising to facilitate domestic recovery, in part through international economic cooperation. But despite his early nod to multilateralism and reticence regarding U.S. entry into World War II (Woods, 1989; Farnham, 1992, 2000),[22] by 1939 he had moved toward a pro-war orientation (Legro, 2000; Berinsky, 2007). In turn, he imbued his rhetoric with nods to unity as he prepared the country for war. After the Pearl Harbor attack, he peppered his fireside chats with unifying language and binary relational comparisons that described how "we" are good whereas our enemies are evil. Americans are "builders," whereas our enemies are "destroyers," "gangsters," and "criminal[s]" fighting a "dishonorable" and "dirty" war.[23]

FDR's nationalist messages conveyed his definition of American norms and values in a time of war. Aiming to make his foreign policies acceptable to the American public (Farnham, 2000), he described the war effort as a logical extension of American identity. Reflecting the "all for one" theme, he stated:

> We are now in this war. We are all in it—all the way. Every single man, woman, and child is a partner in the most tremendous undertaking of our American history. We must share together the bad news and the good news, the defeats and the victories—the changing fortunes of war.[24]

His rhetoric stressed that fellow Americans have a duty to protect the group, both for now and the future, and that they should reject rumors from enemy sources inside or outside of the state. He spoke of sacrifice as

22. See, for example, Fireside Chat 2, where FDR emphasizes joint international suffering: "All of the Nations have suffered alike in this great depression. They have all reached the conclusion that each can best be helped by the common action of all." Roosevelt, Franklin Delano, 1933. "Fireside Chat 2: On Progress During the First Two Months," 7 May. Accessed via the University of Virginia Miller Center Presidential Speech archives. URL: https://millercenter.org/the-presidency/presidential-speeches/may-7-1933-fireside-chat-2-progress-during-first-two-months.

23. Roosevelt, Franklin Delano, 1941. "Fireside Chat 19: On the War with Japan," 9 December. Accessed via the University of Virginia Miller Center Presidential Speech archives. URL: https://millercenter.org/the-presidency/presidential-speeches/december-9-1941-fireside-chat-19-war-japan.

24. Roosevelt, Franklin Delano, 1941. "Fireside Chat 19: On the War with Japan," 9 December. Accessed via the University of Virginia Miller Center Presidential Speech archives.

a privilege—people should relish the chance to contribute to the national defense. In a time of war, unity offered a route to achieve domestic stability and U.S. national security. He later paired pleas for internal unity with binary contrasts against America's enemies.[25] For example, his references to "the Japanese" did not differentiate between ordinary citizens and elites—a stance that trickled down through the media, which painted Japanese people as inherently untrustworthy and deserving of punishment (Schildkraut, 2002, 521-23). When he wanted the public on his side as the United States went to war, FDR called for unity.

By contrast, when a 2015 terrorist attack killed 14 Americans in San Bernardino, California, Barack Obama had a different goal: Tamp down demands to escalate the fight against ISIS (Baker, 2016). Obama used a rare Oval Office address to call for inaction (Yglesias, 2015), or limited action, rather than escalation.[26] He asked Americans to support his existing policies—sustained air strikes on ISIS targets coupled with efforts to create peace in Syria (Prokop, 2015). He emphasized the costs from committing to a ground war against an organization that poses a limited threat to Americans (Inskeep, 2015). He wanted continuity after the deadly but small-scale attack.[27]

Obama then used equality-laden rhetoric to reinforce his vision of American identity. Indeed, the 2015 speech followed his long-standing habit of describing justice, equality, and diversity as essential American values (Augoustinos and De Garis, 2012). In the televised address, he rejected binary relational comparisons and called for inclusion: "We cannot turn against one another by letting this fight be defined as a war between America and Islam" and must instead enlist Muslim communities to counteract extremists. Americans, he asserted, must "reject discrimination," because the United States was "founded upon a belief in human dignity—that no matter who you are or where you come from, or what you look like, or

25. Roosevelt, Franklin Delano, 1942. "Fireside Chat 21: On Sacrifice," 28 April. Accessed via the University of Virginia Miller Center Presidential Speech archives. URL: https://millercenter.org/the-presidency/presidential-speeches/april-28-1942-fireside-chat-21-sacrifice.

26. Obama, Barack. 2015. "President Obama's address to the nation on the San Bernardino terror attack and the war on ISIS," 6 December.

27. His decision to use an Oval Office address reflected terrorism's renewed salience in the U.S. after a deadly year in other Western states. For example, Gallup found that the percentage of Americans who mentioned terrorism as the "most important" problem for the country increased from November to December by 13 percentage points. The 16% of Americans who reported terrorism as the most important problem represented the highest proportion since 2005 (Riffkin, 2015).

what religion you practice, you are equal in the eyes of God and equal in the eyes of the law."[28] In striving to "meet the *psychological* needs of a nation under attack" (Yglesias, 2015, para. 4), Obama used the bully pulpit to convince his audience that American ideals called for restraint. Despite ample criticism about whether the speech did "enough" to quell citizens' fears (Inskeep, 2015), the approach appeared to work. Public support for sending ground troops to Iraq and Syria remained muted—rising a mere 3 percentage points in the wake of the attack compared to July 2015 (Pew Research Center, 2015).

Leaders like Roosevelt and Obama *can* act as identity entrepreneurs, and peddle nationalist themes. But testing whether their rhetoric moves individuals' identity content or shifts foreign policy attitudes requires additional research beyond these illustrative anecdotes. Some scholars contend that effective leaders can be "masters of identity" (Haslam, Reicher and Platow, 2011, 162), but, to my knowledge, public opinion scholars rarely put these claims to the test. An interested researcher could take inspiration from experimental studies about the effects of elite cues to randomly assign participants to receive a unity- or equality-laden message. Measuring participants' self-reported identity content posttreatment could determine whether perceptions shift after effective messaging. Given the important role played by co-partisanship in research on elite messaging (Guisinger and Saunders, 2017), studies should also vary the leader's partisan identity. Or, following Helbling, Reeskens and Wright (2016), future research could track the relationship between party platforms and aggregate perceptions of national identity content in the public.

Case studies and text analyses, too, could provide important insights into the relationship between leader rhetoric, identity content, and foreign policy attitudes. A qualitative discourse analysis could investigate whether and how specific leaders shift the broader conversation about the meaning of group membership. Did Obama's presidential campaign trigger a renewed commitment to equality among his supporters? To what extent have elites succeeded in their efforts to instill competing narratives about European values in their home audiences (Risse, 2010, ch. 3)? Alternatively, pairing computerized text analysis with longitudinal public opinion data could tell us whether public sentiment follows a leader's words. Leaders make statements that reference identity content at annual holidays and

28. Obama, Barack. 2015. "President Obama's address to the nation on the San Bernardino terror attack and the war on ISIS," 6 December.

events, like the EU's 9 May "Europe Day" celebration, France's Bastille Day, or the Independence and Loyalty Days recognized in the United States. Analyzing the correlation between the norms a leader espouses and subsequent trends in the values and national identities endorsed by members of the public could illuminate connections between leaders and followers.

Of course, leaders lack a monopoly on cue-giving and identity entrepreneurship. Nationalist norms might also emerge from the bottom up. Social cues come from peers and fellow citizens rather than elites, and reliably shift attitudes about both domestic and foreign policy (Rothschild and Malhotra, 2014; Kertzer, 2017; Toff, 2018). Indeed, top-down efforts to push ideas about national identity content often meet resistance from the masses, like the Russians who rejected elite efforts to instill a new neoliberal identity in the country (Hopf, 2013) or Egyptians who rejected Nasser's charismatic bid for Arab unity (Karawan, 2002, 159). People adjust their policy positions to match the polls, and likely also take cues about nationalist norms from fellow citizens. As the United States witnessed mass protests against racial injustice in 2020, for example, some citizens concluded that protest is patriotic.

One complicating factor: Successful identity entrepreneurship, from leaders or peers, may resonate with some individuals but fall flat to others. Obama's Oval Office address appears to have backfired, for example, among Republicans who did not appreciate that he "lectured us . . . about tolerance" (Rubin, 2015, para. 6). This group—consisting of individuals who rejected the President's vision for who Americans are and how they ought to behave toward outsiders—believed that Obama had failed to unite the United States against its enemy. To fully understand the antecedents of nationalisms, then, we need to incorporate research on individual dispositions.

DISPOSITIONAL FACTORS

Context provides intellectual and historical fodder that elites and others can use to advance different nationalisms. But if nationalisms entail individual-level commitments and perceptions, these identities partially emanate from within. Individual differences can influence the particular norms a person tends to adopt, as well as how strongly she commits to the group.

The U.S. and EU respondents in chapters 4 and 5 held different views about both content and commitment, for example; situational cues about "the" American or European identity do not fully explain why some people prioritize equality whereas others prioritize unity. Visualizing country-level contestation in the IntUne surveys revealed, for example, that unity- and equality-oriented Europeans reside throughout the EU. And indeed, we know from previous work that some people are more likely to set "hard" or "soft" boundaries on their identities than others (Theiss-Morse, 2009; Schildkraut, 2007; Bonikowski and DiMaggio, 2016; Bruter, 2003; Cram, Patrikios and Mitchell, 2011).

Moreover, people prefer certain relational styles over others. When people categorize preferred norms for relationships with friends, colleagues, authority figures, and family members, the dual dispositional and cultural influences appear: Most Americans adopt unity at home and equality at work (context), but stable average differences separate people who prefer either solidarity or reciprocity across a wider range of relationships (dispositions). Individual differences in these "generic construal tendencies" suggest that dispositional factors determine how people connect to national and supranational groups, and how strongly they commit (Caralis and Haslam, 2004; Haslam, Reichert and Fiske, 2002; Simpson and Laham, 2015a).[29]

Who, then, embraces unity- or equality-oriented nationalisms at greater rates than others? I integrate research on identification and political attitudes to distill plausible dispositional correlates. I select three sets of factors—moral foundations, personal values, and personality traits—that share two important features: (1) Each precedes nationalism in the causal chain, either because it refers to abstract, higher-order beliefs or trans-situational personality traits; and (2) Scholars routinely invoke each as antecedents for the foreign policy attitudes that I examined in this book. Crucially, the fact that dispositions directly affect foreign policy attitudes does not undermine nationalisms' role. Commitment sets the stage for social influence, such that unity- and equality-oriented nationalisms supplement and exacerbate any direct effects of dispositional traits. Attitudes and behavior reflect who we are (our dispositions), but also our expectations about how we should act as a parts of—and on behalf of—our groups.[30]

29. Psychologists who research development, attachment styles, and social value orientations note similar variance in *interpersonal dispositions*, "actor-specific inclinations to respond to particular situations in a specific manner across numerous partners" (Rusbult and Van Lange, 2003, 367).

30. See, for example, White and Laird (2020) on how racialized social constraint shapes Black Americans' voting behavior in ways that sometimes contradict their individual-level preferences.

Moral values

The constitutive norms that characterize unity- and equality-oriented nationalisms imply distinct moral commitments. Maintaining unity requires that group members care for one another and protect the group from insidious forces that seek to divide it, whether from within or outside the group's boundaries. Equality-oriented groups prescribe fairness and reciprocity—if I do my part, you should do yours. And everyone should have an equal opportunity to thrive. In turn, I expect that individual beliefs about what is right and wrong—moral values—shape nationalisms. People attempt to project their own morals onto their group; if a citizen prioritizes fairness and identifies as "American," she will want her group to match her equality-oriented disposition. If she perceives a match between her own morals and group norms, she will commit (Roccas and McCauley, 2004), and in turn endorse policies that conform to those values. Moral commitments combine with these perceptions about the group to create equality- and unity-oriented nationalists.

Theoretical links and conceptual convergence connect what moral psychologists call the "binding" moral principles—authority/tradition, in-group/loyalty, and sanctity/degradation—to unity-oriented nationalism.[31] Binding foundations imply that the collective itself merits moral consideration, and that societal harmony, group maintenance, and community protection should often override individual autonomy (Graham, Haidt and Nosek, 2009; Graham et al., 2011). These values emphasize solidarity and the "ethic of community" that correspond to the "all for one and one for all" ethos associated with national and supranational unity—like unity, homogeneity, and solidarity (Shweder et al., 1997). For example, people who score high on the in-group/loyalty foundation abhor actions that betray the group's unity, the sanctity/degradation foundation requires that people adhere to a set of homogeneous sacred standards, and authority/respect

---

31. My discussion and expectations depend on theory and evidence from psychology's Moral Foundations Theory (MFT). MFT posits that people draw from a set of 5 moral systems to make quick, intuitive judgments about right and wrong (Haidt, 2001). Familiar to many political scientists, research implicates the moral foundations in everything from political ideology to culture wars and foreign policy orientations (Graham, Haidt and Nosek, 2009; Koleva et al., 2012; Weber and Federico, 2013; Kertzer et al., 2014; Rathbun, Powers and Anders, 2019). And indeed, MFT intertwines with my theory of identity content as we draw inspiration from the same source: Haidt and Joseph (2004, 58) used relational models theory to create the foundations. Each relational model implicates moral judgments—caring and altruism within communal sharing groups and fairness and reciprocity in equality matching groups.

encapsulates ideas about societal continuity and cohesive traditions. Moreover, existing research links the binding foundations to support for the U.S. war in Iraq, militant internationalism (Kertzer et al., 2014), "cooler" attitudes toward other countries, "tough" foreign policy stances (Gries, 2014), and disproportionate nuclear retaliation (Rathbun and Stein, 2017).

By contrast, fairness/reciprocity corresponds to equality. One of two "individualizing" foundations, people committed to fairness respect individual rights, punish cheaters who do not reciprocate, and believe that laws and institutions should offer equal protection to all citizens. People who value fairness—especially those who rank fairness as more important than other moral foundations—should adopt stronger equality-oriented nationalism (or, alternatively, shun nationalism when they believe that unity prevails among their co-nationals or key elites). And indeed, fairness/reciprocity correlates with dovish orientations (Kertzer et al., 2014), "warmer" feelings toward other countries (Gries, 2014), and support for intra-European financial bailouts (Rathbun, Powers and Anders, 2019).

The final foundation, harm/care, obligates people to alleviate others' suffering—a principle that could relate to either unity or equality. Researchers typically lump harm/care with fairness because it entails individual autonomy. But some people apply moral caring parochially. Indeed, although unity-oriented nationalism predicts out-group aggression, solidarity requires that group members help each other (Wong, 2010). People maintain an obligation to care for co-nationals or co-Europeans, at least insofar as they reflect the key traits associated with "good" representatives for the group.[32] Indeed, Simpson and Laham (2015a) find a positive relationship between the care foundation and individuals' tendency to construe relationships around unity norms. Yet others apply moral caring to a circle that extends beyond borders and even across species (Waytz et al., 2016), a pattern that corresponds to equality's more permeable boundaries. The relationship between the harm/care foundation and identity content likely depends on other values. Previous public opinion work associates harm/care with dovish orientations but support for humanitarian interventions (Kreps and Maxey, 2018), and support for financial bailouts among Germans who have a larger moral circle (Rathbun, Powers and Anders, 2019), highlighting the contingent effects of this moral system.

---

32. For example, Americans who identify strongly with the national community believe that it is important to help co-nationals via disaster relief, volunteer work, and support for welfare programs (Theiss-Morse, 2009, 104–5).

Personal values

Personal values also shape how we relate to social groups and form our political attitudes (Schwartz, 1994, 1999; Jacoby, 2006; Goren et al., 2016; Rathbun et al., 2016; Biber, Hupfeld and Meier, 2008). The relative importance of each value helps people to resolve trade-offs between competing goals—like the tension between unity and equality that divides nationalisms.[33]

Conservation values—which include security, tradition, and conformity—correspond to unity-oriented nationalisms. Conservation prioritizes homogeneity. People who hold these values prize stability, aim to preserve societal conventions, and adopt behaviors and beliefs that allow the group to persist across generations (Feldman, 2003; Jost et al., 2003; Rathbun et al., 2016). Consistent with a commitment to national unity, survey research shows that Americans who embrace conservation values reject conationals who deviate from cultural traditions, and hold conservative views about race (Goren et al., 2016). Moreover, cross-national research finds consistent evidence for a positive relationship between conservation values and hawkish foreign policy views (Goren et al., 2016; Rathbun et al., 2016; O'Dwyer and Çoymak, 2020; Gravelle, Reifler and Scotto, 2020).

By contrast, openness values and universalism (one of two self-transcendence values) likely inspire equality-oriented nationalism. Although neither openness nor universalism tap fairness or reciprocity norms directly, they nevertheless implicate the relational comparisons that correspond to equality. People who value self-direction, stimulation, and hedonism believe that humans should each share in the same opportunities to seek pleasure, and universalism leads people to care about and embrace outsiders. Together these values should facilitate individuals' ability to conceive of more permeable group boundaries and to accommodate heterogeneity. Existing research on the relationship between openness,

---

33. Schwartz (1994) argues that values share five features: (1) they are abstract, (2) refer to desirable end states, (3) transcend specific situations, (4) guide attitudes and behavior, and (5) entail individual-level rank ordering. His "universal circumplex" contains 10 values that represent the complement of personal values that people adhere to: benevolence, universalism, self-direction, stimulation, hedonism, achievement, power, security, conformity, and tradition. In turn, these values constitute four superordinate sets—openness to change, self-transcendence, conservation, and self-enhancement. The Schwartz circumplex is the most widely accepted values theory in social psychology, and has been validated cross-nationally (Davidov, Schmidt and Schwartz, 2008).

universalism, and foreign policy attitudes reveals inconsistent results—openness values sometimes correlate with militarism (Rathbun et al., 2016), and sometimes do not (Gravelle, Reifler and Scotto, 2020; O'Dwyer and Çoymak, 2020); universalism (together with benevolence) correlates with support for multilateral cooperation, dovish foreign policy attitudes, and opposition to armed drones (Goren et al., 2016; O'Dwyer and Çoymak, 2020).[34] Of course if personal values are associated with equality-oriented nationalism, this inconsistency makes sense—based on the evidence in chapter 4, equality-oriented nationalism increases militarism in situations where force entails a reciprocal response.

Personality traits: Open and closed types

Whereas values help people match abstract beliefs to nationalism and foreign policy attitudes, personality traits connect stable characteristics and behavioral tendencies to political preferences. I expect that traits associated with "open" and "closed" personalities correlate with equality- and unity-oriented nationalisms, respectively (Johnston, Lavine and Federico, 2017).[35]

People who possess closed personality traits likely embrace unity-oriented identities at greater rates than open personalities. Closed types perceive their environment as more threatening than open types. Like unity-oriented nationalists, closed types desire certainty, order, and security (Johnston, 2017, 21). They see the world as a threatening place (Altemeyer, 1988), a mindset that makes them comfortable in familiar settings and skeptical about cultural change (Hetherington and Weiler, 2018).[36] People with closed dispositions should find unity attractive because this nationalism solidifies group boundaries and implies that group members will sacrifice to protect each other.

34. Others find a positive relationship between self-transcendence and hawkishness (Gravelle, Reifler and Scotto, 2020). Given that benevolence hews closer to norms associated with community-level altruism and unity-oriented nationalism, these results underscore the need to separate universalism from benevolence in theories and analyses that relate values to nationalisms and foreign policy attitudes.

35. I follow Johnston, Lavine and Federico (2017) to use "open" and "closed" as shorthand for broad clusters of related personality traits.

36. I employ Hetherington and Weiler's (2018) terminology to refer to people who score high and low on the right-wing authoritarianism scale as having fixed and fluid worldviews, respectively.

By contrast, "open" personalities predispose people to embrace the norms and relational comparisons that characterize equality-oriented nationalism. Open personality types hold fluid worldviews, for example, that prioritize novelty and welcome heterogeneity. They value individualism and perceive dissimilar in-group members as benign. Open types actively seek new experiences, view the world as a friendly, non-threatening place, and value both cultural diversity and fairness (McCrae and Costa Jr, 1991; Johnston, Lavine and Federico, 2017). In turn, I expect them to adopt nationalist commitments that reject binary comparisons and facilitate heterogeneity.

And indeed, past work also implicates personality traits in foreign policy public opinion. Traits associated with closed personalities predict hawkishness: "Closed" people with "fixed" worldviews believe that leaders should respond to foreign threats with shows of strength, support torture to combat terrorism (Hetherington and Suhay, 2011; Hetherington and Weiler, 2018), and were more likely to support both Iraq wars than their "open," "fluid" counterparts (Doty et al., 1997; McFarland, 2003). Closed types supported the deployment of nuclear weapons during the Persian Gulf War more than open types—an escalatory tactic similar to what I expect from unity-oriented nationalists. "Fixed" Europeans oppose the European Union and object to supranational cooperation (Tillman, 2013; Bakker and de Vreese, 2016; Peitz, Dhont and Seyd, 2018), whereas "open" Europeans who score high on openness to experience—one of the"Big 5" personality traits—support EU expansion and European government (but not intra-European trust) (Bakker and de Vreese, 2016). Similarly, "open" Germans opposed the Iraq war (Schoen, 2007), and American presidents who score high on altruism are less likely to act on opportunities to use force (Gallagher and Allen, 2014).[37]

To summarize: I expect that context, elite cues, and dispositions combine to shape nationalist inclinations. Complex interactions between situations and dispositions affect which nationalisms individuals adopt, when they update their beliefs about content, and the strength of nationalist commitments. Nationalisms, in turn, shape foreign policy attitudes.

---

37. Interestingly, Gallagher and Allen (2014) find that presidents who score high on openness to action—a trait associated with "open" personalities—exhibit more volatility in their foreign policy decisions. The trait is associated with more variance in use of force decisions, a result that could implicate their willingness to test the waters with cooperation but use force when directly threatened, in line with what I would expect from equality-oriented nationalists.

These wide-ranging propositions present promising avenues for future research.

Policy Implications

International relations scholarship interweaves with foreign policy practice. Research on nationalism and war emerged from scholars trying to comprehend tragic conflicts like World War I, just as political scientists joined policymakers in pursuing supranationalism as one path to cooperation in anarchy. Indeed, the recent rise in research on nationalism and European supranationalism reflects growing concerns about a nationalist tidal wave that might engulf the globe as economic and migration crises mount and strain the EU's capacity. This landscape invites critical thinking on how varieties of nationalism matter for policymakers.

My research suggests that some of our concerns about rising nationalism may be overblown. Nationalist surges, on their own, do not necessarily produce policy preferences that motivate international militarism and crisis escalation. For instance, the first two decades of the twentieth century featured growing competition between the United States and China, and observers feared that nationalism on both sides puts these great powers on a collision course. But one lesson from my research: Equality-oriented American nationalism facilitates a more diplomatic approach toward China on security matters. If the next decades witness rising equality-oriented nationalism in the United States—perhaps in part from popular reactance against present-day nativist, unity-oriented rhetoric—the American public may oppose tactics that risk escalating simmering conflicts over control of the South China Sea, for example. Equality-oriented nationalism gives the American foreign policy establishment breathing room to gamble on coexistence, rather than confrontation.

A second implication concerns the European Union and its identity-building projects. EU elites prioritize building a European identity (European Commission, 2012), but face pushback from political parties—and member-states—that reject supranationalism. Ultimately, the EU has adopted a compromise position that seeks to advance unity and equality at the same time. The EU "CULT" committee, for example, has been charged with both preserving European heritage (unity) and creating an inclusive society (equality),[38] akin to the various EU treaties that simultaneously

---

38. See, for example, statements made by Mariya Gabriel, Commissioner-designate for Innovation and Youth, during a September 2019 hearing before the European Parliament.

endorse solidarity and tolerance. These competing messages may explain why scholars sometimes conclude that European identification is "fragile and shallow" (McNamara and Musgrave, 2020, 172), as citizens struggle to reconcile unity with equality. If policymakers want to establish foundations for sustained cooperation, their current little-bit-of-everything approach risks backfiring. EU investments into programs that center commitments to fairness, equality, and tolerance in place of unity may clash with the idealistic visions for a European family that have captivated leaders from Monnet to Macron, but offer a more viable path for sustained security cooperation on the continent.

———

In this book, I made the case that nationalisms carry distinct implications for attitudes about conflict and cooperation in international politics. My framework was motivated by theoretical and empirical puzzles scattered throughout existing research on how these commitments affect foreign policy; and by the need for a generalizable typology to describe how nationalisms vary. This book advances an important research agenda by providing a theoretical framework that synthesizes expectations for whether and when unity- and equality-oriented nationalisms relate to attitudes about militarism, conflict escalation, and transnational security cooperation. This project is designed to place the first paving stones rather than mark the end of the road—and I hope that future scholars will travel down it and inject new ideas into the discussion.

Selected comments and specific quotes, in English, available from the European Parliament at https://www.europarl.europa.eu/RegData/etudes/BRIE/2019/638438/IPOL_BRI(2019)638 438_EN.pdf.

Fredonia Experiment

STIMULUS MATERIALS

All participants received the following introduction, and then received one of the three treatments via random assignment:[1]

> People relate to one another in different ways, with various norms or guidelines for how to behave. Think about how your relationships with close family members, supervisors, friends, or merchants, for example, are distinct. On the next page, you're going to read a paragraph asking you to think about a specific way that you and other members of a country interact. Read it over carefully, so that you're able to answer questions about it later.

Control

Imagine that you are a citizen of a country, Fredonia. Fredonia is about 297,000 square miles in area with a population of approximately 34 million people.

(On the next page)

Now, think about a meal that you enjoy. Please spend the next 3 minutes writing about this meal and how to prepare it.

Unity

Imagine that you are a citizen of a country, Fredonia. Fredonia is about 297,000 square miles in area with a population of approximately 34 million people.

1. The introduction appeared immediately following the informed consent procedure. This study was part of a broader project, and elsewhere participants reported information on traits and values alongside cooperative foreign policy preferences.

In Fredonia, typical relationships among citizens are organized as follows. In the past, there were multiple cultural groups that didn't get along. Now, most individuals in your country are unified as one community and think of themselves as Fredonians—you share a common history, speak the same language, and have similar values. As a society, you generally share with one another, freely giving to others in need without expecting anything in return. When you need to make a decision for the country, you decide by reaching a consensus about what is best. You are a typical citizen of Fredonia, sharing in the cultures and traditions. You can think of your relationships with other Fredonians as you do your close family members—a group with which you share a close bond.

(On the next page)

Now, think about Fredonia's social structure as just described. Please spend the next 3 minutes writing about the benefits of Fredonian society, and how the establishment of community is optimal for the country.

Equality

Imagine that you are a citizen of a country, Fredonia. Fredonia is about 297,000 square miles in area with a population of approximately 34 million people.

In Fredonia, typical relationships among citizens are organized as follows. In the past, there were multiple cultural groups that didn't get along. Now, individuals in your country recognize that you differ in many ways, but you generally think of one another as equals or peers, each with even chances. As a society, people generally keep track of what they give to one another so that they can reciprocate in the future. When you need to make a decision for the country, you do so through a voting procedure where each person gets one vote. You are a typical citizen of Fredonia, respecting the differences but equality of others. You can think of your relationships with other Fredonians as you do your casual friendships, co-workers, or classmates—a group where there is even balance and equivalent give and take.

(On the next page)

Now, think about Fredonia's social structure as just described. Please spend the next 3 minutes writing about the benefits of Fredonian society, and how the establishment of equality is optimal for the country.

NATIONALISM

Now, we are interested in finding out how you would feel about being a Fredonian.

National Chauvinism ($\alpha = 0.58$)

1. How superior do you think Fredonia is compared to other nations? [*not at all superior, not so superior, very superior, vastly superior*]
2. How many things about Fredonia make you ashamed? [*none, not many, many, very many*]
3. How much better would the world be if people from other countries were more like Fredonians? [*not better at all, somewhat better, much better, vastly better*]
4. Patriots should support Fredonia even if it is in the wrong. [*strongly disagree, somewhat disagree, neither agree nor disagree, somewhat agree, strongly agree*]

National Attachment ($\alpha = 0.8$)

1. If someone said something bad about Fredonian people, how strongly would you feel it is as if they said something bad about you? [*not strongly at all, not too strongly, strongly, very strongly, extremely strongly*]
2. How much would being a Fredonian have to do with how you feel about yourself? [*not at all, not too much, somewhat, a lot, a tremendous amount*]
3. How much do you feel that what happens to Fredonia in general would be your fate as well? [*not at all, not too much, somewhat, a lot, a tremendous amount*]

CONFLICT VIGNETTE

Stage 1:
Fredonia is currently in the midst of a conflict with a neighboring country, Rusburg. Rusburgians are culturally different than Fredonians, speaking a distinct language and following different traditions.

Historically, both countries have claimed ownership over a piece of territory that lies between them. While it used to be largely uninhabited, over the past few years citizens from both countries have been moving into the area. As space there is becoming scarce, there have been some isolated skirmishes between the two countries in which each has tried to claim complete ownership. Recently, things have escalated with citizens from each country attempting to use their own police presence to establish the territory as fully Fredonia's or Rusburg's—often resorting to violence.

It has always been the position of your government and citizens that the territory belongs to Fredonia, and the government from Rusburg makes the same claim.

Stage 2:

The [*negotiations/sanctions/threats/actions*] were unsuccessful, in that Rusburg and Fredonia both continue to claim ownership over the territory. Now, clashes between police trying to enforce their rights over the area have resulted in the deaths of 45 people, with both Fredonians and Rusburgians included in the total.

Stage 3:

The [*negotiations/sanctions/threats/actions*] were unsuccessful, in that Rusburg and Fredonia both continue to claim ownership over the territory. Now, 6 months later, several bombs exploded at the local farmer's market, resulting in 113 deaths as well as dozens of more injuries, to both Fredonians and Rusburgians. Right now, there is no evidence to say who planted the bombs.

Policy Choices

How should Fredonia respond? (*stage 1*)/How should Fredonia respond in light of this escalation? (*stages 2 and 3*)

1. Welcome Rusburgians and draft an agreement to make the territory a shared space.
2. Negotiate to partition the territory into Fredonian and Rusburgian portions.
3. Formally announce a request that Rusburg withdraw their claim.
4. Threaten economic sanctions against Rusburg to pressure them to withdraw their claim to the territory.
5. Threaten the use of force in the disputed territory to pressure them to withdraw their claim.
6. Break off diplomatic relations with Rusburg and begin military exercises near the territory.
7. Launch a targeted strike against Rusburgian military bases.
8. Declare war against Rusburg in order to fully reclaim the territory.
9. Escalate the existing war by moving troops in and beginning a military takeover of the territory. (*This option only appeared in stages 2 and 3*)

Between stages 1 and 2, participants completed questions about their views of Rusburgians and strategy as part of the broader survey.

MILITANT INTERNATIONALISM

Militant Internationalism ($\alpha = 0.88$)

Please read the following statements and indicate the extent to which you agree or disagree [*strongly disagree, disagree, somewhat disagree, neither agree nor disagree, somewhat agree, agree, strongly agree*]:

1. The United States should take all steps including the use of force to prevent aggression by any expansionist power.
2. Rather than simply countering our opponents' thrusts, it is necessary to strike at the heart of an opponent's power.
3. Going to war is unfortunate but sometimes the only solution to international problems.
4. In dealing with other nations our government should be strong and tough.
5. The United States must demonstrate its resolve so that others do not take advantage of it.

DEMOGRAPHIC CONTROLS

Table A.1 replicates the models from chapter 3, but includes control variables for individual characteristics. The demographic controls include age, gender, race (dummy variable coded 1 for white and 0 otherwise), education (dummy variable coded 1 for bachelor's degree or higher and 0 otherwise), and political knowledge. I measured political knowledge with a 5-item scale ($\alpha = 0.7$).[2] I find that the results hold when I control for these characteristics—models 2–4 show significant, negative interactions between equality and nationalism. The results suggest that older participants promote slightly less conflict, and consistent with research on the gender gap in foreign policy public opinion (Silverman and Kumka, 1987; Eichenberg and Stoll, 2012; Eichenberg, 2016; Lizotte, 2019), men endorse militant internationalism at higher rates than women.

2. The 5 questions: "Who is the Speaker of the U.S. House of Representatives?"; "Which country is currently led by Hamid Karzai?"; "What does NATO stand for?"; "Who is the Prime Minister of the United Kingdom?"; "Name five countries that *currently* have nuclear weapons."

TABLE A.1. Models with Demographic Controls.

	Stage 2 (1)	Stage 3 (2)	Total Escalation (3)	Militant Internationalism (4)
Equality	0.183	0.335**	0.194**	0.220**
	(0.132)	(0.157)	(0.093)	(0.096)
Nationalism	0.241	0.441**	0.295**	0.328***
	(0.168)	(0.199)	(0.118)	(0.122)
Equality x Nationalism	−0.268	−0.523*	−0.326**	−0.444***
	(0.231)	(0.273)	(0.161)	(0.167)
Age	−0.001	−0.004**	−0.003**	0.003**
	(0.002)	(0.002)	(0.001)	(0.001)
Male	0.048	0.028	−0.001	0.084***
	(0.041)	(0.048)	(0.028)	(0.029)
White	0.007	−0.016	−0.018	−0.058*
	(0.047)	(0.056)	(0.033)	(0.034)
University	−0.021	0.019	−0.002	−0.048
	(0.041)	(0.048)	(0.029)	(0.030)
Political Knowledge	0.030	−0.030	−0.030	−0.021
	(0.066)	(0.078)	(0.046)	(0.048)
Constant	0.165	0.365**	0.567***	0.394***
	(0.120)	(0.142)	(0.084)	(0.087)
N	190	190	190	190
R^2	0.029	0.058	0.075	0.114

$^*p < .1; ^{**}p < .05; ^{***}p < .01$

Note: Main entries are OLS coefficients. Unity is the reference group for Equality. Continuous variables, except for Age, rescaled from 0 to 1.

SAMPLE COMPOSITION AND NATIONALISTS

In chapter 3, I described results from an analysis designed to assess whether the treatments moderate the relationship between dispositional traits and nationalist commitments. Table A.2 presents the results, which show no significant interactions between the treatment and participant characteristics. This model suggests that observed traits do not produce distinct nationalists in the unity and equality treatment groups.

PLACEBO TESTS

My theory leads me to expect an interaction between the equality treatment and nationalism. But if the nationalism scale at the center of my

TABLE A.2. Individual Characteristics Do Not Moderate
the Effect of the Treatments on Nationalism.

	Nationalism
Age	0.001 (0.002)
White	−0.024 (0.044)
Male	−0.068* (0.037)
University	0.045 (0.039)
Political Science Class	0.001 (0.038)
Political Knowledge	0.051 (0.061)
Party Id	−0.064 (0.072)
Equality	−0.072 (0.119)
Equality x Age	−0.0004 (0.002)
... x White	−0.0003 (0.060)
... x Male	0.061 (0.053)
... x University	−0.073 (0.054)
... x PS Class	−0.052 (0.053)
... x Knowledge	0.043 (0.086)
... x Party Id	0.148 (0.099)
Constant	0.556*** (0.090)
N	190
R^2	0.077

$^*p < .1; ^{**}p < .05; ^{***}p < .01$

Note: Main entries are OLS coefficients, standard errors in parentheses. The reference group for Equality is the Unity condition.

analyses proxies some other dispositional trait—like political ideology or a propensity to comply with experimental treatments—it would threaten my ability to draw inferences about equality- and unity-oriented nationalisms' effects.

Figure A.1 depicts models that test this possibility using four alternative variables that might feasibly confound the interactions I observe between equality and nationalism: 7-point scales for ideology and partisanship (higher values indicate more liberal/Democratic), a 5-item political knowledge scale, and national attachment (3-item scale). Importantly, past research concludes that "national attachment" has no bearing on conflict attitudes, likely because the intergroup context activates concerns about group superiority (Herrmann, Isernia and Segatti, 2009; Brewer, 1999). But if the nationalism scale taps treatment compliance or reflects an ostensibly more benign aspect of national identification, I should find interactions between equality and attachment. Similarly, if the results depend

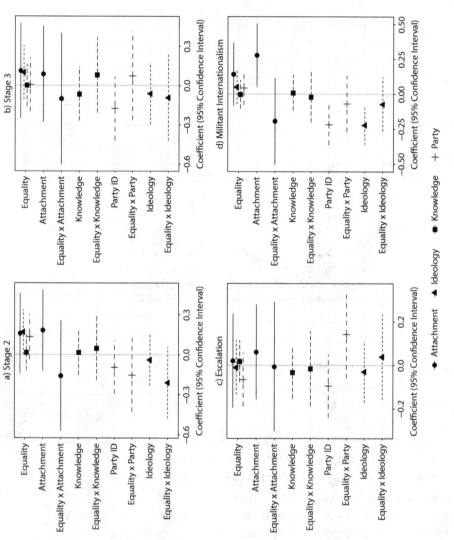

FIGURE A.1. Alternative moderators do not account for the interaction between treatments and nationalism.

Note: Figures display OLS coefficients and 95% confidence intervals.

on political differences between strong and weak nationalists in the two groups, I would expect ideology, partisanship, or knowledge to moderate the treatments. But if the nationalism scale taps specific nationalist commitments—which can rest on unity or equality—these placebo tests should produce null results. And indeed, I find no evidence for significant interactions between the respective "placebo" moderators and equality, increasing confidence in my claims about nationalisms' effects in the Fredonia experiment.

American Nationalisms Experiment

STIMULUS MATERIALS

All participants received a common introduction, followed by random assignment to the unity, equality, or control condition:[3]

All Groups

On the next page, you're going to read a selection from an American history textbook. Read it over carefully, so that you're able to answer questions about it later.

This selection is taken from the introduction to *A Concise History of the American People* by Alan Brinkley.

> The United States of America is a large country, measuring 3.7 million square miles, with a population of over 313 million people.

Unity

> Historically, the U.S. has been composed of many different groups— people of different faiths, ethnic and racial backgrounds, and cultures. Now, though, we think of Americans as part of one community.

> Being American means relating to one another as part of a community, and the central theme is one of unity and solidarity. Americans feel a sense of belonging and closeness with one another—they share common responsibilities. The individual does not matter so much, instead what matters is America as a whole. The phrases "All for one, one for all" and "We're all in this together" describe what it means to be part of the American community.

---

3. The introduction appeared after the informed consent procedure and demographic questions. This study was part of a broader project, and elsewhere participants reported information on cooperative and economic foreign policy preferences.

Americans experience a sense of solidarity, communality, and compassion toward each other. Americans share a common history and language, making them similar in important respects. When Americans make a decision, they can do so by consensus and act in solidarity as a group.

Equality

Historically, the U.S. has been composed of many different groups—people of different faiths, ethnic and racial backgrounds, and cultures. Now, though, we think of Americans as a diverse group of equals.

Being American means relating to one another as equals, and the central theme is one of balance and equality. Americans are regarded as equal in terms of certain qualities—like responsibilities, rights, and opportunities. Americans tend to share things equally, and one-for-one reciprocity matters for them. The phrase "All men are created equal" describes what it means to be part of the American group.

Americans experience a sense of fairness, reciprocity, and balance with each other. Americans may speak various languages or have distinct histories, making them different in important respects but equals as Americans. When Americans make a decision, they do so with one-person one-vote rules.

Step 2
Please list 3 reasons that you think that [community/equality] is a good description of what it means to be American. [*followed by 3 text entry boxes*] Please list 3 of your favorite foods. [control group; *followed by 3 text entry boxes*]

Step 3
Table A.3 displays the 5 reasons that appeared on lists for participants in the unity and equality groups, respectively.

Attention Check

Which of the following is an important part of being an American, according to the passage that you read? [Community, Equality, Neither]

NATIONALISM

Now, we are interested in finding out how you feel about being an American.

TABLE A.3. Lists for Unity and Equality Treatments

Unity	Equality
It is best to work together. United we stand divided we fall.	Political decision-making is based on one-person, one-vote procedures.
Everyone shares the same past and the same language so it is easy to co-exist with one another.	It is expected that if someone does you a favor you should reciprocate when you can, to keep things equal.
Americans hold to the idea that "we are all family" and watch out for each other all the time.	Citizens are fair in their treatment of each other and have a reciprocal method of helping each other and being good neighbors.
In a close community people look out for each other and are also more unified against any foreign enemy. The identity of "us" in regards to community is beneficial in many ways to the group as a whole.	The benefits of this society allow for people to have more individual ideas and thoughts toward the country rather than being a completely unified group.
They look after the needs of another as if they are one big family. No one is left out and they all pull each other up as though another's struggles were their own.	I think this is beneficial to American society because they can treat each other fairly while not pretending to be oblivious of differences.

National Chauvinism ($\alpha = 0.65$ for items 1–3)

1. How superior is America compared to other nations? [*not at all superior, not so superior, very superior, vastly superior*]
2. How much better would the world be if people from other countries were more like Americans? [*not better at all, somewhat better, much better, vastly better*]
3. Patriots should support America even if it is in the wrong. [*strongly disagree, somewhat disagree, neither agree nor disagree, somewhat agree, strongly agree*]
4. How many things about America make you feel ashamed? [*none, not many, many, very many*]

National Attachment ($\alpha = 0.8$)

1. If someone said something bad about the American people, how strongly would you feel it is as if they said something bad about you? [*not strongly at all, not too strongly, strongly, very strongly, extremely strongly*]

2. How much does being an American have to do with how you feel about yourself? [*not at all, not too much, somewhat, a lot, a tremendous amount*]
3. How much do you feel that what happens to America in general would be your fate as well? [*not at all, not too much, somewhat, a lot, a tremendous amount*]

DEPENDENT VARIABLES

Militant Internationalism ($\alpha = 0.81$)

Please read the following statements and indicate the extent to which you agree or disagree [*strongly disagree, disagree, somewhat disagree, neither agree nor disagree, somewhat agree, agree, strongly agree*]:

1. The United States should take all steps including the use of force to prevent aggression by any expansionist power.
2. Rather than simply countering our opponents' thrusts, it is necessary to strike at the heart of an opponent's power.
3. Going to war is unfortunate but sometimes the only solution to international problems.
4. In dealing with other nations our government should be strong and tough.
5. The United States must demonstrate its resolve so that others do not take advantage of it.

China

Thinking about U.S. policy towards China, do you agree or disagree that it is important to be tough with China on military issues? [*strongly disagree, disagree, somewhat disagree, neither agree nor disagree, somewhat agree, agree, strongly agree*]

ISIS ($\alpha = 0.77$ for items 2–5)

Now here are a few questions about the Islamic militant group often referred to as ISIS that controls some areas of Iraq and Syria. As you may know, the U.S. has conducted airstrikes against ISIS forces in Iraq and Syria. Please indicate whether you support or oppose each of the following actions by the U.S. [*strongly oppose, oppose, somewhat oppose, neither support nor oppose, somewhat support, support, strongly support*]:

1. Negotiating with ISIS to address their territorial claims (*reverse coded*).
2. Continued airstrikes against ISIS members in Iraq and Syria.
3. Using unmanned aircraft (or "drones") to carry out targeted attacks against militants.
4. Imposing a "no fly zone" in Syria.
5. Sending ground troops into combat operations against ISIS forces in Iraq and Syria.

Russia ($\alpha = 0.82$)

Some people think that Russia might attempt to invade the Baltic countries on its border, like Estonia and Latvia, who are U.S. allies. If that happens, would you support or oppose the U.S. taking the following actions to protect their allies [*strongly oppose, oppose, somewhat oppose, neither support nor oppose, somewhat support, support, strongly support*]:

1. Imposing international economic sanctions against Russia?
2. Increasing the number of NATO troops in Estonia and Latvia?
3. Launching targeted strikes against Russian military bases?
4. Stationing American troops on the ground in Estonia and Latvia?
5. Declaring war against Russia?

PLACEBO TESTS

Figure A.2 presents results from models that regress militant internationalism and China postures—the two with significant interactions between equality and nationalism—on the treatments and interactions between national attachment, party identification, and ideology. These analyses follow the same logic that I discussed regarding the Fredonia experiment. If an unmeasured factor confounds scores on the nationalism scale, for example, I would expect it to manifest in other measures for national identification like attachment or in political dispositions. Again, the results reveal little evidence to support that interpretation of the nationalism scale. I find non-significant interaction coefficients in 11 of 12 tests, increasing my confidence that the results I report in chapter 4 reflect an interaction between the treatments and nationalism. Results in the supplemental appendix similarly show no evidence for placebo interactions with the Russia and ISIS scales as dependent variables.

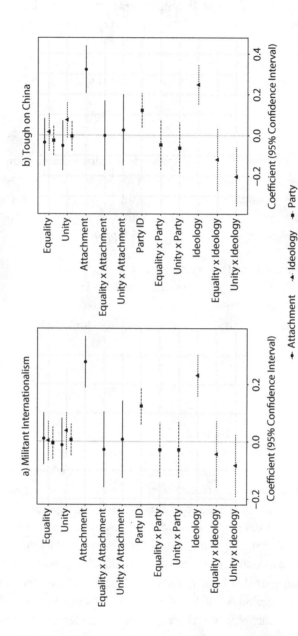

FIGURE A.2. Alternative variables do not account for the interaction between treatments and nationalism.

Note: Figures display OLS coefficients and 95% confidence intervals.

IntUne Surveys: Mass Public

SURVEY ITEMS

Dependent Variables

- **European Trust**: Please tell me on a scale of 0 to 10, how much you personally trust each of the following groups of people. '0' means that you do not trust the group at all and '10' means you have complete trust... People in other European Countries. (*0- No trust at all.... 10- Complete trust*)
- **CFSP and Economic Support**: Thinking about the European Union over the next ten years or so, can you tell me whether you are in favour or against the following.... (*strongly in favour, somewhat in favour, somewhat against, strongly against, neither in favour nor against*)
  — A single EU foreign policy toward outside countries.
  — More help for EU regions in economic or social difficulties.
- **European Army Support**: Some say that we should have a single European Union Army. Others say every country should keep its own national army. What is your opinion? (*national armies, European army, Both national and European, neither nor*)[4]

Independent Variables

My IntUne analyses use factor scores to measure unity- and equality-oriented supranationalisms. To create these independent variables, I conducted an exploratory factor analysis on responses to the following prompt: "People differ in what they think it means to be European. [For] being European, how important do you think each of the following is?" Participants responded to eight characteristics on a 4-point scale from "Not at all important" to "Very important." These items appeared in random order. They followed questions about national identity content on the instrument.

- To be a Christian.
- To share European cultural traditions.
- To be born in Europe.
- To have European parents.
- To respect European Union's laws and institutions.
- To feel European.

4. For analysis, I removed participants who chose "neither nor," though including it as a 4th category does not change the results for the categorical responses that my theory implicates.

- To master any European language.
- To exercise citizens' rights, like being active in politics of the European Union. (*only in the mass surveys*)

To create the factor scores, I first completed a parallel analysis and examined eigenvalues and the scree plot. This process suggested a two-factor solution. I then completed an iterative series of exploratory factor analyses to estimate one-factor, two-factor, and three-factor solutions, and present the results in Table A.4. Consistent with both my theory and what the parallel analysis suggested, the one-factor solution represented a poor fit for the data (TLI=0.66, RMSEA=0.153 [0.151, 0.156]). The three-factor solution incrementally improves model fit (TLI=0.99, RMSEA=0.02, [0.017, 0.02]) compared to the two-factor solution (TLI=0.96, RMSEA=0.051 [0.049, 0.054]). I use the two-factor solution in my analyses based on theoretical guidance and methodological concerns about retaining factors that contain only one strongly loading item.

RESULTS ROBUST TO DROPPING SCALE COMPONENTS

Chapter 5 includes a detailed theoretical and conceptual rationale for including all eight content items from the IntUne public surveys in my analyses. Of course, readers might worry that one specific item fails to cohere with my conceptualization of unity and equality—suggesting perhaps that participating in European cultural traditions taps unity among citizens who perceive "culture" as a homogenizing force, despite its achievable nature and emphasis on equal participation.

I find consistent results when I drop one scale item at a time from the independent variable models: Each iteration produces a negative and significant coefficient on unity, and a positive and significant coefficient on equality. I estimated 8 separate factor analyses to produce new scales for unity and equality that drop each item in turn, and regress trust and CFSP support on these independent variables. Panels a and b in Figure A.3 plot these sequential coefficient estimates for unity and equality, alongside the full-scale version for comparison ("all items"). I find minimal deviations from the dashed reference lines that represent estimates from the models in chapter 5, though the effect of unity on support for the CFSP appears more strongly negative when I drop either the European parents or born in Europe items from the scale. In general, the results show remarkable overlap across scale iterations.

TABLE A.4. Factor Analyses for Equality and Unity in the Mass Public

	One Factor	Two Factor Solution		Three Factor Solution		
	All Items	Equality	Unity	Equality	Unity	Christian
To be Christian	0.33	−0.04	0.43	0.00	0.05	0.68
Born in Europe	0.65	0.01	0.81	0.04	0.75	0.04
European Parents	0.66	0.01	0.83	−0.02	0.88	0.01
Master European Language	0.45	0.52	−0.01	0.51	0.02	−0.04
Cultural Traditions	0.61	0.51	0.16	0.55	0.02	0.19
Respect European Laws	0.51	0.71	−0.12	0.69	−0.06	−0.07
Feel European	0.65	0.61	0.12	0.60	0.18	−0.07
Exercise Citizens' Rights	0.47	0.49	0.04	0.51	−0.06	0.14
RMSEA	0.15 (0.15, 0.16)	0.05 (0.049, 0.054)		0.02 (0.017, 0.024)		
TLI	0.66	0.96		0.99		

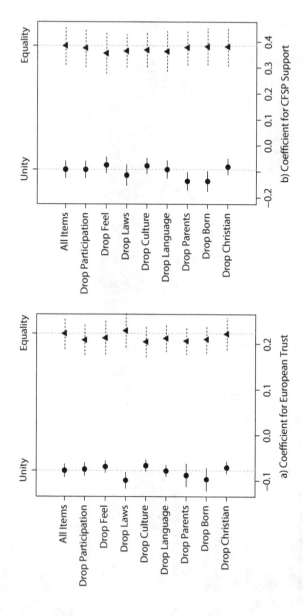

FIGURE A.3. Results robust to alternative specifications for unity and equality.

Note: Black circles represent the coefficients for unity factor scores, and triangles represent the coefficients on equality factor scores. Lines represent 95% confidence interval standard errors clustered by country. The dependent variables have been rescaled to range from 0 to 1, and higher values indicate greater support. Models include controls and incorporate population weights.

TABLE A.5. Should There Be a European Army?

	European Army Only	European & National Armies
Unity	−1.277**	−0.959**
	(0.255)	(0.169)
Equality	3.034**	2.324**
	(0.625)	(0.308)
National Attachment	−1.098**	−0.260*
	(0.091)	(0.113)
Eur. Identification	0.792**	0.597**
	(0.136)	(0.077)
Generalized Trust	0.414**	0.407**
	(0.131)	(0.100)
EU Visits	0.580**	0.297**
	(0.041)	(0.055)
Ideology (right)	−0.759**	−0.176*
	(0.119)	(0.086)
Male	0.501**	0.061
	(0.093)	(0.085)
University	0.393**	0.332**
Age dummies	✓	✓
Country/Year Fixed Effects	✓	✓
Intercept	−1.170**	−0.690**
	(0.292)	(0.150)
N	27431	

$*p < .05; **p < .01$

Note: Table displays estimates from a multinomial logistic regression with standard errors clustered by country; coefficients are relative to the baseline choice of having a national army only. Models incorporate population weights and include 16 dummy variables for n-1 countries represented in the data and controls for gender, age, and university education—France is the reference category.

REGRESSION TABLE: EUROPEAN ARMY

Table A.5 presents results from the multinomial logit model used to produce the predicted probability plots in chapter 5.

IntUne Surveys: Elites

FACTOR ANALYSIS FOR UNITY AND EQUALITY

Elites received the same questions that appeared on the mass survey probing whether they favor the common foreign policy for the EU, and whether they support a European army.

TABLE A.6. Equality and Unity in European Elites

Variable	Factor Analysis Results, Elite Sample				
	Unity	Equality	h2	u2	com
To be Christian	**0.40**	−0.01	0.16	0.84	1.00
Born in Europe	**0.80**	0.01	0.65	0.35	1.00
European Parents	**0.86**	0.00	0.74	0.26	1.00
Master European Language	0.04	**0.42**	0.19	0.81	1.02
Respect European Laws	−0.10	**0.53**	0.27	0.73	1.08
Feel European	0.08	**0.55**	0.33	0.67	1.05
RMSEA	0.009 (0, 0.03)				
TLI	0.999				

TABLE A.7. Support for a European Army among Elites

	European Army Only	European & National Armies
Unity	−1.111**	−0.359
	(0.276)	(0.292)
Equality	1.202**	1.192**
	(0.436)	(0.408)
European Attachment	1.572**	1.144**
	(0.388)	(0.240)
EU Contacts	0.029	0.047
	(0.036)	(0.037)
Political Elite	−0.657**	−0.498**
	(0.132)	(0.122)
Ideology (right)	−0.611	−0.383
	(0.313)	(0.232)
Male	0.263*	0.065
	(0.132)	(0.112)
National Attachment	−1.705**	−0.941*
	(0.431)	(0.373)
2009 Wave	0.023	0.258
	(0.121)	(0.174)
Country Fixed Effects	✓	✓
Intercept	0.111	0.567
	(0.546)	(0.505)
N	3374	

*p < .05; **p < .01

Note: Table displays estimates from a multinomial logistic regression with standard errors clustered by country; coefficients are relative to the baseline choice of having a national army only. Models include 16 dummy variables for n-1 countries represented in the data, omitted for space—France is the reference category.

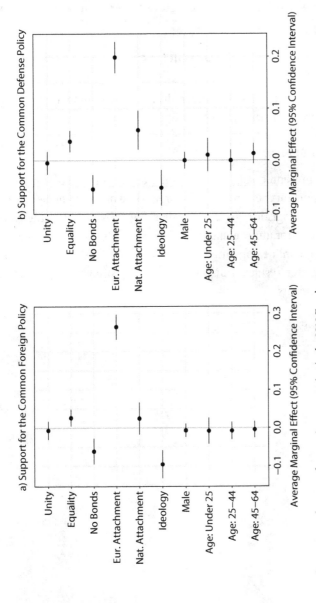

FIGURE A.4. Equality, unity, and support for security cooperation in the 2019 Eurobarometer.

Note: Figure displays the average marginal effects from logistic regression models that regress support for either the common EU foreign policy (CFP) or common EU defense and security policy (CDP) on the independent variables. Models include country fixed effects, omitted for presentation, and incorporate population weights. The reference category for the identity content measures is the mixed group, and the reference category for age is 65 and older. Data from the 2019 Eurobarometer surveys (European Commission, 2020). N=21,022 for CFP and N=21,530 for CDP.

To create the independent variables for unity and equality in the elite sample, I again conducted an exploratory factor analysis. Elites received the same prompt asking about what it means to be European, without the item about exercising citizens' rights. Table A.6 displays the results from the factor analysis that I used to create factor scores for unity and equality in the elite sample.

REGRESSION TABLE: ELITE SUPPORT FOR A EUROPEAN ARMY

Table A.7 displays full results from the multinomial logit model estimating support for a European army among European elites.

Eurobarometer Surveys

In chapter 5, I presented substantive results for the effects of unity and equality on support for the common EU foreign and defense policies based on results from two logistic regression models. Figure A.4 displays the average marginal effects for unity, equality, and the controls (excluding country fixed effects). The online appendix contains logit model estimates for the 2019 Eurobaromater results, and a table of OLS estimates for the 2014 Eurobarometer results.

REFERENCES

Abdelal, Rawi, Yoshiko Herrera, Alastair Iain Johnson and Rose McDermott. 2009. Identity as a variable. In *Measuring Identity: A Guide for Social Scientists*, ed. Rawi Abdelal, Yoshiko Herrera, Alastair Iain Johnson and Rose McDermott. Cambridge: Cambridge University Press, pp. 17–32.

Abdelal, Rawi, Yoshiko M Herrera, Alastair Iain Johnston and Rose McDermott. 2006. "Identity as a variable." *Perspectives on Politics* 4(4):695–711.

Acharya, Amitav. 2001. *Constructing a Security Community in Southeast Asia: ASEAN and the Problem of Regional Order*. London: Routledge.

Acharya, Amitav. 2009. *Whose Ideas Matter? Agency and Power in Asian Regionalism*. Ithaca, NY: Cornell University Press.

Acharya, Amitav. 2014. "Global international relations (IR) and regional worlds: A new agenda for international studies." *International Studies Quarterly* 58(4):647–59.

Acharya, Amitav. 2016*a*. "Advancing global IR: Challenges, contentions, and contributions." *International Studies Review* 18(1):4–15.

Acharya, Amitav. 2016*b*. Regionalism beyond EU-centrism. In *Oxford Handbook of Comparative Regionalism*, ed. Tanja Börzel, Thomas Risse. Oxford: Oxford University Press, pp. 109–30.

Acharya, Amitav, and Alastair Iain Johnston. 2007. *Crafting Cooperation: Regional International Institutions in Comparative Perspective*. Cambridge: Cambridge University Press.

Adler, Emanuel, and Michael Barnett. 1998. *Security Communities*. Cambridge: Cambridge University Press.

Aldrich, John H, Christopher Gelpi, Peter Feaver, Jason Reifler, and Kristin Thompson Sharp. 2006. "Foreign policy and the electoral connection." *Annual Review of Political Science* 9:477–502.

Alesina, Alberto, and Eliana La Ferrara. 2002. "Who trusts others?" *Journal of Public Economics* 85(2):207–34.

Altemeyer, Bob. 1988. *Enemies of Freedom: Understanding Right-wing Authoritarianism*. San Francisco, CA: Jossey-Bass.

Althaus, Scott L, and Kevin Coe. 2011. "Priming patriots: Social identity processes and the dynamics of public support for war." *Public Opinion Quarterly* 75(1):65–88.

Altman, Daniel. 2015. "The strategist's curse: A theory of false optimism as a cause of war." *Security Studies* 24(2):284–315.

Ambrose, Emma, and Cas Mudde. 2015. "Canadian multiculturalism and the absence of the far right." *Nationalism and Ethnic Politics* 21(2):213–36.

Anderson, Benedict. 1983. *Imagined Communities: Reflections on the Origin and Spread of Nationalism*. London: Verso.

Ariely, Gal. 2016. "Does national identification always lead to chauvinism? A cross-national analysis of contextual explanations." *Globalizations* 13(4):377–95.

Aronson, Elliot, Marilynn B. Brewer, and J. Merill Carlsmith. 1985. Experimentation in social psychology. In *Handbook of Social Psychology*, ed. Gardner Lindzey and Elliot Aronson. 3rd ed. New York: Random House.

Aspelund, Anna, Marjaana Lindeman, and Markku Verkasalo. 2013. "Political conservatism and left–right orientation in 28 Eastern and Western European countries." *Political Psychology* 34(3):409–417.

Augoustinos, Martha, and Stephanie De Garis. 2012. "'Too black or not black enough': Social identity complexity in the political rhetoric of Barack Obama." *European Journal of Social Psychology* 42(5):564–77.

Bahry, Donna, Mikhail Kosolapov, Polina Kozyreva, and Rick K Wilson. 2005. "Ethnicity and trust: Evidence from Russia." *American Political Science Review*, pp. 521–32.

Baker, Peter. 2016. "Balancing terror and reality in State of the Union address." *New York Times*, p. 1. https://www.nytimes.com/2016/01/12/us/politics/president-obama-seeks-balanced-message-on-terrorism.html.

Bakker, Bert N, and Claes H de Vreese. 2016. "Personality and European Union attitudes: Relationships across European Union attitude dimensions." *European Union Politics* 17(1):25–45.

Balliet, Daniel, and Paul A M Van Lange. 2013. "Trust, conflict, and cooperation: A meta-analysis." *Psychological Bulletin* 139(5):1090.

Bankert, Alexa, Leonie Huddy, and Martin Rosema. 2017. "Measuring partisanship as a social identity in multi-party systems." *Political Behavior* 39(1):103–32.

Barnett, Michael, and Emanuel Adler. 1998. Studying security communities in theory, comparison, and history. In *Security Communities*, ed. Emanuel Adler and Michael Barnett. Cambridge: Cambridge University Press, pp. 413–41.

Barnett, Michael, and Etel Solingen. 2007. Designed to fail or failure of design? The origins and legacy of the Arab League. In *Crafting Cooperation: The Design and Effect of Regional Institutions in Comparative Perspective*, ed. Amitav Acharya and Alastair Iain Johnston. Cambridge: Cambridge University Press.

Barnett, Michael N. 1995. "Sovereignty, nationalism, and regional order in the Arab states system." *International Organization* 49(3):479–510.

Bauhr, Monika, and Nicholas Charron. 2020a. "The EU as a savior and a saint? Corruption and public support for redistribution." *Journal of European Public Policy* 27(4):509–27.

Bauhr, Monika, and Nicholas Charron. 2020b. "In God we trust? Identity, institutions and international solidarity in Europe." *JCMS: Journal of Common Market Studies* 58(5):1124–43.

Baum, Matthew A, and Philip B K Potter. 2008. "The relationships between mass media, public opinion, and foreign policy: Toward a theoretical synthesis." *Annual Review of Political Science* 11:39–65.

Bayar, Yeşim. 2016. "Constitution-writing, nationalism and the Turkish experience." *Nations and Nationalism* 22(4):725–43.

Bayram, A Burcu. 2015. "What drives modern Diogenes? Individual values and cosmopolitan allegiance." *European Journal of International Relations* 21(2):451–79.

Bayram, A Burcu. 2017. "Good Europeans? How European identity and costs interact to explain politician attitudes towards compliance with European Union law." *Journal of European Public Policy* 24(1):42–60.

Beaton, Ann M, John F Dovidio, and Nadine Léger. 2008. "All in this together? Group representations and policy support." *Journal of Experimental Social Psychology* 44(3):808–17.

Bell, Mark S, and Joshua D Kertzer. 2018. "Trump, psychology, and the future of U.S. alliances." *GMF Asia Program: Assessing the U.S. Commitment to Allies in Asia and Beyond* 11:6–13.

Berinsky, Adam J. 2007. "Assuming the costs of war: Events, elites, and American public support for military conflict." *The Journal of Politics* 69(4):975–97.

Berinsky, Adam J. 2009. *In Time of War: Understanding American Public Opinion from World War II to Iraq*. Chicago: University of Chicago Press.

Berinsky, Adam J, Eleanor Neff Powell, Eric Schickler, and Ian Brett Yohai. 2011. "Revisiting public opinion in the 1930s and 1940s." *PS: Political Science & Politics* 44(3):515–20.

Berinsky, Adam J, Gregory A Huber, and Gabriel S Lenz. 2012. "Evaluating online labor markets for experimental research: Amazon.com's Mechanical Turk." *Political Analysis* 20(3): 351–68.

Berinsky, Adam J, Michele F Margolis, and Michael W Sances. 2014. "Separating the shirkers from the workers? Making sure respondents pay attention on self-administered surveys." *American Journal of Political Science* 58(3):739–53.

Berry, John A, and Carol Pott Berry. 1999. *Genocide in Rwanda: A Collective Memory*. Washington, D.C.: Howard University Press.

Bertoli, Andrew. 2017. "Nationalism and conflict: Lessons from international sports." *International Studies Quarterly* 61(4):835–49.

Best, Heinrich, György Lengyel, and Luca Verzichelli, eds. 2012. *The Europe of Elites: A Study into the Europeanness of Europe's Political and Economic Elites*. Oxford: Oxford University Press.

Biber, Pascal, Jörg Hupfeld, and Laurenz L Meier. 2008. "Personal values and relational models." *European Journal of Personality* 22(7):609–28.

Bitzinger, Richard A. 2015. "China's double-digit defense growth." *Foreign Affairs* 19.

Bjereld, Ulf, and Ann-Marie Ekengren. 1999. "Foreign policy dimensions: A comparison between the United States and Sweden." *International Studies Quarterly* 43(3):503–18.

Blainey, Geoffrey. 1988. *Causes of War*. New York: Simon and Schuster.

Blank, Thomas, and Peter Schmidt. 2003. "National identity in a united Germany: Nationalism or patriotism? An empirical test with representative data." *Political Psychology* 24(2):289–312.

Blois, Keith, and Annmarie Ryan. 2012. "Interpreting the nature of business to business exchanges through the use of Fiske's relational models theory." *Marketing Theory* 12(4): 351–67.

Bonikowski, Bart. 2016. "Nationalism in settled times." *Annual Review of Sociology* 42:427–49.

Bonikowski, Bart, and Paul DiMaggio. 2016. "Varieties of American popular nationalism." *American Sociological Review* 81(5):949–80.

Börzel, Tanja A, and Thomas Risse. 2020. "Identity politics, core state powers and regional integration: Europe and beyond." *JCMS: Journal of Common Market Studies* 58(1):21–40.

Börzel, Tanja, and Thomas Risse. 2007. "Europeanization: The domestic impact of European Union politics." *Handbook of European Union Politics*, pp. 483–504.

Bostdorff, Denise M. 2003. "George W. Bush's post-September 11 rhetoric of covenant renewal: Upholding the faith of the greatest generation." *Quarterly Journal of Speech* 89(4):293–319.

Branscombe, Nyla R, and Daniel L Wann. 1994. "Collective self-esteem consequences of outgroup derogation when a valued social identity is on trial." *European Journal of Social Psychology* 24(6):641–57.

Brehm, Jack W. 1966. *A Theory of Psychological Reactance*. New York: Academic Press.

Breidahl, Karen N, Nils Holtug, and Kristian Kongshøj. 2018. "Do shared values promote social cohesion? If so, which? Evidence from Denmark." *European Political Science Review* 10(1):97–118.

Brewer, Marilynn B. 1991. "The social self: On being the same and different at the same time." *Personality and Social Psychology Bulletin* 17(5):475–82.

Brewer, Marilynn B. 1999. "The psychology of prejudice: Ingroup love and outgroup hate?" *Journal of Social Issues* 55(3):429–44.

Brewer, Marilynn B. 2001*a*. "The many faces of social identity: Implications for political psychology." *Political Psychology* 22(1):115–25.

Brewer, Marilynn B. 2001*b*. Social identity, intergroup conflict, and conflict reduction. In *Ingroup Identification and Intergroup Conflict*, ed. Richard D. Ashmore, Lee Jussim, and David Wilder. Vol. 3. Oxford: Oxford University Press, pp. 17–41.

Brewer, Marilynn B, and Linnda R Caporael. 2006. An evolutionary perspective on social identity: Revisiting groups. In *Evolution and Social Psychology*, ed. Mark Schaller, Jeffry A. Simpson, and Douglas T. Kenrick. New York: Psychology Press, pp. 143–61.

Brinegar, Adam P, and Seth K Jolly. 2005. "Location, location, location: National contextual factors and public support for European integration." *European Union Politics* 6(2): 155–80.

Brinkley, Alan. 2014. *The Unfinished Nation: A Concise History of the American People, Volume I*. 7th ed. NewYork: McGraw-Hill.

Brooks, Stephen G, and William C Wohlforth. 2016. *America Abroad: The United States' Global Role in the 21st Century*. Oxford: Oxford University Press.

Brown, David. 1999. "Are there good and bad nationalisms?" *Nations and Nationalism* 5(2): 281–302.

Brown, Rupert. 2000. "Social identity theory: Past achievements, current problems and future challenges." *European Journal of Social Psychology* 30(6):745–78.

Brown, Rupert. 2020. "The social identity approach: Appraising the Tajfellian legacy." *British Journal of Social Psychology* 59(1):5–25.

Brubaker, Rogers. 1992. *Citizenship and Nationhood in France and Germany*. Cambridge: Harvard University Press.

Brubaker, Rogers. 2004. *Ethnicity Without Groups*. Cambridge: Harvard University Press.

Bruter, Michael. 2003. "Winning hearts and minds for Europe: The impact of news and symbols on civic and cultural european identity." *Comparative Political Studies* 36(10):1148–79.

Bruter, Michael. 2004. "On what citizens mean by feeling 'European': Perceptions of news, symbols and borderless-ness." *Journal of Ethnic and Migration Studies* 30(1):21–39.

Bruter, Michael. 2009. "Time Bomb? The dynamic effect of news and symbols on the political identity of European citizens." *Comparative Political Studies* 42(12):1498–1536.

Brutger, Ryan, and Joshua D Kertzer. 2018. "A dispositional theory of reputation costs." *International Organization* 72(3):693–724.

Burst, Tobias, Werner Krause, Pola Lehmann, Jirka Lewandowski, Theres Matthieß, Nicolas Merz, Sven Regel, and Lisa Zehnter. 2020. "Manifesto Corpus. Version: 2020-b."

Butt, Ahsan I. 2019. "Why did the United States invade Iraq in 2003?" *Security Studies* 28(2): 250–85.

Byman, Daniel. 2000. "Forever enemies? The manipulation of ethnic identities to end ethnic wars." *Security Studies* 9(3):149–90.

Caprioli, Mary. 2005. "Primed for violence: The role of gender inequality in predicting internal conflict." *International Studies Quarterly* 49(2):161–78.

Caralis, Dionyssios, and Nick Haslam. 2004. "Relational tendencies associated with broad personality dimensions." *Psychology and Psychotherapy: Theory, Research and Practice* 77(3):397–402.

Carey, Sean. 2002. "Undivided loyalties: Is national identity an obstacle to European integration?" *European Union Politics* 3(4):387–413.

Carter, Niambi M, and Efrén O Pérez. 2016. "Race and nation: How racial hierarchy shapes national attachments." *Political Psychology* 37(4):497–513.

Cederman, Lars-Erik, Andreas Wimmer, and Brian Min. 2010. "Why do ethnic groups rebel? New data and analysis." *World Politics* 62(1):87–119.

Cehajic, Sabina, Rupert Brown, and Emanuele Castano. 2008. "Forgive and forget? Antecedents and consequences of intergroup forgiveness in Bosnia and Herzegovina." *Political Psychology* 29(3):351–67.

Chandra, Kanchan. 2006. "What is ethnic identity and does it matter?" *Annual Reviews of Political Science* 9:397–424.

Chaudoin, Stephen. 2014. "Promises or policies? An experimental analysis of international agreements and audience reactions." *International Organization* 68(1):235–56.

Checkel, Jeffrey T, and Peter J Katzenstein. 2009. *European Identity*. Cambridge: Cambridge University Press.

Chiozza, Giacomo, and Hein E Goemans. 2004. "International conflict and the tenure of leaders: Is war still ex post inefficient?" *American Journal of Political Science* 48(3):604–19.

Chung, Eun Bin. 2015. "Can affirming national identity increase international trust? Experimental evidence from South Korean, Chinese, and Japanese nationals." *Asian International Studies Review* 16(1):75–97.

Cialdini, Robert B, and Noah J Goldstein. 2004. "Social influence: Compliance and conformity." *Annual Reviews of Psychology* 55:591–621.

Ciorciari, John D, and Jessica Chen Weiss. 2016. "Nationalist protests, government responses, and the risk of escalation in interstate disputes." *Security Studies* 25(3):546–83.

Citrin, Jack, Beth Reingold, and Donald P Green. 1990. "American identity and the politics of ethnic change." *The Journal of Politics* 52(4):1124–54.

Citrin, Jack, Cara Wong, and Brian Duff. 2001. The meaning of American national identity. In *Social Identity, Intergroup Conflict, and Conflict Reduction*, ed. Richard D. Ashmore, Lee Jussim, and David Wilder. Vol. 3. New York: Oxford University Press, pp. 71–100.

Citrin, Jack, and David O Sears. 2009. Balancing national and ethnic identities: The psychology of E Pluribus Unum. In *Measuring Identity: A Guide for Social Scientists*, ed. Rawi Abdelal, Yoshiko Herrera, Alastair Iain Johnson, and Rose McDermott. Cambridge: Cambridge University Press, pp. 145–74.

Citrin, Jack, Ernst B Haas, Christopher Muste, and Beth Reingold. 1994. "Is American nationalism changing? Implications for foreign policy." *International Studies Quarterly* 38(1): 1–31.

Citrin, Jack, and John Sides. 2004. More than nationals: How identity choice matters in the new Europe. In *Transnational Identities: Becoming European in the EU*, ed. Richard K. Herrmann, Thomas Risse and Marilynn B. Brewer. Lanham, MD: Rowman & Littlefield, pp. 161–85.

Citrin, Jack, and John Sides. 2008. "Immigration and the imagined community in Europe and the United States." *Political Studies* 56(1):33–56.

Citrin, Jack, Richard Johnston, and Matthew Wright. 2012. "Do patriotism and multiculturalism collide? Competing perspectives from Canada and the United States." *Canadian Journal of Political Science* 45(3):531–52.

Clements, Kevin P. 2018. Trust, identity and conflict in Northeast Asia—Barriers to positive relationships. In *Identity, Trust, and Reconciliation in East Asia*, ed. Kevin P. Clements. New York: Springer, pp. 1–27.

Clifford, Scott, Justin H Kirkland, and Elizabeth N Simas. 2019. "How dispositional empathy influences political ambition." *The Journal of Politics* 81(3):1043–56.

Coe, Kevin, David Domke, Erica S Graham, Sue Lockett John, and Victor W Pickard. 2004. "No shades of gray: The binary discourse of George W. Bush and an echoing press." *Journal of Communication* 54(2):234–52.

Collingwood, Loren, Nazita Lajevardi, and Kassra AR Oskooii. 2018. "A change of heart? Why individual-level public opinion shifted against Trump's 'Muslim Ban.'" *Political Behavior* 40(4):1035–72.

Collins, Alan. 2007. "Forming a security community: Lessons from ASEAN." *International Relations of the Asia-Pacific* 7(2):203–25.

Cosmides, Leda. 1989. "The logic of social exchange: Has natural selection shaped how humans reason? Studies with the Wason selection task." *Cognition* 31(3):187–276.

Cotta, Maurizio, Pierangelo Isernia, and Paolo Bellucci. 2009. "IntUne Mass Survey Wave 2, 2009." ICPSR34272-v2. Ann Arbor, MI: Inter-university Consortium for Political and Social Research (distributor), 2013-04-22. http://doi.org/10.3886/ICPSR34272.v2.

Cottam, Martha L, and Richard W Cottam. 2001. *Nationalism & Politics: The Political Behavior of Nation States.* Boulder, CO: Lynne Rienner Publishers.

Cram, Laura. 2009. "Identity and European integration: Diversity as a source of integration." *Nations and Nationalism* 15(1):109–28.

Cram, Laura. 2012. "Does the EU need a navel? Implicit and explicit identification with the European Union." *JCMS: Journal of Common Market Studies* 50(1):71–86.

Cram, Laura, Stratos Patrikios, and James Mitchell. 2011. "What does the European Union mean to its citizens? Implicit triggers, identity(ies) and attitudes to the European Union." Unpublished manuscript.

Croco, Sarah E, and Jessica L P Weeks. 2016. "War outcomes and leader tenure." *World Politics* 68(4):577–607.

Cronin, Bruce. 1999. *Community Under Anarchy: Transnational Identity and the Evolution of Cooperation.* New York: Columbia University Press.

Cuhadar, Esra, Juliet Kaarbo, Baris Kesgin, and Binnur Ozkececi-Taner. 2017. "Personality or role? Comparisons of Turkish leaders across different institutional positions." *Political Psychology* 38(1):39–54.

Cumings, Bruce, Richard Falk, Stephen M Walt, and Michael C Desch. 1994. "Is there a logic of the West?" *World Policy Journal* 11(1):113–24.

Curley, Tyler M. 2009. "Social identity theory and EU expansion." *International Studies Quarterly* 53(3):649–68.

Curtis, K Amber. 2014. "Inclusive versus exclusive: A cross-national comparison of the effects of subnational, national, and supranational identity." *European Union Politics* 15(4):521–46.

Davidov, Eldad. 2010. "Nationalism and constructive patriotism: A longitudinal test of comparability in 22 countries with the ISSP." *International Journal of Public Opinion Research* 23(1):88–103.

Davidov, Eldad, Peter Schmidt, and Shalom H Schwartz. 2008. "Bringing values back in: The adequacy of the European Social Survey to measure values in 20 countries." *Public Opinion Quarterly* 72(3):420–45.

Davies, Paul G, Claude M Steele, and Hazel Rose Markus. 2008. "A nation challenged: The impact of foreign threat on America's tolerance for diversity." *Journal of Personality and Social Psychology* 95(2):308.

Davis, Mark H. 1983. "The effects of dispositional empathy on emotional reactions and helping: A multidimensional approach." *Journal of Personality* 51(2):167–84.

Dawes, Robyn M, Alphons J C Van De Kragt, and John M Orbell. 1988. "Not me or thee but we: The importance of group identity in eliciting cooperation in dilemma situations: Experimental manipulations." *Acta Psychologica* 68(1-3):83–97.

De Figueiredo, Rui J P and Zachary Elkins. 2003. "Are patriots bigots? An inquiry into the vices of in-group pride." *American Journal of Political Science* 47(1):171–88.

De Vries, Catherine E. 2020. "Don't mention the war! Second World War remembrance and support for European cooperation." *JCMS: Journal of Common Market Studies* 58(1):138–54.

DeBell, Paul A, and Jason Morgan. 2015. "Party competition and political ideology in post-Communist Europe." Unpublished manuscript.

Deckman, Melissa, and Erin Cassese. 2019. "Gendered nationalism and the 2016 US presidential election: How party, class, and beliefs about masculinity shaped voting behavior." *Politics & Gender*, pp. 1–24.

Delanty, Gerard. 1995. *Inventing Europe*. New York: Springer.

Deutsch, Karl W. 1957. *Political Community and the North Atlantic Area*. Princeton: Princeton University Press.

Deutsch, Karl W. 1961. "Security communities." *International Politics and Foreign Policy*, pp. 98–105.

Devos, Thierry, and Mahzarin R Banaji. 2005. "American = White?" *Journal of Personality and Social Psychology* 88(3):447–66.

Dewey, John. 1916. "Nationalizing education." *Journal of Education* 84(16):425–28.

Diamond, Larry. 2006. What went wrong and right in Iraq. In *Nation-Building: Beyond Afghanistan and Iraq*. Baltimore: Johns Hopkins University Press, pp. 173–95.

Dinesen, Peter Thisted, Merlin Schaeffer, and Kim Mannemar Sønderskov. 2020. "Ethnic diversity and social trust: A narrative and meta-analytical review." *Annual Review of Political Science* 23:441–65.

Doosje, Bertjan, Naomi Ellemers, and Russell Spears. 1999. Commitment and intergroup behavior. In *Social Identity: Context, Commitment, Content*, ed. Naomi Ellemers, Russell Spears, and Bertjan Doosje. Oxford: Blackwell Science, pp. 84–106.

Dorussen, Han, Emil J Kirchner, and James Sperling. 2009. "Sharing the burden of collective security in the European Union." *International Organization* 63(4):789–810.

Doty, Richard M, David G Winter, Bill E Peterson, and Markus Kemmelmeier. 1997. "Authoritarianism and American students' attitudes about the Gulf War, 1990–1996." *Personality and Social Psychology Bulletin* 23(11):1133–43.

Dovidio, John F, Samuel L Gaertner, Ana Validzic, Kimberly Matoka, Brenda Johnson, and Stacy Frazier. 1997. "Extending the benefits of recategorization: Evaluations, self-disclosure, and helping." *Journal of Experimental Social Psychology* 33(4):401–20.

Dovidio, John F, Samuel L Gaertner, and Tamar Saguy. 2009. "Commonality and the complexity of 'We': Social attitudes and social change." *Personality and Social Psychology Review* 13(1):3–20.

Druckman, Daniel. 1994. "Nationalism, patriotism, and group loyalty: A social psychological perspective." *Mershon International Studies Review* 38(1):43–68.

Druckman, Daniel. 2001. Nationalism and war: A social-psychological perspective. In *Peace, Conflict, and Violence: Peace Psychology for the 21st Century*, ed. D. J. Christie, R. V. Wagner, and D. A. Winter. Englewood Cliffs, New Jersey: Prentice-Hall, pp. 49–65.

Druckman, James N, and Cindy D Kam. 2011. "Students as experimental participants." *Cambridge Handbook of Experimental Political Science* 1:41–57.

Duchesne, Sophie. 2008. "Waiting for a European identity ... Reflections on the process of identification with Europe." *Perspectives on European Politics and Society* 9(4):397–410.

Dumont, Muriel, Vincent Yzerbyt, Daniël Wigboldus, and Ernestine H Gordijn. 2003. "Social categorization and fear reactions to the September 11th terrorist attacks." *Personality and Social Psychology Bulletin* 29(12):1509–20.

Durkheim, Emile. 1933. *The Division of Labor in Society*. New York: Free Press. Original publication date 1893.

Dynes, Adam M, Hans J G Hassell, Matthew R Miles, and Jessica Robinson Preece. 2021. "Personality and gendered selection processes in the political pipeline." *Politics & Gender* 17(1):53–73.

Effron, Daniel A, and Eric D Knowles. 2015. "Entitativity and intergroup bias: How belonging to a cohesive group allows people to express their prejudices." *Journal of Personality and Social Psychology* 108(2):234.

Eichenberg, Richard C. 2016. "Gender difference in American public opinion on the use of military force, 1982–2013." *International Studies Quarterly* 60(1):138–48.

Eichenberg, Richard C, and Richard J Stoll. 2012. "Gender difference or parallel publics? The dynamics of defense spending opinions in the United States, 1965–2007." *Journal of Conflict Resolution* 56(2):331–48.

Ellemers, Naomi, Russell Spears, and Bertjan Doosje. 2002. "Self and social identity." *Annual Review of Psychology* 53(1):161–86.

Emerson, Rupert. 1960. *From Empire to Nation: The Rise to Self-assertion of Asian and African Peoples*. Cambridge: Harvard University Press.

European Commission. 2018. "Eurobarometer 81.4 (2014)." TNS Opinion, Brussels. GESIS Data Archive, Cologne. ZA5928 Data file Version 3.0.0. https://doi.org/10.4232/1.12956.

European Commission. 2012. *The Development of European Identity/Identities: Unfinished Business*. Directorate-General for Research & Innovation.

European Commission. 2020. "Eurobarometer 92.3 (2019)." Kantar Public, Brussels. GESIS Data Archive, Cologne. ZA7601. Data file Version 1.0.0. https://doi.org/10.4232/1.13564.

European Union. 1957. "The Treaty of Rome." https://ec.europa.eu/romania/sites/romania/files/tratatul_de_la_roma.pdf.

European Union. 2007. "Treaty of Lisbon." https://eur-lex.europa.eu/legal-content/EN/TXT/HTML/?uri=CELEX:12007L/TXT&from=EN.

Fabrigar, Leandre R, Duane T Wegener, Robert C MacCallum, and Erin J Strahan. 1999. "Evaluating the use of exploratory factor analysis in psychological research." *Psychological Methods* 4(3):272.

Farnham, Barbara. 1992. "Roosevelt and the Munich crisis: Insights from prospect theory." *Political Psychology* 13(2):205–35.

Farnham, Barbara Rearden. 2000. *Roosevelt and the Munich Crisis: A Study of Political Decision-making*. Princeton: Princeton University Press.

Fearon, James, and Alexander Wendt. 2002. Rationalism v. constructivism: A skeptical view. In *Handbook of International Relations*, ed. Walter Carlsnaes, Thomas Risse, and Beth Simmons. London: Sage Publications, pp. 52–72.

Federico, Christopher M, Agnieszka Golec, and Jessica L Dial. 2005. "The relationship between the need for closure and support for military action against Iraq: Moderating effects of national attachment." *Personality and Social Psychology Bulletin* 31(5):621–32.

Feldman, Stanley. 2003. "Enforcing social conformity: A theory of authoritarianism." *Political Psychology* 24(1):41–74.

Feldman, Stanley, and John Zaller. 1992. "The political culture of ambivalence: Ideological responses to the welfare state." *American Journal of Political Science* 36(3):268–307.

Feldman, Stanley, and Karen Stenner. 1997. "Perceived threat and authoritarianism." *Political Psychology* 18(4):741–70.

Feshbach, Seymour. 1987. "Individual aggression, national attachment, and the search for peace: Psychological perspectives." *Aggressive Behavior* 13(5):315–25.

Fielding, Kelly S, and Michael A Hogg. 1997. "Social identity, self-categorization, and leadership: A field study of small interactive groups." *Group Dynamics: Theory, Research, and Practice* 1(1):39.

Fiske, Alan P. 1992. "The four elementary forms of sociality: Framework for a unified theory of social relations." *Psychological Review* 99(4):689–723.

Fiske, Alan P, Nick Haslam, and Susan T Fiske. 1991. "Confusing one person with another: What errors reveal about the elementary forms of social relations." *Journal of Personality and Social Psychology* 60(5):656–74.

Fiske, Alan Page. 1991. *Structures of Social Life: The Four Elementary Forms of Human Relations: Communal Sharing, Authority Ranking, Equality Matching, Market Pricing.* New York: Free Press.

Fiske, Alan Page. 2004. Relational models theory 2.0. In *Relational Models Theory: A Contemporary Overview*, ed. N Haslam Mahwah, NJ: L Erlbour pp. 3–25.

Fiske, Alan Page, and Philip E Tetlock. 1997. "Taboo trade-offs: Reactions to transactions that transgress the spheres of justice." *Political Psychology* 18(2):255–97.

Fiske, Alan Page, and Tage Shakti Rai. 2015. *Virtuous Violence: Hurting and Killing to Create, Sustain, End, and Honor Social Relationships.* Cambridge: Cambridge University Press.

Fligstein, Neil. 2008. *Euroclash: The EU, European Identity, and the Future of Europe.* Oxford: Oxford University Press.

Foyle, Douglas C. 2004. "Leading the public to war? The influence of American public opinion on the Bush administration's decision to go to war in Iraq." *International Journal of Public Opinion Research* 16(3):269–94.

Fursdon, Edward. 1980. *The European Defence Community: A History.* New York: St. Martin's Press.

Gaertner, Samuel L, and John F Dovidio. 2000. *Reducing Intergroup Bias: The Common Ingroup Identity Model.* London: Psychology Press.

Gallagher, Maryann E, and Susan H Allen. 2014. "Presidential personality: Not just a nuisance." *Foreign Policy Analysis* 10(1):1–21.

Gandhi, Mahatma. 1935. *From Yeravda Mandir.*

Gandhi, Mohandas Karamchand. 1925. *Young India.* S Ganesan, Madras.

Gartner, Scott Sigmund. 2008. "The multiple effects of casualties on public support for war: An experimental approach." *American Political Science Review* 102(1):95–106.

Gellner, Ernest. 1983. *Nations and Nationalism.* Ithaca, NY: Cornell University Press.

Gelpi, Christopher, and Joseph M Grieco. 2015. "Competency costs in foreign affairs: Presidential performance in international conflicts and domestic legislative success, 1953–2001." *American Journal of Political Science* 59(2):440–56.

Gelpi, Christopher, Laura Roselle, and Brooke Barnett. 2013. "Polarizing patriots: Divergent responses to patriotic imagery in news coverage of terrorism." *American Behavioral Scientist* 57(1):8–45.

Gelpi, Christopher, and Peter D Feaver. 2002. "Speak softly and carry a big stick? Veterans in the political elite and the American use of force." *American Political Science Review* 96(4): 779–93.

Gibler, Douglas M, Marc L Hutchison, and Steven V Miller. 2012. "Individual identity attachments and international conflict: The importance of territorial threat." *Comparative Political Studies* 45(12):1655–83.

Gilmore, Jason, and Charles M Rowling. 2018. "Lighting the beacon: Presidential discourse, American exceptionalism, and public diplomacy in global contexts." *Presidential Studies Quarterly* 48(2):271–91.

Gilmore, Jason, Penelope Sheets, and Charles Rowling. 2016. "Make no exception, save one: American exceptionalism, the American presidency, and the age of Obama." *Communication Monographs* 83(4):505–20.

Ginges, Jeremy, Scott Atran, Douglas Medin, and Khalil Shikaki. 2007. "Sacred bounds on rational resolution of violent political conflict." *Proceedings of the National Academy of Sciences* 104(18):7357–60.

Glosserman, Brad, and Scott A Snyder. 2015. *The Japan–South Korea Identity Clash: East Asian Security and the United States.* New York: Columbia University Press.

Goemans, Hein E. 2006. Bounded communities: Territoriality, territorial attachment, and conflict. In *Territoriality and Conflict in an Era of Globalization*, ed. Miles Kahler and Barbara F. Walter. Cambridge: Cambridge University Press, pp. 25–61.

Goldstein, Joshua S. 1992. "A conflict-cooperation scale for WEIS events data." *Journal of Conflict Resolution* 36(2):369–85.

Goodman, Sara Wallace. 2012. "Fortifying citizenship: Policy strategies for civic integration in Western Europe." *World Politics* 64(4):659–98.

Goodman, Sara Wallace. 2021. " 'Good American citizens': A text-as-data analysis of citizenship manuals for immigrants, 1921–1996." *Journal of Ethnic and Migration Studies* 47(7): 1474–97.

Goodson, Larry P. 2006. The lessons of nation-building in Afghanistan. In *Nation-Building: Beyond Afghanistan and Iraq*. Baltimore: Johns Hopkins University Press, pp. 145–69.

Goren, Paul, Harald Schoen, Jason Reifler, Thomas Scotto, and William Chittick. 2016. "A unified theory of value-based reasoning and US public opinion." *Political Behavior* 38(4): 977–97.

Graham, Jesse, Brian A. Nosek, Jonathan Haidt, Ravi Iyer, Spassena Koleva, and Peter H. Ditto. 2011. "Mapping the moral domain." *Journal of Personality and Social Psychology* 101(2): 366–85.

Graham, Jesse, Jonathan Haidt, and Brian A. Nosek. 2009. "Liberals and conservatives rely on different sets of moral foundations." *Journal of Personality and Social Psychology* 96(5): 1029–46.

Gravelle, Timothy B. 2018. "Partisanship, local context, group threat, and Canadian attitudes towards immigration and refugee policy." *Migration Studies* 6(3):448–67.

Gravelle, Timothy B, Jason Reifler, and Thomas J Scotto. 2017. "The structure of foreign policy attitudes in transatlantic perspective: Comparing the United States, United Kingdom, France and Germany." *European Journal of Political Research* 56(4):757–76.

Gravelle, Timothy B, Jason Reifler, and Thomas J Scotto. 2020. "Personality traits and foreign policy attitudes: A cross-national exploratory study." *Personality and Individual Differences* 153, article 109607.

Gravelle, Timothy B, Thomas J Scotto, Jason Reifler, and Harold D Clarke. 2014. "Foreign policy beliefs and support for Stephen Harper and the Conservative Party." *Canadian Foreign Policy Journal* 20(2):111–30.

Greene, Steven. 1999. "Understanding party identification: A social identity approach." *Political Psychology* 20(2):393–403.

Greenfeld, Liah. 1992. *Nationalism: Five Roads to Modernity*. Cambridge: Harvard University Press.

Gries, Peter. 2014. *The Politics of American Foreign Policy: How Ideology Divides Liberals and Conservatives Over Foreign Affairs*. Stanford, CA: Stanford University Press.

Gries, Peter Hays. 1999. "A 'China Threat'? Power and passion in Chinese Face 'Nationalism.' " *World Affairs* 162(2):63–75.

Gries, Peter Hays. 2004. *China's New Nationalism: Pride, Politics, and Diplomacy*. Oakland: University of California Press.

Gries, Peter Hays. 2005. "Social psychology and the identity-conflict debate: Is a 'China Threat' inevitable?" *European Journal of International Relations* 11(2):235–65.

Gries, Peter Hays, Derek Steiger, and Tao Wang. 2016. "Popular nationalism and China's Japan policy: The Diaoyu Islands protests, 2012–2013." *Journal of Contemporary China* 25(98):264–76.

Gries, Peter Hays, Qingmin Zhang, H Michael Crowson, and Huajian Cai. 2011. "Patriotism, nationalism and China's US policy: Structures and consequences of Chinese national identity." *The China Quarterly* 205:1–17.

Grinberg, Maurice, Evgenia Hristova, and Milena Borisova. 2012. Cooperation in prisoner's dilemma game: Influence of social relations. In *Proceedings of the Annual Meeting of the Cognitive Science Society* 34:408–13.

Gruffydd-Jones, Jamie. 2017. "Dangerous days: The impact of nationalism on interstate conflict." *Security Studies* 26(4):698–728.

Guisinger, Alexandra, and Elizabeth N Saunders. 2017. "Mapping the boundaries of elite cues: How elites shape mass opinion across international issues." *International Studies Quarterly* 61(2):425–41.

Haas, Ernst B. 1958. *The Uniting of Europe: Political, Social, and Economic Forces, 1950-1957.* Stanford, CA: Stanford University Press.

Hafner-Burton, Emilie M, Brad L LeVeck, and David G Victor. 2017. "No false promises: How the prospect of non-compliance affects elite preferences for international cooperation." *International Studies Quarterly* 61(1):136–49.

Hafner-Burton, Emilie M, Brad L LeVeck, David G Victor, and James H Fowler. 2014. "Decision maker preferences for international legal cooperation." *International Organization* 68(4): 845–76.

Hafner-Burton, Emilie M, D Alex Hughes, and David G Victor. 2013. "The cognitive revolution and the political psychology of elite decision making." *Perspectives on Politics* 11(2):368–86.

Hagström, Linus, and Karl Gustafsson. 2015. "Japan and identity change: Why it matters in international relations." *The Pacific Review* 28(1):1–22.

Haidt, J, and C Joseph. 2004. "Intuitive ethics: How innately prepared intuitions generate culturally variable virtues." *Daedalus* Fall:55–66.

Haidt, Jonathan. 2001. "The emotional dog and its rational tail: A social intuitionist approach to moral judgment." *Psychological Review* 108(4):814–34.

Haidt, Jonathan, and Jesse Graham. 2007. "When morality opposes justice: Conservatives have moral intuitions that liberals may not recognize." *Social Justice Research* 20(1):98–116.

Hainmueller, Jens, Jonathan Mummolo, and Yiqing Xu. 2019. "How much should we trust estimates from multiplicative interaction models? Simple tools to improve empirical practice." *Political Analysis* 27(2):163–92.

Hakhverdian, Armen, Erika Van Elsas, Wouter Van der Brug, and Theresa Kuhn. 2013. "Euroscepticism and education: A longitudinal study of 12 EU member states, 1973–2010." *European Union Politics* 14(4):522–41.

Hamilton, Alexander, James Madison, and John Jay. 2009. The Federalist No. 2 concerning dangers from foreign force and influence. In *The Federalist Papers*, ed. Ian Shapiro. New Haven, CT: Yale University Press.

Hamilton, David L, and Steven J Sherman. 1996. "Perceiving persons and groups." *Psychological Review* 103(2):336–55.

Hanson, Kristin, and Emma O'Dwyer. 2019. "Patriotism and nationalism, Left and right: A Q-methodology study of American national identity." *Political Psychology* 40(4):777–95.

Hartz, Louis. 1955. *The Liberal Tradition in America: An Interpretation of American Political Thought Since the Revolution.* San Diego, CA: Harcourt, Inc.

Haslam, Nick. 2004. Research on the relational models: An overview. In *Relational Models Theory: A Contemporary Overview.* London: Routledge, pp. 27–57.

Haslam, Nick. 2006. "Dehumanization: An integrative review." *Personality and Social Psychology Review* 10(3):252–64.

Haslam, Nick, and Alan Page Fiske. 1999. "Relational models theory: A confirmatory factor analysis." *Personal Relationships* 6(2):241–50.

Haslam, Nick, Therese Reichert, and Alan P Fiske. 2002. "Aberrant social relations in the personality disorders." *Psychology and Psychotherapy: Theory, Research and Practice* 75(1):19–31.

Haslam, S Alexander, Stephen D Reicher, and Michael J Platow. 2011. *The New Psychology of Leadership: Identity, Influence and Power*. London: Psychology Press.

Hassin, Ran R, Melissa J Ferguson, Daniella Shidlovski, and Tamar Gross. 2007. "Subliminal exposure to national flags affects political thought and behavior." *Proceedings of the National Academy of Sciences* 104(50):19757–61.

Hatemi, Peter K, Charles Crabtree, and Kevin B Smith. 2019. "Ideology justifies morality: Political beliefs predict moral foundations." *American Journal of Political Science* 63(4):788–806.

Hayes, Jarrod. 2009. "Identity and securitization in the democratic peace: The United States and the divergence of response to India and Iran's nuclear programs." *International Studies Quarterly* 53(4):977–99.

Hayes, Jarrod. 2012. "Securitization, social identity, and democratic security: Nixon, India, and the ties that bind." *International Organization* 66(1):63–93.

Healy, Andrew, and Gabriel S Lenz. 2014. "Substituting the end for the whole: Why voters respond primarily to the election-year economy." *American Journal of Political Science* 58(1):31–47.

Hechter, Michael. 2000. *Containing Nationalism*. Oxford: Oxford University Press.

Heine, Steven J, and Emma E Buchtel. 2009. "Personality: The universal and the culturally specific." *Annual Review of Psychology* 60:369–94.

Helbling, Marc, Tim Reeskens, and Matthew Wright. 2016. "The mobilisation of identities: A study on the relationship between elite rhetoric and public opinion on national identity in developed democracies." *Nations and Nationalism* 22(4):744–67.

Hemmer, Christopher, and Peter J Katzenstein. 2002. "Why is there no NATO in Asia? Collective identity, regionalism, and the origins of multilateralism." *International Organization* 56(3):575–607.

Henrich, Joseph, Steven J Heine, and Ara Norenzayan. 2010. "Most people are not WEIRD." *Nature* 466(29):29.

Hermann, Margaret G. 1980. "Explaining foreign policy behavior using the personal characteristics of political leaders." *International Studies Quarterly* 24(1):7–46.

Hermann, Margaret G, and Charles W Kegley Jr. 1995. "Rethinking democracy and international peace: Perspectives from political psychology." *International Studies Quarterly* 39(4): 511–33.

Herrmann, Richard K. 1985. "Analyzing Soviet images of the United States: A psychological theory and empirical study." *Journal of Conflict Resolution* 29(4):665–97.

Herrmann, Richard K, Pierangelo Isernia, and Paolo Segatti. 2009. "Attachment to the nation and international relations: Dimensions of identity and their relationship to war and peace." *Political Psychology* 30(5):721–54.

Herrmann, Richard, and Marilynn B Brewer. 2004. Identities and institutions: Becoming European in the EU. In *Transnational Identities: Becoming European in the EU*, ed. Richard K. Herrmann, Thomas Risse, and Marilynn B. Brewer. Washington, D.C.: Rowman & Littlefield Publishers, pp. 1–22.

Hetherington, Marc, and Elizabeth Suhay. 2011. "Authoritarianism, threat, and Americans' support for the war on terror." *American Journal of Political Science* 55(3):546–60.

Hetherington, Marc, and Jonathan Weiler. 2018. *Prius Or Pickup?: How the Answers to Four Simple Questions Explain America's Great Divide*. Boston, MA: Houghton Mifflin.

Hewstone, Miles Ed, and Rupert Ed Brown. 1986. *Contact and Conflict in Intergroup Encounters*. Oxford: Basil Blackwell.

Hinkle, Steve, and Rupert Brown. 1990. "Intergroup comparisons and social identity: Some links and lacunae." In *Social Identity Theory: Constructive and Critical Advances*, ed. Dominic Abrams and Michael A. Hogg. London: Harvester Wheatsheaf, pp.48–70.

Hirschfeld, Lawrence A. 2001. "On a folk theory of society: Children, evolution, and mental representations of social groups." *Personality and Social Psychology Review* 5(2):107–17.

Hixson, Walter L. 2008. *The Myth of American Diplomacy: National Identity and US Foreign Policy*. New Haven, CT: Yale University Press.

Hobolt, Sara B, and Catherine E De Vries. 2016. "Public support for European integration." *Annual Review of Political Science* 19:413–32.

Hoffman, Aaron M. 2006. *Building Trust: Overcoming Suspicion in International Conflict*. Albany, NY: Suny Press.

Hofmann, Stephanie C. 2013. *European Security in NATO's Shadow: Party Ideologies and Institution Building*. Cambridge: Cambridge University Press.

Hofstede, Geert. 1984. *Culture's Consequences: International Differences in Work-related Values*. Beverly Hills, CA: Sage.

Hofstede, Geert, and Michael H Bond. 1984. "Hofstede's culture dimensions: An independent validation using Rokeach's value survey." *Journal of Cross-cultural Psychology* 15(4):417–33.

Hogg, Michael A. 2001. "A social identity theory of leadership." *Personality and Social Psychology Review* 5(3):184–200.

Hogg, Michael A. and Dominic Abrams. 1988. *Social Identifications: A Social Psychology of Intergroup Relations and Group Processes*. London: Routledge.

Hogg, Michael A John C Turner, and Barbara Davidson. 1990. "Polarized norms and social frames of reference: A test of the self-categorization theory of group polarization." *Basic and Applied Social Psychology* 11(1):77–100.

Holsti, Ole R. 1979. "The three-headed eagle: The United States and system change." *International Studies Quarterly* 23(3): 339–59.

Holsti, Ole Rudolf. 2004. *Public Opinion and American Foreign Policy*. Ann Arbor: University of Michigan Press.

Hooghe, Liesbet, and Gary Marks. 2004. "Does identity or economic rationality drive public opinion on European integration?" *PS: Political Science & Politics* 37(3):415–20.

Hooghe, Liesbet, and Gary Marks. 2005. "Calculation, community and cues: Public opinion on European integration." *European Union Politics* 6(4):419–43.

Hooghe, Liesbet, and Gary Marks. 2009. "A postfunctionalist theory of European integration: From permissive consensus to constraining." *British Journal of Political Science* 39(1):1–23.

Hooghe, Liesbet, Gary Marks, and Carole J Wilson. 2002. "Does left/right structure party positions on European integration?" *Comparative Political Studies* 35(8):965–89.

Hopf, Ted. 2013. "Common-sense constructivism and hegemony in world politics." *International Organization* 67(2):317–54.

Hopf, Ted, and Bentley Allan. 2016. *Making Identity Count: Building a National Identity Database*. Oxford: Oxford University Press.

Höpner, Martin, and Bojan Jurczyk. 2015. "How the Eurobarometer blurs the line between research and propaganda." MPIfG Discussion Paper 15/6.

Hornsey, Matthew J. 2008. "Social identity theory and self-categorization theory: A historical review." *Social and Personality Psychology Compass* 2(1):204–22.

Hornsey, Matthew J, and Michael A Hogg. 2000. "Subgroup relations: A comparison of mutual intergroup differentiation and common ingroup identity models of prejudice reduction." *Personality and Social Psychology Bulletin* 26(2):242–56.

Horowitz, Donald L. 1985. *Ethnic Groups in Conflict*. Oakland, CA: University of California Press.

Horowitz, Donald L. 2001. *The Deadly Ethnic Riot*. Oakland, CA: University of California Press.

Horowitz, Michael C, Allan C Stam, and Cali M Ellis. 2015. *Why Leaders Fight*. Cambridge: Cambridge University Press.

Howell, William G, and Jon C Pevehouse. 2007. *While Dangers Gather: Congressional Checks on Presidential War Powers*. Princeton: Princeton University Press.

Huber, Gregory A, Seth J Hill, and Gabriel S Lenz. 2012. "Sources of bias in retrospective decision making: Experimental evidence on voters' limitations in controlling incumbents." *American Political Science Review* 106(4):720–41.

Huddy, Leonie. 2001. "From social to political identity: A critical examination of social identity theory." *Political Psychology* 22(1):127–56.

Huddy, Leonie, and Alessandro Del Ponte. 2019. National identity, pride, and chauvinism–Their origins and consequences for globalization attitudes. In *Liberal Nationalism and Its Critics*, ed. G Gustavsson and D. Miller. Oxford: Oxford University Press.

Huddy, Leonie, Lilliana Mason, and Lene Aarøe. 2015. "Expressive partisanship: Campaign involvement, political emotion, and partisan identity." *American Political Science Review* 109(1):1–17.

Huddy, Leonie, and Nadia Khatib. 2007. "American patriotism, national identity, and political involvement." *American Journal of Political Science* 51(1):63–77.

Huddy, Leonie, Stanley Feldman, Charles Taber, and Gallya Lahav. 2005. "Threat, anxiety, and support of antiterrorism policies." *American Journal of Political Science* 49(3):593–608.

Huff, Connor, and Joshua D Kertzer. 2018. "How the public defines terrorism." *American Journal of Political Science* 62(1):55–71.

Huntington, Samuel P. 1997. "The erosion of American national interests." *Foreign Affairs* 76(5): 28–49.

Huntington, Samuel P. 2004. *Who Are We? The Challenges to America's National Identity*. New York: Simon and Schuster.

Hurwitz, Jon, and Mark Peffley. 1987. "How are foreign policy attitudes structured?" *American Political Science Review* 81(4):1099–1120.

Hurwitz, Jon, and Mark Peffley. 1990. "Public images of the Soviet Union: The impact on foreign policy attitudes." *The Journal of Politics* 52(1):3–28.

Hutcheson, John, David Domke, Andre Billeaudeaux, and Philip Garland. 2004. "US national identity, political elites, and a patriotic press following September 11." *Political Communication* 21(1):27–50.

Hutchinson, John. 1994. *Modern Nationalism*. London: Fontana Press.

Hutchinson, John. 2017. *Nationalism and War*. Oxford: Oxford University Press.

Hymans, Jacques E C. 2002. Applying social identity theory to the study of international politics: A caution and an agenda. In *Annual Meeting of the International Studies Association*.

Hymans, Jacques E. C. 2006. *The Psychology of Nuclear Proliferation: Identity, Emotions and Foreign policy*. Cambridge: Cambridge University Press.

Inskeep, Steve. 2015. "Video and transcript: NPR's interview with President Obama." www.npr.org/2015/12/21/460030344/video-and-transcript-nprs-interview-with-president-obama.

ISSP Research Group. 2013. "International social survey program (ISSP): National identity III." doi:10.4232/1.12312.

Jackson, Jay W, and Eliot R Smith. 1999. "Conceptualizing social identity: A new framework and evidence for the impact of different dimensions." *Personality and Social Psychology Bulletin* 25(1):120–35.

Jacoby, William G. 2006. "Value choices and American public opinion." *American Journal of Political Science* 50(3):706–23.

Janmaat, Jan Germen. 2006. "Popular conceptions of nationhood in old and new European member states: Partial support for the ethnic-civic framework." *Ethnic and Racial Studies* 29(1):50–78.

Jervis, Robert. 1976. *Perception and Misperception in International Politics*. Princeton: Princeton University Press.

Jetten, Jolanda, Tom Postmes, and Brendan J McAuliffe. 2002. " 'We're all individuals': Group norms of individualism and collectivism, levels of identification and identity threat." *European Journal of Social Psychology* 32(2):189–207.

Johnston, Alastair Iain. 2005. "Conclusions and extensions: Toward mid-range theorizing and beyond Europe." *International Organization* 59(4):1013–44.

Johnston, Alastair Iain. 2012. "What (if anything) does East Asia tell us about international relations theory?" *Annual Review of Political Science* 15:53–78.

Johnston, Alastair Iain. 2017. "Is Chinese nationalism rising? Evidence from Beijing." *International Security* 41(3):7–43.

Johnston, Christopher D, Howard G Lavine, and Christopher M Federico. 2017. *Open Versus Closed: Personality, Identity, and the Politics of Redistribution*. Cambridge: Cambridge University Press.

Johnston, Richard, Keith Banting, Will Kymlicka, and Stuart Soroka. 2010. "National identity and support for the welfare state." *Canadian Journal of Political Science* 43(2):349–77.

Jones, Calvert W. 2014. "Exploring the microfoundations of international community: Toward a theory of enlightened nationalism." *International Studies Quarterly* 58(4):682–705.

Jones, Michael E. 2004. "Forging an ASEAN identity: The challenge to construct a shared destiny." *Contemporary Southeast Asia* 26(1):140–54.

Jost, John T, Jack Glaser, Arie W Kruglanski, and Frank J Sulloway. 2003. "Political conservatism as motivated social cognition." *Psychological Bulletin* 129(3):339–75.

Jung, Jai Kwan. 2008. "Growing supranational identities in a globalising world? A multi-level analysis of the World Values Surveys." *European Journal of Political Research* 47(5): 578–609.

Kahl, Colin H. 1998. "Constructing a separate peace: Constructivism, collective liberal identity, and democratic peace." *Security Studies* 8(2-3):94–144.

Kalin, Michael, and Nicholas Sambanis. 2018. "How to think about social identity." *Annual Review of Political Science* 21:239–57.

Kane, John V, and Jason Barabas. 2019. "No harm in checking: Using factual manipulation checks to assess attentiveness in experiments." *American Journal of Political Science* 63(1):234–49.

Kang, David C. 2003. "Getting Asia wrong: The need for new analytical frameworks." *International Security* 27(4):57–85.

Kang, David C. 2020. "International order in historical East Asia: Tribute and hierarchy beyond Sinocentrism and Eurocentrism." *International Organization* 74(1):65–93.

Kang, David C, and Alex Yu-Ting Lin. 2019. "US bias in the study of Asian security: Using Europe to study Asia." *Journal of Global Security Studies* 4(3):393–401.

Karasawa, Minoru. 1991. "Toward an assessment of social identity: The structure of group identification and its effects on in-group evaluations." *British Journal of Social Psychology* 30(4):293–307.

Karawan, Ibrahim A. 2002. Identity and foreign policy: The case of Egypt. In *Identity and Foreign Policy in the Middle East*, ed. Shibley Telhami and Michael Barnett. Ithaca, NY: Cornell University Press, pp. 155–68.

Katsumata, Hiro, and Takeshi Iida. 2011. "Popular culture and regional identity in East Asia: Evidence from the Asia Student Survey 2008." http://www.waseda-giari.jp/sysimg/imgs/wp 2011_e3.pdf.

Katzenstein, Peter J, and Jeffrey T Checkel. 2009. Conclusion: European identity in context. In *European Identity*, ed. Jeffrey T Checkel and Peter J Katzenstein. Cambridge: Cambridge University Press, pp. 213–27.

Kemmelmeier, Markus, and David G Winter. 2008. "Sowing patriotism, but reaping nationalism? Consequences of exposure to the American flag." *Political Psychology* 29(6):859–79.

Keohane, Robert O. 1986. "Reciprocity in international relations." *International Organization* 40(1):1–27.

Kertzer, Joshua D. 2016. *Resolve in International Politics.* Princeton: Princeton University Press.

Kertzer, Joshua D. 2017. "Microfoundations in international relations." *Conflict Management and Peace Science* 34(1):81–97.

Kertzer, Joshua D. 2020. "Re-assessing elite-public gaps in political behavior." *American Journal of Political Science.*

Kertzer, Joshua D, Jonathan Renshon, and Keren Yarhi-Milo. 2021. "How do observers assess resolve?" *British Journal of Political Science* 51(1):308–30.

Kertzer, Joshua D, Kathleen E Powers, Brian C Rathbun, and Ravi Iyer. 2014. "Moral support: How moral values shape foreign policy attitudes." *The Journal of Politics* 76(3):825–40.

Kertzer, Joshua D, and Kathleen Powers. 2020. Foreign policy attitudes as networks. In *The Oxford Handbook of Behavioral Political Science*, ed. Alex Mintz and Lesley Terris. Oxford: Oxford University Press.

Kertzer, Joshua D, and Thomas Zeitzoff. 2017. "A bottom-up theory of public opinion about foreign policy." *American Journal of Political Science* 61(3):543–58.

Kinder, Donald R, and Cindy D Kam. 2010. *Us Against Them: Ethnocentric Foundations of American Opinion.* Chicago: University of Chicago Press.

King, Gary, and Langche Zeng. 2007. "When can history be our guide? The pitfalls of counterfactual inference." *International Studies Quarterly* 51(1):183–210.

Kitayama, Shinobu, and Ayse K Uskul. 2011. "Culture, mind, and the brain: Current evidence and future directions." *Annual Review of Psychology* 62:419–49.

Kivimäki, Timo. 2010. "East Asian relative peace and the ASEAN way." *International Relations of the Asia-Pacific* 11(1):57–85.

Klar, Samara. 2013. "The influence of competing identity primes on political preferences." *The Journal of Politics* 75(4):1108–24.

Klar, Samara, Thomas Leeper, and Joshua Robison. 2020. "Studying identities with experiments: Weighing the risk of posttreatment bias against priming effects." *Journal of Experimental Political Science* 7(1):56–60.

Kleider, Hanna, and Florian Stoeckel. 2019. "The politics of international redistribution: Explaining public support for fiscal transfers in the EU." *European Journal of Political Research* 58(1):4–29.

Knafo, Ariel, Sonia Roccas, and Lilach Sagiv. 2011. "The value of values in cross-cultural research: A special issue in honor of Shalom Schwartz." *Journal of Cross-Cultural Psychology* 42:178–85.

Ko, Jiyoung. 2019. "Not so dangerous? The impact of nationalistic sentiments on foreign policy preferences." Unpublished manuscript.

Kocher, Matthew A, Adria K Lawrence, and Nuno P Monteiro. 2018. "Nationalism, collaboration, and resistance in occupied france." *International Security* 43(2):117–50.

Koenig-Archibugi, Mathias. 2004. "Explaining government preferences for institutional change in EU foreign and security policy." *International Organization* 58(1):137–74.

Kohn, Hans. 1944. *The Idea of Nationalism.* New York: Macmillan Company.

Koleva, Spassena P, Jesse Graham, Ravi Iyer, Peter H Ditto, and Jonathan Haidt. 2012. "Tracing the threads: How five moral concerns (especially purity) help explain culture war attitudes." *Journal of Research in Personality* 46(2):184–94.

Koremenos, Barbara, Charles Lipson, and Duncan Snidal. 2001. "The rational design of international institutions." *International Organization* 55(04):761–99.

Kosterman, Rick, and Seymour Feshbach. 1989. "Toward a measure of patriotic and nationalistic attitudes." *Political Psychology* 10(2):257–74.

Krebs, Ronald R, and Jennifer K Lobasz. 2007. "Fixing the meaning of 9/11: Hegemony, coercion, and the road to war in Iraq." *Security Studies* 16(3):409–51.

Kreps, Sarah, and Sarah Maxey. 2018. "Mechanisms of morality: Sources of support for humanitarian intervention." *Journal of Conflict Resolution* 62(8):1814–42.

Kreuzer, Peter. 2006. "Violent civic nationalism versus civil ethnic nationalism: Contrasting Indonesia and Malay(si)a." *National Identities* 8(1):41–59.

Krosnick, Jon A. 2018. Questionnaire design. In *The Palgrave Handbook of Survey Research*, ed. D. Vannette and J. Krosnick. New York: Springer, pp. 439–55.

Krosnick, Jon A, and Duane F Alwin. 1987. "An evaluation of a cognitive theory of response-order effects in survey measurement." *Public Opinion Quarterly* 51(2):201–19.

Krupnikov, Yanna, and Adam Seth Levine. 2014. "Cross-sample comparisons and external validity." *Journal of Experimental Political Science* 1(1):59–80.

Kuhn, Theresa, and Florian Stoeckel. 2014. "When European integration becomes costly: The Euro crisis and public support for European economic governance." *Journal of European Public Policy* 21(4):624–41.

Kunst, Jonas R, John F Dovidio, and Lotte Thomsen. 2019. "Fusion with political leaders predicts willingness to persecute immigrants and political opponents." *Nature Human Behaviour* 3(11):1180–89.

Kupchan, Charles A. 2010. *How Enemies Become Friends: The Sources of Stable Peace*. Vol. 121. Princeton: Princeton University Press.

Kupchan, Charles A, and Clifford A Kupchan. 1991. "Concerts, collective security, and the future of Europe." *International Security* 16(1):114–61.

Kuzio, Taras. 2002. "The myth of the civic state: A critical survey of Hans Kohn's framework for understanding nationalism." *Ethnic and Racial Studies* 25(1):20–39.

Kydd, Andrew. 2005. *Trust and Mistrust in International Politics*. Princeton: Princeton University Press.

Kymlicka, Will. 1998. *Finding Our Way: Rethinking Ethnocultural Relations in Canada*. Toronto: Oxford University Press.

Kymlicka, Will. 2001. *Politics in the Vernacular: Nationalism, Multiculturalism and Citizenship*. Oxford: Oxford University Press.

Kymlicka, Will. 2003. "Being Canadian." *Government and Opposition* 38(3):357–85.

Kymlicka, Will. 2004. "Marketing Canadian pluralism in the international arena." *International Journal* 59(4):829–52.

Laffan, Brigid. 1996. "The politics of identity and political order in Europe." *JCMS: Journal of Common Market Studies* 34(1):81–102.

Lange, Matthew. 2013. When does nationalism turn violent? A comparative analysis of Canada and Sri Lanka. In *Nationalism and War*, ed. John A Hall and Siniša Malešević. Cambridge: Cambridge University Press, pp. 124–44.

Larson, Deborah Welch, and Alexei Shevchenko. 2010. "Status seekers: Chinese and Russian responses to US primacy." *International Security* 34(4):63–95.

Lebow, Richard Ned. 2016. *National Identities and International Relations*. Cambridge: Cambridge University Press.

Lee, Hyo Won, and Sijeong Lim. 2020. "Public feelings toward ASEAN: One vision, one identity, one community?" *Asian Survey* 60(5):803–29.

Lee, Siu-yau, and Kee-lee Chou. 2020. "How nation building backfires: Beliefs about group malleability and anti-Chinese attitudes in Hong Kong." *Political Psychology* 41(5): 923–44.

Legro, Jeffrey W. 2000. "Whence American internationalism." *International Organization* 54(2):253–89.

Lengyel, György, and Stefan Jahr. 2012. Surveying elites: Information on the study design and field report of the IntUne elite survey. In *The Europe of Elites: A Study into the Europeanness of Europe's Political and Economic Elites*, ed. Heinrich Best, György Lengyel, and Luca Verzichelli. Oxford: Oxford University Press, pp. 242–68.

Lepore, Jill. 2019. "A new Americanism: Why a nation needs a national story." *Foreign Affairs* 98(2):10–19.

Levendusky, Matthew S. 2018. "Americans, not partisans: Can priming American national identity reduce affective polarization?" *The Journal of Politics* 80(1):59–70.

Levy, Jack S. 1994. "Learning and foreign policy: Sweeping a conceptual minefield." *International Organization* 48(2):279–312.

Li, Qiong, and Marilynn B Brewer. 2004. "What does it mean to be an American? Patriotism, nationalism, and American identity after 9/11." *Political Psychology* 25(5):727–39.

Liberman, Peter. 2006. "An eye for an eye: Public support for war against evildoers." *International Organization* 60(3):687–722.

Liberman, Peter, and Linda J Skitka. 2017. "Revenge in US public support for war against Iraq." *Public Opinion Quarterly* 81(3):636–60.

Lieven, Anatol. 2016. "Clinton and Trump: Two faces of American nationalism." *Survival* 58(5):7–22.

Lind, Jennifer. 2020. "Narratives and international reconciliation." *Journal of Global Security Studies* 5(2):229–47.

Lindstam, Emmy, Matthias Mader, and Harald Schoen. 2021. "Conceptions of national identity and ambivalence towards immigration." *British Journal of Political Science* 51(1):93–114.

Lizotte, Mary-Kate. 2019. "Investigating the origins of the gender gap in support for war." *Political Studies Review* 17(6):124–35.

Lopez, Anthony C, Rose McDermott, and Michael Bang Petersen. 2011. "States in mind: Evolution, coalitional psychology, and international politics." *International Security* 36(2):48–83.

Lupton, Danielle. 2020. "The reputational costs and ethical implications of coercive limited air strikes: The fallacy of the middle-ground approach." *Ethics & International Affairs* 34(2):217–28.

Lupton, Danielle L. 2019. "The external validity of college student subject pools in experimental research: A cross-sample comparison of treatment effect heterogeneity." *Political Analysis* 27(1):90–97.

Lyall, Jason, Yuki Shiraito, and Kosuke Imai. 2015. "Coethnic bias and wartime informing." *The Journal of Politics* 77(3):833–48.

Macdonald, Julia, and Jacquelyn Schneider. 2017. "Presidential risk orientation and force employment decisions: The case of unmanned weaponry." *Journal of Conflict Resolution* 61(3):511–36.

Mader, Matthias, Thomas J Scotto, Jason Reifler, Peter H Gries, Pierangelo Isernia, and Harald Schoen. 2018. "How political are national identities? A comparison of the United States, the United Kingdom, and Germany in the 2010s." *Research & Politics* 5(3):1–9.

Mansfield, Edward D, and Jack Snyder. 2002. "Democratic transitions, institutional strength, and war." *International Organization* 56(2):297–337.

Mansfield, Edward D, and Jack Snyder. 2007. *Electing to Fight: Why Emerging Democracies Go to War*. Cambridge, MA: MIT Press.

Mansfield, Edward D, and Jack Snyder. 2009. "Pathways to war in democratic transitions." *International Organization* 63(2):381–90.

Mantena, Karuna. 2012*a*. "Another realism: The politics of Gandhian nonviolence." *American Political Science Review* 106(2):455–70.

Mantena, Karuna. 2012*b*. "On Gandhi's critique of the state: Sources, contexts, conjunctures." *Modern Intellectual History* 9(3):535–63.

Marks, Gary, and Liesbet Hooghe. 2003. National identity and support for European integration. Technical report WZB Discussion Paper.

Markus, Hazel R, and Shinobu Kitayama. 1991. "Culture and the self: Implications for cognition, emotion, and motivation." *Psychological Review* 98(2):224–53.

McCrae, Robert R, and Paul T Costa Jr. 1991. "Adding Liebe und Arbeit: The full five-factor model and well-being." *Personality and Social Psychology Bulletin* 17(2):227–32.

McDaniel, Eric L., Irfan Nooruddin, and Allyson F Shortle. 2016. "Proud to be an American?: The changing relationship of national pride and identity." *Journal of Race, Ethnicity and Politics* 1(1):145–76.

McDaniel, Eric Leon, Irfan Nooruddin, and Allyson Faith Shortle. 2011. "Divine boundaries: How religion shapes citizens' attitudes toward immigrants." *American Politics Research* 39(1):205–33.

McDermott, Rose. 2002*a*. "Experimental methodology in political science." *Political Analysis* 10(4):325–42.

McDermott, Rose. 2002*b*. "Experimental methods in political science." *Annual Review of Political Science* 5(1):31–61.

McDermott, Rose. 2009. Psychological approaches to identity: Experimentation and application. In *Measuring Identity: A Guide for Social Scientists*, ed. Rawi Abdelal, Yoshiko M Herrera, Alastair Iain Johnston, and Rose McDermott. Cambridge, Cambridge University Press, pp. 345–68.

McDermott, Rose. 2011. Internal and external validity. In *Cambridge Handbook of Experimental Political Science*, ed. James N. Druckman, Donald P. Green, James H. Kuklinski, and Arthur Lupia. Cambridge: Cambridge University Press, pp. 27–40.

McDermott, Rose, and Jonathan A Cowden. 2001. "The effects of uncertainty and sex in a crisis simulation game." *International Interactions* 27(4):353–80.

McFarland, Sam. 2003. "The effects of authoritarianism and social dominance upon American students' attitudes toward attacking Iraq." *Psicología Política* 27:119–30.

McFarland, Sam G. 1981. "Effects of question order on survey responses." *Public Opinion Quarterly* 45(2):208–15.

McFarland, Sam, Justin Hackett, Katarzyna Hamer, Iva Katzarska-Miller, Anna Malsch, Gerhard Reese, and Stephen Reysen. 2019. "Global human identification and citizenship: A review of psychological studies." *Political Psychology* 40:141–71.

McFarland, Sam, Matthew Webb, and Derek Brown. 2012. "All humanity is my ingroup: A measure and studies of identification with all humanity." *Journal of Personality and Social Psychology* 103(5):830–53.

McGuire, William J, Claire V McGuire, Pamela Child, and Terry Fujioka. 1978. "Salience of ethnicity in the spontaneous self-concept as a function of one's ethnic distinctiveness in the social environment." *Journal of Personality and Social Psychology* 36(5):511–20.

McNamara, Kathleen R. 2015*a*. "JCMS annual review lecture: Imagining Europe: The cultural foundations of EU governance." *JCMS: Journal of Common Market Studies* 53:22–39.

McNamara, Kathleen R. 2015*b*. *The Politics of Everyday Europe: Constructing Authority in the European Union*. Oxford: Oxford University Press.

McNamara, Kathleen R, and Paul Musgrave. 2020. "Democracy and collective identity in the EU and the USA." *JCMS: Journal of Common Market Studies* 58(1):172–88.

McRoberts, Kenneth. 1997. *Misconceiving Canada: The Struggle for National Unity*. Oxford: Oxford University Press.

Mead, Walter Russell. 1999. "The Jacksonian tradition and American foreign policy." *The National Interest* 58:5–29.

Mead, Walter Russell. 2002. *Special Providence. American Foreign Policy and How It Changed the World*. New York: Routledge.

Mearsheimer, John J. 2014. *The Tragedy of Great Power Politics (Updated Edition)*. New York: W. W. Norton & Company.

Meernik, James David. 2004. *The Political Use of Military Force in US Foreign Policy*. London: Ashgate.

Mendelberg, Tali. 2001. *The Race Card: Campaign Strategy, Implicit Messages, and the Norm of Equality*. Princeton: Princeton University Press.

Mercer, Jonathan. 1995. "Anarchy and Identity." *International Organization* 49(2):229–52.

Mintz, Alex, Yi Yang, and Rose McDermott. 2011. "Experimental approaches to international relations." *International Studies Quarterly* 55(2):493–501.

Miron, Anca M, and Jack W Brehm. 2006. "Reactance theory—40 years later." *Zeitschrift für Sozialpsychologie* 37(1):9–18.

Mitchell, Kristine. 2015. "Rethinking the 'Erasmus Effect' on European identity." *JCMS: Journal of Common Market Studies* 53(2):330–48.

Mols, Frank, and Martin Weber. 2013. "Laying sound foundations for social identity theory-inspired European Union attitude research: Beyond attachment and deeply rooted identities." *JCMS: Journal of Common Market Studies* 51(3):505–21.

Monnet, Jean. 1952. "The United States of Europe has begun. The European coal and steel community—Speeches and addresses by Jean Monnet, 1952–1954." Reproduced from microfiche. http://aei.pitt.edu/14365/.

Monnet, Jean. 1978. *Memoirs*. Garden City, NY: Doubleday & Company, Inc.

Monroe, Kristen Renwick. 2008. "Cracking the code of genocide: The moral psychology of rescuers, bystanders, and Nazis during the Holocaust." *Political Psychology* 29(5):699–736.

Monroe, Kristen Renwick, and Rose McDermott. 2010. "Nicole's father is NOT German! The immutability of differences, and the social construction of their moral and political salience." *PS: Political Science & Politics* 43(1):77–81.

Montgomery, Jacob M, Brendan Nyhan, and Michelle Torres. 2018. "How conditioning on post-treatment variables can ruin your experiment and what to do about it." *American Journal of Political Science* 62(3):760–75.

Moorthy, Ravichandran, and Guido Benny. 2012. "Is an 'ASEAN community' achievable?" *Asian Survey* 52(6):1043–66.

Moorthy, Ravichandran, and Guido Benny. 2013. "Does public opinion count? Knowledge and support for an ASEAN community in Indonesia, Malaysia, and Singapore." *International Relations of the Asia-Pacific* 13(3):399–423.

Morgenthau, Hans. 1948. *Politics Among Nations: The Struggle for Peace and Power*. New York: Knopf.

Morton, Rebecca B, and Kenneth C Williams. 2008. Experimentation in political science. In *The Oxford Handbook of Political Methodology*, ed. Janet Box-Steffensmeier, David Collier, and Henry Brady. Oxford: Oxford University Press, pp. 339–56.

Morton, Rebecca B, and Kenneth C Williams. 2010. *Experimental Political Science and the Study of Causality: From Nature to the Lab*. New York: Cambridge University Press.

Moss, Sigrun Marie. 2017. "Identity hierarchy within the Sudanese superordinate identity: Political leadership promoting and demoting subordinate groups." *Political Psychology* 38(6): 925–42.

Mudde, Cas. 2007. *Populist Radical Right Parties in Europe*. Cambridge: Cambridge University Press.

Mudde, Cas, and Cristóbal Rovira Kaltwasser. 2013. "Exclusionary vs. inclusionary populism: Comparing contemporary Europe and Latin America." *Government and Opposition* 48(2):147–74.

Müller, Wolfgang C, Marcelo Jenny, and Alejandro Ecker. 2012. The elites–masses gap in European integration. In *The Europe of Elites: A Study into the Europeanness of Europe's Political and Economic Elites*, ed. Heinrich Best, György Lengyel, and Luca Verzichelli. Oxford: Oxford University Press, pp. 167–91.

Mullinix, Kevin J, Thomas J Leeper, James N Druckman, and Jeremy Freese. 2015. "The generalizability of survey experiments." *Journal of Experimental Political Science* 2(2):109–38.

Mummendey, Amelie, and Michael Wenzel. 1999. "Social discrimination and tolerance in intergroup relations: Reactions to intergroup difference." *Personality and Social Psychology Review* 3(2):158–74.

Mummendey, Amélie, and Sven Waldzus. 2004. National differences and European plurality: Discrimination or tolerance between European countries. In *Transnational identities: Becoming European in the EU*, ed. Richard K. Herrmann, Thomas Risse, and Marilynn B. Brewer. Lanham, MD: Rowman & Littlefield, pp. 59–72.

Mutz, Diana C. 2011. *Population-based Survey Experiments*. Princeton: Princeton University Press.

Mutz, Diana C, and Eunji Kim. 2017. "The impact of in-group favoritism on trade preferences." *International Organization* 71(4):827–50.

Mutz, Diana C, and Robin Pemantle. 2015. "Standards for experimental research: Encouraging a better understanding of experimental methods." *Journal of Experimental Political Science* 2(2):192–215.

Mylonas, Harris. 2012. *The Politics of Nation-building: Making Co-nationals, Refugees, and Minorities*. Cambridge: Cambridge University Press.

Mylonas, Harris, and Kendrick Kuo. 2017. Nationalism and foreign policy. In *Oxford Research Encyclopedia of Politics*. Oxford: Oxford University Press.

Narang, Vipin, and Rebecca M Nelson. 2009. "Who are these belligerent democratizers? Reassessing the impact of democratization on War." *International Organization* 63(2): 357–79.

Nettle, Daniel, Karthik Panchanathan, Tage Shakti Rai, and Alan Page Fiske. 2011. "The evolution of giving, sharing, and lotteries." *Current Anthropology* 52(5):747–56.

Neumann, Iver B. 1999. *Uses of the Other: "The East" in European Identity Formation*. Minneapolis: University of Minnesota Press.

Nieguth, Tim. 1999. "Beyond dichotomy: Concepts of the nation and the distribution of membership." *Nations and Nationalism* 5(2):155–73.

Nissen, Sylke. 2014. "The Eurobarometer and the process of European integration." *Quality & Quantity* 48(2):713–27.

Nomikos, William G, and Nicholas Sambanis. 2019. "What is the mechanism underlying audience costs? Incompetence, belligerence, and inconsistency." *Journal of Peace Research* 56(4):575–88.

O'Dwyer, Emma and Ahmet Çoymak. 2020. "Basic human values and their contexts: A multilevel analysis of support for the use of armed drones in the United States, United Kingdom, and Turkey." *Political Psychology* 41(2):249–64.

O'Leary, Brendan, and Nicholas Sambanis. 2018. Nationalism and international security. In *The Oxford Handbook of International Security*, ed. Alexandra Gheciu and William C. Wohlforth. Oxford: Oxford University Press, pp. 415–31.

Oneal, John R, and Bruce Russett. 2001. *Triangulating Peace: Democracy, Interdependence, and International Organizations*. New York: Norton.

Osaghae, Eghosa E. 1999. "Democracy and national cohesion in multiethnic African states: South Africa and Nigeria compared." *Nations and Nationalism* 5(2):259–80.

Osborne, Danny, Petar Milojev, and Chris G Sibley. 2017. "Authoritarianism and national identity: Examining the longitudinal effects of SDO and RWA on nationalism and patriotism." *Personality and Social Psychology Bulletin* 43(8):1086–99.

Osborne, Jason W, and Anna B Costello. 2009. "Best practices in exploratory factor analysis: Four recommendations for getting the most from your analysis." *Pan-Pacfic Management Review* 12(2):131–46.

Osgood, Charles E. 1962. *An Alternative to War or Surrender*. Urbana: University of Illinois Press.

Ostrom, Thomas M, and Constantine Sedikides. 1992. "Out-group homogeneity effects in natural and minimal groups." *Psychological Bulletin* 112(3):536–52.

Paluck, Elizabeth Levy, and Donald P Green. 2009. "Prejudice reduction: What works? A review and assessment of research and practice." *Annual Review of Psychology* 60:339–67.

Park, Benjamin E. 2018. *American Nationalisms*. Cambridge: Cambridge University Press.

Parker, Christopher S. 2010. "Symbolic versus blind patriotism: Distinction without difference?" *Political Research Quarterly* 63(1):97–114.

Parsons, Craig. 2002. "Showing ideas as causes: The origins of the European Union." *International Organization* 56(1):47–84.

Peitz, Linus, Kristof Dhont, and Ben Seyd. 2018. "The psychology of supranationalism: Its ideological correlates and implications for EU attitudes and post-Brexit preferences." *Political Psychology* 39(6):1305–22.

Perreault, Stephane, and Richard Y Bourhis. 1999. "Ethnocentrism, social identification, and discrimination." *Personality and Social Psychology Bulletin* 25(1):92–103.

Pew Research Center. 2015. "Views of government's handling of terrorism fall to post-9/11 low: Little change in views of relationship between Islam and violence." https://www.people-press.org/2015/12/15/views-of-governments-handling-of-terrorism-fall-to-post-911-low/.

Posen, Barry R. 1993. "Nationalism, the mass army, and military power." *International Security* 18(2):80–124.

Postmes, Tom, and Russell Spears. 1998. "Deindividuation and antinormative behavior: A meta-analysis." *Psychological Bulletin* 123(3):238–59.

Pouliot, Vincent. 2007. "Pacification without collective identification: Russia and the transatlantic security community in the post–Cold War era." *Journal of Peace Research* 44(5): 605–22.

Prather, Lauren. 2014. "Values at the water's edge: Social welfare values and foreign aid." Unpublished manuscript.

Pratto, Felicia, Jim Sidanius, Lisa M Stallworth, and Bertram F Malle. 1994. "Social dominance orientation: A personality variable predicting social and political attitudes." *Journal of Personality and Social Psychology* 67(4):741–63.

Prokop, Peter. 2015. "Why Obama gave an Oval Office address on terrorism without saying anything new." *Vox*. https://www.vox.com/2015/12/6/9859792/obama-address-san-bernardino-isis.

Prutsch, Martin J. 2017. *Research for CULT Committee – European Identity*. Directorate-General for Internal Policies: Policy Department for Structural and Cohesion Policies, Culture and Education.

Putnam, Robert D. 1995. "Bowling alone: America's declining social capital." *Journal of Democracy* 6(1):65–78.

Putnam, Robert D. 2007. "*E Pluribus Unum*: Diversity and community in the twenty-first century the 2006 Johan Skytte Prize Lecture." *Scandinavian Political Studies* 30(2):137–74.

Quek, Kai. 2017. "Type II audience costs." *The Journal of Politics* 79(4):1438–43.

Quick, Brian L, and Michael T Stephenson. 2007. "Further evidence that psychological reactance can be modeled as a combination of anger and negative cognitions." *Communication Research* 34(3):255–76.

Rai, Tage Shakti, and Alan Page Fiske. 2011. "Moral psychology is relationship regulation: Moral motives for unity, hierarchy, equality, and proportionality." *Psychological Review* 118(1): 57–75.

Raney, Tracey, and Loleen Berdahl. 2009. "Birds of a feather? Citizenship norms, group identity, and political participation in Western Canada." *Canadian Journal of Political Science* 42(1):187–209.

Rathbun, Brian C. 2007. "Hierarchy and community at home and abroad: Evidence of a common structure of domestic and foreign policy beliefs in American elites." *Journal of Conflict Resolution* 51(3):379–407.

Rathbun, Brian C. 2009. "It takes all types: Social psychology, trust, and the international relations paradigm in our minds." *International Theory* 1(3):345–80.

Rathbun, Brian C. 2011a. "Before hegemony: Generalized trust and the creation and design of international security organizations." *International Organization* 65(2):243–73.

Rathbun, Brian C. 2011b. "The 'Magnificent Fraud': Trust, international cooperation, and the hidden domestic politics of American multilateralism after World War II." *International Studies Quarterly* 55(1):1–21.

Rathbun, Brian C. 2012. "From vicious to virtuous circle: Moralistic trust, diffuse reciprocity, and the American security commitment to Europe." *European Journal of International Relations* 18(2):323–44.

Rathbun, Brian C. 2015. Chinese attitudes toward Americans and themselves. In *Perception and Misperception in American and Chinese Views of the Other*, ed. Alastair Iain Johnston and Mingming Shen. New York: Carnegie Endowment for International Peace, pp. 9–21.

Rathbun, Brian C, Joshua D Kertzer, Jason Reifler, Paul Goren, and Thomas J Scotto. 2016. "Taking foreign policy personally: Personal values and foreign policy attitudes." *International Studies Quarterly* 60(1):124–37.

Rathbun, Brian C, Kathleen E Powers, and Therese Anders. 2019. "Moral hazard: German public opinion on the Greek debt crisis." *Political Psychology* 40(3):523–41.

Rathbun, Brian C, and Rachel Stein. 2017. "The greater good: Public opinion on the morality of using nuclear weapons." *Journal of Conflict Resolution*.

Reagan, Ronald. 1983. "Transcript of address by president on Lebanon and Grenada." *New York Times*. https://www.nytimes.com/1983/10/28/us/transcript-of-address-by-president-on -lebanon-and-grenada.html.

Reeskens, Tim, and Marc Hooghe. 2010. "Beyond the civic–ethnic dichotomy: Investigating the structure of citizenship concepts across thirty-three countries." *Nations and Nationalism* 16(4):579–97.

Reeskens, Tim, and Matthew Wright. 2013. "Nationalism and the cohesive society: A multilevel analysis of the interplay among diversity, national identity, and social capital across 27 European societies." *Comparative Political Studies* 46(2):153–81.

Reicher, Stephen D, Russell Spears, and Tom Postmes. 1995. "A social identity model of deindividuation phenomena." *European Review of Social Psychology* 6(1):161–98.

Reicher, Stephen D, S Alexander Haslam, and Michael J Platow. 2007. "The new psychology of leadership." *Scientific American Mind* 18(4):22–29.

Reicher, Stephen, and Nick Hopkins. 2001. *Self and Nation: Categorization, Contestation and Mobilization*. London: Sage.

Reicher, Stephen, S Alexander Haslam and Nick Hopkins. 2005. "Social identity and the dynamics of leadership: Leaders and followers as collaborative agents in the transformation of social reality." *The Leadership Quarterly* 16(4):547–68.

Reicher, Stephen, S Alexander Haslam, and Rakshi Rath. 2008. "Making a virtue of evil: A five-step social identity model of the development of collective hate." *Social and Personality Psychology Compass* 2(3):1313–44.

Reifler, Jason, Thomas J Scotto, and Harold D Clarke. 2011. "Foreign policy beliefs in contemporary Britain: Structure and relevance." *International Studies Quarterly* 55(1):245–66.

Renshon, Jonathan. 2009. "When public statements reveal private beliefs: Assessing operational codes at a distance." *Political Psychology* 30(4):649–61.

Renshon, Jonathan. 2017. *Fighting for Status: Hierarchy and Conflict in World Politics*. Princeton: Princeton University Press.

Richeson, Jennifer A, and Richard J Nussbaum. 2004. "The impact of multiculturalism versus color-blindness on racial bias." *Journal of Experimental Social Psychology* 40(3):417–23.

Riffkin, Rebecca. 2015. "Americans name terrorism as no. 1 U.S. problem." *Gallup*. https://news.gallup.com/poll/187655/americans-name-terrorism-no-problem.aspx.

Risse-Kappen, Thomas. 1995. "Democratic peace—Warlike democracies? A social constructivist interpretation of the liberal argument." *European Journal of International Relations* 1(4): 491–517.

Risse, Thomas. 2001. A European identity? Europeanization and the evolution of nation-state identities. In *Transforming Europe: Europeanization and Domestic Change*, ed. Maria Green Cowles, James A Caporaso and Thomas Risse-Kappen. Ithaca, NY: Cornell University Press, pp. 198–216.

Risse, Thomas. 2004. European institutions and identity change: What have we learned? In *Transnational Identities: Becoming European in the EU*, ed. Richard K. Herrmann, Thomas Risse, and Marilynn B. Brewer. Washington, D.C.: Rowman & Littlefield, pp. 247–71.

Risse, Thomas. 2010. *A Community of Europeans?: Transnational Identities and Public Spheres*. Ithaca, NY: Cornell University Press.

Roberts, Margaret E, Brandon M Stewart, and Dustin Tingley. 2014. "stm: R package for structural topic models." *Journal of Statistical Software* 10(2):1–40.

Roberts, Margaret E, Brandon M Stewart, Dustin Tingley, Christopher Lucas, Jetson Leder-Luis, Shana Kushner Gadarian, Bethany Albertson, and David G Rand. 2014. "Structural topic models for open-ended survey responses." *American Journal of Political Science* 58(4): 1064–82.

Robinson, Amanda Lea. 2014. "National versus ethnic identification in Africa: Modernization, colonial legacy, and the origins of territorial nationalism." *World Politics* 66(4):709–46.

Robinson, Amanda Lea. 2016. "Nationalism and ethnic-based trust: Evidence from an African border region." *Comparative Political Studies* 49(14):1819–54.

Roccas, Sonia, and Clark McCauley. 2004. Values and emotions in the relational models. In *Relational Models Theory: A Contemporary Overview*, ed. Nick Haslam. New York: Routledge, pp. 263–85.

Roose, Jochen. 2013. "How European is European identification? Comparing continental identification in Europe and beyond." *JCMS: Journal of Common Market Studies* 51(2):281–97.

Rosch, Eleanor. 1975. Principles of categorization. In *Cognition and Categorization*, ed. E. Rosch and B. B. Lloyd. Hillsdale, NJ: Lawrence Erlbaum, pp. 27–48.

Rothschild, David, and Neil Malhotra. 2014. "Are public opinion polls self-fulfilling prophecies?" *Research & Politics* 1(2):1–10.

Rousseau, David L. 2006. *Identifying Threats and Threatening Identities: The Social Construction of Realism and Liberalism*. Stanford, CA: Stanford University Press.

Rousseau, David L, and Rocio Garcia-Retamero. 2007. "Identity, power, and threat perception: A cross-national experimental study." *Journal of Conflict Resolution* 51(5):744–71.

Rubin, Jennifer. 2015. "Obama's speech: Pieties and platitudes, but no policy." *Washington Post*. https://www.washingtonpost.com/blogs/right-turn/wp/2015/12/07/obamas-speech -pieties-and-platitudes-but-no-policy/.

Ruggie, John Gerard. 1992. "Multilateralism: The anatomy of an institution." *International Organization* 46(3):561–98.

Rusbult, Caryl E, and Paul A M Van Lange. 2003. "Interdependence, interaction, and relationships." *Annual Review of Psychology* 54(1):351–75.

Sadowski, Yahya. 2002. The evolution of political identity in Syria. In *Identity and Foreign Policy in the Middle East*, ed. Shibley Telhami and Michael Barnett. Ithaca, NY: Cornell University Press, pp. 137–54.

Saideman, Stephen M. 2013. When nationalists disagree: Who should one hate and kill? In *Nationalism and War*, ed. John A Hall and Siniša Malešević. Cambridge: Cambridge University Press, pp. 341–55.

Saideman, Stephen M, and R William Ayres. 2008. *For Kin or Country: Xenophobia, Nationalism, and War*. New York: Columbia University Press.

Sambanis, Nicholas. 2001. "Do ethnic and nonethnic civil wars have the same causes? A theoretical and empirical inquiry (part 1)." *Journal of Conflict Resolution* 45(3):259–82.

Sambanis, Nicholas, and Moses Shayo. 2013. "Social identification and ethnic conflict." *American Political Science Review* 107(2):294–325.

Sambanis, Nicholas, Stergios Skaperdas and William C Wohlforth. 2015. "Nation-building through war." *American Political Science Review* 109(2):279–96.

Sapolsky, Robert. 2019. "This is your brain on nationalism." *Foreign Affairs* 98(2):42–47.

Sartori, Giovanni. 1970. "Concept misformation in comparative politics." *The American Political Science Review* 64(4):1033–53.

Saunders, Elizabeth N. 2011. *Leaders at War: How Presidents Shape Military Interventions*. Ithaca, NY: Cornell University Press.

Schafer, Mark. 1999. "Cooperative and conflictual policy preferences: The effect of identity, security, and image of the other." *Political Psychology* 20(4):829–44.

Schatz, Robert T, Ervin Staub, and Howard Lavine. 1999. "On the varieties of national attachment: Blind versus constructive patriotism." *Political Psychology* 20(1):151–74.

Schatz, Robert T, and Howard Lavine. 2007. "Waving the flag: National symbolism, social identity, and political engagement." *Political Psychology* 28(3):329–55.

Schilde, Kaija E, Stephanie B Anderson, and Andrew D Garner. 2019. "A more martial Europe? Public opinion, permissive consensus, and EU defence policy." *European Security* 28(2):153–72.

Schildkraut, Deborah J. 2002. "The more things change . . . American identity and mass and elite responses to 9/11." *Political Psychology* 23(3):511–35.

Schildkraut, Deborah J. 2005. *Press "ONE" for English: Language Policy, Public Opinion, and American Identity*. Princeton: Princeton University Press.

Schildkraut, Deborah J. 2007. "Defining American identity in the twenty-first century: How much 'There' is there?" *Journal of Politics* 69(3):597–615.

Schildkraut, Deborah J. 2011. *Americanism in the Twenty-first Century: Public Opinion in the Age of Immigration*. Cambridge: Cambridge University Press.

Schildkraut, Deborah J. 2014. "Boundaries of American identity: Evolving understandings of Us." *Annual Review of Political Science* 17:441–60.

Schimmelfennig, Frank. 2007. Functional form, identity-driven cooperation: Institutional designs and effects in post–Cold War NATO. In *Crafting Cooperation-Regional International Institutions in Comparative Perspective, Cambridge, MA*, ed. Amitav Acharya and Alastair Iain Johnston. Cambridge: Cambridge University Press, pp. 145–79.

Schlenker, Andrea. 2013. "Cosmopolitan Europeans or partisans of fortress Europe? Supranational identity patterns in the EU." *Global Society* 27(1):25–51.

Schoen, Harald. 2007. "Personality traits and foreign policy attitudes in German public opinion." *Journal of Conflict Resolution* 51(3):408–30.

Schoen, Harald. 2008. "Identity, instrumental self-interest and institutional evaluations explaining public opinion on common European policies in foreign affairs and defence." *European Union Politics* 9(1):5–29.

Schrock-Jacobson, Gretchen. 2012. "The violent consequences of the nation: Nationalism and the initiation of interstate war." *Journal of Conflict Resolution* 56(5):825–52.

Schwartz, Shalom H. 1994. "Are there universal aspects in the structure and contents of human values?" *Journal of Social Issues* 50(4):19–45.

Schwartz, Shalom H. 1999. "A theory of cultural values and some implications for work." *Applied Psychology: An International Review* 48(1):23–47.

Schweller, Randall. 2018. "Opposite but compatible nationalisms: A neoclassical realist approach to the future of US–China relations." *The Chinese Journal of International Politics* 11(1): 23–48.

Sekhon, Jasjeet S. 2011. "Multivariate and propensity score matching software with automated balance optimization: The matching package for R." *Journal of Statistical Software* 42(7): 1–52.

Senese, Paul D. 1996. "Geographical proximity and issue salience: Their effects on the escalation of militarized interstate conflict." *Conflict Management and Peace Science* 15(2):133–61.

Sheppard, Blair H, and Marla Tuchinsky. 1996. "Interfirm relationships: A grammar of pairs." *Research in Organizational Behavior* 18:331–31.

Shweder, R A, N C Much, M Maharpatra, and L. Park. 1997. The "Big Three" of morality (autonomy, community, and divinity), and the "Big Three" explanations of suffering. In *Morality and Health*, ed. A Brandt and P Rozin. New York: Routledge, pp. 119–69.

Sides, John, and Jack Citrin. 2007. "European opinion about immigration: The role of identities, interests and information." *British Journal of Political Science* 37(3):477–504.

Sides, John, Michael Tesler, and Lynn Vavreck. 2019. *Identity Crisis: The 2016 Presidential Campaign and the Battle for the Meaning of America*. Princeton: Princeton University Press.

Silverman, Jane M, and Donald S Kumka. 1987. "Gender differences in attitudes toward nuclear war and disarmament." *Sex Roles* 16(3-4):189–203.

Simpson, Ain, and Simon M Laham. 2015a. "Different relational models underlie prototypical left and right positions on social issues." *European Journal of Social Psychology* 45(2):204–17.

Simpson, Ain, and Simon M Laham. 2015b. "Individual differences in relational construal are associated with variability in moral judgment." *Personality and Individual Differences* 74: 49–54.

Sindic, Denis, and Stephen D Reicher. 2009. " 'Our way of life is worth defending': Testing a model of attitudes towards superordinate group membership through a study of Scots' attitudes towards Britain." *European Journal of Social Psychology* 39(1):114–29.

Sinopoli, Richard C. 1996. *From Many, One: Readings in American Political and Social Thought*. Washington, D.C.: Georgetown University Press.

Skjelsbæk, Inger, and Torunn Lise Tryggestad. 2020. "Pro-gender norms in Norwegian peace engagement: Balancing experiences, values, and interests." *Foreign Policy Analysis* 16(2):181–98.

Smith, Anthony D. 1991. *National Identity*. Reno: University of Nevada Press.

Smith, Anthony D. 1992. "National identity and the idea of European unity." *International Affairs* 68(1):55–76.

Smith, Anthony D. 1993a. "The ethnic sources of nationalism." *Survival* 35(1):48–62.

Smith, Anthony D. 2000. *The Nation in History: Historiographical Debates about Ethnicity and Nationalism*. Hanover, NH: University Press of New England.

Smith, Rogers M. 1993b. "Beyond Tocqueville, Myrdal, and Hartz: The multiple traditions in America." *American Political Science Review* 87(3):549–66.

Smith, Rogers M. 1997. *Civic Ideals: Conflicting Visions of Citizenship in US History*. New Haven, CT: Yale University Press.

Snyder, Jack. 1991. *Myths of Empire: Domestic Politics and International Ambition*. Ithaca, NY: Cornell University Press.

Snyder, Jack. 2019. "The broken bargain." *Foreign Affairs* 98(2):54–60.

Snyder, Jack, and Karen Ballentine. 1996. "Nationalism and the marketplace of ideas." *International Security* 21(2):5–40.

Snyder, Jack. 2000. *From Voting to Violence: Democratization and Nationalist Conflict*. New York: Norton.

Staub, Ervin. 2000. "Genocide and mass killing: Origins, prevention, healing and reconciliation." *Political Psychology* 21(2):367–82.

Steffens, Niklas K, Sebastian C Schuh, S Alexander Haslam, Antonia Perez, and Rolf van Dick. 2015. " 'Of the group' and 'for the group': How followership is shaped by leaders' proto-typicality and group identification." *European Journal of Social Psychology* 45(2):180–90.

Stein, Rachel M. 2019. *Vengeful Citizens, Violent States*. Cambridge: Cambridge University Press.

Stoeckel, Florian. 2016. "Contact and community: The role of social interactions for a political identity." *Political Psychology* 37(3):431–42.

Tajfel, Henri, and John Turner. 1979. An integrative theory of intergroup conflict. In *Differentiation Between Social Groups: Studies in the Social Psychology of Intergroup Relations*, ed. Henri Tajfel. New York: Academic Press, pp. 33–47.

Tajfel, Henri. 1981. *Human Groups and Social Categories: Studies in Social Psychology*. Cambridge: Cambridge University Press.

Tajfel, Henri. 1982. "Social psychology of intergroup relations." *Annual Review of Psychology* 33(1):1–39.

Tajfel, Henri, and John C Turner. 1986. The social identity theory of intergroup behavior. In *Psychology of Intergroup Relations*, ed. S Worchel and W G Austin. Chicago: Nelson-Hall, pp. 7–24.

Tamir, Yael. 2019. *Why Nationalism?* Princeton: Princeton University Press.

Tankard, Margaret E, and Elizabeth Levy Paluck. 2016. "Norm perception as a vehicle for social change." *Social Issues and Policy Review* 10(1):181–211.

Telhami, Shibley. 2013. *The World Through Arab Eyes: Arab Public Opinion and the Reshaping of the Middle East*. New York: Basic Books.

Terry, Deborah J, and Michael A Hogg. 1996. "Group norms and the attitude-behavior relationship: A role for group identification." *Personality and Social Psychology Bulletin* 22(8): 776–93.

Terry, Deborah J, Michael A Hogg, and Katherine M White. 1999. "The theory of planned behaviour: Self-identity, social identity and group norms." *British Journal of Social Psychology* 38(3):225–44.

Theiss-Morse, Elizabeth. 2009. *Who Counts as an American? The Boundaries of National Identity*. New York: Cambridge University Press.

Thomsen, Lotte. 2010. Seeing social relations. PhD thesis. Harvard University.

Tillman, Erik R. 2013. "Authoritarianism and citizen attitudes towards European integration." *European Union Politics* 14(4):566–89.

Toff, Benjamin. 2018. "Exploring the effects of polls on public opinion: How and when media reports of policy preferences can become self-fulfilling prophesies." *Research & Politics* 5(4):1–9.

Toff, Benjamin, and Elizabeth Suhay. 2019. "Partisan conformity, social identity, and the formation of policy preferences." *International Journal of Public Opinion Research* 31(2):349–67.

Tomz, Michael, Jessica L P Weeks, and Keren Yarhi-Milo. 2020. "Public opinion and decisions about military force in democracies." *International Organization* 74(1):119–43.

Tomz, Michael, and Jessica Weeks. 2013. "Public opinion and the democratic peace." *American Political Science Review* 107(3):849–65.

Transue, John E. 2007. "Identity salience, identity acceptance, and racial policy attitudes: American national identity as a uniting force." *American Journal of Political Science* 51(1): 78–91.

Trautsch, Jasper M. 2016. "The origins and nature of American nationalism." *National Identities* 18(3):289–312.

Triandis, Harry C, Christopher McCusker, and C Harry Hui. 1990. "Multimethod probes of individualism and collectivism." *Journal of Personality and Social Psychology* 59(5):1006–20.

Triandis, Harry C, and Richard W Brislin. 1984. "Cross-cultural psychology." *American Psychologist* 39(9):1006–16.

Tudor, Maya, and Dan Slater. 2020. "Nationalism, authoritarianism and democracy: Historical lessons from South and Southeast Asia." *Perspectives on Politics*, pp. 1–17.

Turner, John C. 1985. "Social categorization and the self-concept: A social cognitive theory of group behavior." *Advances in Group Processes: Theory and Research* 2:77–122.

Turner, John C. 1991. *Social Influence*. Pacific Grove, CA: Thomson Brooks/Cole Publishing Co.

Turner, John C, Michael A Hogg, Penelope J Oakes, Stephen D Reicher, and Margaret S Wetherell. 1987. *Rediscovering the Social Group: A Self-categorization Theory*. Oxford: Basil Blackwell.

Tusicisny, Andrej. 2017. "Reciprocity and discrimination: An experiment of Hindu-Muslim cooperation in Indian slums." *Political Psychology* 38(3):409–26.

Uslaner, Eric M. 2002. *The Moral Foundations of Trust*. Cambridge: Cambridge University Press.

van Evera, Stephen. 1994. "Hypotheses on nationalism and war." *International Security* 18(4): 5–39.

Van Vugt, Mark, and Claire M Hart. 2004. "Social identity as social glue: The origins of group loyalty." *Journal of Personality and Social Psychology* 86(4):585–98.

Vasquez, John A. 2009. *The War Puzzle Revisited*. Cambridge: Cambridge University Press.

Verhaegen, Soetkin, Marc Hooghe, and Ellen Quintelier. 2017. "The effect of political trust and trust in European citizens on European identity." *European Political Science Review* 9(2):161–81.

Verkuyten, Maykel. 2009. "Self-esteem and multiculturalism: An examination among ethnic minority and majority groups in the Netherlands." *Journal of Research in Personality* 43(3):419–27.

Voci, Alberto. 2006. "The link between identification and in-group favouritism: Effects of threat to social identity and trust-related emotions." *British Journal of Social Psychology* 45(2): 265–84.

Vodosek, Markus. 2009. "The relationship between relational models and individualism and collectivism: Evidence from culturally diverse work groups." *International Journal of Psychology* 44(2):120–28.

Waldzus, Sven, Amelie Mummendey, and Michael Wenzel. 2005. "When 'Different' means 'Worse': In-group prototypicality in changing intergroup contexts." *Journal of Experimental Social Psychology* 41(1):76–83.

Walker, Stephen G, Mark Schafer, and Michael D Young. 1999. "Presidential operational codes and foreign policy conflicts in the post–Cold War world." *Journal of Conflict Resolution* 43(5):610–25.

Walt, Stephen M. 1996. *Revolution and War.* Ithaca, NY: Cornell University Press.

Waltz, Kenneth Neal. 1979. *Theory of International Politics.* Vol. 5. New York: McGraw-Hill.

Ward, Steven Michael. 2017. "Lost in translation: Social identity theory and the study of status in world politics." *International Studies Quarterly* 61(4):821–34.

Waytz, Adam, Ravi Iyer, Liane Young, and Jesse Graham. 2016. Ideological differences in the expanse of empathy. In *Social Psychology of Political Polarization,* ed. Piercarlo Valdesolo and Jesse Graham. New York: Psychology Press, pp. 61–79.

Weber, Christopher R, and Christopher M Federico. 2013. "Moral foundations and heterogeneity in ideological preferences." *Political Psychology* 34(1):107–26.

Weber, Eugen. 1976. *Peasants into Frenchmen: The Modernization of Rural France, 1870–1914.* Stanford, CA: Stanford University Press.

Weeks, Jessica L P. 2014. *Dictators at War and Peace.* Ithaca, NY: Cornell University Press.

Weinberg, Jill D, Jeremy Freese, and David McElhattan. 2014. "Comparing data characteristics and results of an online factorial survey between a population-based and a crowdsource-recruited sample." *Sociological Science* 1:292–310.

Weiss, Jessica Chen. 2013. "Authoritarian signaling, mass audiences, and nationalist protest in China." *International Organization* 67(1):1–35.

Weiss, Jessica Chen. 2014. *Powerful Patriots: Nationalist Protest in China's Foreign Relations.* Oxford: Oxford University Press.

Weiss, Jessica Chen. 2019. "How hawkish is the Chinese public? Another look at 'rising nationalism' and Chinese foreign policy." *Journal of Contemporary China* 28(119):679–95.

Wellen, Jackie M, Michael A Hogg, and Deborah J Terry. 1998. "Group norms and attitude-behavior consistency: The role of group salience and mood." *Group Dynamics: Theory, Research, and Practice* 2(1):48–56.

Wendt, Alexander. 1992. "Anarchy is what states make of it: The social construction of power politics." *International Organization* 46(2):391–425.

Wendt, Alexander. 1999. *Social Theory of International Politics.* Cambridge: Cambridge University Press.

Wendt, Alexander. 2003. "Why a world state is inevitable." *European Journal of International Relations* 9(4):491–542.

Wendt, Alexander. 2004. "The state as person in international theory." *Review of International Studies* 30(2):289–316.

Wenzel, Michael, Amélie Mummendey, and Sven Waldzus. 2007. "Superordinate identities and intergroup conflict: The ingroup projection model." *European Review of Social Psychology* 18(1):331–72.

Wenzel, Michael, Amélie Mummendey, Ulrike Weber, and Sven Waldzus. 2003. "The ingroup as pars pro toto: Projection from the ingroup onto the inclusive category as a precursor to social discrimination." *Personality and Social Psychology Bulletin* 29(4):461–73.

Wheeler, Nicholas J. 2018. *Trusting Enemies: Interpersonal Relationships in International Conflict.* Oxford: Oxford University Press.

White, Ismail K, and Chryl N Laird. 2020. *Steadfast Democrats: How Social Forces Shape Black Political Behavior.* Princeton: Princeton University Press.

Whitehead, Andrew L, and Samuel L Perry. 2020. *Taking America Back for God: Christian Nationalism in the United States*. Oxford: Oxford University Press.

Whitman, Alden. 1979. "Jean Monnet, 90, architect of European unity, dies." *New York Times*, p. 1–5.

Wills, Garry. 1992. *Lincoln at Gettysburg: The Words that Remade America*. New York: Simon and Schuster.

Wimmel, Andreas. 2006. "Beyond the Bosphorus? Comparing German, French and British discourses on Turkey's application to join the European Union." https://nbn-resolving.org /urn:nbn:de:0168-ssoar-245750.

Wimmer, Andreas. 2013. *Waves of War: Nationalism, State Formation, and Ethnic Exclusion in the Modern World*. Cambridge: Cambridge University Press.

Wimmer, Andreas. 2019. "Why nationalism works." *Foreign Affairs* 98(2):27–34.

Wittkopf, Eugene R. 1990. *Faces of Internationalism: Public Opinion and American Foreign Policy*. Durham, N.C.: Duke University Press.

Wohlforth, William C. 1999. "The stability of a unipolar world." *International Security* 24(1): 5–41.

Wohlforth, William C. 2008. Realism. In *The Oxford Handbook of International Relations*, ed. Chritian Reus-Smit and Duncan Snidal. Oxford: Oxford University Press.

Wohlforth, William C. 2009. "Unipolarity, status competition, and great power war." *World Politics* 61(1):28–57.

Wohlforth, William C, Benjamin De Carvalho, Halvard Leira, and Iver B Neumann. 2018. "Moral authority and status in international relations: Good states and the social dimension of status seeking." *Review of International Studies* 44(3):526–46.

Wolak, Jennifer, and Ryan Dawkins. 2017. "The roots of patriotism across political contexts." *Political Psychology* 38(3):391–408.

Wolsko, Christopher, Bernadette Park, Charles M Judd, and Bernd Wittenbrink. 2000. "Framing interethnic ideology: Effects of multicultural and color-blind perspectives on judgments of groups and individuals." *Journal of Personality and Social Psychology* 78(4):635–54.

Wong, Cara J. 2010. *Boundaries of Obligation in American Politics: Geographic, National, and Racial Communities*. Cambridge: Cambridge University Press.

Woods, Randall Bennett. 1989. "FDR and the triumph of American nationalism." *Presidential Studies Quarterly* 19(3):567–81.

Woodward, Bob. 2012. *Bush at War*. New York: Simon and Schuster.

Woodwell, Douglas. 2007. *Nationalism in International Relations: Norms, Foreign Policy, and Enmity*. New York: Springer.

Wright, Matthew. 2011. "Diversity and the imagined community: Immigrant diversity and conceptions of national identity." *Political Psychology* 32(5):837–62.

Wright, Matthew, Jack Citrin, and Jonathan Wand. 2012. "Alternative measures of American national identity: Implications for the civic-ethnic distinction." *Political Psychology* 33(4):469–82.

Wright, Matthew, and Tim Reeskens. 2013. "Of what cloth are the ties that bind? National identity and support for the welfare state across 29 European countries." *Journal of European Public Policy* 20(10):1443–63.

Xi, Jinping. 2014. *The Governance of China*. Beijing: Foreign Languages Press.

Yarhi-Milo, Keren. 2018. *Who Fights for Reputation: The Psychology of Leaders in International Conflict*. Princeton: Princeton University Press.

Yglesias, Matthew. 2015. "With his speech on San Bernardino, Obama is confronting a problem he's long feared." *Vox*. https://www.vox.com/2015/12/6/9859686/obama-speech-isis -nightmare.

Zhao, Suiseheng. 2000. "Chinese nationalism and its international orientations." *Political Science Quarterly* 115(1):1–33.

Zimmer, Oliver. 2003. "Boundary mechanisms and symbolic resources: Towards a process-oriented approach to national identity." *Nations and Nationalism* 9(2):173–93.

Zogby, James. 2010. *Arab Voices: What They are Saying to Us, and Why it Matters*. New York: St. Martin's Press.

A NOTE ON THE TYPE

This book has been composed in Adobe Text and Gotham.
Adobe Text, designed by Robert Slimbach for Adobe,
bridges the gap between fifteenth- and sixteenth-century
calligraphic and eighteenth-century Modern styles.
Gotham, inspired by New York street signs, was designed
by Tobias Frere-Jones for Hoefler & Co.